ITOYA

H. TANAKA.
EXCHANGE TRANSACTOR
SILK SELLING AGENT
BENTEN DOR NICHOME
YOKOHAMA JAPAN

為換方

生絲賣込商

糸屋 田中平八

My Families and Other Samurai

My Families and Other Samurai

A Memoir

Haruko Fukuda

First published in Great Britain in 2023
by Richfield and Barr Publishing Limited

Edited, designed and produced by Tandem Publishing
http://tandempublishing.yolasite.com

Endpaper illustrations. Front: Image of Itohei's first shop in Yokohama.

Back: Painting of Aburatsubo by Dugald Barr.

ISBN: 978-1-3999-5905-6

10 9 8 7 6 5 4 3 2 1

A CIP catalogue record for this book is available from the British Library.

Printed and bound in Great Britain by CPI Group (UK) Ltd, Croydon CR0 4YY.

For my parents

CONTENTS

PREFACE

~

When I was seventeen my grandmother said to me "Please don't become a bluestocking; you are never going to have to work." My life turned out to be quite the opposite, forging a lifelong career in finance. It was not because of personal ambition, design or even choice. I was indeed fortunate to have been offered interesting opportunities at every turn, but, born Japanese yet making my life mostly in England in the fiercely competitive and male-dominated world of finance, I have been regarded as unusual and a one-off. Over the years a number of people have urged me to write my autobiography. I have until now refused to make such an audacious move. The Japanese in me has whispered that it would be bad manners to talk about myself. But I decided that I could start to write down where I came from, and tell some of the history of my families on both father's and mother's sides, and what life was like in Japan in the twentieth century.

My father was a senior official of the powerful Japanese Ministry of Finance (MoF); his career took him to serve as a minister in Washington and London, and to Manila, where as the first Executive Director for Japan he was instrumental in the launch of the Asian Development Bank. In the capitals of America and Europe he played an important role in significant episodes of international financial diplomacy for Japan in the early postwar period. Our family, unexpectedly, ended up living an international life across the globe, often separated for long

I

periods. My sisters and I all married foreigners – not something that could have been contemplated by our grandmother – and made our lives abroad. How I made my life alone in England will be the subject of another book.

I have felt for a long time how little is known in the West about what Japanese life was really like before the war, or even in the latter half of the twentieth century. This story of my families and ancestors, albeit dealing with a relatively well-off section of society, is a contribution to the social history of Japan and I hope it will go some way to redress that imbalance. I witnessed myself what was left of the transition from the Meiji Restoration of 1868 to the Second World War and its aftermath, including the period of Allied Occupation. One of my grandparents' houses was commandeered for US Air Force personnel during that latter period. My forebears include some notable historical figures: one of them built Japan's first railway tunnel in the early Meiji period; another, a legendary speculator and entrepreneur, was the founding father of Japan's principal financial markets, in foreign exchange, commodities and futures contracts, and stocks and shares. There was an admiral, who as head of the Navy forced Japan to sign the crucial Naval Limitation Treaty and who saved the imperial system at the end of the war. Also, a Cambridge graduate who introduced rugby football to Japan at the end of the nineteenth century; a great horticulturist who supplied the 2,000 cherry trees that line the shores of the Potomac Basin in Washington; and one of the greatest haiku poets of the last century.

From the latter part of the nineteenth century to the inter-war years, life for an enterprising and outward-looking part of Japanese society was more sophisticated – indeed luxurious and leisured – than is often depicted in the West. It was still closer to Europe than to America; however, it retained many unique Japanese philosophical tenets of an earlier time. My father's family had been samurai since the Middle Ages, but my

2

mother's family, quite different, were the new rich of the Meiji Restoration, having made their fortune in mining, commerce and finance. Two different cultures melded together in the arranged marriage of my parents. Defeat in the Second World War then changed their lives for ever.

Events impact the lives and fortunes of families. In this story, the Meiji Restoration, the Second World War and the economic crash of 1990 in Japan were catalysts in altering the lives of my family. This story is drawn from the extensive family archives, writings of my father and private family letters. Reading some of my own letters to my parents I have been reminded of thoughts and feelings from my youth. But letters between my parents, and those of my grandparents and my aunts to my mother, are more than revelatory and moving. They reveal their expectations within an arranged marriage, how they coped with events that defied their lifetime expectations and the courage with which they faced new realities. They tell the story of daily preoccupations and a way of life in mid-twentieth-century Japan. More than this, my father's writings of the 1950s, 1960s and 1970s, up to his death, express how passionately he and his generation of government officials worked to recover Japan's position in the international arena. They were eager to learn from the victors of the war and to bring wisdom to bear in the reconstruction efforts, and most of all to effect a cordial reconciliation with former foes. My father did not squander his chance to make a real difference to Japan's standing when posted to Washington and London; he met people in positions of influence at the highest level, and helped effect ground-breaking achievements in international diplomacy.

Before the Second World War, Japan had been a significant power; after all, it had the third largest navy in the world. After the Meiji Restoration the Japanese adopted Western habits and technological advances with amazing rapidity. My forebears were no exception and made significant contributions to the development of modern Japan at that time. They lived a comfortable and sophisticated life on a magnificent estate in central Tokyo, which I myself remember well; they toured Europe, hunting, shooting and fishing, enjoying gourmet dining. The war and the defeat in 1945 changed all that they had taken for granted. Some would say the situation was not much different in Britain after the war. But Japan had to recover not just her economic strength but also her reputation.

And it was to that end – to recover Japan's reputation – that my parents and their colleagues aspired throughout my childhood, and that ambition framed our family life as well. I have myself always been conscious of my heritage. I wanted to write about it before embarking on a description of my own life and career that have resulted in my British citizenship.

The Families: Masaru and Yoko on 28th February 1944.

INTRODUCTION

~

The vestiges of snow on the ground around the well-placed ancient rocks in the gardens glisten in the sharp sunlight of winter, but the tiny buds of *ume* blossom appearing on the bare black branches signal the coming of spring, the season of hope. It is perhaps the most beautiful time of year in Japan. The air begins to soften soon after for the next blossom, the peach, and mothers look forward to the annual festival of *momonosekku* (桃の節句), a legacy dating from the Heian period, displaying fine dolls to celebrate their daughters' wellbeing. It was at that time of year, when rosaceae prunus *ume* were coming into bloom, that Masaru and Yoko were married in a grand ceremony with Shinto ritual in Tokyo.

My parents married in February 1944, just over two years after Japan's entry into the Second World War. My mother, Tanaka Yoko (田中洋子), had finished her course at the Tokyo Woman's Christian University. She was twenty-two years old. My father, Fukuda Masaru (福田勝), was a young official of the Ministry of Finance, the most powerful of all government ministries. Following the fiercest battles of the Guadalcanal campaign the previous year, the US offensive in the western Pacific was gathering momentum; soon after their marriage it was beginning to tilt the balance of probability towards Japan's eventual defeat. For my father it was crisis time, with severe divisions within the government, eventually leading to the fall of the Tojo Cabinet less than six months later. For my mother, the hardship and

7

austerity of the war years brought an end to the lifestyle she had been raised to expect. The months after their wedding saw dark and frightening days, her husband often working till late at night at the Ministry, she waiting alone in a large house, splitting firewood for bathwater and growing vegetables in the garden. Not the bed of roses the newlyweds would have expected, but one of mental discipline and arduous physical effort. An inner wish – 'When the war is over, it will be back to normal' – kept her going, but it was to prove in vain. The defeat and surrender the following year changed all expectations.

It is often said that events change lives and fortunes. That could not have been truer in Yoko's life. Had it not been for the social upheaval of the Meiji Restoration nearly a century earlier, Yoko probably would never have married Masaru. Her family was a product of that social revolution, which enriched self-made opportunist entrepreneurs, founding *zaibatsu* dynasties. In the prevailing caste system, an ancient samurai family such as my father's would not normally have contemplated a union with a commoner. The ambitious new rich climbed the social ladder through aristocratic marriages and by sending their children to the imperial Peers' School. The ethos and values of the merchant class were at odds with the austere but proud culture of the samurai. For Yoko it was at times perplexing and hard to conform. She accepted and obeyed, doing as she was told by her husband and mother-in-law, even if she resented the implied condescension. Masaru wrote to her in one of his letters that he was aware of the differences of culture and tradition between their families, but was grateful how readily she had accepted and adhered to his family's ways. They enjoyed a successful marriage and, despite those differences, they were loyal to each other and to their respective families; the two distinct cultures melded together eventually to build a truly international family. The origins of each family and how they evolved are described over the following chapters.

It is not fashionable in the modern world to discuss the lives of well-endowed people and their families; rather we hear more often of successes achieved in the face of adversity, financial and otherwise. This, though, is not a story of poverty to wealth; it is more a story of wealth to relative poverty, as old money gave way to a new social order in postwar Japan. From the Meiji Restoration of 1868 to the collapse of the 'bubble' economy in 1990, many Japanese dynasties succumbed to the pressures of the moment; the Second World War was of course the most devastating of these. My paternal and maternal families were no exception, though both contained personalities who played significant roles at the turning points of history.

The lifestyle of prewar Japan is too little known even amongst aficionados of Japanese history. By 1920, the country was a major force on the world stage, rivalling many Western powers. Two hundred years of feudal hierarchy had come to an end, bringing wealthy merchants and commercial interests into the governing class, as the Meiji Emperor created many new members of the House of Peers in the national legislature; they were quick to adopt Western ways of life and culture. The Taisho period that followed the death of the Meiji Emperor was a time of hope and economic prosperity; Japan had won the Russo-Japanese war in 1905 and had joined the ranks of the major powers, with high levels of capital accumulation on the national accounts. Japanese society before the war was far more international than has often been supposed – in some respects even more so than in today's 'globalised world'. It was sophisticated and cosmopolitan. Through the stories of my families, based on their archives, private letters and the writings of principal members, the following chapters capture what life was like both before the war and in its aftermath. I too have personally witnessed how life changed after the war, amid the years of the Allied Occupation and decades of reconstruction.

War and defeat were a watershed moment in Japan. My

parents' response to the dramatic change in their fortunes was to adapt to the new circumstances with innovation, as well as a tenacious ambition to recover lost ground and to participate fully in a new internationalism; in some ways the situation was analogous to the end of the *sakoku* ('locked period' under the Tokugawa shogunate) and opening up of the country a century before. My father's commitment to this aspiration, as a senior government official, changed the course of his career and of our family life.

It was 'destiny', as my great-uncle, who was head of the Navy, would have said, that in the second half of the twentieth century my family lived in America, Europe and south-east Asia. He himself had sacrificed his own career in untiring efforts to prevent Japan from entering a war that he believed could not be won. Other close relations in the family diaspora responded with similar determination to the new challenges of a dramatically changed world. Members of my family had close relations with Britain throughout the twentieth century and I myself ended up becoming a British citizen. My childhood memories of arriving in Washington and in London not so long after the war, having to integrate in what was a new and at times hostile world, and then being separated from my parents for many years for reasons of economic necessity, are not just youthful nostalgia; the story tells the struggle and the earnest intent of the Japanese leadership to regain their position in world affairs. Their values rested intuitively within the culture and customs of old Japan, of the samurai and of a hierarchical society. Ultimately, while remaining a staunch patriot, my father led his family to live a truly international life, with a firm belief that peoples of different nations were guided by common fundamental human values.

The Marriage

As was then customary in Japan, my parents were introduced by respective family friends who regarded the union of the two families as 'a good match'. The introduction was made by a school friend of Yoko's mother, Mrs Ohno Atsuko, and Admiral Takei Daisuke and his wife, who were friends of the Fukuda family. The two families came from different classes: until the end of the war, Japan had a rigid caste system; families were classified as nobility, samurai or commoners. The marriage certificate clearly marked their caste rankings. The union exemplifies the social aspirations of both classes at the time, one to rise in status and the other to gain wealth to maintain status – not dissimilar to that then prevailing in Britain, with dukes marrying American heiresses.

The wedding, with several hundred guests, was held opposite the Imperial Palace at the Imperial Hotel in Tokyo, the iconic building designed by Frank Lloyd Wright. It was the grandest hotel in Tokyo at the time, priding itself on fine Western cuisine. Most society weddings took place there, including all my mother's siblings'. The war was on, and group photographs of the occasion show everyone looking serious. My grandmother lamented that the wartime scarcity made it difficult to kit my mother out with the standard of trousseau expected of a family of their social standing and wealth. My father's parents never held that against her and welcomed her into the family; an old samurai dynasty such as theirs was firmly grounded in the traditional virtue of contempt for money. Nevertheless, the papers relating to the wealth tax returns that the Occupation government imposed soon after the war show that in her bank account Yoko held as much cash as my father and his mother put together, which she must have brought into the marriage. After the wedding my parents went on honeymoon to the grand and elegant Fujiya Hotel in Hakone on the foothills of Mount Fuji, still clad in deep snow, a favoured honeymoon destination in their circle.

The practice of *omiai*, 'arranged marriage', was almost universal in Japan in those days and Yoko would not have expected anything else. Eligible young people had beautiful portrait photographs taken for the purpose of *omiai* and these were presented to prospective families by close friends who would act as the *onakodo* ('go-between'). Introductions could be refused or rejected even after the meeting. These friends would let the families know about background and personality. Parents would quietly ask around amongst friends to canvass opinion, making sure no skeletons lurked in any cupboards. They would then broach the subject with their son or daughter to see if they would like a meeting. It would be unusual for parents to force their children into marriage, however suited they believed them to be. The couple, once intrigued, and if the photographs passed the test, would meet, together with the parents; if both sides then considered that the marriage might be suitable, the couple would meet from time to time for tea or lunch and eventually make the decision for themselves. That was the Japanese tradition, with marriage to a foreigner considered completely out of order. It persisted at least until the 1970s, and it was rare for upper-middle-class families to agree to their children marrying for love. That is not to say that there weren't exceptions: one of my mother's first cousins, who later became a famous politician, married for love. But he wrote in his memoirs that it was considered an *actus reus*, and his mother was exceptionally demanding of her daughter-in-law, even though she had been at the Peeresses' School and came from a well-known upper-class family. Even in the twenty-first century *omiai* marriages are not that unusual, though becoming less common, and with young couples more often meeting at university, at work or through their own friends. Even so, at the wedding ceremonies they often have had 'stand-in *onakodo*' from amongst family friends to lend formality. *Onakodo* also indicated the social standing of the families.

'Good families' did not allow their daughters to go out to work; it was thought to lower their status. Most daughters of well-to-do families went to university: it was considered an important qual-ification for a bride to be well educated. But parents made sure their daughters did not stay out late or have close boyfriends. To prepare for marriage, daughters would not only go to university, but also needed to learn the art of flower-arranging and the tea ceremony, as well as go to cookery school. It may seem unbeliev-able today that family background mattered so much.

Arranged marriages were in the first instance a union of two families. A daughter married *into* the bridegroom's family; her duties would then be to his family. In Japanese they say the bridegroom's family 'got' or 'was given' the bride. An engagement would be sealed with a *Yuinoo* (結納) ceremony at which both families gathered in the bridegroom's house. The bride's parents would commit to bring gifts of considerable value, described on a piece of paper, wrapped inside a ceremonial envelope and tied with gold and silver strings knotted in an elaborate manner. The actual gift would then be delivered separately. Another envelope, similarly elaborately tied, would contain the list of the bride's trousseau. The envelopes would be presented on a lacquered salver on a stand, and the visitors would bow deeply to the receiving family. Significantly, there were also exchanges of the lists of close relations – an important testimony to the respectability of the families. Yoko kept her lists carefully in the top drawer of her chest of drawers all her life. Her trousseau list included several pieces of furniture: a lacquered dressing table and matching chests of drawers, several *tansu* (tallboys with drawers) that would contain her kimono and clothes, and other furniture for her own possessions. She was given her own room in the house for her personal use. Her parents expected that her new family would protect her just as much as she would be expected to serve the bridegroom's family faithfully. That would bring with it obligations and the requirement for mutual respect in financial as well as personal terms. Yet the relationship between the two families remained formal; mutual respect, but always a distance between them.

As shown later in this book, American intellectuals during the Occupation frowned upon the practice of arranged marriages as being retrograde and argued that free marriage was superior. Some wrote expressing their views very directly to my father. Within a couple of decades, as the Americanisation of Japanese lifestyle relentlessly took hold, the American dream of free love became the norm. It is now almost taboo for parents to discuss the family background of the prospective son- or daughter-in-law. My father was a liberal thinker and he was given to saying to us when we were young: "I won't be able to find you a husband; so you find your own..." But it is worth recalling that even in Britain, a more traditional society than America, it was a form of social etiquette and a mark of good upbringing that girls were 'introduced' by someone and that they did not just casually meet their partners, even though the introductions were not so for-malised or ritualistic as in Japan.

Divorce was frowned upon and carried a social stigma, but was not that uncommon. Indeed, on both sides of my family some marriages failed; the families then ceased all communication. Often these divorces resulted from incompatibilities of families, rather than issues with the couple themselves.

My parents had a happy marriage. There were stresses for my mother that might have come from the nature of *omiai* marriages. But she followed the tradition of wifely obedience dictated by custom; her personality, groomed to be compliant, was also accompanied by a learnt forbearance. My father loved her, as we know from his letters, and he also knew of the strains that she might have been put under. Whether such stresses and strains were greater than in a Western-style love match is difficult to tell, but in the context of the conventions of Japanese marriages of the time, Yoko lived her married life as it was expected of her and found happiness on her own terms.

Only seven months into her marriage Yoko fell ill with pleurisy and went home to her parents to recuperate. My father was shocked and desolate. He wrote to her of his sadness in the most expressive way: he could feel her presence in every room and felt bereft to see her small room empty but for her personal possessions – handbags on her dressing table. On returning from the office in the evenings she was not there to welcome him back at the entrance to the house as she always had done; how much he cherished the memory of her walking with him each morning to the top of the road to see him off to the Ministry; how much he was touched to find her still waiting for him with their dinner even well after 10.30 at night; how much he enjoyed their walks around the neighbourhood together at weekends. The memories of walking in the hills together at Hakone on their honeymoon were engraved on his heart. It might be that habits and customs in his family differed from hers, and that might have been stressful for her, but how greatly he appreciated her readiness to accept them. Mother kept this letter in the drawer of her dressing table all her life, together with another he wrote in the early years of their marriage which tells her of his personal convictions and philosophy.

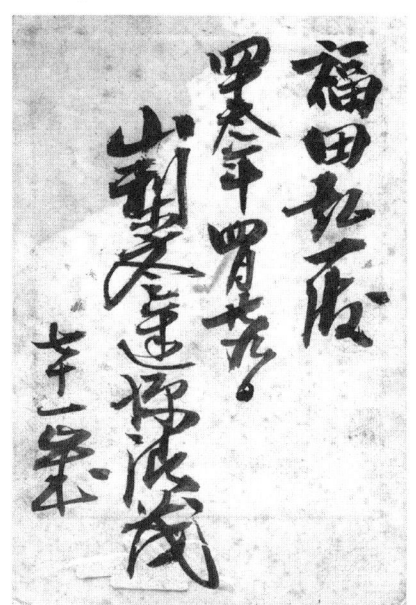

'The Last Samurai': my great-grandfather, Yamanashi
Bunnoshin of the Daté clan; photo studio, Sendai, 1910.

1. The Samurai Tradition and the Fukuda Family

~

Who Were the Samurai?

Generations of Fukuda ancestors were samurai, going back to the thirteenth century. Family records show that in the sixteenth century one of them served at the Court of Toyotomi Hideyoshi (豊臣秀吉) as a senior adviser on strategy – something like a Cabinet minister in today's government. My father descended from that distinguished samurai ancestry, but his mother's family were also an ancient samurai retainer of the Daté clan in Sendai. He was therefore of the *shizoku* (士族) caste at birth and when he married, before the caste system was abolished at the end of the war. The history of the samurai is much romanticised in the West and remains something of an enigma to students of Japanese history, or at least a curiosity. The cinematic representations – the stories of the *Kagemusha*, which depicted the historic Battle of Sekigahara which brought Tokugawa Ieyasu (徳川家康) to power at the end of the sixteenth century, and of the *Seven Samurai*, a moral tale of an earlier period, – are legendary. The elaborate samurai armour, made of lacquer and silk, and the fine metalcraft of the swords immortalise the romance of the samurai. Yet it would be a mistake to reduce the history of the samurai to something worthy only of a television drama, or state simply that the time of the samurai was abruptly brought to an end by the Meiji Restoration. First, the relationship between the successive shoguns and the emperor was not one of rivalry, as is often imagined in the West. The events that led to the Meiji Restoration constituted a struggle between the samurai clans themselves rather than a confrontation between the samurai class and the emperor. As S. R. Turnbull wrote in his authoritative volume on the history of the samurai: '... there was little that was radical or revolutionary about the Meiji Restoration ... for it was engineered by members of the samurai class itself and the Emperor remained what he had been since ancient times, a legitimizer of government by others...'

'Samurai' is often translated simply as 'warrior' in the West, but in fact they were a hereditary military nobility and officer caste of Japan from the Middle Ages until the designation of samurai was abolished in the Meiji Restoration; but its caste ranking remained until the US Occupation government abolished the class system in 1946. For centuries until the Tokugawa shogunate gained control and the allegiance of all the clan chiefs of the whole country, the chiefs, the *daimyo* as they were called, had been principally engaged in territorial aggrandisement to bring greater areas under their control and into their fiefdoms. The daimyo were the feudal landowners, served by their retainer samurai who belonged to the clan and were paid in rice according to their rank. The daimyo and senior samurai more often than not built huge fortified castles and lived in them with their families, surrounded by the more senior of their retainers, within the castle or close by. They were wealthy and were distinguished by being allowed to carry two swords. They remained the highest-ranking social caste of Japan throughout the Edo period.

For five centuries until the Tokugawa clan established its hegemony (in the early seventeenth century), Japan went through a period of continuous fighting between various clans – rather like

Scotland and much of Europe in the Middle Ages. The Heian period that preceded that saw three centuries of Fujiwara clan dominance: the Fujiwara family, having sprung from northern Japan, gained predominant influence in the governing of Japan by establishing a regency through marrying their daughters into the imperial family; a child emperor would be retired on gaining maturity and successive child emperors reigned, but only in name. The Fujiwara lived in splendour, more magnificent than the Imperial Palaces, espousing the sophisticated lifestyle of the Imperial Court – music, poetry, banquets, the refined culture of the Heian period. It is beautifully depicted by Murasaki Shikibu in her *Tale of Genji*, considered to be the world's first ever novel, written in the eleventh century. She herself was of samurai descent and had married a Fujiwara and become lady-in-waiting at the Imperial Court. Meanwhile the Taira family descended from Emperor Kanmu (AD 782–805) established a powerful clan; by the order of that emperor, the descendants of previous emperors from several generations before, as well as of future emperors who were not eligible for the throne, would be given the surname Taira/Heike. Several successive emperors therefore had descendants who were Tairas.

By the late eleventh century, factionalism at Court between different branches of the Fujiwara family whose power was on the decline by then, as well as of the imperial family itself, erupted in a struggle between the powerful samurai clan of Minamoto (related by marriage to the Fujiwara) and that of Heike/Taira (their offspring being imperial themselves); by then the main line of the Taira family had for two centuries taken the leading positions of government. It is considered that Taira no Kiyomori created the first samurai government of Japan by 1156 in Kyoto. The war between separate branches of the imperial family has some similarity to the Wars of the Roses in England a few centuries later. The epic *Tale of the Heike* (平家物語) tells of the long-fought struggle which ended in the victory of the

Minamoto clan and its leader becoming shogun. The Heike clan was destroyed. Minamoto no Yoritomo set up his Court in Kamakura, leaving the Imperial Court in Kyoto. My Fukuda ancestors were originally members of the Heike clan. Yoritomo was the first shogun of the first *bakufu* (military government) in Japan's history.

The Kamakura period, and the Ashikaga and Momoyama periods that followed, spanned five centuries of territorial wars (*sengoku jidai* – 戦国時代). Students of Japanese history will be familiar with the names of Takeda Shingen (武田信玄), an Ashikaga shogun who sprang from the mountainous region of Shinshu (now Nagano prefecture) and of Oda Nobunaga (織田信長). Takeda Shingen was a member of the Minamoto clan. My mother's ancestors from that region were retainers of the Takeda shogunate, but the consequence of defeat in battle sent them fleeing to the hills, robbed of samurai status for good. In the sixteenth century Oda Nobunaga, an enlightened but ambitious samurai of the Heike clan, attempted to unify Japan, but was assassinated by the forces of a treacherous retainer. His ambitions were inherited by his follower, Toyotomi Hideyoshi, who avenged his master by defeating the traitor in battle and assumed Nobunaga's authority and power.

Hideyoshi unified Japan, becoming its *de facto* ruler, appointed Chancellor of the Realm and Imperial Regent. By then, he had subjugated the area that is now Kyushu, the Satsuma domain of the Shimazu clan. He staged a long but inconclusive war against Korea, which gave him national kudos. He opened a port at Imahama on the shores of Lake Biwa, east of Kyoto, and built his castle there. It is no surprise that my father's family, residing at Miyazu castle not far away in the territorial suzerainty of the Shimazu clan, should have been senior members of his Court. Hideyoshi left lasting legacies for Japan in many ways: Momoyama Castle, Osaka Castle, the class system itself, the restriction on the possession of swords to two for the clan samurai retainers but only one for the *ronin* (masterless) warriors. He also restored many important temples in Kyoto, still to be seen today. During his shogunate Zen Buddhism was introduced to Japan from China. Hideyoshi was of the view that the samurai's military skills must be matched and enhanced by cultural achievements and values. The stoical philosophy of Zen was disseminated among their ranks, and it was Hideyoshi who embedded the practice of tea ceremonies and Noh plays that were to become lasting cultural hallmarks of Japan. He himself took the lead in Noh plays, staged with his retainer samurai playing supporting roles. His principal tea master was the legendary Sen no Rikyū (千利休) whose descendants continue to this day as the leading tea ceremony masters, Senge (千家).

It was with the philosophy of Zen that the stoical values of the *bushi* (武士), were adopted and cultivated until they became synonymous with samurai. Bushi were the *shizoku* (士族), a caste that survived until the end of the Second World War within Japan's class system; *bushido* (武士道) is the 'way of the samurai', the unwritten code of behaviour and lifestyle that encompasses not only the martial arts of kendo (剣道), karate (唐手) and judo (柔道), but also the philosophical values of self-discipline, loyalty, self-sacrifice, humility, austere aestheticism and modesty of dress in everyday life with formal preparedness for ceremonies.

Throughout these centuries of successive shogunates, the imperial family at Kyoto held a parallel authority, all the time recognising the military government of the shogun. The Imperial Court at Kyoto awarded the title of shogun to the head of the *bakufu* (幕府) – characteristically this meant the 'field headquarters of the army' while on the battlefield, the temporary command post. The emperor could still issue imperial orders to the *bakufu*, which theoretically had to be followed. But the effective power and actual administration were in the hands of the hereditary shoguns. Thus, the emperors and their advisers were often silenced or coerced by threats of military force. As already seen, certain samurai families exercised enormous influence over the imperial government: the Fujiwara, the Taira and the Minamoto, not least because they were often related or partly imperial themselves. The jealousies between them produced numerous regional and large-scale wars of alliances, betrayals and transitions of power. The Meiji Restoration merely returned the central authority to the emperor. Samurai lost their occupation as warrior-governors, but former samurai became the administrators and officer caste of the imperial government of Japan. My father came from one of those families and continued that tradition, becoming a senior government official and never forgetting his heritage. He instinctively lived by the code of behaviour of the bushi or samurai, reinforced by his upbringing by parents both descended from distinguished samurai families.

The Nagasaki Years and the Mitsubishi Shipyard

Masaru was born in Nagasaki in September 1914. His father, Fukuda Koichi (福田弘一), was a senior naval architect at the Mitsubishi shipyard there, the largest shipyard in Japan. His parents named him Masaru, which means 'victory', as the First World War was underway and Japan had declared war on Germany the previous month. Masaru's uncle, Yamanashi Katsunoshin (山梨勝之進), a young officer of the Imperial Japanese Navy, had just arrived in Singapore to serve as the Liaison Officer with the Royal Navy in its Pacific campaigns. (The one and only time in history that the Imperial Japanese Navy served under Royal Navy command.)

The family lived in a large house with gardens in the hillside residential district of Nagasaki, Otomegawacho (夫婦川町) at the foot of Shironokoshi (城残) mountain, overlooking the bay. There were tall gateposts and walls, a long avenue from the gate to the house, verandahs and a garden with mature trees. There was a Zen Buddhist temple, Shuntokuji (春徳寺), very close. The outstanding views from the house were an inspiration for young

Masaru as he saw ships on the horizon. One day a pre-Dreadnought battleship, HIJMS *Katori* (香取) came into port; soon two sailors came to the house to say they had been ordered by the Captain to take the family on board to visit. *Katori*, the then pride of the Imperial Navy, was the first battleship that Masaru's uncle had been given to command, at the young age of forty. It was the flagship of the Taisho Emperor and was the last but one battleship built for Japan in Britain, commissioned just before the Russo-Japanese War (1904–05) to be built by the Vickers shipyard at Barrow-in-Furness. The last battleship built in Britain was *Katori*'s sister ship *Kashima*, built at Elswick by the Armstrong Whitworth shipyard. He arranged for the family to inspect it and visit him on board. My father often told us that for a boy aged nearly four it was an unimaginable excitement.

On Sundays during the summer months, a special boat was prepared for the families of the shipyard to take them to an island across the bay. They picnicked and bathed on lovely white sand; my grandmother was a strong swimmer. My father recalled that though Nagasaki was the prefectural capital and home to the Supreme Court of Western Japan, the city was dominated by the Mitsubishi shipyard. Naval ships were launched with members of the imperial family and the Minister of the Navy always in attendance; red and white ceremonial balls (薬玉) would be broken to release white pigeons. There was a clubhouse for the senior employees of the shipyard: my father told us of his happy memories of being taken there to be served delicious cocoa and Western cakes and to play billiards. He loved the sea and when he retired went on many drives with my mother along the coast of Sagami Bay from their holiday flat in Hayama.

My father was the youngest of the three children of my grandparents. The eldest daughter, Michiko (道子), died aged three of diphtheria while her father was away on business in Hong Kong. As Masaru was born after her death my grandparents could not have been more assiduous in protecting his wellbeing.

He had another sister, Naoko (直子), two years older. They were very close. From the upstairs bedroom windows they could see the entire extent of Nagasaki Bay and together they watched the daily shuttle boats to Shanghai arrive and depart; the hulls of the British warships were painted entirely in white, indicating peacetime, and the French sailors would be strolling the quays, bright red pompoms on their caps. The Chinese navy came in, painted in the bright Chinese colours. To escape the oppressive heat, foreign residents of Shanghai frequently came for sojourns in Nagasaki, which they found cleaner and more sophisticated. The British, the Dutch, the French and the Russians strolled the streets of Nagasaki, which was at that time an international city.

Shuntokuji was to become a lasting link for my family with Nagasaki. When Michiko died, the priests at the Zen Buddhist temple came to my grandparents and asked if they could have her buried in the temple grounds. Although they understood that the family was Christian, they said young Michiko came to play at the temple and had become their friend. They loved her and would like to have her buried there. They built on her grave in the front garden of the temple grounds a large stone monument of a Buddha cradling an infant girl. Years later, Aunt Naoko visited the temple and discovered that Shuntokuji was one of the temples which hid Christians during the persecutions in the seventeenth century when the Tokugawa shogunate came to power. The well behind the temple buildings has a cross carved into the stone below ground and the hidden Christians gathered around the well to worship. Aunt Naoko told us when we were at our summer house in Karuizawa in the early 1970s how moved she was to find it; being a devout Catholic herself with deep belief in fate, she found the coincidence more than touching.

Nagasaki was of course historically one of the principal Christian communities in Japan. It was where the first foreigners, Portuguese and Spanish Jesuit missionaries led by St Francis

Xavier, arrived in Japan in the sixteenth century, and the scene of Christian persecution under the Tokugawa shogunate in the following century. I myself have visited Shuntokuji twice on my visits to Nagasaki, and my father sent an annual contribution to the temple throughout his life. Masaru also instructed the family that he wanted to have his funeral conducted by the priests of Shuntokuji; though he was brought up a Christian, towards the end of his life he renounced it. So it was that my father's funeral at our home in Tokyo was conducted by the principal priest of Shuntokuji and he received his *kaimyou* – the Buddhist name given at death – from the temple. My mother has said that she too would like a Buddhist funeral when her time comes at our temple, Kotokuji in Tokyo, which is associated with Shuntokuji and whose chief priest played a part in my father's funeral.

Fukuda Origins: Miyazu Castle since the Middle Ages

Nagasaki was not the ancestral base of the Fukuda family; my grandfather was sent there by his employer, Mitsubishi Shipbuilding (now Mitsubishi Heavy Industries). The samurai seat of my father's ancestors was Miyazu Castle (宮津城) in the Kyoto prefecture. The family owned extensive areas to the west of Miyazu, which included large mines.

Historical records show that the Fukuda family were already samurai by the thirteenth century. Their name was Fukutomi until the early nineteenth century when the name of Fukuda was bestowed on Fukutomi Jūzaemon (福富重左衛門), my father's great-great-grandfather, as reward for exceptional service by the clan chief, Lord Shimazu of the Satsuma domain. The earliest known ancestor was Fukutomi Kibei (福富喜兵衛), six generations before Jūzaemon. He would have been in the Heike clan. One of his successors, Fukutomi Heizaemon (福富平左衛門), during the Momoyama period of the sixteenth century, already residing at Miyazu Castle, was what we might today call 'minister' in charge of strategy in the government of Toyotomi Hideyoshi.

As the samurai's governing role under the military shogunate ended with the Meiji Restoration, my great-grandfather wrote out in his own hand the family history, delving into early records verifying the lineage of the early generations of the Fukutomi/ Fukuda family at Miyazu Castle. It was customary in the Edo period for senior samurai families to engage in mining, to give them credibility and bolster their power and social position; the family had, eight generations before, expanded their land ownership to Tajimakoku Choraigun Seino Ginzancho, west of Miyazu, in order to develop an extensive mining operation – probably silver mining judging from the address, 'Ginzancho'. Successive generations of the family continued to own and operate those mines. The family also produced *sake* from the newly harvested rice on the extensive farmland in their domain around Miyazu city; they continued this business for hundreds of years until the mid-nineteenth century. It was for the owner-ship of this extensive territory, with precious metal mining and rice and sake production adding to the territorial suzerainty of the clan as a whole, that its chief, Lord Shimazu, bestowed the name of Fukuda on Fukutomi Jūzaemon. The area of Miyazu was prosperous in the Edo period; in 1899, by imperial decree, Miyazu became an open port for trade with Great Britain and the USA.

My great-grandfather, Fukuda Jōnosuke (福田譲之助) – samurai name Minamoto Chuushin/Tadanao (源忠直) – was the last samurai of the Fukuda family. When the Meiji Restoration ended the samurai hierarchy, my great-grandfather became a master of swordsmanship and taught it to the younger gener-ation. I remember my youngest sister Eiko asking our father what she was to write as her great-grandfather's occupation in her school homework in Washington; he said "Fencing teacher." But father was being modest about his forebear's achievements. His grandfather also became a civil engineer as modernisa-tion in Japan gathered momentum. He was the instructor for engineering technique in the building of Japan's first mountain tunnel, the Osakayama tunnel in Shiga prefecture. He then took charge of the management of the tunnels of the Hokuriku line, one of the first railways built in Meiji Japan.

By the time my grandfather, Fukuda Koichi, was born in 1880, Jōnosuke had moved the family along the coast from Miyazu eastwards to Echizen, an area rich in Japanese history, and the birthplace of Sei Shōnagon, the author of *The Pillow Book* (*Makura no Soshi*). Echizen is also known as the centre of fine *uchihamono*, hand-beaten blades. When he compiled the family tree, Jōnosuke wrote a note saying that Koichi was brought up in his early years near the sea in Echizen. It was there that Jōnosuke honed his knowledge of engineering and the railway transport system that required tunnels to carry the lines through the mountainous terrain. But the family moved again for Koichi's schooling when he was six years old, establishing themselves in the northern outskirts of Osaka, known as Sugaharacho. Jōnosuke and his father, Fukuda Iemon (福田伊右門), and their wives are buried in the family grave in the great Tennōji temple (天王寺) in Osaka. The temple, thought to have been founded by Shōtoku Taishi in AD 593, is the oldest official temple in Japan. Having sold the vast estate in Miyazu the family was wealthy, and with the building of the tunnel my great-grandfather made a fortune.

Grandfather Koichi (福田弘一): *Scion of the Samurai*

My grandfather, the eldest son, was brought up in wealth: he recalled to his son Masaru that he had a succession of sailing boats, played tennis, learnt the arts of flower-arranging and tea, played the violin, and indulged in every luxury pastime of that generation. He was academically gifted and an honour student at school. He became proficient in French and studied its literature; our summer house in Karuizawa called Tsubaki-So (椿荘), which he had designed and built, had walls lined with bookcases full of French classics. The main room had a potbellied stove with a flying chimney on the pine floor. He loved classical music and played the violin himself, but it became his abiding ambition that his daughter Naoko should become a concert pianist. At our family home in Tokyo he had a large collection of records of all the major works of eighteenth- and nineteenth-century European composers; we played them every day on the HMV gramophone in a mahogany case. As a young child I was always intrigued by the picture of a dog inlaid in its inside lid. For his profession he chose to be a naval architect, studying shipbuilding and qualifying at the Imperial University of Tokyo. His life and lifestyle were appropriately those of a scion of a wealthy aristocratic family, and he kept to these ways throughout his life.

Yet my grandfather was proud of his own achievements; he told his son Masaru that the Meiji Emperor always attended the graduation ceremonies of the Imperial Tokyo University and, when he was recruited into Mitsubishi Shipbuilding, the founder and Chairman, Iwasaki Koyata, interviewed him personally. The company represented the epitome of Japan's naval engineering – the symbol of power that provided to officers and men alike a profound sense of confidence in the Imperial Navy. He joined it as Japan was basking in the glory of victory in the Russo-Japanese War the year before. He was there in the best years of the Japanese Imperial Navy and of Japan's naval shipbuilding. Even before the Meiji Restoration, the last shogun recognised the supreme importance of the Navy as the primary defence force of the nation. The Meiji Emperor introduced a long-lasting collaboration with the Royal Navy, not only inviting instructors to the naval academy but also ordering the most up-to-date warships from Britain. Amongst Koichi's peers were some who rose to become President of the company, but together with many of his colleagues he was to fall victim to the naval limitation treaties, which in the 1920s and 1930s restricted naval expansion by Japan. He was an authority on calculations of the Plimsoll line, and known to be so at Lloyd's of London: he told his family it was his pride that the submissions bearing his signature were never once returned by Lloyd's. But, as my father recounted, his weakness was that he did not drink alcohol – not good for corporate ladder-climbing.

His younger brother Takashi (孝, my father's uncle) was adopted at birth as the eldest son of Shimazu Seinosuke (島津 政之助). The Fukuda/Fukutomi family had a long association with the Shimazu family and are related. Masanosuke himself was the third son of Fukuda Iemon, and my great-grandfather Jōnosuke's younger brother. So Fukuda Takashi was adopted by his uncle. It was common practice in those days for aristocratic families to adopt children to secure the succession. For successive generations my father's ancestors were samurai of the Shimazu clan: my great-great-great-grandfather, Jūzaemon (samurai name Minamoto Chuujuu/Tadashige 源忠重), his son Iemon and grandson Jōnosuke were all feudal warriors in the Shimazu clan until Jōnosuke retired in 1872. As is well known to historians, the Shimazu clan were the daimyo of the Satsuma domain, instrumental in the Meiji Restoration. Until his death my father kept in contact with his Shimazu cousins, childhood playmates from Nagasaki.

Koichi's sisters, Miyoko and Kiyoko (my father's aunts), married well into the Okamoto and Matsuno families, and Miyoko's daughters (my father's first cousins) eventually married men who became leading industrialists in Japan's postwar period: Mima Toshiyuki as President of Nippon Mining, and Haruyama Shigeo as President of Asahi Life Insurance.

In his late teens, Koichi went to school in Sendai, partly because his uncle Ainosuke (愛之助、brother of Jōnosuke) had established a separate line (*bunke* 分家) of the Fukuda family there, and the Sendai Daini High School was the second most academically acclaimed high school in Japan. His own father had retired by then and the family fortune was somewhat in decline; his parents continued to live at their home in Osaka. He worked during school holidays delivering newspapers. He espoused Christianity there, becoming a Methodist. It was during those years that he was introduced to my grandmother at the family seat of the Yamanashi family.

Grandmother Sada (山梨貞) and the Yamanashi Family: Christian Samurai

Yamanashi Sada (山梨貞), who was to become Koichi's wife, was the eldest daughter of a senior samurai – Yamanashi Bunnoshin (山梨文之進) of the Daté clan. Sendai was the only city in Japan that allowed Christian worship throughout the Edo period. It was home to the legendary Will Adams, the first Englishman to arrive in Japan (in 1604), who became a confidant of the Shogun, impressing him with his account of Protestant England's victory over the Catholic Armada of Spain. In 1582, the chief of the Daté clan had sent a youth mission to the Vatican. It was not long after the death of Michelangelo and Rome was still enjoying the legacy of Pope Julius II's art patronage; they were welcomed at sumptuous banquets, and presented with beautiful ornaments of gold and silver and Christian paraphernalia. The sadness of their return home was that, by the time they arrived back, the Tokugawa shogunate had closed all ports to foreigners and to Christians. Nevertheless, the Daté family remained Christian throughout the Edo period and after. Their house in Tokyo was in Ikedayama, an upmarket central residential district, close to the family home in Shiroganedai bought by my grandmother; the choice of location might well have been due to proximity to her friends.

Koichi would approach the imposing gates of the Yamanashi estate, the drive rising beyond, with several kitchens on the left before one reached the house. He recalled that there were five kitchens, each cooking for different parts of the household. It was a major establishment, and he arrived in a state of awe.

The estate extended to over 3,000 *tsubo* (around 10,000 square metres). There were deer roaming in the park and mature trees, giving a certain grandeur to the estate. It is now the site of a girls' high school. Sada, the eldest daughter, was organising various members of the household in their tasks. She was a beauty in her twenties, with unusually deep-set pale brown/green eyes and high cheekbones, several years senior to Koichi. She always had a kindly gaze. We learnt from his cousin after my father died that she had been married before and divorced, with a child who died young. Why my father never told us is a mystery, but perhaps he had put it out of his mind. Koichi went on to university in Tokyo but returned to marry her after he qualified as a naval architect. It is not clear whether they first lived in Tokyo or in Osaka, but by 1910 they were in Nagasaki, and his mother Tsugi went to live with them.

Sada was a devout Christian, and a Baptist lay preacher. My grandfather died six months before I was born so I never knew him. But I remember my grandmother saying her prayers every morning and evening with me beside her before a small altar in her room. She would tell me to be good so I would not be sent to hell; the graphic descriptions of what hell might be like are etched on my mind. We often went to church together, to the Misakicho Church (三崎町教会) in the Kanda district of Tokyo. It was originally built in stone in Gothic style, later replaced in the 1920s by a more neo-classical edifice, also in stone. Today it remains a beautiful modern church of serenity and calm. Not only did Sada follow all Christian virtues and deeply believe in the teachings of the church, she was also an exceptionally able woman. She was always ready to help anyone in need: she would sew the wedding attire for a neighbour's daughter's ceremony overnight; she was quick-witted, a perfectionist in everything she approached and ultra-efficient in all matters of housekeeping, much to the annoyance of her daughter-in-law! She would hurry Yoko to have a quick lunch and cook regional dishes from the North that were unfamiliar to Yoko. She maintained very high standards in the choice of clothes and indeed all possessions, her taste discreet but espousing the highest quality. She bought for her daughter-in-law grand kimonos with the Fukuda family crest sewn on.

She adored and protected me, lest her granddaughter by her most treasured son should fall into any danger. She bought the most lovely clothes for me from the moment I was born. She would send my mother out during the period of wartime austerity to buy food from the top-branded manufacturers, never accepting what was generally available from the local groceries. Yoko found this very hard. Often my grandmother walked to visit her friends, the Daté family from Sendai, and sometimes she would take me with her. I found those visits somewhat intimidating. But she was a woman of great courage and generosity of spirit, and mother said she admired her. She had received an award from the Japan Red Cross for helping the injured and the displaced in the earthquake and tsunami that shook the Sendai area in 1892. Aunt Naoko said when her mother died, that she could hear her saying from the coffin: "Is it possible that I would die?"

An Anglophile Samurai: Yamanashi Katsunoshin KBE (勝之進) – *the 'Treaty Admiral'*

The Yamanashi family had a long and distinguished history as samurai dating back to the Middle Ages. The family is now remembered mostly through Sada's younger brother, Katsunoshin (勝之進). Of all the members of my immediate family, it was he who carried the torch for the samurai philosophy even a century after the abolition of that status. He also held a lifelong affection for Britain and a close association with the country throughout his career. He was one of the first cadets of the Imperial Naval Academy at Etajima, taught by the Royal Navy. Although he went to a Christian school established by American missionaries of the Congregational denomination, and was educated there in English, his desire to join the Imperial Navy made him attend night school to become even more proficient in the English language, as was required at the Etajima Academy. His masters included Archibald Douglas (later Admiral) with whom he kept in contact until Douglas's death. I met Douglas's granddaughter who came to visit me at my home, Creems, in Suffolk by helicopter; she was still piloting it herself, at the age of nearly eighty. She brought with her some copies of letters Yamanashi had written to Douglas and left them with me. Yamanashi's naval career is much recorded and posthumous biographies of him tell of his distinguished career and important contributions. His personality was well described by Mrs Elizabeth Vining, an American Quaker whom Yamanashi had selected to go to Japan in 1946 to tutor the Crown Prince in English and helped to settle in. He had initially preferred to have a Briton because of his natural affinity with Britain, but for political reasons at the end of the war he determined that it would be important to have an American for this role. She wrote in her book of recollections: 'There can be few left today who had themselves lived out the philosophy of the samurai as Mr Yamanashi has done … the samurai virtues of loyalty, contempt for money, frugality, simplicity, stoicism… He had all the qualities of the ideal samurai: courage, a stern sense of duty, loyalty, truthfulness, love of beauty, an ascetic grace of living in the face of poverty, kindness, dignity. In addition he had a Navy man's experience of great spaces and broadening knowledge of other lands, other navies, other ways of life and thought, which the land-bound warrior seldom has and without which he is blind and fatally prone to hubris…'

Yamanashi is remembered as the 'Treaty Admiral', the man who as Vice Minister of the Navy and First Sea Lord in 1930 committed the Japanese government to sign the second Naval Limitations Treaty, which restricted the building of support ships. (The first Naval Limitation Treaty of 1921 had limited the number of capital ships.) He had a long association with the Royal Navy and the *Times* obituary of him on his death aged ninety described him as 'a friend of the Royal Navy'. He had come to Britain in 1902 to oversee the building of the battleship *Mikasa* (the flagship at the decisive Battle of Tsushima in the Russo-Japanese War) at Barrow-in-Furness and sailed her back; he was at Dartmouth on an exchange programme in 1912; he served as the Liaison Officer with the Royal Navy in Singapore at the outbreak of the First World War; he was on tour to Scapa Flow a few days after the Battle of Jutland and attended the victory banquet on the *Iron Duke*; he was a friend of Admiral Jellicoe and particularly close to Admiral Jerram, and on this visit to Scapa Flow his old friends invited him to stay with them on their ship (Jerram's flagship HMS *King George V*) rather than with the Japanese naval officers on the ship they came in. It was those friendships that played a crucial role during negotiations for the two Naval Limitation Treaties. He was the principal escort on the visit by the then Prince of Wales to Japan in 1923, leading his squadron to the Indian Ocean to escort the Prince's squadron to Japan and likewise on the Prince's return journey. For this service he was awarded an Honorary KBE.

The Naval Limitation Treaties of 1921 and 1930
The power struggle between the 'Treaty Faction' of which Yamanashi was a leading member and the 'Fleet Faction' led by another admiral within the Navy, as well as that between the Army and the Navy, characterised the political conflicts of the 1930s in Japan. In his lectures to the students of the Maritime Self-Defence Force in the 1960s Yamanashi, by then in his eighty-fifth year, explained the fierce arguments exchanged between the principal protagonists. He stressed his key role in the two Naval Limitation Treaties of 1921 and of 1930; by that stage all others concerned were dead. In that theatre of political struggle, he put into practice his most profoundly held belief, that morality must

be the basis of warriors' conduct in their use of weapons and that the most dangerous thing in life is the pursuit of personal glory. The realism with which he approached the conferences reveals that he was not a pacifist. He demonstrated the essential qualities of a statesman – a never-flagging determination based on the firm convictions of a patriot – in the face of a complex web of political rivalries in Japan viewed against the background of those between the major powers abroad.

In 1921 Yamanashi was deputy chief of the Special Commission on Arms Limitation and was a plenipotentiary member of the delegation to Washington, led by Admiral Kato Tomosaburo. In his own account he characterised the Washington Treaty, which determined the capital ships tonnage ratio at 5:5:3 for Britain, America and Japan respectively, as the 'peaceful overture' to the eventual war against America. For him the negotiations were themselves a form of war without recourse to weapons. The treaty had its origins in the American desire to build the strongest navy in the world, rivalling the British, and in her ambitions in China and the western Pacific. In 1900 the relative naval strengths of Britain, Japan and the US had been in the approximate ratio of 100: 25: 20. However, Theodore Roosevelt's administration had begun the build-up of American sea power, so that by 1921 the ratio had changed to Britain 100, the United States 75 and Japan 49. In 1908 Yamanashi had been one of the officers who entertained the Sperry mission, coming to Japan to flaunt America's new naval strength. By 1915, while the European powers were engaged in the First World War in which Japan was with the Allies against Germany, the United States Navy Board was announcing that the US Navy 'should be equal to the most powerful Navy maintained by any other nation in the world.' Meanwhile, the issue of Japanese immigration into California had begun to be troublesome; successive legislation had been passed either limiting the number of immigrants or prohibiting them from owning farmland, until eventually any further immigration from Japan was prohibited in 1926. And despite facilitating the Treaty of Portsmouth to end the Russo-Japanese War conclusively in 1905 and recognising the terms of that treaty, within a very few years the United States started to challenge these over Japan's control of the railways in Manchuria, a major prize for winning the war, wanting to have similar access to them and eventually to start building its own there. Altogether, over thirty years US–Japanese relations had become ever more difficult and mutually antagonistic. Britain on the other hand, having been fearful of the Russian advance into China after its earlier conquest of Manchuria, was not pleased about the US's overt intentions in China with its insistence on an 'open door policy', and supported Japan's annexation of the Korean peninsula as her protectorate in return for a Japanese agreement to honour British strongholds on the Chinese mainland, forsaking the Anglo–Korean treaty of alliance. In this climate of rising mistrust amongst the major powers, the Japanese Navy was becoming increasingly nervous. Budget discussions in the 1910s were dominated by the so-called 'eight-eight plan' calling for the building of eight battleships and eight cruisers (see more below). This was finally approved in 1920, though the burden on the exchequer amounted to two-thirds of all government expenditure at the time. Kato Tomosaburo, Yamanashi and others felt that a naval limitation treaty was inevitable – Japan had reached the limit of taxation, and thus of the naval budget.

Meanwhile fiscal constraints were also mounting for Britain. Yamanashi stated in his lectures that Britain's position was never very clear to the Japanese at the start of the talks; they didn't know whether Britain had already reached an understanding with the United States. It had seemed so during the negotiations over the creation of the League of Nations in the Versailles Treaty, as Britain had sided with the United States, abandoning the Anglo-Japanese Alliance of 1902, which had been renewed twice before. It was because of the existence of that alliance that Japan had supported the British in the First World War. An important issue that annoyed the Japanese was the British rejection of their demand for racial equality in the terms of the Versailles Treaty, in order to suppress the Kaiser's assertion of the notion of 'the Yellow Peril'. Britain had her colonies with inhabitants of different races, and she had a large population of different colours and races living in the homeland; Britain was also wary of Japanese sympathy towards the nascent independence movement in India. Yamanashi himself lectured to students years later that Gandhi and Nehru had been inspired by Japan's victory in the Russo-Japanese war. In that lecture he speculated that had Japan been able to resolve the migration issue in California with an alternative immigrant destination, perhaps on the Chinese mainland, history might have been different.

In Washington in 1921 his old friend Admiral Beatty visited his room and said abruptly "We have no money." Dispensing with conventional salutations he launched forth on how it was essential to maintain naval superiority for the defence of widely scattered colonies but that the lack of financial resources meant inevitable concession to American demands. He urged Yamanashi that Japan must follow suit. It was imperative that Britain agreed to equality with the United States, but it could not accept a superior Japanese Navy; eventually the Japanese had to accept the ratio of 5:5:3. There were also discussions on the definition of capital ships and on the bases, on which the status quo was to be maintained. But no agreement could be reached on the tonnage ratios for cruisers and other supporting vessels, mostly because of the intransigence of the French and the Italians. And it was on this subject of the support ships that talks continued without agreement throughout the 1920s, with Britain strongly opposing the United States' proposals of equality and Japan trying to mediate between them.

In 1930 another meeting was called by Britain to be held in

London, following the failure of a conference in Geneva in 1927. Japan sent former Prime Minister Wakatsuki Reijiro, supported by Navy minister Takarabe Akira; Yamanashi as the Navy vice-minister was the effective head of the Navy Ministry and was to play the principal role in Japan signing the London Treaty of 1930. In his memoirs of his father, his son Shinichi records the size of that task. Not only did he weave together the various strands of opinion within the Navy itself, but he devoted tireless efforts to handling public opinion through the Press, lest the opportunity to preserve peace be lost. His son remembers late-night calls from the Press at his home, the official residence of the First Sea Lord, which he fielded unhesitatingly, telling his wife that the public had the right to know and understand the progress of the negotiations and Japan's position. For him personally, as well as for those who worked closely with him at the Ministry, there were numerous assassination threats, and Yamanashi declared he was prepared to confront them.

Those threats were real; the Prime Minister of that time, Hamaguchi Osachi, who from the start was totally committed to coming to terms with the other powers, and who appealed to Yamanashi "I am prepared to stake my life over this issue for the Country, the Emperor and the people. Vice Minister, please help me," was indeed assassinated. Yamanashi's task was principally to reconcile the interests of the Navy and the country at large, but also to gain the acquiescence of those who were opposed to the Naval Limitation Treaties, including Prince Fushimi, a leading Fleet faction member who had posed the loaded question: "Is Yamanashi wearing a military uniform?" Yamanashi had suggested that the delegation to London might include someone from the opposing camp, since he feared that the London Conference would spark a political confrontation within Japan, but his suggestion was rejected. The Japanese wish was to achieve 70 per cent of American (and British) tonnage for cruisers and support vessels and 78,000 tons for submarines.

With Yamanashi's insistence, despite various objections, this remained the basis of agreement. Wakatsuki's delegation managed to negotiate up the ratio from 10:10:6 to 10:10:6.975. The minuscule difference between this and 10:10:7, even with the final submarine tonnage of 78,000 tons, was to lead to disastrous political divisions in Japan. Britain insisted on no further building of submarines, thus by the end of 1936 the existing Japanese submarine tonnage of 78,000 tons, with no replacements allowed, would fall to 52,000 tons.

Yamanashi made the point that, at the Navy Ministry, the decision to agree to the terms of the second Naval Limitation Treaty put forward by the United States was based on practical considerations of available financial and other resources. Not just budgetary constraints, but also shortages of trained men and shipbuilding capacity were determining factors. He took the view that it was not the appropriate time to be arguing about constitutional theories on the meaning of the much-debated notion of 'Supreme Command'; rather, to focus on how to avoid being drawn into a war they had no hope of winning. He managed to corral the opinions of divergent interest groups and finally sent a telegram instructing the delegation in London to sign. He admitted that its sending was like spitting blood. He had arranged for the imperial family's agreement through Prince Fushimi, then the most senior member of the imperial family in the Navy, and also personally obtained the agreement of the chief opponent of the treaty, Admiral Kato Kanji, on condition that he would obtain the Prime Minister's agreement that the savings arising from the treaty would be spent on qualitative improvements in the Navy and quantitative upgrading of its air strength. But at a meeting between the Prime Minister, Admiral Kato Kanji and Yamanashi to communicate the Navy's position officially, Kato, who had agreed to remain silent, suddenly stated that from the standpoint of military manoeuvres the US proposal was unacceptable. Thus the Navy's wholehearted acceptance of the treaty was brought into question and the government was in crisis. Yamanashi nevertheless resolved to push the treaty through and sent the decisive telegram to Wakatsuki. He then engineered the apparently triumphant return of the delegation by sending his deputy to Harbin to forewarn them of the difficult atmosphere at home. As the celebratory banqueters sat down at table, Kato Kanji was not present; he had offered his resignation from the Navy.

Yamanashi in his lecture regrets that nothing could have been done to prevent the build-up of a political crisis. The issue of the legal interpretation of the constitutional relationship between the government and the armed forces – the meaning of 'Supreme Command' – is too complex a matter to delve into here. The arguments, hotly debated by parliamentarians and political-ly-oriented academic lawyers, were stoked by a constitutional requirement that ministers of the Navy and the Army be serving officers of the two armed forces, while these were of course at the same time members of the government. To some, especially the opponents of the treaty, the Navy had lost face on behalf of Japan. Yamanashi offered his resignation as vice-minister in June 1930. He wrote to the Prime Minister that it was the Navy that was placed in a sacrificial position, and in order to avoid further damage to its morale and to stem the conflict of opinion he felt it necessary to leave his post. He asked the Prime Minister to remember the understanding they had reached on the naval budget with the reduced naval capacity; and his final request was to bear in mind the achievements of Kato Kanji.

Yamanashi became Commander-in-Chief at Sasebo, then at Kure. As the militarists gained strength and political ten-sions mounted, involving violent confrontations, he offered his resignation in 1933 as full Admiral and Commander-in-Chief. Almost all senior serving officers of the Navy and of the Army who had had close relations with either Britain or the US were systematically removed as early retirees then. Many political leaders regretted this decision; the former Prime Minister and the leader of the delegation to London, Wakatsuki Reijiro, as often quoted, wrote that he said to Yamanashi "In any normal circumstance a person of your ability would have become the Admiral of the Combined Fleet and Minister of the Navy; that you should resign from your post makes me fear for the country." But Yamanashi replied that a decision of such magnitude would inevitably have involved personal sacrifice and that in committing Japan to the treaty he was fully prepared to be that sacrifice; he had no regrets. One of Yamanashi's protégés, Yamamoto Isoroku – one of Japan's greatest Second World War admirals – often quoted Yamanashi, arguing passionately but unsuccessfully for the continuation of the treaties after 1936, when they were scheduled to expire.

This simplified account does little justice to those who were deeply concerned about the geopolitical situation around the Pacific between the major powers. In the background were the consequences of the First World War which cost the European nations not just lives but their financial future; the coming into force of the Versailles Treaty and the League of Nations which undermined the Anglo-Japanese Alliance of 1902, which was not renewed, leaving Japan feeling insecure; rivalry between Britain and the United States in terms of sea power, when the British were under financial pressure; escalating tensions between the US and Britain during the 1920s and 1930s, mostly over their respective interests in the Far East and the Pacific; Soviet intentions on the mainland of China, where Japan had started to win territorial suzerainty; Japanese intentions of countering or defending themselves from US interventions in China and the Pacific; and increasing US animosity towards Japan, due both to its commercial ambitions in mainland China and to the Japanese influx into California. Japan was on the back foot in 1921 in Washington and in 1930 in London. By the time my maternal great-grandfather, Watase Torajiro, was sending saplings of cherry trees to thank the Americans in 1911 for assisting in concluding the peace with Russia at the end of the Russo-Japanese War of 1904–5, the Americans under President Taft were already thinking that the Treaty of Amity and Commerce of half a century earlier was irrelevant to their future prosperity or to their power base and were curbing Japanese immigration. Cherry trees were welcome but not the people. The Americans were insisting during the First World War that the enemy was German 'militarism' rather than the country itself, and that henceforward global diplomacy must be based on a community of nations (via the League) rather than the hitherto prevalent basis of a balance of power. But in reality it was still balance of power considerations that dominated throughout the 1920s and 1930s. Indeed, even soon after the end of the Second World War, the American Occupation government said to Japan that it could just destroy the country's industry and livelihood and give it to the Soviets, but that would increase, at least 'slightly', the Soviets' power against the US and for now she preferred to keep Japan on her side. The manner in which the US–Japan Security Treaty of 1951 was imposed says it all.

Retirement from the Navy: President of the Peers' School
Yamanashi on his resignation from the Navy spent the following seven years in retirement at home, tending to his rose garden and pursuing other pastimes. He particularly liked reading Shakespeare and often quoted "There is a tide in the affairs of men…" His son wrote that he brought back from Washington many records of classical music and books on English literature. As if in anticipation of his change of fortune, he had purchased in 1929 a piece of land on the outskirts of Tokyo on which he built a new house to compensate for the loss of his official residence. But he must have known that his service to the nation had not ended with resignation from the Navy.

In 1939 Yamanashi returned to public life, appointed President of the Peers' School (Gakushuin). This was a highly political appointment at the time and in the context of the Japanese Empire: the following year the Crown Prince was to enter the school. The Navy put Yamanashi's name forward as successor to Admiral Nomura Kichisaburo, who became Foreign Minister in the new government of Abe Nobuyuki. The presidency of the Peers' School was always held by a senior military officer, the most notable of whom was General Nogi. The Asahi newspaper scooped Yamanashi's appointment in its evening edition. Public reaction was one of wholehearted acceptance. The journalist Sugimoto Ken (杉本健) wrote in his history of the Imperial Navy that the appointment further enhanced the sparkle of the 'star' of the Treaty Faction. Prime Minister Abe's government was short-lived, and by 1940 he was succeeded by Yonai Mitsumasa, previously a naval officer and Yamanashi's protégé.

The Showa Emperor (Emperor Hirohito) asked Yamanashi personally to take charge of the education of his elder son, the then Crown Prince Akihito, who later succeeded as Heisei Emperor. For Yamanashi it meant he was now responsible for Akihito's safety during war years. As the conflict intensified, Yamanashi evacuated the school to the mountains at Nikko, where they took over the legendary Kanaya Hotel. Today there are photographic displays there of the young boys of Gakushuin in their life of dormitories and classroom study.

Yamanashi served as the President of this august institution until October 1946. As the war ended, Yamanashi's priority was to try to save the school from being disbanded by the Allied Occupation government, as it was an imperial institution owned by the Imperial Household Agency. By then, the Crown Prince's younger brother, Prince Yoshinomiya, was also a pupil there. On his own initiative, with skilful but difficult negotiations with General Headquarters (GHQ) and the Imperial Household Agency, Yamanashi obtained an agreement that the school would be reorganised as a private educational institution, outside government control. The task was harder than was immediately apparent: he had to raise the funding single-handed to meet the cost of the required purchase of the school and its landed assets from the imperial household. Having successfully completed his task he relaunched the school, opening it to the public with competitive examinations for entry, and persuading Abe Nosei (安倍能成) to succeed him as President. Subsequently he retired. Yamanashi of course knew that, as a military man, it would be incumbent on him to withdraw from any educational establishment. He must have had the agreement of GHQ to that condition before completing his mission. It is ironic that the Allies, for whatever reasons of their own, purged a man so vehemently opposed – at the highest echelon of government – to Japan entering into war with the United States and its European allies, so sacrificing his career. He was appointed Honorary Life President of the school in 1964.

The Imperial Edict of January 1946

Yamanashi's public service did not end with the saving of the imperial school from potential demise. As soon as the Instrument of Surrender was signed on 2 September 1945 aboard USS *Missouri*, Yamanashi felt compelled to act; unconditional surrender threw into question the whole future of the imperial system and the Emperor's life. Yamanashi started secret negotiations with GHQ. He was a deft hand at manoeuvring political protagonists, as shown during negotiations for the London Treaty of 1930, skills once more to the fore as he masterminded this dramatic moment in history. His lips remained sealed about what happened at this pivotal moment throughout his life, but it is now incontrovertibly recognised by historians that Yamanashi was the author of the 'Declaration of Humanity', the Imperial Edict of 1 January 1946 in which 'His Majesty disavows entirely any deification or mythologising of his own Person…' The imperial system was therefore saved as a constitutional monarchy.

44

Yamanashi had sent an Englishman – R. H. Blyth of Ilford, employed at Gakushuin to teach English – on his bicycle to MacArthur's GHQ one cold day in December 1945, three months after the signing of the Surrender. Blyth was a haiku expert and a friend of Suzuki Daisetsu, a scholar of Zen philosophy, whom Yamanashi also employed at the school. Yamanashi entrusted to Blyth a sealed envelope, inside which was a handwritten note on a yellow piece of paper proposing his initiative; he asked that the reply, if in the affirmative, should be given by burning the yellow paper in front of his messenger. Blyth reported back to him in shock that the paper had been set alight before his eyes. Yamanashi negotiated with the support of the Prime Minister, Shidehara Kijuro, the Imperial Household Minister, Iwashita Sotaro, Blyth and his friends at GHQ (General Dyke) and one Dr Henderson, himself a haiku scholar. A pocket diary was uncovered in 2021 which made headlines in the Mainichi Newspaper. In it, Yamanashi had recorded his movements during this period, including his visits to GHQ and other places. Some entries are in English, typical of the man.

When an American historian, William P. Woodward – author of the authoritative history of the American Occupation of Japan – visited him in his eighties and broached the subject, Yamanashi was ready with a characteristic response. He clapped his hands loudly above his head and asked "Which of my hands produced that sound?" The historian, in search of a definitive answer to the enduring mystery of how the Declaration of Humanity came about, went straight to the point, broaching the subject of the piece of yellow paper. Yamanashi was definitely not going to play ball. And with a neat sense of humour he rebuffed it with another well-known riddle – "What is the sound of one hand clapping?" To this there is both no answer and an obvious answer. Yamanashi then asked the historian if he knew of the whereabouts of the piece of yellow paper to which he had referred. "You asked for that paper to be burnt!" came the reply, indicating the historian equally appreciated the supreme importance of the non-reply reply in this matter. Yamanashi was satisfied. The piece of yellow paper was the crucial evidence that the message to GHQ was written by Yamanashi in his own hand, and therefore that the suggestion for the Declaration came from the Japanese side close to the Emperor. Yamanashi had asked that the paper be burnt in front of the messenger as a failsafe way of preventing the Emperor committing himself on record one way or another. The old Admiral then explained that it would not have been appropriate had the Emperor pronounced words dictated directly by the Americans; yet, by the same token, had his words not been acceptable to the Americans then the whole project would have failed. He was on the ball even at that advanced age, showing astuteness and everlasting discretion.

One has to wonder if the Allies, in purging Yamanashi, had ever fathomed his deep understanding of the meaning of peace. As the journalist Sugimoto wrote, when he thought of Yamanashi, the two characters for 'peace', 平和, came to mind, as he was someone who recognised the true meaning of peace as not merely the cessation of combat. When the Showa Emperor was asked by a well-known Court journalist whom among his many advisers His Majesty respected most, he replied unhesitatingly: "Yamanashi Katsunoshin." A year before his death the Emperor sent him a personal gift of a walking stick with the imperial crest to be used at Court – the highest honour that the Emperor could bestow.

There is a stone monument to Yamanashi in Sendai at the site of his old family home, now a high school, and a memorial oak. The battleship *Mikasa*, whose construction he oversaw at Barrow-in-Furness, is preserved as a museum ship in Yokosuka, and contains a memorial display of Yamanashi, including a fine bronze bust. He had devoted much attention to the restoration and preservation of the ship in his last decade. He was honoured to be the first President of the *Mikasa* Preservation Society and invited his old pupil HIH Prince Yoshinomiya to represent the Emperor at the ship's inauguration as a museum in 1961. It touched him very much, as if closing the circle of his long career.

In 1917 Yamanashi had asked his elder sister, Sada, if it would be acceptable to sell the family estate to a school, as the Miyagi prefecture wanted it for the establishment of a girls' high school and local government offices. My grandmother replied that she would agree if it was to be an educational institution, but not for any commercial purpose. As she bade farewell to the centuries-old family estate, she planted a flowering cherry tree in the grounds which survives to this day.

Yamanashi devoted much effort to persuading the Yoshida Cabinet to establish a Maritime Self-Defense Force and to restore military pensions. I remember visiting him at home during the 1950s with my mother on numerous occasions; his house was almost spartan, the only ornament being a framed example of calligraphy by Crown Prince Akihito hanging in the place of honour in his drawing room, the *tokonoma*. He exuded warmth in private, and whenever he came to our school he would seek me out and greet me, but his dignity was awesome. As President of the school he knew every student by name, and also their parents' names and occupations: passing them in the street many years later he would amaze them with his instant recognition and by addressing personal matters of concern. He was known never to criticise another man, and despised self-serving comments by others. He habitually told his son that one must never speak of oneself or one's own achievements; it was for others to judge.

My father said to me in his final days at the hospital, when I was at his bedside throughout the night, that "The two people I admired most in my life were my mother and Uncle Yamanashi."

Aunt Naoko (直子) and the Haiku Poet

Aunt Naoko inherited many of her mother's Yamanashi characteristics. She too was a *grande dame* of immense abilities. Her facial features were those of the Yamanashi; like her mother fair in complexion with deep-set brown eyes above high cheekbones. She was handsome and tall. Her name Naoko is taken from her grandfather's samurai name, Minamoto Chuushin/Tadanao. As was her father's abiding ambition, she became a concert pianist, taught by a famous Japanese pianist of the time, and played at concerts conducted by Rudolf Kempe on his visit to Japan. On her untimely death in her early sixties, at Koyasan temple where her husband Kusatao and his circle were on a haiku retreat, innumerable people wrote to remember the kindnesses she had bestowed on them. One young neighbour wrote that when she was in distress over matrimonial proposals pressed on her by her parents, Naoko had said to her "Come and talk to me whenever you want and remember that I will always be your ally." She had the gift of being able to show her compassion in very direct ways.

In the early 1930s she married Nakamura Kusatao (中村草田男), one of the greatest haiku poets of the twentieth century. He had the demeanour of an artist and looked unusual with his wavy long hair; at that time no man in Japan went around with hair blowing behind him, and my cousins found it embarrassing to walk with him in public. My father respected him greatly and they were close friends. Naoko supported her husband in every aspect of work and life. She gave up the piano, believing that two artists in one house would not work. She was a devout Catholic, having decided to convert from her Baptist family faith while at Sacred Heart School.

Naoko's life centred on religion; she worked tirelessly for the local church and would never miss a service. She brought up her four daughters to be equally devout and required that their marriage partners should consent at least to children being brought

48

up in the faith. When her daughter Yumiko considered not going to mass one Sunday as she was preparing for the entrance examination for the University of Tokyo the following day, Naoko told her that going to mass and taking communion were all the more important in preparation for the exams. Naoko's second daughter, Ikuko, wrote a year before her death of ovarian cancer in her early sixties a heart-rending note to her family, which told of her lifelong convictions as taught by her mother: when asked at school aged seven what the most important thing in life was she had replied, after a little thought, "love". She had reflected for many years that perhaps the answer was a little audacious, but facing death (she had been told of the true nature of her illness and that the chemotherapy itself could kill her) she reaffirmed in her mind that it was love that was the most important thing in life; Ikuko told of her gratitude to her family, her sisters and her parents, also friends; and most of all that it must be what God had prepared for her and that there can be no fear in death if it is to be near her Lord. She had asked her younger sister, Yumiko, to pray for her ahead of the eight-hour surgery, because she said Yumiko's prayers were the most powerful.

Yumiko wrote in the Epilogue to her major work on Henri Bergson, the French philosopher, that when Ikuko asked her she contemplated for many hours the meaning of prayer; she wrote that she had struggled for many years to reconcile the desire for greater knowledge with her firm belief, as a devout Catholic, in the teachings of the church. Clearly she was influenced by Bergson's thinking on the dichotomy between 'dynamic religion' and 'static religion'. She came to believe, if I am not doing her an injustice by this simplification, that the words of St Benedict *ora et labora* (pray and work) provided at least a part of the answer. She translated it, though, in her book as 'Pray well and work hard.' Naoko and her family made an enormous contribution to the life of the church in Kichijoji near their Tokyo home, as well as in the resort of Karuizawa where we had summer homes. Her mother had worried that Naoko might have difficulty marrying as a Catholic: not many men would accept 'only fish on Fridays'. Kusatao's parents – diplomats at times stationed at the Embassy in London – were concerned that not many women would marry a young poet of slender means.

But together they built a close-knit and lively household; at mealtimes the family would engage in lively discussion and debate on all matters of current interest, and each daughter had no hesitation in expressing her independent views, often strongly arguing against their father and telling him to be quiet. There was definitely free speech there, unafraid of parental diktats: my sisters and I were always amazed at the lively verbal combat. A few moments before his death, Kusatao became a Christian and was able to receive the last rites. As befits a great poet, the family had a death mask made.

Aunt Naoko had perceptive and artistic taste – she often presented my mother with kimono fabrics or outfits that had caught her eye. She organised the finances of the family and built three separate houses for their four daughters in the grounds of their home. In this compound all the daughters, their husbands and their children lived together all their lives. In many ways it was enviable, providing a harmonious, warm and secure environment in which to flourish, all in their own ways. The two younger daughters still live there. When Naoko was young she would get up at 5 o'clock every morning to practise the piano for two hours before going to school. That early rising habit must have stuck with her ever after, as even at the holiday home in Karuizawa she would be up at 5, hours before the rest of the family, to clean the house and prepare breakfast as well as do her make-up and hair. She took away in her trousseau the Steinway grand piano. For many years she taught all her children to play, also some neighbours who wanted to learn. But ultimately Kusatao's work took over her life.

Leaving Nagasaki

Grandfather Koichi was relocated by Mitsubishi Shipbuilding from Nagasaki, where he had become head of shipbuilding, to the company's headquarters in Marunouchi, Tokyo in October 1923, the year the Washington Treaty of Naval Limitation was ratified, limiting the ratio of capital ships between Britain, the USA, Japan, France and Italy. As described in detail above, his brother-in-law Yamanashi was a plenipotentiary member of the mission to Washington and had played a significant role in the negotiations of 1921–22. My father was told by his uncle Yamanashi that the treaty put an end to the grand ambition, then in place, to build the Eight-Eight Fleet (八八艦隊) of eight battleships and eight cruisers. Construction of the battleship *Tosa* (土佐) at Nagasaki shipyard, then in progress, had to be abandoned. The treaty meant no further capital ships to be built in Japan; by 1926 there was no more work for my grandfather. What had once been an illustrious shipyard at Nagasaki now languished in such hardship that they used the teak procured for shipbuilding to make bookcases and furniture to be sold to staff members.

The President of the Imperial University of Kyushu asked Koichi to abandon his employer and accept a professorship in shipbuilding at the university. However, he declined this offer; my father regretted this decision and told him it was foolish of him, but Koichi told his son that the education of his children must come first and that had to be in Tokyo. He left the company in search of other employment, which was hard to find. He eventually became a lecturer at the Imperial University of Tokyo in shipbuilding engineering and design from 1927 to 1929. The 1930 Second Naval Limitation Treaty on support ships then halted Japan's naval shipbuilding altogether, at least for a while. My father has always said that the years of unemployment that followed were difficult ones for the family. In his memoir of his father, he wrote that, even so, Koichi enjoyed a better life than himself – continuing the wealthy lifestyle in which he had been raised, indulging in sophisticated pastimes, playing the violin and reading the French classics, sending his daughter to study piano with the then top pianist in Japan, and being able to spoil his grandchildren, whom he adored, whenever they came to visit. My father held this against him throughout his life until, with his own death approaching, he finally felt that he wanted to give his father a proper memorial service at the graveside.

One of Koichi's last achievements in his shipbuilding career at Nagasaki was to repair the German passenger and cargo vessel given to Japan at the end of the First World War as reparations. He spent the five months from June to October of 1920 in Tokyo and Yokohama, staying at the Tokyo Station Hotel opposite the company's headquarters in Marunouchi, to supervise the repair; the ship's balance was not secure. Koichi successfully restored the ship to seaworthiness and it was relaunched as *Taiyō Maru*. A model of it is in the Transport Museum in Tokyo. It was an irony of history that, on the eve of the attack on Pearl Harbor, *Taiyō Maru* was used by the Japanese military as a reconnaissance ship around the islands of Hawaii for the war that his family so much opposed. It would be difficult to know what his feelings were in the final month of 1941 as the Pacific War unfolded.

A very large framed photograph of the ship, together with another of its relaunch as *Taiyō Maru*, bearing the imperial chrysanthemum crest on its bow, always hung in the corridor of my childhood home in Tokyo. Just outside grandmother's bedroom was also an almost life-sized framed photograph of the infant Michiko, dressed in a beautiful kimono with a ribbon tied in a bow around her long hair. They were the perpetual reminders of my grandparents' Nagasaki years.

A Grand House in Tokyo
When they moved to Tokyo the family first lived briefly in Shimo Ochiai in the Shibuya district. But soon they bought a

plot of land in the upmarket residential district which is now called Shiroganedai. Grandfather Koichi designed and built a large house. It was customary at the time for wealthy families to have a twin house, one in Western style and the other in traditional Japanese *sukiya* style, but connected, so our family home was built in that fashion, with gardens set around. Naoko went to her wedding from that house and came home to give birth to her daughters. There was a long wall along the road, and a gate with tall gateposts on the slip road. On entering the main gate, a tall stone lantern stood, with large ancient stones set nearby surrounded by bamboo and Bergenia 'elephant ears', with large leaves of dark green. Pine trees, camellias and the ornamental Japanese maple that graced the front garden with colour in the autumn remain in my memory. The Western house was of fine silvery pebbledash with a tiled roof, set with tall sash windows in wooden frames painted dark brown. Being a ship architect, Koichi designed it with a very strong steel frame to withstand earthquakes; he had steel girders set in below the floors so that two concert grand pianos could be rolled around without vibrations.

The beautiful drawing room had a parquet floor, French windows with etched smoked glass opening onto the garden, three bays of sash windows and another two at the side of the room. A large two-tier chandelier of yellow crystal hung in the middle of the room. The walls were lined with smokey-coloured textured wallpaper in *moiré* and the windows were dressed with full-length dark gold velvet curtains fringed with tassels, as were the pelmets. There was an Edwardian mahogany inlaid suite of furniture on a soft green, thickly tufted carpet. Before Naoko married, there were two Steinway grands for her to practise on. A year before my father died, he had a plan to pay for one of the pianos to be refurbished and re-tuned, but the cost proved prohibitive. One end of the drawing room had a pair of full-length mahogany panelled doors surrounded by classical architraves opening onto the living room, also floored in parquet, with sash windows on two sides. It was a lovely grand room that all visitors admired; when my father decided to demolish this house on his return from assignment abroad in 1972, my mother's sister Setsuko (節子) said it was sacrilege to destroy that beautiful room. When I was a child I spent a lot of time in it, listening to music on the gramophone, looking at American magazines with lovely photographs (my father's friends in America had given him subscriptions), making telephone calls to friends and listening to the wireless. Father bought a gadget to practise putting, which he put under the sash windows overlooking the garden, and used in the evenings and at weekends. He had taken up golf when he married my mother, whose father was a keen and expert golfer, and he joined the exclusive Tokyo Golf Club, where my grandfather became Captain and President, playing with a handicap of one; my father was quite good, but not as good as his father-in-law or his brother-in-law.

The garden was surrounded by mature shrubs – azaleas, rhododendrons, fatsias, Japanese maple, gardenias, philodendrons and tall trees – with a swing on the lawn for me. When I was four my sister Sakiko (咲子) was born, and later she and I played together on the swing and picnicked on a rug. She was a high-spirited girl: when she learnt to speak she would pronounce proudly that having been born in the Year of the Tiger she was strong, and in her baby talk called herself *Chahchah*. This stuck as her nickname; we always call her Chahchah in our family, and that's how I refer to her in this book.

During the war my father would go on a risky journey amid constant air raids to my mother's family farm in Angyo, Saitama, travelling on the train with her father, to bring back potatoes and vegetables in a rucksack. After the war food was still scarce; my mother grew vegetables, cultivating a small patch in the garden, and we sometimes made bonfires so that we could cook sweet potatoes in the embers.

Before Chahchah was born, my parents decided to sell one half of the twin houses; the large Japanese house that linked to the Western house with a long wooden corridor was separated and sold with its surrounding garden. The asset tax that the Occupation government brought in forced many families to sell their land and houses. We also sold some forested land in Karuizawa. We were fortunate in finding a congenial family to move into the Japanese house. They had just returned from a posting in England; Mr Iwata was an executive of Ishikawajima Harima Heavy Industries. They had three daughters much older than me, whose grandmother also moved in. I loved going to visit her to play. I would borrow my mother's make-up, put on lipstick and a nice dress, try to walk in Mummy's high heels, and push my pram with my favourite doll through the garden gate. I brought my colouring book to show her and my doll's new clothes that my mother had made. Grandmother Sada became a close friend of hers, and she would come with me, helping to manoeuvre the pram.

It must have been hard for my father to make the decision to sell the house, but I have no doubt that his mother would have offered total support. My grandfather had died in January 1946 in the mountain resort of Karuizawa, at our summer house, to which he and Grandmother had evacuated in 1945 as the war intensified with the bombing of Tokyo by the Americans. He died of a heart attack aged sixty-eight. On receiving a telegram from his mother which read 'Father dies', Masaru immediately set off for Karuizawa with his brother-in-law Kusatao, travelling by train through snowy mountains in extreme cold. The scenery was still bleak with the ravages of war; winds howling, forests bare and snowy mountains on the horizon. There were no supplies or adequate services for cremation and funerals, so with the help of a neighbour and friend, Mr Tohyama, they waited in the wilderness for his body to be entirely cremated. Masaru and Kusatao brought back Grandfather's ashes in a box on the train. Though he had often said to his son that he wanted his ashes to be scattered in the Pacific Ocean, a simple ceremony at the family grave in Tama Bochi (多摩墓地) followed, after a funeral service at home in the freezing cold drawing room. Much later, Masaru felt that he must offer a proper memorial service for his father, and arranged this for 28 January 1984 (the thirty-eighth anniversary of Grandfather's death). He engaged a Protestant minister, Mr Kikuchi, from the nearby Shoei Church (頌栄教会) to conduct the service, chose the hymns which were those frequently sung at home by Grandmother, and arranged for his father's particular favourite Castella from Fukusaya to be distributed to all the Fukuda relations (Castella is a Nagasaki speciality of rich sponge cake, presumably introduced by the Portuguese). He wrote a simple account of his father, and had it printed and bound for circulation with the Castella. However, he himself died a few weeks before that ceremony was to take place. On the singing of the hymn 'God be with you till we meet again…' around the family grave, my sister Eiko burst into tears.

Masaru – a boy in Nagasaki; c. 1917.

2. MY FATHER MASARU: AN 'ENVOY EXTRAORDINARY'

~

Prodigy and a Naval Interlude

When the family moved to Tokyo, Masaru was nine years old and went to a local primary school. One of his neighbourhood friends was Tsuchiya Yōzaburo, whose father was a leading stockbroker. Yōzaburo told me that they walked to school holding hands every day. After school they swapped homework; Masaru would do Yōzaburo's maths and Yōzaburo would do Masaru's crayon paintings. Masaru's pictures were always of the sea with a ship on the horizon, but Yōzaburo's were almost always of Mount Fuji. He continued to paint to the end of his life and he had many of his paintings of Mount Fuji and the *koi* fish he collected cast in *shippo* enamel dishes. The young boys played tennis and spent summer holidays together when Yōzaburo came to stay at our mountain lodge in Karuizawa.

Masaru went on to the academically top schools in Tokyo, while his sister Naoko went to the Sacred Heart International School, within walking distance of our house. He attended 'Itcchu' (東京府立第一中學校), the top middle school for boys in Japan. In those days there were several elite schools, which were

59

government-owned, and competitive entrance examinations dictated the academic rankings. Itcchu was the top school for the elite. Masaru was a brilliant student; the report cards his parents kept show he came top of his class each and every year. He went on to the Senior High School at Urawa and then to the Imperial University of Tokyo to read Jurisprudence, with the added difficulty of it being taught (as an option) in German. He graduated with Honours and received a leaving scholarship from the university. He took the civil service entrance examination in 1938 and applied for the Ministry of Finance (大蔵省), but Uncle Yamanashi advised him that he might not be good enough for that and should instead try for the Ministry of Commerce and Industry (商工省). But Masaru was determined: he came top in the civil service exams and naturally he went to the Ministry of Finance. His first appointment there was to the Banking Bureau (銀行局), from April 1939.

Those were the years of the Great Depression and Japan's serial moves onto the Chinese mainland; by 1937 Japan had not only invaded Manchuria but was engaged in full-scale war with China. National conscription started in Japan in 1938. Masaru took the officers' exams to take up a short service commission in the Imperial Navy. As he came top in the Navy exams, his name is listed first in the directory of the *Tangen 2* (短現), the second-year intake of the short service commission from May 1939.

Masaru's first job in the real world was therefore to join the war: a spell during 1939–42 with the Navy, first on board the battle-ship HIJMS *Chōkai* in the South China Sea around Shanghai and Amoy, and off the coast of French Indochina, followed by a spell at Kure Naval Arsenal on procurement. Kure Arsenal was then one of the largest naval dockyards in the world. In a contri-bution to the volume commemorating the fortieth anniversary of the Tangen 2 officer intake, my father described the secret construction at Kure of the battleship *Yamato*, the heaviest and most powerfully armed battleship ever constructed. He recalled that it was entirely shrouded so that no one could see it from the outside, and the windows of nearby buildings and houses were boarded up. *Yamato* was the flagship of the Combined Fleet in 1942, from which Admiral Yamamoto Isoroku directed the fleet in the Battle of Midway, one of the most decisive battles in naval history.

HIJMS *Chōkai* was the flagship of the Second Fleet of the Imperial Japanese Navy. Masaru spent fourteen months on her – an unusually long time aboard ship – in the intolerably humid heat of the South China Sea, living in extremely cramped conditions; then followed the gruelling schedule at Kure, which eventually affected his health. At a regular medical inspection he was warned that he would be unsuited to naval combat service at sea and was moved to the finance administration division at Kure in August 1941. At the time of the attack on Pearl Harbor he was a duty officer on watch. After that fateful day of 8 December it was he who received the return of the First Carrier Division to Kure. He recorded that the dinner for the returning men he hosted was a sombre occasion, with no other officers present. Soon afterwards he was issued with his transfer to a reserve role. He was then assigned to the Governor's Secretariat of the Cabinet Planning Board until its closure in September 1943. This was the time of the Guadalcanal campaign, and Japan had realised the need to concentrate on building up its air strength. The Cabinet Planning Board became the centre for coordinating national strategy. Though Masaru always said later that he felt he had not fulfilled his patriotic duty, as he never served in theatres of combat during the war, he enjoyed his time with the Navy: there was a fine camaraderie among the men aboard ship. Satsuki-kai (五月会), the alumni society of the *Chōkai*, met every year throughout the postwar period well into the new millennium, in remembrance of the youthful patriotism that bound them together. *Chōkai* was heavily involved in the battles in the south-west Pacific and Indochina after Masaru had left the ship; eventually she was damaged and scuttled in October 1944. Seeing the news, six months after his marriage, must have been distressing.

Masaru remembered in the commemorative volume years later that the most nerve-wracking thing he had to do on *Chōkai* was being the officer chosen to salute Prince Fushimi, the Chief of Staff of the Imperial Navy, during his inspection, without putting a foot wrong – walking backwards, but looking straight ahead, was not something he was used to! Masaru, who was not in any way 'clubbable' and mostly avoided reunions, attended these ones whenever he could. He kept the memories of the time in the Navy close to his heart, with touching loyalty to his fellow men. Commemorative photograph albums of the *Chōkai* show their sorties and landings in Shanghai and Amoy, as well as their daily lives aboard ship. He particularly enjoyed the golden sunsets across the bay of Canton. A close and distinguished colleague at the Ministry of Finance and in the Navy a year senior to him, Tanimura Hiroshi (谷村裕), wrote to my father shortly before his death that the years at sea gave him the inspiration to look beyond the horizon and search for the international dimension in Japan's policies in finance. He said in that letter that he wept as he wrote, remembering the time spent together in his room at Kure late into the night when my father was organising very methodically the procurement budget for the Navy in 1941. As Tanimura wrote, his Navy experience caused my father to follow an international career at the Ministry; he regretted, however, that someone of his ability should thus have been diverted from the mainstream. When I went to Shanghai in 1979 with my James Capel colleagues, my father was particularly keen to hear what Shanghai now looked like. I was surprised by this display of nostalgia, as he was generally not keen on things Chinese. But his party song was 'A Dancer of Shanghai', presumably a song from that period.

A Dapper Family Man

It was never expected that members of my father's family would involve themselves in commercial activities. They regarded themselves as of the governing class, who served in the ministries, politics, armed forces or academia. To live by commerce was thought vulgar, though banking was just about acceptable. Indeed, all of the immediate Fukuda family followed that tradition, including my father's uncle and his children, as well as his sister and her children. Grandfather's profession in naval architecture was highly respectable, as it was the principal means of national defence. Even in my youth after the war, I would never have expected to marry someone from a family engaged in trade, however rich, especially if self-made. Such attitudes rapidly evaporated in the 1970s as the phenomenal expansion of the economy dictated change in Japan's social order: 'Economic growth first, social provisions second, inherited virtues forgotten'. However, in the determined national effort to recover from the devastation of the war, Japan adopted a highly regulated form of government, and so the status of that governing class survived for at least four more decades within the state bureaucracies, with the Ministry of Finance at the pinnacle. Thus the prewar samurai ethos actually continued in certain circles well into the second half of the twentieth century – my father was a typical product of that class. But, unlike the ever-multiplying mini-bureaucrats of the postwar era, from central government to the municipalities, who proudly pushed paper around as if the paper encapsulated essential truths, my father knew the true meaning of honour. With that he was well aware of the responsibilities and obligations accompanying this elite status.

Brought up in the samurai tradition, Masaru had qualities inherited from his parents and his uncle: humility, honesty, directness, contempt for money, love of humanity, a strong sense of honour and moral courage. There was an instinctive refusal to compromise; he was forthright with what he considered to be right. He tirelessly tried to teach junior colleagues to exercise moral judgement, not to be swayed by the general policy diktats. That kind of directness became outdated and impermissible in the modern consensus-based approach of postwar Japan. In 'Japan and the Asian Development Bank', Dennis T. Yasumoto quotes a colleague describing him: 'Mr Fukuda was the kind of person who would single-handedly charge the enemy even if the odds were 10,000 to one.' He was indeed known to be outspoken and independent, with an excellent command of English, quick to capture nuances. His writings were always salient and expressive, showing a very precise mind. Yasumoto, though, could not have implied that he was reckless; my father was the most cautious of men, always justifying any decision with his convictions.

But Masaru was, unlike his mother, essentially a shy person, and a romantic idealist. Early in his marriage he wrote to his young wife explaining his life's philosophy, that he was a senti-mentalist, and that this might be his weakness. He said it was easier to write than to tell her. On his death, Gyohten Toyoo (行天豊雄), internationally perhaps the best-known Ministry of Finance official of that generation, who worked closely with my father over many years, wrote in a tribute in the *Nikkei* news-paper that 'Mr Fukuda was most frightening, yet so very kind.' That sums up his personality well. He did not suffer fools gladly, but even those who were shouted at understood that his inten-tions were sincere and not self-serving. He took immense care to look after the careers and personal well-being of those who worked with him at the Ministry. They never forgot his human-ity and compassion; many of them shared their memories with me in later years. Even twenty years after the war Japan was too poor to allow home leave for families, and officials' duty-visits to Ministry headquarters were strictly limited. Masaru gave up his turn to a younger colleague whose father was gravely ill; the col-league's parents wrote to the head of the Ministry to record how much they appreciated his action. He held distinguished men of achievement in admiration and great respect. It was as though he regretted his own apparent lack of comparable achievement and distinction. He held no class prejudices; he was a democrat and firmly meritocratic, even with women. So he did not object to his daughters having jobs. But he did not necessarily regard women as intellectual equals and did not believe that women had to be clever; for him looks and sophistication were more important.

Greatly spoilt by his mother, Masaru had an inwardly nervous nature; mollycoddled and pampered to avoid catching a chill, he was indulged and could harbour selfish likes and dislikes. He was a fussy eater, giving my mother a hard time at table. He disliked all poultry, mostly because he did not like the look of the skin, refused pork in any form, such as sausages, bacon or ham (which, in any case, were down-market foods in those days), hated the smell of garlic, and did not like lamb because of the smell of its fat. Had he found such things in the house there would have been divorce! He never ate Chinese food; he did not like messed-up mixtures, and garlic was prevalent in Chinese cooking. He would even refuse an invitation to an official banquet if it was to be Chinese food. He liked grilled white fish such as Dover sole or turbot (but not mackerel), eggs, beef (but only fillet, sirloin and rump steaks), soups (but only consommé or creamed potage), smoked salmon and certain vegetables. He was a man of habit and routine. His breakfast was always porridge, two soft-boiled eggs, toast and marmalade with coffee. Those things were available even during and immediately after the war. Our family never had a Japanese-style breakfast at home. For lunch, after he retired from the Ministry, he would go almost every day to the Tokyo Club and have smoked salmon and an omelette. Like most men, he was fond of sweet puddings and cake; at tea time when he was at home at weekends he would call for eclairs, which he was most fond of having with Lipton's Orange Pekoe tea. He sometimes had a weak whisky and soda in the evenings at home and at cocktail parties, but was not a strong drinker; he disliked big parties and banquets where he would be expected to join in heavy drinking. That included family parties at the in-laws' house, as my mother's father was a heavy drinker and a gourmet with a penchant for unusual and exotic food.

While he was serving in the Embassy in London Masaru almost always lunched at Claridge's, inviting members of the British government or the City. The Ambassador when we first arrived in London, Ohno Katsumi (大野勝己), told the Embassy staff that they must not be seen in any restaurant where white tablecloths were not used: he himself almost always lunched at Brown's Hotel in Dover Street, at the time one of the most discreet upper-class hotels. Having come from Washington, a less formal society by then, my father would secretly go out to buy sandwiches for lunch to save money when not entertaining his British counterparts. But the atmosphere in London in 1960 was one where the wartime enemy Japan was still regarded with suspicion, if not hatred; the Ambassador's strictures made sense in that context.

Masaru liked witty and beautiful women and cared a lot about how people looked. That was a romantic aspect to him. In his letters to my mother from America he encouraged her to look sophisticated and cosmopolitan like American women, and he sent us all lovely dresses for Christmas. When we first arrived in London in the 1960s I remember him taking us to Selfridges to choose himself outfits that he liked and considered up to the mark for his wife. My love of clothes was probably ingrained in me by my father. If he saw us wearing something he disapproved of he would throw it away or even burn it on the bonfire! He was himself elegant and always dressed correctly in the best suits from the top tailors wherever we were. In London he had his shirts made at Hawes & Curtis in Burlington Gardens, and his suits and other requirements at Henry Poole in Savile

Row, which Emperor Haile Selassie and other dignitaries of the international scene frequented. Saying a blue range suited him best, he never wore greys or browns. It was not that he was extravagant; he looked after his clothes meticulously and wore them for a long time. He was brought up to buy only the best quality of anything from the top purveyors, be it formal or casual attire, and always looked smart. To him it was a mark of social standing to be properly dressed, as it had always been in his family. When I was a child in Tokyo he always wore a hat: what used to be called 'soft'. Most men wore hats in those days. He was of middle height, handsome with his facial features clearly delineated.

Finances were tight for the family after his father became unemployed in the 1930s. I often heard Masaru complaining, even decades later, how despite his lack of a job, his father indulged his daughter and the granddaughters born at home in the large house at Shiroganedai with what seemed an almost abnormal degree of affection. His eternal respect for his mother stemmed partly from those years when she managed the finances of the family with skill and without compromising standards. I suppose that was the confidence of the 'landed gentry' as it were, asset-rich but cash-flow poor; the ancient senior samurai families such as the Fukudas were still in that category of the old rich living off inherited wealth in large *ozashiki* houses. When he came to have a job of his own in wartime, salaries of Ministry officials as servants of the nation were meagre, and continued to be so compared with those of industry and commerce in the postwar period. After the war, devaluation of the currency by the Occupation government brought home the devastating reality of defeat in war: the New Yen was now worth a hundredth of the old. Everyone was now equally poor, as the Occupation government deprived the old rich of their assets with the introduction of the penal asset tax. We were brought up to be ultra-careful with money and we never asked our parents to buy things for us.

Some Sundays my father would take the family out to Ginza for window-shopping and to afternoon tea at the Shiseido Parlour, an elegant and fashionable restaurant and tearoom; but his stricture was that we were allowed to have only vanilla ice cream. I longed to have the colourful ice cream sundae or banana split, but my wishes were never fulfilled as my father said those things are 'common' and not for the likes of us; presumably they were more expensive! The Shiseido Parlour was built in the Colonial style, with whirling fans hanging from high ceilings and aspidistras and palm trees in pots in the corners of the large salons. On those occasions he would march ahead, leaving wife and daughters shouting "Wait for us!" He would not be seen dead carrying his wife's shopping, let alone holding hands.

When my father was posted abroad in 1960 finances became even harder, because the low exchange rate for the Japanese yen meant that, even with overseas allowances, we were relatively poor. The requirement in his international appointments to have a set of ceremonial clothes – *veste noir*, morning coat, black and white dinner jackets (in Washington called a white tuxedo, which famously Sir Edward Heath sported throughout his life), white tie and tails for state occasions in London – was a heavy expenditures for the meagre salaries of Japanese officials. My sisters and I had to be kitted up with winter and summer school uniforms – a major outlay. Conversations about economising were legion amongst the Japanese diplomats of the time. Some enterprising senior diplomatic wives would even fit snow chains on the tyres of their cars by themselves to save money. My father, however, maintained his high standards and his tastes: for holidays we went to stay at the grandest hotels of Europe in suites and had the expensive dishes that he liked – caviar, fillet steaks, smoked salmon and lobster; he would not allow us to try strange alternatives he did not like the look of. As he told us, we only had holidays infrequently and for short periods so we could afford those luxuries. My mother spent her entire married life being allowed to eat only what her husband would eat himself; after his death she felt liberated in her diet.

Despite being a stickler for detail and having selfish eating habits, Masaru was an amusing conversationalist and a man of social graces. He was particularly good at bestowing flattery both on men and women (but never on members of his own family!). Letters from America show that he was an effective flirt. His conversation was always witty and interesting at table, and at receptions and cocktail parties he was a popular participant. Embassy wives said to my mother how lucky she was to have such an amusing companion, but mother replied "Not at home!" He was of course meticulous in his manners and was always polite except when angry, and certainly never rude to any woman. He spoke in a loud voice; his mother said disapprovingly that he developed that habit in the Navy. But when reproached by his wife he said that people who spoke in whispers might have something to hide and be less than totally honest.

He was fastidious in the extreme when it came to tidiness and cleanliness. No papers or pens and pencils on his desk were ever out of alignment. He would never tear open an envelope but always slice it neatly with a pair of scissors. His handwriting was as if printed, each character perfectly formed and of uniform size. Nothing irrelevant was allowed to remain; books were perfectly aligned in bookcases according to their size and subject; he absolutely hated untidiness. He polished his own shoes to military perfection and had all garments cleaned after one wearing. By contrast, my mother was a hoarder and not so tidy. He would try to throw things away and mother would shout at him: "It might come in useful one day!"

Though my father was strong in his friendships, and warm with acquaintances, he did not look for companionship or want to meet frequently. The war years intervened and made social gatherings difficult, even with fairly close relations. Transport was inadequate and everyone was too hard-up to waste money on socialising after the war. Apart from his sister and nieces, and mother's sisters, his Yamanashi first cousin Okami Yoshiko was the only relation who came to visit us at home. She often came to see her aunt Sada. Yoshiko had married the heir to a rich family, the Okamis, who owned a vast estate in Kami-Osaki near our home in Shiroganedai. He talked of her as a beauty and said that when he was young he was 'in love' with her. Yoshiko was an accomplished concert pianist and held her first cousin Naoko as a friendly rival.

Decades later, I came to know her son, Yoshiaki, through another relation, Okami Masako, who married Orita Masaki who became Ambassador to London. We all became good friends together and I have been lucky to enjoy this rekindling of family ties in Japan. It is often said that Japanese do not invite friends into their homes and foreigners find it difficult to make close friendships. That was certainly true, partly for cultural reasons related to the sharp distinction made between things 'within' and things 'without'. Matters that are 'within' the family are kept strictly within the family, not to be imparted to others. My father, though, did invite his American friends to visit us at home even in the early 1950s. He even took them to visit his father-in-law at my mother's old home. And when we went abroad he arranged many dinner parties at home.

With close colleagues at the Ministry, he was assiduous at keeping in contact: paying his respects through visits and letters to those who had been his mentors and supporters; and exchanging written works with contemporaries who shared his intellectual interests. He was meticulous in correspondence, always responding to letters from old colleagues in the Navy and the Ministry, and always writing to them on their promotions and achievements.

The Elite: the Ministry of Finance
The Ministry of Finance – *Okurasho* – was his life and anchor.

Once a career Okurasho official, always an Okurasho official. The old Okurasho was collegiate and despite internal rivalries it was like a family. They shared the pride of being Ministry officials and were highly conscious of the position and influence they commanded. Highly competitive, Masaru in his youth set his sights high for life: nothing more natural than for him to join the Ministry of Finance. From his childhood he had always come first in class at school and at university, so it was no surprise that he should come first in the civil service examinations. He doubled that by coming top in the officers' examinations for the short service commission in the Navy. He would have expected to follow the same trajectory throughout his career, though he was always aware that, while he was among the most brilliant of his generation, others might nevertheless rise further. He was not one for sucking up to his senior bosses or currying favours nor indeed for being jealous of others' successes; but he kept his relationships well manicured. He would tell his wife of the competitive landscape and his position in it, confiding in her his fears and aspirations. As he recalled in an essay towards the end of his life, there was something noble about the pride of ambitious young officials standing before the wooden gates in the 1930s, looking up at the Ministry in awe; they were aware of a cardinal responsibility owed to the Emperor, and their youthful aspirations of what they might achieve for him and the country. He explained to me when I was older that nobody was naïve enough to believe that the Emperor was God, but he was the symbol of the nation's dignity. The nobility of that shared idealism was the foundation of lifelong friendships.

Masaru was a high flyer amongst his peers at the Ministry, and was on a mainstream career path in the principal bureaux there. On his return to the Ministry from the Navy and the Governor's Secretariat of the Cabinet Planning Board, which was disbanded in 1943, he was first placed in the Banking Bureau, but soon after transferred to the most important department, the

Budget Bureau. When I was a young child he would often be working throughout the night at the Ministry, especially in the busy months of Budget preparation and the passage through the Diet. Yet he felt gravely disappointed that his career at the Ministry of Finance ended in failure, according to his own standards and ambitions. He never had the opportunity to head up a major bureau at Ministry headquarters. His last appointment carried the rank of director-general of a bureau (局長), the rank only just below that of vice minister, the head of the Ministry. How critically he felt this disappointment manifested itself in deep depression. Had he not followed his commitment to duty by going to Manila, it might have ended differently. Had he refused, that might have had other, adverse consequences. Being appointed to represent the Japanese government in the newly founded international organisation for Asia was an honour, and his uncle wrote to congratulate him on the move. But he had to stay there too long, against his wishes. That was fatal for his career, as he knew. Life is cruel in this way, and he always said that luck determines everything.

Bureaucrats rather than politicians were the predominant force in government in postwar Japan. Politicians come and go but bureaucrats remain. For decades after the war, Finance remained the most powerful Ministry, followed by the Ministry of Foreign Affairs and the Ministry of International Trade and Industry (MITI). There was a certain amount of rivalry between them, but in public perception MoF was the one that wielded the baton, and with that power came social cachet.

Almost all Ministry of Finance officials were graduates of the University of Tokyo, and had read Jurisprudence. Many of them went into politics halfway through their careers and some became Prime Minister – Ikeda Hayato, Fukuda Takeo, Miyazawa Kiichi, Ohira Masayoshi, all of my father's generation. My father nurtured similar ambitions; he would tease my mother, saying he might stand as a candidate for the Socialist

Party. He was a liberal thinker in politics as well as in his approach to life. He said that in the Ministry he was probably closest to Ikeda Hayato's group in the 1950s, although he was also close to Fukuda Takeo, as they were colleagues only a few years apart. But my father also respected Tanaka Kakuei, finding it remarkable that someone of little education (Tanaka had only a junior school education) and no social standing should espouse a political philosophy that was to dominate Japanese politics through the late 1960s and 1970s. Tanaka Kakuei was Minister of Finance in the 1960s and Prime Minister in the early 1970s; he managed to raise the political funding through an enormous popular base; he was also known for great personal tenacity.

When Tanaka visited Washington in 1961, as he entered the Japanese Embassy in Massachusetts Avenue, sited next to Lutyens' British Embassy, he was received by officials who stood in line to greet him. When he reached my father he said: "Fukuda Masaru, entered the Ministry of Finance 1939, Budget Bureau, Finance Bureau…" reciting the entirety of his entry in the Ministry Directory. Tanaka had memorised the Directory so that he could impress the officials and gain their support. He was that sort of man, who never forgot people who had helped him: when in 1974 as Prime Minister he was addressing a meeting of the Asian Development Bank, two years after my father had left the bank, at the start of his speech he said "… the first representative of our government was Fukuda Masaru who is a long-standing friend of mine…" He had asked my father to arrange a personal meeting with Reginald Maudling, then Chancellor of the Exchequer, a decade previously under difficult circumstances and he had not forgotten. When my father died, Tanaka sent a huge floral tribute and a personal representative to the funeral.

The Ministry of Finance, not being a large Ministry in numbers, continued to be a close-knit circle with a collegiate atmosphere of mutual respect. There was a familial feeling amongst the officials, even those of different generations. Once when I was visiting the Ministry during the time I was at James Capel, a middle-ranking official cordially welcomed me and said immediately "You are the daughter of OUR Mr Fukuda, aren't you?"; he had never met my father. Throughout my career in the City, successive MoF officials stationed in London all looked after me as one of their own, and many became close personal friends. There was an instant recognition that we belonged in the same society with shared values.

In my year at the Peers' School, there were two other MoF children: Hatoyama Yukio, whose grandfather became Prime Minister while we were in junior school and whose father later became a leading politician; and Nishihara Kumiko whose father was previously posted to London in the same position as mine in the 1950s and became director-general of the Finance Bureau. We had the sense of a shared family background and Kumiko and I became close friends for life. Both Kumiko's and Yukio's mothers, siblings and cousins were all at the school. Hatoyama Yukio, later to found the Democratic Party of Japan and become Prime Minister himself, and I had our classroom desks next to each other in junior school, as our surnames were close, according to the phonetic 'alphabet'. While I was CEO of the World Gold Council I had a feature interview in the *Nikkei* newspaper with one of the DPJ members of the Diet, Mr Kaieda Banri, who later became leader of that party; upon learning that we had been school friends, he mentioned that to Hatoyama. Hatoyama immediately asked me to a lunch of sushi in a private room at the New Otani Hotel near the Diet building. It was an amusing and happy episode; as I had left the school when my father was posted to Washington in 1960 we hadn't met for forty years. On one occasion, when I was away ill from school, his mother brought my homework to my father at the Ministry. My father remembered, chuckling, that it gave him great kudos with colleagues in the office as a great beauty had approached him! She was tall with exotic features, daughter of the Ishibashi family who owned the Bridgestone Tire Company.

The Ministry of Finance sent my father, as its most senior representative, to America and Britain fifteen years after the end of the war. In those postings he was to have the opportunity to put his abilities to use, and he achieved important milestones for Japan in the international arena. These will be the subject of later chapters. Before that, I must turn my attention to my mother and her antecedents – a very different family.

'Tenka-no-Itohei'; late nineteenth century.

3. THE TANAKA DYNASTY: THE MEIJI NEW WEALTH

~

Yoko was the eldest daughter of an heiress, Tanaka Hanako (田中花子). Hanako was the granddaughter of the legendary entrepreneur Tanaka Heihachi (田中平八), known to history as *Tenka-no-Itohei*, 'Itohei descended from Heaven' (天下の糸平). He was the creator of the Tanaka *zaibatsu*, alongside the Mitsui, Yasuda, Shibusawa and Iwasaki families of the late nineteenth century; they became the oligarchs of post-Meiji Restoration Japan.

Itohei's heir, also named Heihachi, had two daughters; the elder, Hanako, was the successor to the family as there were no sons. My grandfather Watase Jiro (渡瀬次郎) therefore married into the Tanaka family to manage the family enterprises. He was the second child of Watase Torajiro (渡瀬寅次郎) who ran a major horticultural business and was a pioneering educationalist of the Meiji era. Hanako's younger sister, Kimiko (君子), married one of the famous liberal political thinkers of the 1930s and 1940s, Minobe Yohji (美濃部洋次), whose nephew years later became the Governor of Metropolitan Tokyo. Yoko said at the party to celebrate her ninetieth birthday that she was born and brought up in a wealthy family and had had a very fortunate life with everyone being kind to her. As the first child and

77

grandchild, she was endowed with overwhelming affection by all who surrounded her. She was brought up on one of the largest estates in central Tokyo. She had little to fear; she had around her a nanny, a retinue of maids and male servants, and a large household to protect her. On the estate in various houses lived her aunt Kimiko and her family, her mother's uncle Kamakichi (釜吉) and his family, and of course her grandparents. She went to the Peers' School, as did her mother and siblings, and had never left familiar surroundings or the network of family friends until she married Masaru. She was born in 1921, Japan's 'Edwardian' era; upper-class life was elegant, refined and gracious.

Descended from Heaven: Tenka-no-Itohei (田中平八): a Meiji Entrepreneur

Tanaka Heihachi, Tenka-no-Itohei, is the legendary founding father of Japan's foreign exchange market, the Tokyo Commodity Exchange and the Tokyo Stock Exchange. His colourful life and entrepreneurial achievements have been depicted in the novel *Tenka-no-Itohei* by award-winning historical novelist Saotome Mitsugu (早乙女貢) and another with the same title by Shara Soju, well-known author of a twentieth-century novel, *Heike Monogatari*. He has also been the subject of a Kabuki play.

When in the early years of the 1850s Commodore Matthew Perry led a fleet of powerful US naval ships to open trade with Japan and forcibly negotiated over several years the Treaty of Peace and Amity, two centuries of national isolation came to an end. The shogun (Tokugawa Yoshinobu) eventually realised, having learnt of the destruction of the Chinese fleet and the seizure of Canton, Hong Kong and Shanghai in the Opium Wars by the British, that Japan had to make peace with the West. The shogun was by then under pressure as the commercial middle class had been gaining prominence and wealth, rapidly eroding the old feudal structures. These social changes eventually brought about the end of the Tokugawa shogunate through the actions of the rebellious daimyo of Satsuma, Choshu and Tosa; imperial government returned to Japan with the Meiji Restoration.

The Americans were first allowed to land at Kurihama, not far from Yokohama in Edo Bay (now Tokyo Bay). Until then only a limited number of foreigners could trade, through Nagasaki; but the Americans effectively opened up access to the centre of Japan's main island with its capital at Edo (now Tokyo). Several notable personalities of that time had the foresight to open the port at Yokohama (which the Tokugawa shogunate initially opposed) so that imported goods could easily be transported to Edo, which would become the nationwide distribution hub. Foreign merchants quickly congregated in Yokohama and com- mercially-minded Japanese also made their way there. With the Americans arriving in Yokohama, Yoko's great-grandfather Itohei reckoned that they must need yen currency to exchange for dollars. It was in Yokohama that Itohei made his first fortune.

He was born Fujishima Kamakichi (藤島釜吉) but in his late teens was adopted by a well-to-do family engaged in the silk textile business, the Tanaka family, and was given the name Tanaka Heihachi. The Fujishima ancestors were samurai in the sixteenth century and retainers of the Oda Nobunaga clan. However, after defeat in battle they fled to the hills of Nagano. As often with defeated clan retainers, the family disappeared into farming and small-time commercial activities. They lived in the mountains of Nagano near Iida city.

From a young age Itohei was a risk-taker. Never one to give up in defeat, he repeatedly failed in various ventures. When he was about twelve years old, he was sent out to work at a fishmonger's; young Heihachi showed his commercial instincts by starting a raffle to attract customers with the slogan 'Win fish for free'; on occasion he set up a stall outside the popular temple on feast days as worshippers from distant areas gathered there. By the time he was fifteen, having learnt a little about trading in fish, he escaped from his hard fishmonger taskmaster and went to

Osaka to trade in fish and rice on his own. Repeating successes and failures, he returned to his home town to seek work with the silk business of the Tanaka family. He would once again escape and leave for Nagoya to corner the market in rice, but initial success ended in failure and he had to return cap in hand to the Tanaka family in his home town of Iida and marry their adopted daughter Haru.

His break came when he hit upon the idea of going east to Yokohama: he left his wife and young daughter Tora, entrusted to his elder brother in Iida, promising that he would come back to collect them in a few years. He first stayed near Nagoya, where he rescued a young woman who was about to be 'sold' as a concubine and fell in love. Shara's novel makes out that she remained the love of his life. He then went on to Yokohama where he met another woman he married (bigamously!) with a wealthy mother who helped him financially in his early days there. This too was not without its challenges: on the way, Itohei bought and loaded a large quantity of tea on a boat at Yokkaichi city in Ise, but the boat sank in a storm and he lost all his money. Undeterred, he then went back west to Kyoto with a view to gain access to typically Japanese handicrafts and curios that might appeal to foreigners in Yokohama. He managed to persuade a pretty young woman he fancied, on the promise of taking her to Yokohama, to speak to her parents who ran a handicraft business. He succeeded in getting them to let him take their products on a 'sale or return' basis, and set off for Yokohama.

Once Yokohama port was opened, what had previously been a quiet town quickly grew into a hub for foreign trade and flourished with commercial activities. Records show that the largest amount of trade in Yokohama was conducted in silk yarns. Heihachi decided to open a foreign exchange shop and to trade in silk yarns, as his home town in Nagano was a major producer and he was uniquely well-placed to access supplies. His businesses quickly grew to rival the largest in the area. This silk yarns business gave him the nickname Itohei (糸平) – 'a bloke with yarn' – the name that was to make him a legend.

He was tall, nearly six foot, slender, with well-defined facial features: strong bushy eyebrows on a long face with a strong chin. His gaze was penetrating and often fierce. He was gifted with physical strength, an advantage in many close scrapes, and was attractive to women even while a poverty-stricken vagabond in his youth. On arriving in Yokohama, he first earned his keep by pulling rickshaws, and soon a customer asked him for a long ride. On being told the destination was Iida in Nagano, he adamantly refused, claiming that it was too far; in fact he could not possibly show his face in his home town where he had left his wife and daughter and was in a large amount of debt to many investors in his failed ventures over the years. He agreed to take the customer somewhere not too far from Iida, to Suwa also in Nagano prefecture. On the way the customer told him the reason he so desperately wanted to go to Iida was that the price of Japanese silk yarns was rising fast and carried a premium, as foreign merchants quickly discovered the superior quality of silk produced in Japan; also, production shortfalls in China and Italy were pushing the price ever higher. Itohei could not contain his emotions: he had to go to Iida to get the silk yarns himself, not let his customer in the rickshaw take the lead. On a mountain path, where bears, hyenas, apes and boars hid in the bushes waiting for a bite, he decided that the only thing to do was to abandon his customer, faking an accident. He rushed back, abandoning his rich client to his fate, and decided to go to his closest friend in Iida to whom he had entrusted the young woman he had rescued and fallen in love with on his way to Nagoya before arriving in Yokohama. He had promised her that he would come to collect her within two years; his time was not quite up then. On arrival he struck a deal with his friend in whispers that this was a secret mission and the friend was not to tell his brother, who was looking after Itohei's wife and daughter. The friend agreed and collaborated in procuring the silk yarns and shipping them to Yokohama. Itohei told him: "This time it is for real." Itohei gambled on his conviction that the price would continue to rise and borrowed a substantial sum of money. He could then negotiate long-term contracts at the lowest possible prices for bulk orders. He persuaded an acquaintance in Yokohama to finance the purchase of a vacant house in central Yokohama with some land on which he built a large warehouse in clay for the silk yarn inventory that was arriving in abundance. Determined to be his own boss with his own shop, he set up his silk yarn company, Itoya (糸屋) in 1865 and started his foreign exchange business. He put up a billboard: 'ITOYA H. Tanaka Exchange Transactor Silk Selling Agent'.

Apart from exporting silk and tea, he made markets in foreign gold and silver coins as well as in American dollars. Japan's currency was gold but some foreign merchants brought silver coins in exchange (it was said the silver was Mexican), and the Yokohama merchants began exchanging gold and silver coins as well as the paper currency of the dollar. Itohei was the first to both buy and sell, rather than provide a one-way exchange. It was he who realised that the price of gold in yen was different from that in dollars, and the Japanese had been exchanging yen for it too cheaply; he therefore embarked on arbitrage to narrow the differential. Thus he became a leading market maker, perhaps the largest, in foreign exchange. It was a challenge as foreign merchants used different measurements of lengths and weight from the Japanese units, and the dollar was growing as an international unit of exchange. Price fluctuations were extreme and volatile. He eventually set up a private foreign currency exchange in which American, British, Dutch and Russian merchants participated. As the Japanese government started to regulate the foreign exchange market the private foreign exchange company in which Itohei was the major player was turned into Japan's second national bank (Daini Kokuritsu Ginko; 国立第二銀行) in

1872 with Itohei as one of the largest shareholders. He quickly grew rich, and was able to return to his home town to clear all debts and restore his reputation. He brought his wife and daughter, left behind six years previously, to Yokohama and housed them in his new establishment together with his new wife. He went back and forth to Tokyo to secure business opportunities, especially with those foreign merchants who landed in Tsukiji: entertaining them in grand restaurants – where the geisha would ostracise 'smelly and hairy' foreigners, who Itohei assuaged by bringing in prostitutes to spare the geisha. He eventually set up a palatial residence in Saiwaicho next to the Imperial Palace moat, where he brought up his family.

Tokyo had become the political centre and the mecca for finance, while Yokohama remained the commercial hub. Itohei maintained his home base in Yokohama right up to his death. Towards the end of his life, convalescing at his summer house in Atami, he was visited by the newly appointed head of Yokohama Customs. A young man of only twenty-six, Hoshi Tōru (星亨) came to enlist his support in installing better discipline at the port to stop foreigners evading customs duties by under-reporting landed goods. The worst offenders were the British, as they had the backing of the domineering and arrogant Sir Harry Parkes at the British Mission. Characteristically, the Japanese customs officials were too timid to counter them, not least because large and rough British seamen would brandish pistols and knives. The new head of customs, though, was made of sterner stuff: he was not going to be intimidated.

Itohei was much impressed by Hoshi and agreed that he would round up a hundred men to keep watch and pounce on the next arriving ship to offload cargo. British ships had the habit of secretly taking the goods through the back entrance of the nearby hotel to hide them from customs inspection. Itohei's men sealed that route, and when the captain of the British merchant ship *Indian* arrived and presented a report showing only a tenth of the actual volume of goods landed, with the unit price also being set at a tenth of the true value – thereby undervaluing by a hundredfold – Hoshi declared it contraband and sent it off to auction. Itohei had arranged the auction in advance, enlisting cooperative Japanese merchants all prepared to bid. This became a *cause célèbre*, resulting in seamen firing pistols at the Japanese, the British chamber of commerce bribing a Japanese to steal the contraband for them before the auction, and Sir Harry Parkes arriving at the Customs headquarters to engage in a violent argument that ended in a fist fight. Parkes made a formal complaint to the then Minister of Foreign Affairs; being summoned by the minister, Hoshi stood his ground and refused to change the amount of the levy. Customs revenue quadrupled as a result. Making sure that he sidestepped any possible conflict of interest, Itohei paid all the men who had helped at the port personally so that the Customs department would not draw on public funds; he treated them afterwards to dinner with as much sake as the men wanted to drink; and he did not bid at the auction himself. Some time later Hoshi was relieved of his duties when the British government complained that he had used the word *Jo-o* (女王) ('Queen') in referring to Queen Victoria, rather than *Jo-koo* (女皇) ('Queen Empress' in the Japanese translation). The Japanese government sent him to London to study and he chose law and became a qualified barrister there (the first Japanese ever to qualify abroad); he returned to Japan and was elected a member of the Diet, an outspoken and controversial politician, eventually to be appointed Minister for Communications in the Cabinet. He was assassinated at the age of fifty-one.

Itohei's biographies indicate a kindly aspect to his personality. He was not just a brash rogue, despite many adventurous episodes: he would rush to rescue women and children under attack by highwaymen; used his early gains in Yokohama to initiate and fund the infrastructure of the city; and contributed in large measure to charity. He helped many a woman trying to escape the 'hairy barbarians' (毛唐人) as brash European merchants pursued them in the streets, often giving them money from his small savings in the early years. Courtesans and women of easy virtue at the time were said to have found foreign men with blue eyes distasteful, as many of them brought in syphilis from Shanghai and Hong Kong: it was not just that they had strong body odour, but hairy beards, arms and chests to boot. When Itohei had amassed some capital, he turned his mind to a remark of Sir Harry Parkes, who had complained that the water in Yokohama was not properly desalinated and was inferior even to the drinking water in south-east Asia. Itohei was not going to tolerate this affront: "We could not be compared to the black people of the primitive islands." He offered the authorities capital to fund a water system for the whole city. Yokohama honours his legacy with a large stone monument.

In his later years Itohei ran a large estate in Omori on the outskirts of Yokohama for his second wife, Dai, to live in with a retinue of servants. They had eight children. My mother remembers often visiting with her younger sister Setsuko when their great-grandmother would beckon the maid to serve *oshiruko* (Japanese pudding) to the young. She has told us amusing stories of how in very old age her great-grandmother would have Sellotape on her eyelids to keep them from falling down. Plastic surgery for cosmetic purposes had not then been invented!

Itohei had other houses in both Yokohama and Shizuoka where he convalesced from tuberculosis; he ultimately died in Yokohama. While convalescing in Atami, he funded a pipeline there for drinking water, and also the telegraph line between Odawara and Atami. Realising that his days were numbered, he set about building a large palatial residence in the centre of Yokohama so that the mourners, who he reckoned would be not only large in number but nationally respected dignitaries, could be appropriately received. So it was that the newspapers of the day reported the event in large measure. This palatial residence survived the Great Kanto Earthquake of 1923 and bombings during the war, although it had changed hands a number of times after Itohei's death; it was commandeered by the US Occupation to be used as their social club and was called Ko-yo-kaku (紅葉閣) until it was bought by the Japan Public Housing Corporation in 1956 and became the site of large-scale social housing which survives to this day. Itohei is buried in the cemetery of Ryosenji temple (良泉寺) together with tombstones for the members of his own immediate family, including his brother, first wife and their daughter Tora and her husband Kikujiro. The ledgers of his dealings in foreign exchange are preserved in the archives of Waseda University in Tokyo; the family donated them in the 1970s on my father's advice.

As his businesses gained traction, Itohei became close to other leading political and business figures of that time: Shibusawa Eiichi, another self-made industrialist of that generation who was the first President of Japan's first bank, the Daiichi Kokuritsu Bank in Kabutocho, a forerunner of today's Mizuho Bank; Mitsui Hachiroemon, of the most eminent commercial family of the Tokugawa shogunate, co-founder of the Daiichi Kokuritsu Bank; Inoue Kaoru, one of the most notable political figures of the Meiji Restoration, of the Chōshu clan, educated at University College London, becoming Japan's first Minister of Finance; Ito Hirobumi, also of the Chōshu clan, also educated at UCL, becoming Japan's first Prime Minister, and others. Those well-known figures clearly recognised Itohei's financial acumen, but also used his funding abilities in their endeavours for the development of modern Japan at that crucial moment in history. Itohei became the central figure, in collaboration with them, in the establishment of the three principal financial markets of Japan: foreign exchange, commodities, and stocks and shares. He was the largest shareholder amongst the five original instigators of the joint stock company, the Tokyo Stock Exchange, in 1872. It was he who recognised the need for a futures market in rice, a

Fukuda estate in Nagasaki, c. 1915

Top: Aunt Naoko outside the main gate.

Middle: Great-grandfather Fukuda Jōnosuke in bowler hat and crested *hakama* attire.

Right: The long tree-hedged wall at the front.

Top: Into the house: a discreet entrance for a samurai.

Middle: In the house; a young family – Naoko and Masaru, with grandmother Tsugi (seated), and father Koichi (standing behind); c. 1916.

Left: Masaru and Naoko paying a visit to their elder sister Michiko's grave at Shuntokuji, c. 1917.

The Fukuda–Shimazu connection

Top: Brothers Fukuda Koichi and Shimazu Takashi, c. 1920.

Shimazu Reiko, c. 1938.

Taiyō Maru – used for reconnaissance on the eve of the attack on Pearl Harbor

Below: _Taiyō Maru_ had been a German WWI reparation payment to Japan. Repaired under Koichi's instruction.

Left: Relaunch at the Nagasaki shipyard, early 1920s.

Koichi teaching shipbuilding engineering at the Imperial University of Tokyo, late 1920s.

Opposite: Masaru's kindergarten in Nagasaki, c. 1917.

Growing up with grandparents – Fukuda Jōnosuke, his wife Tsugi, Naolo, Sada, Masaru. In the garden of the Nagasaki house, c. 1919.

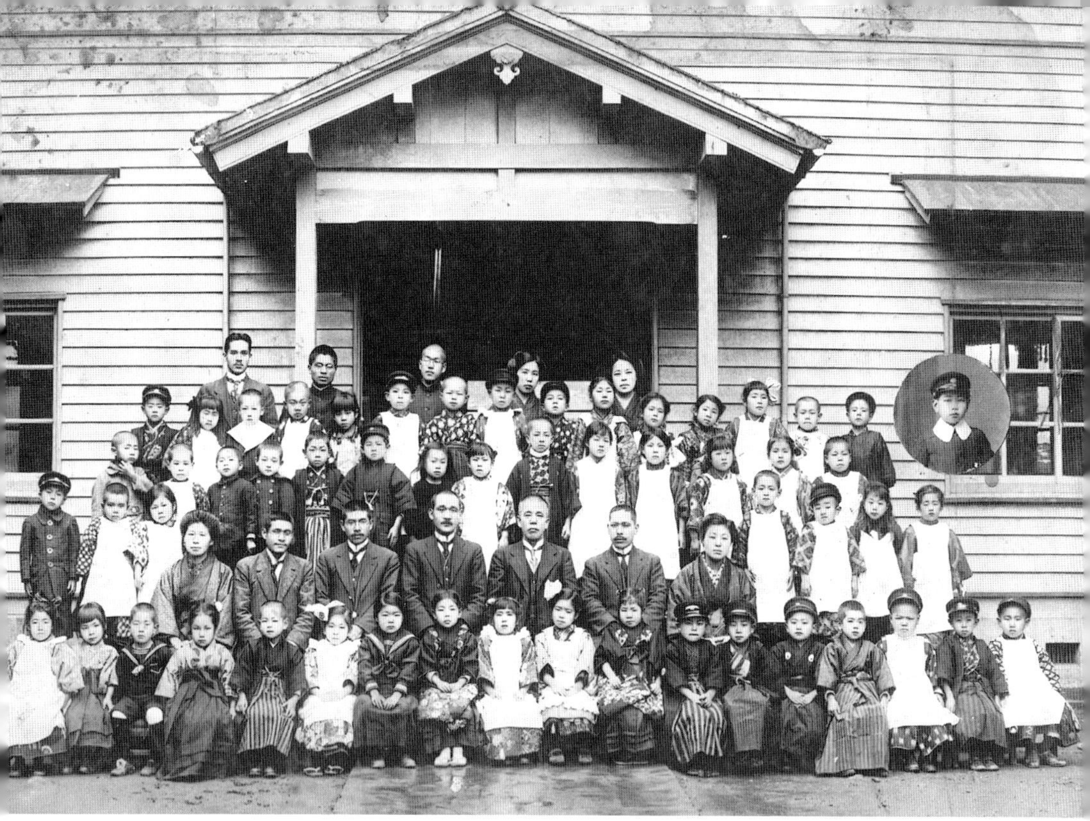

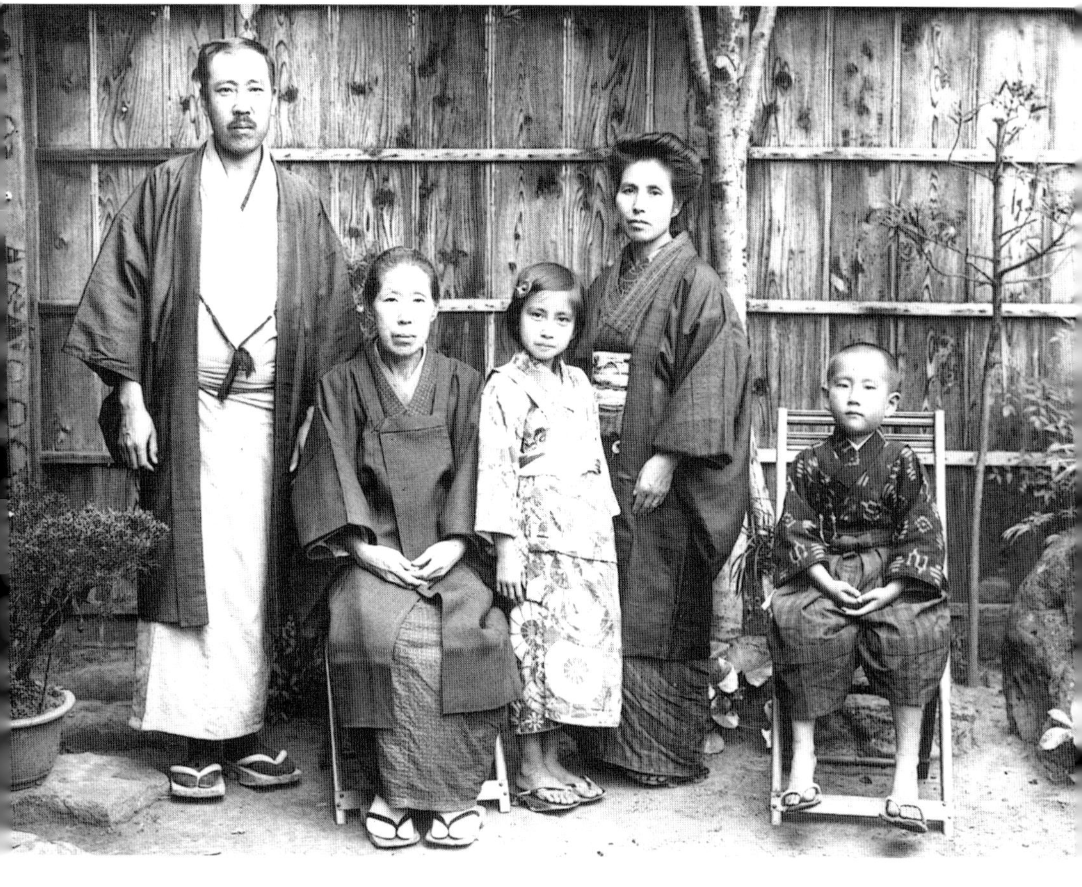

Admiral Yamanashi Katsunoshin in full uniform, 1928; a gift to his brother-in-law Fukuda Koichi.

In his last year, 1966.

HIJMS *Mikasa*.

Bronze bust of Yamanashi on *Mikasa* museum ship.

Clockwise from top left: Western house rear view, early 1920s; entrance to Western house; Masaru and Naoko on the Western house verandah; Masaru doing prep in the Japanese house; garden around the Western house; garden of the estate.

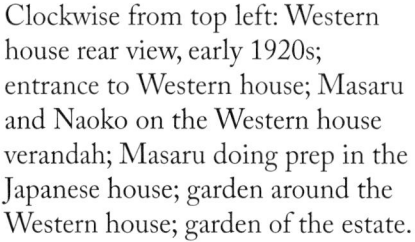

HIJMS *Chōkai* – flagship of the Second Fleet, 1939.

'Ping pong diplomacy' – mess room;
Masaru extreme left.

Officers and men on board, 1939

seasonal product, when he was asked by Mitsui Hachiroemon to set up the exchange and to run it. That was the first commodity futures exchange in Japan. Both these exchanges are sited in the same location to this day.

It is for the part he played in the early years of the Meiji period in those ground-breaking developments that Itohei is known to posterity as 'Tenka no Itohei'. On his death his friends had a giant stone monument installed beside the Sumida River, close to the site of the stock exchange; Ito Hirobumi instructed that the monument be to 'Tenka-no-Itohei' and he himself provided the calligraphy that was carved on the stone. The monument was relocated in 1978 and is now in Mukojima in Tokyo. It is of colossal size, weighing 80 tons, as was discovered when attempts to move it began; national newspapers ran the story, some with comical cartoons.

But Itohei's private ventures extended also to founding the Dai-Hyakujuuni Kokuritsu Bank, a national currency-issuing bank in 1878, and the Tanaka Bank in 1883 (renamed from Tanaka Gumi, established in 1877), both headquartered in Kabutocho, Tokyo; also a mining company, Tanaka Kogyo (田中鉱業), with gold and silver mining assets in various parts of Japan. Thus the family gained its *zaibatsu* status. Tanaka Kogyo's headquarters was unsurprisingly located on a site opposite the Tokyo Stock Exchange in Kabutocho. That remained for well over a hundred and fifty years the headquarters of my mother's family company. In the 1970s and 1980s a large part of the building was let to Yamaichi Securities – one of the Big Four securities companies of Japan. When he died in 1884 Itohei's personal fortune was at a low ebb. Judging by the message he left in his will to his successors, that they must never indulge in speculation, he must have lost money in speculative investments – most likely in cornering the market in foreign exchange during the 'Matsukata Deflation' of the early 1880s. But in any case his speculation had gained him huge wealth, only to be followed by large losses that he then recovered many times over. He knew that luck as well as calculation played its part. But after his death his heir Tanaka Yōnosuke (Tanaka Heihachi II) and his son-in-law Kikujiro (Tora's husband) remained major shareholders of the Tokyo Stock Exchange for a long time. Tanaka Bank was hit by the 1930s Depression and was closed in 1932. The mining enterprise, though, continued to survive as a private company for a hundred years until the mines were closed in the 1990s by my uncle, who by then was running the company. When it closed it was Japan's fourth-largest mining company. Itohei considered that mining was an activity which befitted the life of an industrialist, indicating his social aspirations. During the Tokugawa shogunate, successive shoguns had amassed mining assets across Japan. Daimyo and feudal clan chiefs also engaged in mining (as did my father's family north of Kyoto) as a sign of their wealth and power. The Meiji oligarchs of the *zaibatsu* families were all engaged in mining: Mitsui Mining, Mitsubishi Metal Mining, Sumitomo Metal Mining, all mined gold.

Itohei had courage and foresight; he was also an innovative entrepreneur. He swam with the times, sent his sons to be educated abroad and arranged aristocratic marriages for them. He was only fifty-one when he died.

Itohei's Heirs
Although he had left his first wife and daughter behind when he made his way to Yokohama, and married another woman with whom he had eight children, Itohei did keep in contact with his first family. His first wife, Haru, was the adopted daughter of the Tanaka family, which had also adopted him formally when he was nineteen. They had a daughter, Tora, who married Kitamura Kikujiro; but as she was their only offspring Itohei insisted that Kikujiro be adopted into the Tanaka family. Tora and Kikujiro had three sons. Kikujiro joined his father-in-law in the banking and mining enterprises and his sons and grandsons continued to

work there. Of his nine children and numerous grandchildren, I am introducing one grandson, a granddaughter, and two sons here.

Ginnosuke (田中銀之助): *a British-Educated Sophisticate*
Itohei sent his eldest grandson by Tora, Ginnosuke (田中銀之助), to be educated at the Peers' School and then on to the Leys School and Trinity Hall, Cambridge. It was by no means unusual or unique that he was sent to be educated in England; during the early period of Meiji many aspiring young Japanese men went to study in England. A number of them went to Cambridge and one became an active participant at the Union (the debating society) and became a well-known political activist on his return to Japan. Another, a descendant of Emperor Nijo of the Heian period, came to London and married his landlord's daughter; their eldest daughter married Sir Ralph Richardson, the famous actor. Some others too became well-known political figures of the early twentieth century. It was, though, less common for a teenage youth to be sent to school abroad before university, or without a specific career in mind, but Ginnosuke was just destined to join the family firm. He was instrumental in introducing rugby football to Japan, along with an English friend, Edward Bramwell-Clarke. Rugby was first played in Japan in 1899 by students of Keio University with which Bramwell-Clarke was associated. Back in Japan, Ginnosuke was a socialite, founding the famous Tokyo Club in Kasumigaseki, Tokyo, on similar lines to the gentlemen's clubs of London, and he engaged in upper-class pastimes and consorted with foreigners. He was also a leading tennis player and a black belt in Judo. A well-known geisha of that period wrote in her memoirs that Ginnosuke was a colourful guest at her restaurant. It says a great deal about the position Itohei had achieved in Japanese society in so short a time that his grandson would be accepted by leading aristocratic families as a suitable match for their daughters. Itohei with his

social ambitions arranged for his grandson to be married first to Ayako, the eldest daughter of Baron Hijikata (土方男爵), and secondly to Eiko, daughter of Marquess Hatta (八田裕次郎公爵).

On returning from England, Ginnosuke worked in his grand-father's bank, Tanaka Bank, as a director, and in the family mining company Tanaka Kogyo. Ginnosuke had two daughters and four sons. The sons worked in Tanaka Kogyo all their lives. The daughters married well. Keiko, a year younger than my mother, married Mimura Yohei (三村庸平) who became the Chairman and President of the Mitsubishi Corporation. Kuniko, a year younger, married the eldest son and heir to the daimyo of Niigata, Nishiwaki Kyōzaburo (西脇孝三郎). Both the daughters went to school with my mother and my aunts and they were like cousins. I myself knew them well. Keiko would always get in touch whenever she was in London, accompanying her husband on his business trips, and we met for lunches, teas and shopping. Kuniko was almost like an aunt, as her elder son was in my class at our junior school and we met often. Until they married, Keiko and Kuniko lived with their parents in Uchisaiwaicho.

Though enjoying a thoroughly enviable life, Itohei's family from his first wife Haru was later to be somewhat overshadowed by the dynasty created after he married his second wife Dai. It was the elder of his two sons by her who assumed the dynastic name Heihachi II. His role as 'the heir' and the inheritor of the main family businesses and estates is sufficiently important that it is covered in a separate following chapter. In an inversion of the natural order, therefore, I am first writing of the younger brother, Kamakichi, and his business and other interests, before returning to Heihachi.

Kamakichi (釜吉), *a German-Educated Industrialist, and Takata Shokai*
Kamakichi had been sent to Heidelberg where he read Engineering, and like so many of his contemporaries who had

studied abroad he became a true internationalist and acquired an intimacy with European culture and leisure pursuits. However, it was for his practical engineering proficiency and management skills that he came to the notice of one of Japan's leading industrialists, the owner-president of one of Japan's great *zaibatsu* trading conglomerates, Takata Shokai. The firm was especially notable for dealing in armaments, transport equipment and precision engineering: so Takata 'talent-spotted' Kamakichi as his successor, and also as husband of his only daughter, heiress to the concern. Thus Kamakichi was adopted into the Takata family.

The Takata Shokai company held a commanding position in Japan's international trade, especially in naval armaments. Mitsui was preeminent in Army procurement; Takata with the Navy. At the end of the nineteenth century Takata Shokai had offices in New York and the City of London (at 88 Bishopsgate), engaged in importing drilling equipment for mining, water pumps and naval vessels. It was Takata that the Armstrong-Whitworth shipyard in Britain signed up to be the contracting agent for Japan's procurement of some of the warships for the Russo-Japanese War. In 1899 it became the sole agent in Japan for the Westinghouse Corporation of the US. The company was well placed in the Japan of the boom years of the early twentieth century. Not only was it Takata which laid the electric tram system in Tokyo, but it also imported the essential materials for the building of Japan's largest steel mill, Yahata Seitetsusho KK. Possessing capabilities and know-how in precision equipment and insulation materials, Takata was the contractor for the electrification of the street lights for the whole of Tokyo. The company had partnerships with companies in rolling stock, cotton spinning, banking and mining.

However, the congruence of events – the coming into force of the Naval Limitation Treaty in 1923 which limited the building of capital ships by the leading nations, reducing demand for those areas in which its main commercial strengths lay; a disastrous fire in 1922 at the copper mine that it had acquired in 1911; and the Great Kanto Earthquake of 1923 – conspired to put the company into administration in 1925. Once an illustrious business that rivalled the giants Mitsui and Okura, it was destroyed. Its headquarters in Kojimachi was a fine Classical edifice in stone, designed by Olivier Delalande of Paris; it was badly damaged in the earthquake.

Having spent his youth in Europe, Kamakichi was an internationalist; he was one of the founding members of the League of Nations Association of Japan. Taking after his father, he also frequented the famous restaurants of the day and was a well-known figure among the leading geishas there. His company executives followed suit with a largesse that became notorious. But those aspects of him are not what my mother remembers.

Together with his eldest brother Heihachi (my mother's grandfather), Kamakichi enjoyed the sophisticated lifestyle of that generation of prewar Japanese: duck and pheasant shooting, fishing for the delicious Ayu using tethered cormorants, boar hunting, gourmet cuisine, tea ceremony parties in the pavilions in their gardens, equestrian pursuits, tennis, foreign cars, overseas grand tours, skiing, golf, grand dinner parties at home with chefs brought in from top restaurants. My mother told me that on Christmas Day the chef at the Tokyo Club would bring a hard-crust game pie made with the wild duck from their shoot. Summer months were spent in their country houses in the up-market resort of Karuizawa in the hills to escape the heat of Tokyo. There, they would regroup with their society friends who also had houses there and enjoy the country pursuits of hill-walking, collecting wild flowers, picnics and tennis parties. Heihachi housed Kamakichi and his family on the grounds of his estate in Fukidecho near Toranomon in Tokyo when he moved his own family from Uchisaiwaicho, leaving his step-nephew (though they were more like half-brothers) Ginnosuke there.

The Takata family lived in a splendid house set in a garden, just inside the main gate within the Fukidecho estate, which as Heihachi's creation will be described in the following chapter. The Western-style house was approached through a gravel drive to the fine portico with its glass awning and wrought iron frame; a few steps led up to the grand front door. The house was of pebbledash with windows in dark wood architraves. The hall, with a wide winding staircase with a mahogany balustrade, was floored in parquet. Sash windows on all sides with beautiful drapes and tassels and Edwardian mahogany furniture graced the three-storey house, which connected with the traditional Japanese house beyond.

Kamakichi was a man of taste and culture; he had a fine collection of wares for tea ceremonies and scroll paintings. He was part of the circle of rich tea aficionados in Japan's upper-class society. In those days tea ceremony gatherings were an important aspect of social intercourse, where people could admire fine tea bowls and converse in stylish ways. His wife, Yukiko, was usually seated in the Japanese living room by a lacquered table overlooking the garden whenever I visited them. It was a serene room without any clutter; the *tokonoma* in the far corner displayed a scroll painting suitable for the season, with fine ornaments and flowers in a vase at the base.

Their daughter Aiko and her husband Kitaoka Masami, an internationally known clinical scientist specialising in Japanese encephalitis at what is now called the Kitazato Igaku Kenkyujo in Shiroganedai, lived with their two sons in the Western-style building mentioned earlier. Kamakichi adored my mother, his first great-niece, and showered her with presents; my mother in turn speaks of him to this day with the greatest affection. Aunt Aiko was my mother's favourite and they remained close friends to the end of Aiko's life. She was a free spirit and liked the bohemian style of life, willing to flout convention in all matters including dress. I visited her with my mother often when she would tease me, a defenceless young girl, most unfairly. As they were both of the intellectual elite rather than from 'society', my father became close friends with Aiko's husband, who confessed that he felt small in the Takata family ménage, not coming from upper-class society. Their two sons, who were in their teens when I was little, came to my grandparents' garden with their airguns to shoot pigeons. Years later my aunt Asako (朝子) told me nostalgically how she played with them on their bicycles around the estate.

When my uncle Yuhei got married, he and his wife Mariko lived for a few years in the Western house there. It seemed to me so stylish that Mariko should be wearing stilettos in the house, making clacking noises as she walked on the wooden floors. I would often visit her with my cousin Kinuko to take a small gift of *temari*, that we made from colourful wool yarns into a ball that bounced. We amused ourselves in those days with such inconsequential handicrafts. That house still has an important place in the memories of my childhood. In the 1970s when I was visiting Tokyo, it had been let to the well-known pearl dealer, Jarwood; it was abhorrent to me that they had put up an advertising hoarding on the side of the house. I was so saddened to think that Jarwood had no conception of what an elegant life had been led before his time in what was now his home. Aiko's elder son, Takata Yuichi (who became the principal successor to the Takata family), had a daughter who grew up to be a television 'talent', a famous modern singer, Takata Mayuko. My mother went to her wedding to a well-known musician.

Yuichi and Eiji sold their house when their father died and went to set up their own homes elsewhere; my mother said that their new abodes were worthy of their heritage and had displays of art and *objets d'art* inherited from their parents and grandparents. But Aiko in later life suffered from clinical depression and lived a lonely life elsewhere. By then, my grandparents had died and her generation of the family were no longer around her.

Today the site of their house hosts the Peruvian-Japanese fusion restaurant 'Nobu' and a 7/11 store!

Heihachi II (洋乃助): *the Heir and Creator of Fukidecho*
Itohei's given name was Heihachi and he named his heir the same. Heihachi II was the eldest of Itohei's children by Dai, having been born with the childhood name of Yōnosuke (洋乃助). Heihachi II is not as well-known as his father, but in the history of the Japanese stock market he is not a forgotten figure. He was only nineteen when Itohei died and in accordance with his father's wishes, he assumed the name Heihachi and took over the reins of the family enterprises. His legendary father had left hefty debts for his son to meet. Heihachi II, disregarding his father's wishes, engaged in speculation to meet those debts. He recovered the family fortune, mostly through his stock market activities, and the family firm, Tanaka Kogyo, mining gold, silver and copper, provided the mainstay of family income. Ginnosuke and his father Kikujiro helped him on the Board of Tanaka Kogyo and also of the Tanaka Bank in the management of these enterprises. He also continued to invest in real estate, both in Tokyo and in the provinces. He was of a nervous disposition and not physically robust. He was exceptionally careful with his diet: his morning soup was to be served at exactly the correct temperature – a bit of a challenge for the chef and the servants who carried it down the long corridors from the kitchen to the breakfast table! Tall and handsome, always well dressed, Heihachi is photographed on visits to his mines in a well-tailored suit with a hat. He would be carried in a rickshaw down the mine. My mother told me that every morning after breakfast he would listen to the radio broadcast of the stock market real-time trading and would telephone his broker to give orders. In 1923 he came to London for six months, accompanied by servants and staff, to speculate on the London Stock Exchange.

He inherited from Itohei the estate in Saiwaicho (now

Uchisaiwaicho) near Hibiya on the outskirts of the Imperial
Palace; all grand families lived close to the Imperial Palace. There
he lived with his wife and two daughters. He also arranged that
his step-nephew, Ginnosuke, from his father's first marriage,
should continue to live there with his family. As Itohei was
good at arranging marriages for his children, his eldest son and
heir Heihachi II married Fukuhara Sumiko (澄子), the eldest
daughter of Baron Fukuhara Minoru (福原実男爵). The Fukuhara
family was a hereditary leading clan of Chōshu, in an area
around Hagi in what is now Yamaguchi prefecture. The Chōshu
and Satsuma clans, it is well known, led the events preceding the
Meiji Restoration and their social positions were secured during
the Meiji period. In any case, Baron Fukuhara was an admiral
and ennobled by the Meiji Emperor.

Sumiko was a great beauty, tall with perfect bone structure;
she was well educated at the Jogakkan School in Tokyo, taught
by American missionaries and fluent in English. Her school
notebooks are written in beautiful handwriting in English and
illustrated with skilful watercolours. Ladies of the Meiji era were
educated in art as well as in literature and music. Sumiko was a
talented painter and played the piano. Unlike the daughters of
grand families in Britain who were more often than not educated
privately at home, young Japanese ladies were sent to school.

From all accounts, Saiwaicho was a palace. My grandmother
Hanako and her sister Kimiko were brought up there and went
to their weddings from that house. Ginnosuke and his children
continued to live there after Heihachi moved to another estate
near Toranomon before my mother was born. When, towards
the end of her life, Great-Aunt Kimiko was suffering from
Alzheimer's disease she would in her wandering mind talk of
going to Saiwaicho to visit her parents and we got a glimpse of
the grand and well-served establishment there. Her carers (who
could not have had any idea of the scale of it) asked my mother
on one of her visits to the nursing home if Aunt Kimiko had had

some servants around her in her youth. My mother was bemused by this and said to me "If they only knew ... no one today could possibly even imagine what it was like." I do know that Ginnosuke's daughters, for example, never even put their own stockings on by themselves. I understand that my grandmother tried to bring up her own children to be more independent and my mother and her sisters did don their own clothes by the time they were in their teens. My mother told me that her mother said to her "You never know what circumstances may befall you when you marry; you might not marry someone wealthy; you have to be prepared to be able to look after yourself." In the context of the Taisho era in which she made that remark that was prescient. Yoko ended up marrying during wartime.

One thing that still remains from that Saiwaicho estate is a tea pavilion that has been moved to a garden in Shiroganedai; it is named Muan and is described as the tea pavilion of Tanaka Heihachi. Happōen presumably bought it when the Saiwaicho estate was sold: Happōen was the residence of an old samurai family, the Okubo, and is now a restaurant and functions complex set in old-style Japanese gardens. The main house in *sukiya* style and the surrounding gardens set with lawns and ponds are very reminiscent of my grandparents' house and gardens, but on a smaller scale. As it was within walking distance of our family home in Shiroganedai, we often went there to have meals, and inevitably the conversation turned to the tea house which was visible from the restaurant in the distance. On one occasion when my mother invited her siblings to dine with us there, Uncle Yuhei looked out of the window, saying "It is important for me to see the tea house." I have visited Muan many times with friends and sometimes I would say to the lady conducting the tea ceremony for visitors that I am a descendant of Tanaka Heihachi, to her astonishment. I am happy that it is in this lovely garden. It is an oasis of calm: a stylish Japanese garden in central Tokyo. That it is near the house where I was brought up also makes for a special connection.

Heihachi was a great gardener. When he moved from Saiwaicho to Fukidecho, the subject of the next chapter, he created the large and beautiful garden around his estate. Yoko wrote in her childhood diaries that he would go out to the garden whatever the weather and give instructions personally to the gardeners. For her, it was a haven – an oasis of nature in the middle of a city crowded with concrete buildings and asphalt roads – and her interest in plants and nature was fostered there in her childhood.

Kimiko (君子) and Minobe Yohji (美濃部洋次), a Leading Anti-War Liberal

Kimiko was Heihachi's younger daughter, Itohei's granddaughter. On her marriage to Minobe Yohji, who later became a leading anti-war liberal, Heihachi granted them a part of his estate to build their residence at 16 Fukidecho. It was built into the hillside with woodland at the back that led to the gardens of the main part of the estate, but with the entrance at the bottom of the Kamiyacho side. At the front of the house on the street was a high wall of dark granite stones (presumably to retain the rising lie of the land) with steps up to the front entrance. We normally used the other entrance to the upper part of the house at the side up the hill. Behind the house at the rear was a large kennel for several Alsatian dogs that Great-Aunt Kimiko kept for training. When she was widowed in the early 1950s she decided to donate one trained dog each year to the blind. I was always frightened of these dogs. They barked ferociously from behind the high, strong wire fence beside the path, as I walked up through the woods to visit my grandmother.

Kimiko was very close to her sister, my grandmother, and she would take the same path almost every day to see her and their mother. She was tall and a great beauty, inheriting strong facial features from her father and grandfather. When I was born, she bestowed on me her fine set of *ohinasama* dolls, which her father

Heihachi had given her when she was born. These dolls are now in a display cabinet in the hall at my house in Suffolk, a reminder of my heritage. She came to visit me and my husband in London a few months after we married, on the way to her pilgrimage to Jerusalem with the nuns from the convent in Kojimachi she was associated with; she had converted to Catholicism in her widowhood when she decided to teach young Catholic missionaries the Japanese language. She was widowed very young: her husband Minobe Yohji (美濃部洋次) died in 1953 in mid-career, only a few months after being released from the Allied Occupation purge. He was an official of the Ministry of Commerce and Industry and brother of Minobe Tachikichi (美濃部達吉), a famous liberal academic in the House of Peers, constitutional theorist, and professor of political science at the Imperial University of Tokyo in the prewar period. Tachikichi's son Ryokichi became a famous Mayor of the Tokyo Metropolitan Government in the 1980s.

Minobe Yohji and two other bureaucrats, Sakomizu Hisatsune (迫水久常) and Mohri Hideoto (毛利英於菟), both of the Ministry of Finance, were called the 'triumvirate reformist bureaucrats', well known for their leftist inclinations. They advocated that a planned economy based on Marxist theories as practised in the Soviet Union be introduced in a modified form in wartime Japan. The underlying tenet was that the ownership and management of companies should be separated and industrial production be centrally controlled to save the national economy from total collapse. As Minobe wrote himself, those reformists were at all times looking for an opportunity to end the war as early as 1943. Sakomizu recalled that Minobe was one of the very first to call for the cessation of the war. All three held influential positions in the bureaucracy; they were part of the elite specially selected to join the Cabinet Planning Board (as my father was), which coordinated the policies of the government, the military and the palace and became the engine room of the war. Minobe and Sakomizu were close personal friends.

This book is not the place in which to discuss or even attempt to outline the complex politics of Japan during the war. The following is taken from the first-hand account given by Sakomizu and Kishi Nobusuke (Prime Minister from the late 1950s into 1960) in a book of reminiscences of Minobe published soon after his death. With Kimiko and son Kokichi, they talked for several hours about Minobe's activities during the war and their close friendship. They remember, amongst other things, how Sakomizu and Minobe played a significant role together, covertly, in the overthrow of the government of General Tojo in July 1944. The resignation of the Tojo Cabinet was to provide the critical turning point of the war.

By then, both Sakomizu and Minobe were being watched closely by the Kempeitai – the secret police – on Army Command instructions, and Minobe escaped arrest on a number of occasions. As the war was drawing near to a close, with Japan certain to lose, in July 1945 it was Sakomizu, by then Prime Minister Suzuki Kantaro's Principal Private Secretary, who drew up the report on the devastatingly weak military position of Japan. When the Potsdam Declaration was issued on 26 July 1945 the Army rejected the proposed terms of surrender: that the sovereignty of the government and the Emperor be subordinated to the headquarters of the Allied Occupation. As the United States relentlessly fought on and dropped Little Boy and Fat Man on Hiroshima and Nagasaki on 6 and 9 August respectively, and the Soviet Union declared war on Japan on the 8th, the Supreme Council for the Direction of the War convened, for the first time ever with the presence of the Emperor, in an underground bunker. The Emperor, having heard the Prime Minister, asked the opinion of Foreign Minister Togo Shigenori, who suggested that the full terms of the Potsdam Declaration be accepted. With the Emperor's consenting nod, the process of surrender began. The Emperor is reported to have said he did not mind about his own life or even the imperial system itself but that the lives of his people must be spared; knowing the delicate political background he agreed to make the unprecedented move of addressing the nation in a radio broadcast.

With Mohri looking over his shoulder, it was Minobe who drafted, at Sakomizu's request, the Imperial Proclamation of 15 August, which Sakomizu wrote out in his own hand to present to the Cabinet. It was then worked over by distinguished scholars of *Kanbun* (writing in old Chinese characters) and one or two members of the Cabinet, and presented to the Emperor for his approval. Who knows if the celebrated subtle wording 'The war situation has developed not necessarily to Japan's advantage,' avoiding the use of the word 'defeat', was indeed Minobe's sensitive contrivance? The proclamation in the characteristically courtly language was recorded through the night of 14 August: the Emperor recalled in an interview with Court journalists a decade later that the recording was finally finished a half-hour before midnight. By the early morning of 15 August, the nation was informed by radio news that there would be a broadcast at midday on NHK and that everyone was requested to listen. All national newspapers were told to deliver the morning edition in the afternoon. The people of Japan were told to stand during the broadcast. The national anthem, *Kimigayo*, was played at midday and the Emperor spoke. *Kimigayo* was played again. There followed the recordings of the Prime Minister that elaborated on the Emperor's proclamation. It was the first time that the Emperor's voice had been heard by the ordinary people of Japan.

The dramatic events of that night of 14 August, with the warhawks in the Army and the Imperial Guard at the palace, are much recounted elsewhere: the Imperial Guards and the Army faction that tried to prolong the war occupied the Imperial Palace and tried to seize the NHK tape recording and take the Emperor hostage. Hirohito was in hiding. The tape was not found; it was hidden in a locked safe in amongst a pile of documents. The Lord Chamberlain, held at gunpoint to reveal its location, adamantly insisted on his ignorance. Meanwhile, having finished the Emperor's recording, Sakomizu, with tears flowing incessantly, had gone to sleep in the Prime Minister's official residence in Kasumigaseki at about 2 a.m. He was woken by the sound of machine guns firing at the residence from tanks at the crossroads below its window. He immediately telephoned the Prime Minister who had gone back to his own private residence and told him to leave as his house might be set on fire; and the Prime Minister escaped by a whisker. Sakomizu found his way out of the building by a hidden back route into the street, desperate with fear that he could be arrested imminently. He ran to the nearby home of Minobe at No. 16 Fukidecho. At about 3 a.m., as he remembered, he furiously banged on the door to find Minobe and his wife, Kimiko, still awake. He recalled that the only sustenance Kimiko could offer him was dry bread. Kimiko in this volume recalled that she and her husband desperately tried to think of a safe place for them to hide. The rebels and the Kempeitai were close. By 6 a.m. they decided to go to the police station. At midday the Imperial Proclamation was broadcast to the nation.

Both Sakomizu and Minobe were purged by the Allied Occupation. Two people who risked their lives for years to try to stop the war were purged merely because they held certain positions in the bureaucracy. Only a few months after being released in 1953, Minobe died of a heart attack. On his death, future Prime Minister Kishi Nobusuke (岸信介) gave the eulogy at the Shinto funeral at 16 Fukidecho. It is the only Shinto funeral that I have ever attended. Kishi had been the deputy minister, and then the minister of the Ministry of Commerce and Industry during the war, and had earlier, while a senior official in the Ministry, persuaded Minobe to be stationed in Manchuria to implement industrial development there; throughout the war years the two of them remained close. It was Kishi who led the resistance of the bureaucracy to General Tojo's onslaught against

the 'disloyal' bureaucrats who had argued for an early negotiated peace. In a catalytic turn of events in 1944, Tojo demanded
Kishi's resignation as the head of the Ministry. The Ministry of
Commerce and Industry was significant in that it gave out the
military procurement orders to the manufacturers. Minobe was
head of the machinery division and, putting himself in danger,
played a crucial role in communicating Kishi's determined
refusal to the Cabinet by visiting Admiral Okada Keisuke
(former Prime Minister, in the mid-1930s) at his home. Okada
had been leading the faction in favour of negotiating an end to
the war for three years, and was under the eagle-eyed watch of
the Kempeitai, who were also following Minobe. The Kempeitai
immediately telephoned Kishi to verify whether Minobe was his
messenger; Kishi denied any knowledge, saying how would he
know where a grown-up adult was going – he could have been
visiting a geisha!

Minobe was an exceptionally independent-minded individual and especially outspoken with the Press. When he married
Kimiko he wrote in his diary that it had never been in his mind
to marry; he was opposed to the institution as he regarded it as
a denial of the individual; he married only to please his mother.

My mother said in her speech at the dinner party given for her
ninetieth birthday that she loved Aunt Kimiko almost as much
as she loved her own mother. She has also always treasured the
piece of calligraphy that Yohji's father Minobe Toshikichi had
rendered and given to her at the time of her marriage. I can
picture Aunt Kimiko now, walking up across the large garden
where stood the ancient ginkgo tree that saved the lives of some
200 people during the 1923 Great Kanto Earthquake.

The Upper House and part of the garden, circa 1980. Yuhci's house on the left; Hotel Okura South Wing behind, and its main building on the right.

4. FUKIDECHO: A VANISHED WORLD

~

Fukidecho (葺手町) was where I was born and where my mother came from. The place holds abiding memories for me and all my maternal relations – it was our home, and a special place. All of the family called it 'Fukidecho', though that was actually the address rather than the name of the house. It was true enough that most of the Fukidecho area belonged to the Tanaka family. And it was to Fukidecho that we always returned. For my mother, life there remained her anchor and source of strength. Though she lived for more than sixty years in the Fukuda family home in Shiroganedai, about twenty minutes away by car, Fukidecho remained emotionally and psychologically her real home. We all somehow felt that we could always go home to Fukidecho in moments of desperation and everything would be all right. It had that quality of a fortress. In fact, paradoxically, for that very reason I chose *not* to go back to live there with my grandparents when I came down from Cambridge, fearing I would lose my freedom. I managed to persuade my father that I should remain in London and get a job for a while.

How differently my life would have turned out had I indeed gone back to Japan after graduating, to live with my grandparents and await my parents' return. *Omiai* marriage for sure! At the care home, where sadly she had to retire in her late 90s (still going strong at 102 as I write), my mother's conversations with me are more often than not about life at Fukidecho. She has often said that no one today could possibly understand or imagine what her life had been like in her youth; this makes her lonely, with no one today to understand her personality properly, or share her memories; all her siblings have now died, except for her youngest sister, who has had Alzheimer's for the last twenty years. About ten years ago, Aunt Mariko (by then widowed) asked me "What was Fukidecho like?" I was surprised by the question; but on reflection realised that, of course, I had known it as it was before she married Yuhei, and we kept talking about Fukidecho in terms of a 'kind of life', rather than just as a place.

Though I did not experience prewar life at Fukidecho, I am old enough to have known what it was like immediately after the war and in the 1950s; life there, albeit on a reduced scale, still retaining much of the lifestyle of those prewar days. Fukidecho was special because within its extensive demesne there lived a large upper-class family, with several members each having their own mansion and gardens: a world of its own. Its uniqueness was partly to do with the extent of the demesne, but not many people, even those much richer, could recreate previous lifestyles from before the war, and certainly not in the very centre of Tokyo.

A Grand Estate

Fukidecho was the creation of my mother's grandfather, Heihachi II; my mother was his first grandchild, and he loved her to distraction. She was born there and married from there and all her siblings lived there *en famille* with their parents, grandparents, aunts, uncles and cousins. For me, it was as if it was another home which I went to at least twice a week and often to stay.

Heihachi and Sumiko had moved from Saiwaicho to Fukidecho soon after their elder daughter Hanako got married to Jiro in 1919, and moved their family to this estate. The area came to be known as Tanakayama (Tanaka Hill, 田中山) as the whole hillside encompassed several Tanaka residences. When Uncle Yuhei built a skyscraper on the site of his old house decades later he named it Tanakayama Building. It was near the Toranomon intersection, between Tomoecho and Kamiyacho. Since the Hotel Okura was built in 1962, it has become easier to explain the location. Virtually the whole area next to the main building of the Okura and below its South Wing, going down the hill to the main road around Kamiyacho (神谷町), was called Fukidecho. There were natural woodland gardens with five tea pavilions and several large *oyashiki* residences (御屋敷) within the estate, including one for the Takata family and another for the Minobe family, as already mentioned. After the war, when Yuhei married and started his own family, he had built in another part of the estate a large house and garden; Grandfather also built an apartment block for his children and Asako made her first home in it. The main house on the upper part of the estate was in two parts: one large Western-style house in stone with a large handsome portico, connected by a corridor to a huge traditional *sukiya*-style Japanese house built around an internal garden. My mother was born in the Western part of the house.

A wide gravel drive, flanked by a row of oak trees, led to the inner gateposts. We used to collect acorns under the trees and roasted them for snacks. On the left, opposite the Takata family house, were two small houses: the head gardener lived in one and the chief house servant in the other, with their respective families. The inner gates opened onto a further gravel drive beyond, extended to the main house. The stone-built Western-style house in front was redolent of nineteenth-century residences in Paris. My mother has always said that it was the most lovely house. There were garages and outhouses, including a laundry on the opposite side of the Japanese house beyond. My grandfather had a penchant for American cars and had a succession of Packards and Cadillacs, while my uncle Yuhei was given a Chevrolet. The chauffeur was to be seen polishing those vehicles, kept in

immaculate condition, with feather dusters. In the years immediately after the war my grandfather also kept Angora rabbits
with bright red eyes in the outhouse next to the garage. And
there were chickens running around. Beyond those outhouses
was a traditional two-storey keep – a *kura*. This kura has survived
the complete redevelopment of the area in recent years; it is still
there in amongst the forest of skyscrapers, presumably preserved
for its architectural and historical importance.

My mother has told me that Heihachi bought the main part of
the estate from Baron Aoki, but he added to it a row of terraced
houses at the bottom of the hill to house the servants. The main
gate was on the Tomoecho side of the hill, opposite where the
Hotel Okura is now. The Okura site was a bombsite during my
childhood; destroyed in a raid over Tokyo in 1945, it remained
derelict until the hotel was built in 1962 in readiness for the
Olympic Games of 1964. The Okura family lived there before the
war. Baron Okura Kihachiro was a very wealthy and well-known
industrialist of the Meiji and Taisho eras and a close friend of
Heihachi. The Okura Shukokan – the little museum beside the
hotel – now houses some historic material that depicts their
friendship. Okura Kihachiro was a great collector of antique
artefacts, and it is said that he never asked the price or bargained
but simply offered what he thought was the correct value to the
antique dealer. The museum is a permanent monument to him
and his family in their place of residence; I have often thought
how enviable that is as I have watched through the decades after
my grandfather's death the successive demolition and sales of
our homestead in various stages, so that there is no hint left of
my mother's family domain. Her siblings and cousins continued
to live in various buildings on the estate and some still do, but in
a much-altered environment.

Before I describe life at Fukidecho I will record first what happened to the estate. The Tanaka family fortune did not survive the
vicissitudes of time. First, the Occupation government brought

in a penal asset tax immediately after the war, and that led to the sale of the Western part of the main residence for a corporate guest house. Some years later, the natural woodland garden was sold to become a golf driving range, operated by the Seibu Group. Then with Grandfather Jiro's death in 1970, the main house and its gardens had to be sold to meet inheritance tax obligations. There were many fraught and upsetting family discussions: Aunt Asako wanted to make the main house and gardens into a memorial museum, but my mother thought the contents of the house were not up to the standard of a museum; Aunt Setsuko's husband's construction company, Kajima Corporation, wanted to buy it for redevelopment – a prize site for skyscrapers; Uncle Yuhei wanted to preserve the garden. Asako regretted to her dying day that her suggestion was not taken up, as she felt that a piece of social history had been lost. Eventually it was decided that it would be sold to Kajima on the condition that the site would not be developed during Yuhei's lifetime. Setsuko sent a lorry to take away ancient ornamental stones and specimen trees from the garden to be sited at her own residence, much to the amazement of my mother. Having heard this she decided she would like to have the cornus tree, scion of one of the original ones that President Taft donated to Japan in 1912, in return for the cherry trees gifted by Japan to America, and also the large antique Chinese basin in the garden. The cornus flourished in our garden in Shiroganedai until 2015 when we sold our Fukuda family house; the Chinese basin is now in my garden in Suffolk. With the passage of time, thirty-five years later in 2005, the site was levelled and developed with new skyscrapers, even though Uncle Yuhei was still alive. I never forget: on New Year's Day 2006 I went to the Hotel Okura for lunch with my mother and my friend Dugald (who had just recovered from a major illness) and saw that what had been my mother's home was now a building site. In her characteristically stoical way my mother said, "It can't be helped; life has to move on … I understand that it is sad for you as your memories are wiped out..." But I know that she regretted it deeply: when it was reported in the *Nikkei* newspaper that there was to be a thirty-storey-high luxury apartment block (and other office buildings) she asked me if I could buy an apartment in it as revenge. I wondered if I could possibly afford to do this, but decided it was not practical. The site was developed in a joint venture between the Kajima and Ohbayashi Corporations.

On the estate there remained various other buildings that belonged to the family until finally in 2018 all of the estate but for a few flats went out of family ownership. Uncle Yuhei had rebuilt his residence, No. 20 Fukidecho, three times over with successively beautiful houses surrounded by lovely gardens with koi in the little stream; he was very proud of the koi, saying "those ones were born here!" He had placed in the corner a small shrine that had always been in the family, dedicated to the ancestors, which he visited each morning to clap his hands in prayer. He eventually developed the site with two large skyscrapers, called the Tanakayama Buildings; one of them had three apartments for his family, and the rest was let for offices.

Yuhei also redeveloped other houses on the estate: the lovely Western house where Yoko and her siblings grew up at No. 17, the apartment block Ginnan House that Grandfather Jiro had built for all his children to own where Asako made her home, other smaller old Japanese houses where various relations made their homes over the years were turned into office buildings to let. But by 2005, fifteen years after the collapse of the bubble economy in 1990, with the property market still subdued, it was time to reorganise their asset holdings. That had to include Fukide Building No. 1 at No. 17 Fukidecho. The collapse of the market, to put it into context, resulted in a 75–80 per cent fall in property prices in Japan, never to recover in thirty years. Interest rates have been close to zero or even negative throughout those decades and still are. Tanaka Kogyo, the mining company, had closed its old exhausted mines by the 1990s and the company was reconstituted as Itohei Kosan. My mother and her sisters, and their children, therefore lost their shareholding interest in what had been their principal family firm. The long economic recession following the collapse of the stock market and the property bubble in 1989–90 put great pressure on 'old money and wealth'. Banks were under government pressure to call in long lines of old credit; it was a devastating time. Old wealth based on rentier income from property such as that of the Tanaka family was gradually eroded. My mother, though, said "Never mind, they have led an extravagant lifestyle for a long time … they will be all right."

Japan seemed to get used to low growth, deflation, large public debt, decades of bear market; but with a low level of unemployment and high fiscal spending it appeared to build a civilised modern economy unrivalled by other Western nations. Visitors voiced envy – less social strife, good social provisions, beautiful modern buildings. Investment in infrastructure continued to gather momentum with ever-higher standards of earthquake tolerance in roads and buildings. The collapse and the prolonged decline of asset prices imposed an almost automatic redistribution of wealth. One of my friends said "I look back on our earlier life with much nostalgia, but we have to accept now that we are all equally poor. And I wonder if the country is more peaceful for it." With hardly any interest income, widows and all those who lived on investment income such as my mother have had to make ends meet for the past thirty years by realising their capital.

The Olympic Games were to be held in Tokyo in 2020, which gave a further impetus for the beautification of the city and led to speculation that property prices might rise before the event. In 2017, more than a decade after Yuhei's death, his successor decided that both the Tanakayama Buildings and the adjacent office building, Fukide Building No. 2, that had been built on the site of Ginnan House and other old Japanese houses, together making up a substantial development site, should be sold to Mitsui Residential Development Co. They completed the building of luxury residential tower blocks in 2022, in which Yuhei's widow and children retained several apartments and will continue to live. The sale marked the end of the Tanaka establishment at Fukidecho. The unity of the Tanaka descendants, all sharing a common interest, has thus been broken.

As new owners stamped their marks on the newly developed establishments, the Fukidecho address has disappeared from the map. Grandmother's sister's residence at No. 16 had carried the name Fukide Heights as a mansion block for decades but it has recently been redeveloped into a smart large-scale apartment block where the Minobe family still resides.

The only person, other than family, who knows of my association with that area is the head waiter at the Okura's Toh-Ka-Lin restaurant, Suzuk-san, who always sat me by the window overlooking the site saying "That is your old home, isn't it?" I go to the restaurant often, partly so I can see it with nostalgia and curiosity.

Fukidecho or Tanakayama was one of the largest estates in central Tokyo in the twentieth century, uniquely situated only a stone's throw away from Kasumigaseki, the government district. As a child I was not conscious of its scale nor of how exceptional the beautiful gardens were. The very first reunion of her class after my mother left school before the war was held there, with the young 'debutantes' all beautifully dressed in fine kimonos. One of my mother's Peeresses' School friends told me when I had grown up that no one else lived like that and I must never forget what it was like. While I was at junior school, I would invite my close friends to picnic there. The kitchen would prepare picnic baskets for us and these were brought out to where we spread a rug under a large gingko tree on the perimeter of the woodland garden.

No. 17: Lloyd Wright Style and an Occupation HQ

By the time Yoko was born in 1921, her parents had built a large Western-style house designed by Frank Lloyd Wright's associate, Antonin Raymond, on the Kamiyacho side of the estate at No. 17 Fukidecho, next door to Aunt Kimiko's house. It was Raymond's first commission in Japan. Yoko was brought up in this house and its successor during her childhood and lived there with her parents until she married during the war. I describe this house here before moving on to life at the main residence of the estate; though it remained in family ownership until the early twenty-first century, the family never lived there after the war as the house was promptly commandeered by the US Occupation government as one of its headquarters.

There was a pair of large wooden doors hanging on granite stone gateposts, with a curved gravel drive rising uphill to the house, built of unpolished travertine marble. The house had a central portico and wings on either side at oblique angles. The windows had mullions in the same stone designed in the characteristically Frank Lloyd Wright style. The furniture inside was made in mahogany to suit the style of the house and the floors were parquet. Photographs show it to have been a beautiful residence. All the women are seen in their kimonos, hair in the old Japanese style, piled high with elaborate hairpins. Sadly, my grandmother Hanako did not like this house, and she summoned a soothsayer who declared that its orientation was ill-conceived. She had it demolished, replaced by another Western-style house.

I remember this house well; it was in stucco with dark brown window frames around sash windows. When the house was demolished in 1974 my mother took the lantern that hung in the portico; in 2015, when our house in Shiroganedai was also demolished, I brought it back to England and hung it above the front door of my house, Creems, in Suffolk. My local English builder was impressed by its Art Deco elegance. When US Occupation forces commandeered this house at the end of the war, they used it as their Headquarters 5, and for US Air Force personnel until the late 1950s, when it was returned to the family. Grandmother Hanako much lamented the resultant damage. I remember her saying to me "How barbaric the Americans are; they have no respect for beautiful objects." The US military had nailed aluminium covers over inlaid Edwardian furniture; the house was in a mess when they left. They had very little contact with my grandparents; certainly I never saw any of them. This house remained until 1974 when, after Grandfather's death, my uncle decided to develop this plot and build an office building to let, Fukide Building No. 1. The Shinto priest came to cleanse the site, swinging a stick with pure white folded paper hung from it, I remember, wishing the new building well. The whole family was there. So many memories for my mother and her sisters were buried for good – especially for Asako who lived there through the air raids of 1945, rushing into the shelters with her father and his manservant Ryozo. The two small Japanese houses just inside the gate on the left, which I often visited with my mother when I was little, and where Great-Grandmother Sumiko's relations lived, were also demolished in that process.

No. 24: the Upper House

Grandparents' house, the main or 'upper house' (上の家) as we called it, built in *sukiya* style, had verandahs all around looking onto the large spread of lawns, bordered to the south by ponds with stepping stones that led us into the woodland garden beyond. Grandfather Jiro was very interested in keeping a 'perfect' lawn and the gardeners tended it meticulously, rolling, seeding and fertilising each season; some female garden helpers from the neighbourhood were often seen crouching to weed with hand sickles. The head gardener, Yasu, speaking in an old-fashioned retainer mode, would be in attendance whenever Heihachi and Jiro were in the garden, receiving their instructions. Living on the estate, he worked for the family all his life. I watched him milk the goat, prune the roses and catch chickens for the kitchen when I was little; he followed us children around the large garden lest we fall into the ponds. I remember Grandfather telling me that the varieties of grass he used were bents mixed with the finer fescue, because of the very hot summer in Tokyo. He kept a small area that was all fescue, close to the house outside the drawing room, where there was an area laid with large pebbles on which stood the old Chinese basin, glazed with a phoenix amongst lotus flowers design on the outside and beautiful sky blue on the inside, containing goldfish. Beside the basin were tables with a number of bonsai trees. It was in front of this area that the commemorative photographs were taken of my mother's school classmates and those of the family on the occasion of my parents' engagement. At the time I was not interested in such a subject as lawns, and thought Grandfather self-indulgent in his concern for such trivial matters. But when I came to have my own garden in Suffolk years later, I realised how rewarding such knowledge could be.

The 'natural garden', in the distance beyond the lawns, with unmade paths edged with large pebbles, was a spinney; it had five tea pavilions at various locations. I loved walking there, and as a child often went on my own, roaming through the woodland. It was beautiful, with dappled light: I romanticised imaginary life all around. There was no one else there, only birdsong and wood-pigeons, but it was safe. It took at least twenty minutes to go round this area of the woodland without stopping, so it must have been quite a large area. There was a big gate onto the street at the bottom of this woodland area, where tea party guests for the pavilions would arrive in their carriages. This gate was on the Tomoecho side of the estate at its bottom corner. There were many kinds of ferns, rodgersias, wild astilbes in flower with tiny pink flowers beside the paths, bamboo thickets and tall trees with cicadas on their trunks in the summer, wild cherries in flower in the early spring, climbing camellias, violets of dark purple, and of course dragonflies on the ponds in the summer. For summer holidays we were given holiday 'prep' to collect different kinds of cicadas; that was easy for me since the cicadas in the woodland garden were unworldly and unsuspecting of predators.

The ponds that separated the main part of the garden with lawns from the woodland garden had tadpoles in the spring. My cousin Kinuko, my sister Chahchah and I played by the pond to catch the tadpoles and small frogs. Sometimes one of us would fall into the pond, and a happy time ended in tears.

During the Great Kanto Earthquake and subsequent fire, people who lived in the area just below the estate rushed up to shelter under large trees with firmly grounded roots. The ginkgo tree just on the edge of the woodland was the focal point of this escape. For many days and weeks, people pitched their tents around the tree to survive the devastation. That ginkgo tree, under which I had picnics on innumerable occasions with my school friends, was eventually taken to the UNESCO Village on the outskirts of Tokyo when my grandparents sold the woodland garden to the Seibu group in the late 1950s; Seibu built a golf driving range on that site. By the mid-1960s Seibu had sold it on to the Norinchukin Bank to build a skyscraper – Norinchukin Kinnenkan – with a shopping arcade. My grandmother lamented that development, as it spoilt the view from our garden. The UNESCO Village re-erected the large stone monument commemorating the event beside the tree. On one of my later school outings our class was taken to the UNESCO Village: on spotting our ginkgo I was proudly telling my friends and teachers that the tree came from my grandparents' garden … but no one seemed interested.

The lawns in front of the living room of the house had a rose garden straight ahead that my grandmother laid out herself, and she was often seen cutting roses for the vase; her favourite rose was Peace. Although I preferred to plant Classic roses rather than Hybrid Teas in my own garden when I came to Suffolk,

I have made an exception for Peace. A few yards away was a bamboo fence that separated the garden of the Western part of the house. There was a little gate with a roof in the fence that Kinuko and I used to go through to play there.

Almost always my grandmother was sitting by the low table in the living room overlooking the lawn. That was 'her corner'. She had a small handwarmer *hibachi* beside her. On the table she had her tray of little whatnots, a small pair of scissors, a pen and pencil, a small magnifying glass, her enamelled ashtray and a long cigarette holder and matches. Both Grandmother Hanako and her mother Sumiko smoked, using a cigarette holder of silver and tortoiseshell. Whenever we went to visit in the afternoons we sat around this low table with Grandmother and chatted over tea and cakes. When I was little, the maids would sit beside me to help me eat, squashing strawberries with cream and sugar, peeling apples and cutting them up, peeling and seeding every grape. The verandah had large armchairs with soft covers of white linen and a coffee table and continued along the garden front to the next room, the drawing room.

The living room where the family normally congregated had a large fireplace with a mantel and shelf, in front of which were two large leather-upholstered armchairs. Grandfather Jiro always sat in one of them; he would often beckon young Kinuko to sit on his knee. In one corner of the room stood the dining table where we had breakfast and informal family lunches and dinners. It was made of thick well-polished blond oak with eight beautifully crafted matching chairs of stained mahogany with seats upholstered in green leather. The table and chairs were made specially for the house at No. 17 to a design that was quintessentially 1920s modern. The table had extension leaves that would make it large enough to seat perhaps twenty. For meals, it was set with lacquered trays for each person with a cruet set on each tray. When the Upper House was sold, my mother brought this dining table and the chairs to our home and for the following forty years my family used them for all our meals. When in 2015 we decided to sell our home in Shiroganedai, I agonised about what to do with this table and the chairs: it seemed a pity to throw them away, imbued with memories of innumerable happy meals throughout my life. It was difficult to find a home for them, as they were too large for most Japanese houses of today, and antique dealers were reluctant to take them. I tried to persuade my sister Sakiko to take them back to America, but her husband Francis vetoed it. I found a dealer who was interested to hear that they were designed by Antonin Raymond in the 1920s and eventually offered me a few hundred pounds. I had no choice but to accept.

Family dinner parties were held to celebrate grandparents' birthdays; they would bring in a chef from famous Japanese restaurants to cook in the kitchen. But Aunt Mariko, a very accomplished cook, would bring some special dish to add to the menu. I particularly remember on one occasion, soon after she married Uncle Yuhei, she made a large jellied terrine with colourful pieces of vegetables set in aspic which looked amazing. I always made a cake for my grandmother's birthday present and brought it to those parties; I loved decorating a large sponge cake my mother helped me to bake, with cream and caramelised fruit on top with the appropriate number of candles. Making such things, handicrafts, painting in watercolours and playing the piano were the habitual ladies' pastimes at Fukidecho.

On my way back from school, halfway to home, I would get off the tram at Kamiyacho and walk up the street, passing the Minobe house and No. 17; sometimes I would drop in at Uncle Yuhei's house at No. 20 to see Aunt Mariko and go up through the garden, but more often I would walk past and follow the road round to the Tomoecho side to the main gate. On the gravel drive, I would hear dogs barking in the Takatas' garden, which posed a challenge. I was terrified of dogs: I would try to walk silently, but, this not being possible on gravel, try running down to the inner gate, the noise of my approach on gravel bringing out a manservant from the house. Safe at last from the dogs!

Ryozo, the chief manservant, would come out by the back door and acknowledge that I was approaching; he would quickly go to the *genkan*, the front entrance of the house, and open the door. Inside on the *tatami* were sitting two or three maids in a line, one of whom would stand up and come forward to help me to take off my shoes on the pebble-laid floor of the front entrance. She would offer me slippers to get up into the tatami-matted house. Meanwhile, another maid would have gone quickly down the corridor along the glazed screens beside the internal garden to the living room where my grandmother would be sitting and announce my arrival. I would then walk down the same corridor to my grandmother. The house was built around an internal garden with a verandah along it.

As one entered the house, there was a waiting room on the left for visitors before they were shown to the drawing room. Certain tradesmen, such as shoemakers or kimono couturiers, would be received by my grandparents in that waiting room. It was not for the fishmongers and grocers, who came to the kitchen door to get their daily orders. Fishmongers would bring the day's offering handwritten in ink on *kyogi* – the skin of the bamboo bark. One of the maids would take it to Grandmother who chose the menu for the day. The large kitchen had what people these days call an 'island' in the middle with cupboards underneath; Grandmother would go there to taste the sauces being prepared. A large Westinghouse fridge had exactly the same sound of whirling motor and smell of old fridges I encountered in old country houses in England. It always contained bottles of freshly-drawn goat's milk and ice-cold water for the table. Behind the kitchen were maids' rooms where they were ironing and sewing. When I was a child there were five live-in maids and a *shosei* who lived in a small room next to the maids' rooms. Shosei were student lodgers who worked as house servants in return for accommodation and meals; that was a prewar phenomenon that soon became an anachronism after the war. Ocho was our cook, who was originally Great-Aunt Kimiko's wet-nurse from the Saiwaicho days and lived in a small house on the estate. A tiny old woman, having been with the family for decades, she was a confident and bossy leader of the servants and we were rather frightened of her. Her domain was the kitchen and service rooms around it and she never came into the main part of the house.

Many of the servants from the prewar days stayed in service with my grandparents all their lives; my mother's nanny Takemi was always there at Fukidecho, though living in her own house with her brother and his family, and when I was born she came daily to our house to look after me. She was a trained nurse and cared for Heihachi in his later life. I was very fond of her; when I got married, she presented me with a pair of silver napkin rings with our initials engraved on them. My mother at her care home, feeling helpless, says often "If Takemi was alive, she would come rushing to help me…" Oshige was my grandmother's personal maid and she lived in one of the terraced houses at the bottom of the hill that Heihachi had provided for the servants' families. Oyuki was my aunt Setsuko's nanny: by the time I was born, she had married well, into a family with a large temple in Shiba and she came to visit Fukidecho often. Ryozo stayed with the family till well past his retirement age into the 1990s, continuing to work for my uncle Yuhei, and lived in a small house provided for him and his family in the grounds. His first duty in the mornings was to open all the full-length shutters, of which there were many, and dust all around the house before anyone rose. At Akiya (the seaside resort near Hayama), Osué lived in a small house on the grounds, looking after the family estate there with her husband, and cooking for us whenever we went there. They were all loyal and the sense of mutual dependence made them, as it were, a part of the family; certainly their existence gave us all a sense of security that would be difficult to find today. In turn, they were looked after by the family, who provided their livelihood. Aunt Asako, who had a house of her own in Akiya, always said that she would look after Osué to the end.

Next to the maids' room were two staircases that led up to bedroom suites for my uncle and my three aunts, overlooking the internal garden. The main corridor flanked that garden – a little landscape of rocks and ponds, streams and islands with well-placed moss and ferns and small ornamental trees. The corridor was lined with glazed screens with a narrow verandah all the way along. My great-grandmother Sumiko had a suite in this corridor where she spent most of the day; my mother would never fail to visit her there. Beyond her suite were the prayer room with the large *Butsudan* altar and its anteroom (a mini-chapel as it were). There Hanako said prayers every morning. Reaching the main part of the house on the principal corridor, to the left were several rooms: first the wardrobe room with several large wardrobes and tallboys; and beyond it the master bedroom with a dressing room. Dressing rooms in Japanese houses had to be of some size, since wearing a kimono meant that there had to be a large enough area to lay out the kimono, obi etc., and for the *iko* stand on which to hang the kimono before donning it, and for the dresser to help with the tying of the obi. There would be beautifully crafted large trays of polished wood or lacquer in which the chosen accoutrements of the costume would be carefully placed. The lady would stand on a special sheet of cloth, bound on its edge with silk braid, placed on the tatami, and the dresser would put the clothes on her.

As one arrived on another side of the inner garden, there was a passage that led to the drawing room quarter with a small ante-room, then the large drawing room flanked by a wide verandah with tatami, but with a suite of large upholstered armchairs and sofas, and glazed screens to the garden on two sides. There was a piano in the anteroom beside a window overlooking the lawn.

Mother played the piano when we were visiting and Setsuko taught Sakiko to play. In this complex was the living room where my grandmother sat during the day. The main corridor led to the Western part of the house. That part of the corridor was carpeted and lined with floor-to-ceiling bookcases; at the end was a door that opened into the Western house. There were also cloakrooms with Western-style lavatories, one of which my grandfather said was his proprietary cloakroom; all the rest of us had to walk down the long and often very cold main corridor to the cloakroom at the other end of the house. The Western house was sold after the war to Nittetsu Kogyo for entertaining guests, presumably to meet the asset tax.

There was a wing to the left of the main entrance of the house beyond the guests' waiting room. A corridor led down to the two-storey rooms with galleries above, which were the store-rooms. Hanako kept everything: she had trunks and wardrobes full of old clothes there; we would find clothes that had belonged to my aunts for me to wear as we were growing up. Beside it there was the bathroom complex and the dressing room, with five dressing tables each with three-way mirrors, at which ladies had their hair combed and did their make-up. Whenever I went to stay, a maid would plait my hair, using camellia oil to keep it in good condition. A maid would always be in attendance to help with the bath and soap our backs, dry us with towels as we stood in the anteroom in our dressing gowns. There was also the cloakroom with five separate lavatory cubicles. Opposite the cloakroom was a large basin under the window where Grandfather did his morning ablutions, usually singing Schubert Lieder very loudly. I was always intrigued by the various types of loofahs that hung around it.

In the 1920s, the Japanese part of the mansion was even larger, with another wing, but this was taken to Akiya to become one of the houses on the family holiday enclave. It was there that we spent our spring and summer holidays, as the main house there was let to the US Navy to house the Commander-in-Chief at nearby Yokosuka.

Grandfather Jiro (次郎): a Worldly Gentleman
The creator of this vast estate, my great-grandfather Heihachi, had died the year before I was born. The house as I knew it after the war was dominated by Grandfather Jiro's presence. Life had revolved around Heihachi while he was alive; servants would be always at the ready should he call with his bell. He had his nurse with him in his later years who kept an eye on his fragile constitution. Yoko and his other grandchildren would visit most days, and he adored and spoilt them. Yoko was the first grandchild and he and Sumiko would always be calling for her – "Yo-chan, Yo-chan". In her teens Heihachi would take her to their mines in the mountains and take her underground with him. In the early days he would be carried down the mine on a sedan chair, dressed in a suit and a hat. After his death, Jiro was to stamp his personal preferences and style on the life of the house and the estate.

If Heihachi was a keen gardener, Jiro was a keen horticulturalist. He studied agriculture at Hokkaido University, also his father's alma mater. It was not just because of the food shortages during and after the war that he had large kitchen gardens. It was his hobby. They were in the lower part of the garden as one approached it via winding steps of large stones from the west end of the lawns. You could not see this area from the house as it was on lower ground on the Kamiyacho side of the estate. When I was a child, until my uncle Yuhei built a house there for his family, there were pigsties with perhaps a dozen pigs and turkey pens, and an extensive vegetable garden. The rest of the area was given over to a golf practice range with high nets to catch the balls. Grandfather also kept chickens below the laundry in front of the garage, and two goats tied to a tree beside the *kura*. I was given goat's milk as a child which I hated; to this day I dislike goat's cheese, which has become more prevalent on restaurant menus in Europe. I was also appalled to see turkeys change colour – their wattles would turn red and purple from white if they got excited. I still do not like eating turkey. Grandfather would walk down to the kitchen garden every morning with scissors to collect vegetables, which he would give to the kitchen for his breakfast. All this husbandry in the very centre of Tokyo, only a stone's throw from the epicentre of government, Kasumigaseki, was not just rare but unique. After Uncle Yuhei built his house where the pigs and turkeys had been, Grandfather would walk down the stone steps clacking the scissors to alert the little girls in the house who would joyfully rush out to greet him. A mountain of fresh salad was prepared and he always had French dressing on it. He also invariably had a glass of fresh vegetable juice made from that morning's harvest; much better than V8! One is always encouraged these days to eat fresh vegetables for health and long life; my grandfather had more than a normal serving of it but it did not help him to live beyond the age of seventy-three. But that might have been because of other habits.

Jiro brought to Fukidecho a cosmopolitan lifestyle. Unlike Heihachi, a conventional and a nervous eater, he was a gourmet and a very heavy drinker, but he did not smoke. I don't know what he had for lunch because he would go out after his large breakfast in his chauffeur-driven Cadillac to his office in Kabutocho. For breakfast, though, apart from his huge salad of fresh vegetables, he had eggs, cold meat, toast and marmalade, the vegetable juice, fruit, coffee and goat's milk. In the evenings, my aunt Asako, who dined with him at home to the end of his life, told me that without fail he had hors d'oeuvres, soup, fish, meat, salad, cheese and pudding. No course was ever omitted; he had to have a fish course as well as meat, as was the practice in formal meals. He was fond of game such as wild boar, venison, wildfowl and all kinds of preserved food such as bottarga, which he brought back from Taiwan, caviar, and little crabs marinated live in Chinese rice wine. The cook would prepare these every evening according to the menu that Grandmother (or after her death my aunt) would plan in the morning.

His sons-in-law, with more conservative tastes, would find these evenings something of an ordeal. My grandmother would often offer alternatives – a beef steak instead of wild boar, for example – while Grandfather tucked into his favourite dish, bemused by the less-than-adventurous eating habits of his in-laws. Anything that was novel or unusual would intrigue him. He loved to try foreign dishes, though English, French, Japanese or Chinese of different regional kinds were the usual daily diet. And he was very knowledgeable about food. Quite often, he would take his family out to his favoured restaurants in Ginza. One of these was Honten Hamasaku, a famous family-run establishment since the 1920s. It was the first restaurant in Japan to have an open kitchen; there are only a few tables and a small counter next to the kitchen on the ground floor but there are several private rooms upstairs for banquets. I myself have frequented this very pure Japanese restaurant for many years; the owner/chef remembered my grandfather as well as my uncle over the years and I have loved going there, sometimes alone, and chatting with him and his family. Being a long-standing veteran of the trade in Ginza, he is a well-known figure amongst Japanese industrialists. His business acumen, probably gained from studying economics at Keio University before joining his father's restaurant, makes him an interesting conversationalist; that they own their own building in the prime site of Ginza has probably given the family financial stability in a volatile industry. My mother loved going there to talk with the old lady, widow of the original founder, who is a year younger than her; even in her nineties in her kimono she would be serving in the restaurant, looking after old customers. The restaurant specialises in *okoze*, one of the most expensive fish in Japan (known in the West as 'reef stonefish'). It is rare to find places which serve this delicacy.

Jiro was a family man. He took his family skiing in winter in the mountains of the Japan Alps; spent the summer months to-ing and fro-ing from Tokyo to Karuizawa, the resort where the family spent the summers. In the 1920s he took Hanako on European tours to Paris, Rome and other cultural capitals where they bought wonderful souvenirs; he had portrait photographs of his wife taken by famous photographers in Paris, and bought her jewellery and dresses by fashionable couturiers of the time. During their tours abroad they would have photographs of their children taken at studios back in Tokyo and couriered to them. Everywhere they went, they bought souvenir spoons with the badge of the city enamelled on the handle and had them mounted in frames; Uncle Yuhei followed that example, and put together a second collection with his wife in more recent years. For his own and his wife's birthdays Jiro organised family banquets at home, bringing in chefs from leading restaurants to prepare fabulous meals. Such extravagance was pretty much unheard of in postwar Japan. Since Grandmother's birthday fell in early December, it was always *fugu* (blowfish). After Jiro's death, Uncle Yuhei made sure that the tradition was kept up, but at restaurants in private rooms rather than at home. On these occasions we, the grandchildren, were seated at a separate smaller table; I rather resented routinely being put together with younger cousins – I wanted to be with the grown-ups and join in their conversation. Jiro made sure when two of his daughters with their families were living abroad on their husbands' overseas assignments to visit them, knowing that his wife would miss her daughters and grandchildren; my mother, their eldest, was abroad with her family for eleven years, and their youngest, Aunt Noriko (範子), also with her family, for even longer in California. As a child I was always rather afraid of him but my mother said "How can you be afraid of him? He is the kindest and the gentlest man in the world."

Certainly, his grandchildren as well as his children inherited

Jiro's love of food and probably also of alcoholic drink. He was a great drinker; it is probable that he got through a bottle of whisky a day. Uncle Yuhei continued the tradition! He also liked dry martini cocktails. When at a family gathering years later I ordered a dry martini, Aunt Mariko (Yuhei's widow) immediately remarked "That's proof you are Tanaka Jiro's granddaughter! Let's all have martinis." So we did, with a big laugh. How Jiro would have loved to see that. Was it with a twist or an olive? I would not put it past him to like Gibsons!

Watase's (渡瀬寅次郎) *Heritage*

Jiro was the second child of Watase Torajiro, an early student of the American missionary William S. Clark, at Sapporo Agricultural College (now Hokkaido University). Torajiro is remembered as an educationalist as well as the founder of a horticultural enterprise, Kōnō-en (興農園). His wife, Jiro's mother, was accomplished in her own right: the first Japanese woman to fly in an aeroplane, and an early suffragette. Torajiro and his horticultural company supplied over 2,000 cherry trees to flank the Potomac Basin in Washington DC. That was the initiative of the then Mayor of Tokyo, Ozaki Yukio (尾崎行雄), a well-known politician. The first batch sent in 1910 was diseased and had to be destroyed. The second batch of over 3,000 was sent in 1912 from Kōnō-en. These were grafted with stock from the banks of the Arakawa River in Tokyo. In return, in 1915 President Taft sent a batch of flowering dogwood saplings as an expression of gratitude.

Jiro and his family were all Congregationalist Christians, but in marrying into the Tanaka family he followed the family faith of Buddhism. He was the second of eleven children – rich families had many offspring in those days as they could afford it. They remained closely in touch with him after he married away into the Tanaka family and met often. My mother Yoko played with her many cousins – twenty-eight in all – and went on holidays with them. Some are still in touch with her. She was very fond of her uncles Saburo and Masakatsu. Masakatsu had a holiday home in Akiya too and Yoko would go on swimming expeditions with his children to Chojagasaki. I knew only one of them, Hanako. She was Jiro's elder sister and often came to visit Fukidecho. She had married into a well-known political family: her husband, Kosaka Junzo, was a member of the House of Peers before the war. He also founded Shin-Etsu Chemical Corporation, which became one of the largest chemical companies in the world with the largest market share in PVC resins and semiconductor silicon. The family retains a close management involvement in it.

Hanako's two sons (my mother's first cousins) became leading politicians of the postwar era. The elder, Kosaka Zentaro (小坂善太郎), was Foreign Minister twice (under Prime Ministers Ikeda and Miki), Minister for Labour (under Prime Minister Yoshida), as well as Minister in charge of the Economic Planning Agency (under Prime Minister Tanaka). His younger brother, Kosaka Tokusaburo (小坂徳三郎), also became a member of the Diet later for the LDP (the Liberal Democratic Party, which has governed Japan for much of the postwar period) and served in the Cabinet holding various portfolios, including the Economic Planning Agency and the Ministry for Transport. He was for some time the President of Shin-Etsu Chemical. Their father told them that combining a political career with running an industrial company would result in succeeding at neither; so he told his sons that Zentaro should concentrate on politics and Tokusaburo on industry.

I knew the Kosaka (pronounced Kozaka) family well. Aunt Kosaka, as she was called by our family, was a *grande dame* of prewar political society. She was large in stature, with a distinguished aura and quite clearly socially gifted. We saw her often when she visited Fukidecho and we also visited her at her large *besso* (holiday home) in Karuizawa during summer holidays there. The Kosaka besso was situated close to the Kumoba-no-ike lake (雲場の池) in central Karuizawa surrounded by forests. (It is worth noting that their original besso in Karuizawa had been the Shaw House, built by Alexander Shaw, an Anglican missionary, which Zentaro's father had bought but eventually gave up to be a museum which is open to this day.) My mother took us boating on the lake, rowing skilfully herself, and on the way back we visited Aunt Kosaka for tea. When I got married she sent me a beautiful Japanese traditional doll in a glass display case that I still have. But she was so accomplished a woman that the rather unworldly Grandmother Hanako was somewhat frightened of her elder sister-in-law, and was always deferential to her.

Being the eldest son of a major political family, Zentaro was smart but somewhat reticent. He mentioned in his autobiography that when the Hotel Okura was built in 1962 its first President, Noda Iwajiro, a respected businessman, asked him to name the Chinese restaurant and execute the calligraphy to be hung at its entrance. Then Foreign Minister, Zentaro accepted at once and considered that a name redolent of the beautiful peach forest near his home town in Nagano prefecture would be suitable: Toh 桃 (peach) Ka 花 (flower) Lin 林 (forest). He was nervous that the restaurant might not succeed, which could have had repercussions for him as a politician, but – phew! – it turned out to be one of the best, if not the best, Chinese restaurants in Tokyo and flourishes to this day.

His younger brother, Tokusaburo, was an affable character, immediately friendly and easy to get on with. On one of my visits to Tokyo in the early 1980s my father suggested I should visit him. My father telephoned and Tokusaburo immediately invited me to come and see him in his office in Nagatacho – Tokyo's political district. He was very genial, offered me a cigarette and we chatted for about an hour on all matters of mutual interest, including the stock market. As I was about to leave he gave me a new packet of cigarettes that was his brand. One could easily see that he was a real politician; he knew how to please anyone he met with a smile; he sent me immediately afterwards a kind letter to say how much he enjoyed meeting me, and for many years until his death always a New Year greeting letter. Sadly he died young in his early seventies with Alzheimer's disease. His wife was the daughter of the main Mitsui family and was a great golfer; she was the champion for successive years at the women's tournament at the Tokyo Golf Club.

Gentlemanly Pursuits

One of Jiro's most important pastimes was golf and he played a major role at all the golf clubs he belonged to. He played off a handicap of one until he died in his seventy-third year. There were (and are) two major golf clubs near the capital: the Tokyo Golf Club and Hodogaya Golf Club. He was Captain of the former for many years and was a Trustee of the latter. Tokyo Golf Club, like no other in Japan, did not allow memberships to be sold on to others, and that fine tradition still continues. Uncle Yuhei, of course, was also a keen player and when he married Mariko she too took up the game seriously. The joy of my grand-father when Mariko scored a 'hole in one'! They never stopped talking about it. Conversation at Fukidecho was so often about golf and who did what where in which tournament etc. – it was all too boring for us children. They had a golf practising range at Fukidecho with high nets and a putting green. My mother never played golf but her sisters Asako and Noriko did. Asako, though, joined her own clubs of choice and never played with her family at the Tokyo Golf Club; she wanted to be independent! There were tennis courts in the grounds of Fukidecho as well as at the Karuizawa estate. We all played, as did my parents. Aunt Noriko and her husband were great tennis players. It was an important feature of life at the Peers' School, as were equestrian pursuits; there was a tennis club in the Imperial Palace grounds

called the Palace Club, to which all serious players from the
school belonged. I too played while at school and Grandfather
let me join the Palace Club just before we went to America. I
do not know if they had stables at Fukidecho before the war, but
my mother and her siblings certainly enjoyed riding and there
are many photographs of them on horseback on holidays in
Karuizawa. In my childhood some of my friends at school took
up dressage seriously, also at the Palace Club. Though my father
could not afford to let us take up riding in Tokyo, when we came
to England he was much pleased that Chahchah went riding
with her school friend at local stables.

Jiro was a man of many interests, not just golf and food; he
found his pleasures in classical music, knew Schubert Lieder by
heart in German and often sat in the living room listening to
the gramophone. He also spoke English quite well, as there was
a strong tradition of English teaching at Hokkaido University.
With Uncle Takata, also an internationalist with sophisticated
hobbies, he went shooting and fishing before the war. Fishing
for *Ayu* fish with cormorants continued after the war, and when
I was a child he would tell me about his catch, but for a young
girl it sounded frightening and I worried about the cormorants
lest they be strangled. Having taken on the duty to perpetuate
the Tanaka *zaibatsu*, he took this responsibility more than seriously. During the war, my mother told me, he always carried in
his pocket a phial of cyanide, in case he might ever have to take
his own life. That was the prevailing atmosphere of fear and it
required discipline. In the darkest days of the war in Tokyo he
organised the evacuation of his wife and children to a mountain
retreat with servants, while himself remaining in Tokyo with
one of his daughters. Aunt Asako told me how, as the sirens
sounded across Tokyo, she and her father would rush into the
bomb shelter he had had dug into the bank at the side of the
garden at No. 17, with helmets and buckets prepared for such
occasions. He had the idea that if the shelter was dug into the

rising ground, they could walk into it without having to go down into a shelter as was the norm.

During the war the family was fortunate in having a large mining enterprise in the hinterland, so vegetables from the surrounding farms could be sent to Tokyo in the period of food scarcity. Jiro had also cultivated a farm the family owned in Angyo (Saitama prefecture) outside Tokyo and went there on the train with rucksacks to collect produce for the family. My father would go with him to bring back potatoes and other root vegetables on very risky and cold journeys. This farm was later sold and it became the site of a large market. Decades later, in 2003, a plot from this market site was sold to a German food wholesale company, Metro Cash & Carry GmbH, to build an outlet. I was Adviser to Metro Cash & Carry from late 2002 to 2012 on their Japanese operations, but I had no knowledge of the area or that my family had originally owned the site. When I told my mother that we had opened a second outlet in Angyo and told her where it was, she said in astonishment that the site had been our farm many many years ago. The personal connection delighted my German colleagues, and they talked of the fortuitous connection as a good omen.

Friendships

Jiro was gregarious by nature and was blessed in his friendships. When at the end of the war some of his close friends were incarcerated in Sugamo Prison he assiduously paid them regular visits. I often heard him telling his wife how he had found them. As with most other Japanese, while saddened by the unfortunate fate of those close friends held as war criminals in prison, he did not hold that against his old American friends from before the war. He frequented the Tokyo Club where his social circle gathered, and there he also made friends with foreigners who had been put up for membership. Indeed, it was he who nominated in the 1920s the first ever foreign member in Antonin Raymond, the architect associate of Frank Lloyd Wright. Jiro gave Raymond his first commission in Japan, for No. 17 Fukidecho. They remained friends throughout the war and, as the conflict ended, Aunt Asako went to work with Mrs Raymond, an interior designer.

I discovered, quite by chance and from someone totally unconnected, that Raymond had in fact worked for US Intelligence. It was an extraordinary encounter at a drinks party given by a university friend of Dugald's at the Oxford and Cambridge Club in London a few years ago. Someone (son of another American who lived in Japan in the immediate postwar period) unknown to either of us struck up a casual conversation. As we chatted, he revealed that he and his parents had been in Japan in the 1950s, and somehow that led to his saying that they were close friends of the Raymonds. His father was also working for US Intelligence at the time. Another such coincidence was that, while I was serving as Chairman of the Japan Society in the late 1990s, at a function I had organised I sat next to a Mr Gadelius. As we chatted it became clear that he was one of the children of the Gadelius family to whom my grandfather had let a house in the seaside resort of Akiya before the war, and also in Tokyo in the Western part of the Takata family house in Fukidecho. The name Gadelius was often mentioned in my childhood; he said with a smile "I am Goro Gadelius" and remembered his brothers and himself playing with Yoko and her sisters. When I told my mother of my encounter with Goro she was more than amused. The Gadeliuses ran an important Swedish trading company with a deep relationship with Japan. They gave their children Japanese names: Goro means the fifth child in Japanese. Goro said that he had a large collection of *inro* at his home in Eaton Square. Given the length of time that the Gadelius family had lived in Japan I imagined that it must be a very fine collection. Inro are small cases, more often than not made of papier-mâché, lacquered with fine gold particles in the highest standard of *makié* to hold medicine and small articles that samurai carried, hung with a silk rope on the obi sash. At the end of the war, former samurai families had many of these lying around in their attics. I remember my mother saying when I was about five years old "They are two a penny; apparently foreigners want to have them." We promised to meet again and for me to see the collection. Life is full of such coincidences; in my case in very surprising ways they took me back to my grandfather Jiro's cosmopolitan outlook and his open-minded friendships with foreigners.

A close friend and distant relation of Jiro's was a gynaecologist called Dr Higuchi. He had a private clinic and nursing home just opposite our estate in Kamiyacho. It was a small house built of grey stone behind a forecourt flanked with a wide gate. Beside the gatepost was a board with a picture of the legendary Momotaro – a peach opening up with a healthy baby springing out. Higuchi Byoin, as it was called, was where I and Chahchah were born and my cousins also. When I was three years old Aunt Setsuko gave birth to Kinuko there. Setsuko asked me "Would you like to eat some cheese?" It was unusual to have such luxuries as cheese so soon after the war and I was delighted to be given it. It was American and wrapped in silver paper. We also had it at home sometimes, but not very often.

Aunt Asako told me that one treasured memory for her was that when I was born she was the first in the family to walk down the garden and across the road to the clinic bearing beautifully prepared food in lacquered tiered boxes to my mother. She was entrusted by Grandmother to bring the *osashiire* (お差し入) for her. The word has no exact translation in English; it means more than just a 'present'; it encompasses the feeling of appreciation for someone who has been working hard under pressure. She recalled the excitement of the family, as I was the first child of my generation: she had never seen such an adorable baby. I was always her favourite niece and we were great friends, especially later in my adult life. It was a custom in Japan in those days that women went home to their parents for childbirth. So it was that my mother went home to Fukidecho, and spent several weeks there with her parents after giving birth.

I was taken home to our house in Shiroganedai with my mother, and Grandmother made sure that Takemi, who had been my mother's nanny, came with us. So Takemi looked after me in the first few years of my life.

Grandmother Hanako (田中花子): an Heiress

People said of her that she was unworldly. That could be taken as a criticism; but at times it was said in her defence. Certainly my mother often defended her, explaining the true nature behind her apparent unworldliness: it was not that she was unfeeling or arrogant, but rather reserved. She was an *ojosan* (お嬢さん) which does not just mean a daughter; the word has the connotation of a young lady who is not expected to work, a well-behaved girl whom others care for and look after in a well-to-do family. Yet it is not a derogatory description, rather it is used in a deferential and respectful manner. Being the elder of the two daughters of Tanaka Heihachi II, she was an heiress destined to inherit the family fortune and business. She went to the Peers' School, where by and large all the girls were 'unworldly'; most of them were imperial princesses or daughters of noble families. To be 'worldly' was considered vulgar and not of their kind. The Joshi-Gakushuin, as the girls' division of the Peers' School was called, was established in 1885 by the Meiji Empress for daughters of the imperial family and the nobility.

Here I digress and write briefly about the Peers' School: our family life was much influenced by it, with our social circle almost entirely consisting of prewar Gakushuin alumni, and all of us speaking the Gakushuin 'language'. Grandmother Hanako was the first female member of our family to attend this school, though Ginnosuke (銀之助) as well as her other cousins of the Kurachi and Kosaka families and their spouses also all went there, and it was central to our family life, as all Hanako's children and most of her grandchildren went to the school, including myself.

Gakushuin: the Peers' School

Gakushuin today is just one of the private schools of Japan, but it has a distinguished history. It was established by the Emperor Ninko in 1847 in Kyoto to educate the sons of the imperial aristocracy. After the Meiji Restoration, the Meiji Emperor moved the school to Tokyo in 1877. The school was administered by the Imperial Household Agency and it was the property of the imperial household. Very few commoners were accepted for the limited places: the Meiji Emperor, having created many new peerages for those instrumental in the political transition, decreed that the school was for the education of the children of the 'modern aristocracy'; and he made it compulsory by legislation through the Diet for them to enrol their children at Gakushuin. All the successive Presidents of the school were from the nobility, often of senior military rank.

Emperor Ninko had inscribed on the walls of the Gakushuin building in Kyoto four maxims for its students:

WALK IN THE PATHS TRODDEN BY THE FEET OF
THE GREAT SAGES
REVERE THE RIGHTEOUS CANONS OF THE EMPIRE
HE THAT HAS NOT LEARNED THE SACRED DOCTRINES,
HOW CAN HE GOVERN HIMSELF?
HE THAT IS IGNORANT OF THE CLASSICS,
HOW CAN HE REGULATE HIS OWN CONDUCT?

When in 1946 peerages were abolished by the Americans, the future of the school was thrown into doubt. As mentioned, its last President under imperial ownership was my father's uncle, Admiral Yamanashi; he embarked on a tortuous negotiation with the American Occupation GHQ and the imperial household to take the school out of imperial ownership and open it to the wider public, introducing competitive entrance examinations, and so re-established it as a private educational institution. All members of the imperial family continued to attend, and the offspring of its alumni also continued their family tradition. The social network of Gakushuin therefore lived on throughout the postwar period. Families with connections that went back generations provided a spirit of kinship that gave us a sense of security and belonging, especially in the years following the war when the former aristocratic way of life was forcibly abandoned. That sense of belonging should not be underestimated: as the war ended, the former nobles, princes and princesses lost not only their titles but all their possessions, which were confiscated by the American Occupation, including assets and jewellery that had been hidden in bank vaults during the war. They were suddenly commoners, indistinguishable from ordinary people; only their fellow Gakushuin students knew who they were. It has been recorded that the Showa Emperor gave a farewell banquet at the Akasaka Detached Palace on the eve of them being robbed of their *miyake* (宮家) princely status.

In the immediate postwar period, my generation of students was told never to mention that we were at Gakushuin and, when wearing our uniform, not to speak in public places but always conduct ourselves with proper manners; we were told that we were a target of popular criticism based on class prejudice. Throughout my childhood, we went around in a self-effacing manner, feeling embarrassed lest the taboo became known. But now, in the twenty-first century, the school has become just another private school and not all imperial family children attend it. In the prewar period, however, mother's cousin Kosaka Zentaro wrote in his memoirs that being a commoner he was bullied at school by boys from the noble families, yet ostracised as a toff outside it.

But links to the imperial family remained strong in the postwar period. All of the Showa Emperor's children, his brothers and their wives had been at the school. His youngest brother Prince Mikasa's children were my contemporaries. On the Showa Emperor's birthday, a national holiday, the whole school gathered at the university campus to celebrate, standing in line, and the Crown Prince came to address us. The Empress sent us all a token of the celebration: a piece of cake embossed with the imperial chrysanthemum seal, wrapped in special paper in a box. When the Crown Prince attended the Queen's coronation in London in 1953, on his return he came to address the whole school to report back on his travels. He held up a scroll from which he read out his report. This was broadcast on NHK news that evening. I remember listening to it with my parents on the wireless in our drawing room; my mother remarked that the chorus of 'Banzai, the Emperor, banzai' by the assembled school contained my voice too. All of us graduates of Gakushuin have a special affection and feeling of closeness to the imperial family as we met its members often at alumni gatherings and other school events.

On the occasion of Their Majesties the Emperor and Empress's state visit to the UK in 1998, one of my friends suggested that we should have a gathering with the Emperor in London. I asked Uncle Yuhei, who was then the President of Oyukai (the school alumni association) if I should arrange such a meeting. My uncle said emphatically that we must and he contacted the Imperial Household Agency. I then discussed with the Household officials in charge of the visit the logistics of this event and agreed that it would be over tea in a private function room at Grosvenor House. Security arrangements were very strict, as it was expected that there would be hostile demonstrations by former prisoners of war; it was important that His Majesty should enter the building from a discreet back door, invisible to the public. It was a wonderful occasion for us; His Majesty seemed relaxed and enjoying informal conversations, as we sat around on sofas and armchairs. Many reminiscences were shared and some of the courtiers found their own relations amongst us as well. It went on past the scheduled time and the Lord Chamberlain leading the party was anxious that His Majesty should return to his lodgings (Buckingham Palace) before the Empress, who was meeting the alumnae of her own school, Sacred Heart, at the same time.

In 1885, the Meiji Empress had established the women's division as Joshi-Gakushuin (Peeresses' School) in a separate location, and successive Empresses attended its ceremonial occasions as the Emperors did at the main school. The Meiji and Taisho Empresses bestowed on the school anthems of their own composition, which we continued to sing on our graduation days. The anthems *Kongoseki* and *Hana Sumiré* are heart-rending verses of our past that evoke the tenderest of emotions; I often think of them nostalgically and of my mother, as we used to sing them together in my childhood.

In 1947, when the school was taken out of the imperial household, the two institutions were merged; the junior school and the university became coeducational, but the high schools continued to operate at separate locations, so boys and girls are educated separately for those six years and meet only at school festivities or on ceremonial days. The first postwar President, Abe Nosei (or Yoshishige), wrote an anthem for the whole school: it reflects the emotions of defeat in the moment at the end of the war, calling for the *new* Gakushuin to arise like a phoenix that had died in the embers of destruction to live again on the debris of sorrow. As a child I was unaware of the significance of the verse, too young to understand the defeat, but, reading it later in adult life, it is historically significant, invoking the emotions of a nation that lost a devastating war.

Gakushuin pupils spoke in a particular way with their use of honorifics. Even today it is immediately recognisable amongst ourselves. Women spoke in the third person singular when addressing each other, never using the word 'you'; it seemed too direct and rude. In Spanish and in Italian that form of speech is still prevalent. Our language at home was basically Gakushuin and I was brought up in it. But by the 1960s everyone became conscious that such a manner of speaking would be considered haughty, and adapted to ordinary ways. Whenever my mother is with people from the school, she reverts instantly to that language and returns to her old self amongst her equals. The imperial family at Court spoke in yet another way. (I suspect this has become much diluted by now.) In my mother's time, for ceremonial days, they went to school dressed in *hakama* and kimono with the family crest on both sides on the front below the shoulders, in a particular shade of sombre purple that was their colour; black was considered by the school to be too audacious.

The school emblem is the cherry blossom: for boys single-petalled light pink, for girls double-petalled dark pink, sewn onto our uniforms. All school sites have avenues of cherry trees from the gate to the school buildings. School stationery and other equipment all bore the emblem. My mother would carry silver mirrors, tissue holders and other portable necessities of toilette embossed with the school emblem. For school outings to the countryside, they brought their picnics in lacquered picnic boxes and telescopic chopsticks in silver engraved with their family *mon* (crest). I was amazed to see the fine craftsmanship on such items amongst my mother's possessions.

Gakushuin today is much like other private schools. But for those of us who were there decades ago there is a bond that will never be severed; for some unidentifiable reason we, the girls, recognise each other even by the look or the aura of persona and know we can trust each other. Quite recently a concert violinist approached me at a reception and asked which school I had attended in Japan? I was more than surprised – when I said Gakushuin, she smiled and said she thought so: "You have that aura … I did too." Like my own, her mother and grandmother had also attended. We immediately fell back into our old school lingo in our chatter and became instant friends. Alumnae of Gakushuin have a society called Tokiwakai (常盤会) while the men have Oyukai (桜友会). There are international branches in various major capitals of the world and we hold regular get-togethers for dinners.

When the present Reiwa Emperor was Crown Prince and studying at Oxford, Oyukai and Tokiwakai held a joint dinner in his honour at the Oxford and Cambridge Club in London. He seemed self-confident and distinguished and also friendly. On that same visit to London, I had the honour of showing him around the London Stock Exchange floor, as I was its only Japanese member. We took him to the jobbers' pitch of White and Cheeseman, who had made a quote in the Japanese government bond of 1963 which my father had arranged, of which more shortly.

Of my maternal family, all my aunts and uncles went to the school. On New Year's Day each year Uncle Yuhei went there to participate in the customary New Year kendo contest: that was a tradition in our school for men. He was at the school when Mishima Yukio, the author, was there; Mishima, as is well known, was very adept at kendo and other martial arts. Some of the masters from his schooldays were still teaching when I got into junior school. A number of long-serving mistresses in the girls' section of the high school had taught my aunts. I was not particularly good academically – rather, average in all subjects; the only things in which I got better marks were English and composition, but I was hopeless at maths, science subjects and sports except tennis. I was shy and not very gregarious or in any way an exceptional student. The school enforced strict discipline and we were not to put our hands on the desks or speak without being called. Those who misbehaved were told to stand outside in the corridor. In every Presidential address, we were unfailingly told that human beings must be honest and sincere. I did not know until much later as an adult that the world was full of dishonest and deceitful people who would tell outright lies out of self-interest, to the detriment of others. In the jungle of the fiercely competitive world of financial markets I found myself a victim rather too often; I was a naïve *ojosan*.

As with other students from old Gakushuin families, my grandmother provided my aunts' old uniforms for me to wear; as I grew out of one she would bring out another, larger, one, much to my disappointment – I longed to have a new one. I and the other girls who had to bear the same fate consoled ourselves, saying it was superior to have old uniforms! Many of the newcomers to the school seemed to be very wealthy. Their parents drove foreign cars and lived in newly built comfortable houses; they brought luxurious lunch boxes while my mother more often than not made me mince and scrambled eggs; they went ice-skating and joined equestrian clubs which my parents definitely could not afford. The lifestyle of the prewar Gakushuin families was austere by comparison with the modern ways of the postwar new industrialists.

Refined and Reserved

My mother and grandmother had gone to school accompanied by their personal maids, who waited for them in the designated waiting room and took them home in private cars (or sedan chairs in my grandmother's case in the earlier period). They never ever went out alone. The war changed everything for my mother, who had to face the reality of a new life in war-torn Japan, including going out shopping for groceries and attending to housekeeping herself; she and her generation went on public transport – unimaginable before the war. But Grandmother never did; the local shops came to take orders each day from the kitchen and the suppliers of clothes called at the house with patterns of fabrics and samples. That was not unique; one of my friends from school said that even in the 1970s and 1980s her father had his shoemaker come to the house to take measurements and he would never go to a shop. That was the old way. Grandmother remained an *ojosan* all her life. That made her seem aloof to those who were not part of that society. It was considered bad manners to show too much emotion. And Peeresses' School women were much less demonstrative than those who attended the Sacred Heart School or the other educational institutions where well-to-do families sent their daughters. Those women generally seemed more extrovert and socially adept. We were not very good at paying false compliments or at flattery. It must be emphasised, though, that Grandmother was not in any way haughty or arrogant. Nor did she flaunt her wealth: that would have been thought vulgar.

Uncle Yasushi, Aunt Noriko's husband, said she was *suteki*, meaning sophisticated and attractive. Both she and her younger sister Kimiko were beautiful, as their mother Sumiko was – probably the best-looking of them all. It mattered to them that they were *bijin* (美人) beautiful women – they took immense care over their hairdos, make-up and clothes. Takemi told me that Grandmother had a new kimono made every time she was invited to a party. Being well dressed was *de rigueur*, showing respect to the host. She was certainly refined, and kind and gracious to her sons-in-law, but not overly emotionally demonstrative.

Grandmother was not extravagant; she kept everything in the storage room and old clothes were never thrown away but handed down and worn by a succession of her children and grandchildren. This hoarding habit had a silver lining – it has meant that there are some valuable 'antique' kimonos and obis dating from the prewar period and the earlier twentieth century that could never be reproduced or replaced today. We are proud of these possessions and my mother has treasured them all her life. Hanako did not like waste; she would keep old postcards to fold into strips and 'weave' to make baskets, which she then had lacquered to make a nice box. We spent afternoons together in this form of handicraft. She never threw away any remnants of material; she would cut them into triangles or squares and sew them onto the corners of boxes to protect them; the maids were taught how to do these tasks and nothing was wasted. Some of them became dolls' clothes; our dolls were dressed in *montsuki* (紋付) kimono – the most formal attire, with the family crest on them!

I spent a lot of time with Grandmother throughout my childhood at Fukidecho, sitting in the living room; at Akiya; and at our summer house in Karuizawa where we spent each August. My enduring memory of her is the fact that she displayed no favouritism, despite my being the very first grandchild (and for three years the only one), in contrast to Sada – my father's mother whom we lived with and who very much mollycoddled me and poured out affection every minute of the day. But my mother thought she was being over-protective and that I would not grow up robust.

When we were little, our Great-Grandmother Sumiko was still alive; we would call on her in her room and chat together. When I arrived on my way back from school, Grandmother Hanako and I would sit together across the low table and maids would bring in *oyatsu* (mid-afternoon cakes and fruit) and tea for us. We talked about the affairs of the day; when I was a little older in my early teens we would talk about politics and she would say in a satisfied tone "Haruko-chan and I agree about politics." She was an intelligent woman and was careful not to spoil her grandchildren. I suspect she felt I was greatly spoilt in the Fukuda household.

I know that she had a special place in her heart for my mother, who was her first child, and she felt for her during and after the war, having to do a lot of housework that she had not been used to before marriage. But such was the fate of the young women of my mother's generation. Grandmother made sure that my mother always had a live-in maid at home, whom she sourced for us. When we left for Washington in the early autumn of 1960 my grandparents took us all out to a tempura restaurant in Ginza. Grandmother was in tears, holding my mother in her arms and saying "Yo-chan, be careful and take care"; she handed her a farewell present of a solitaire diamond ring.

Art and Jewellery

Hanako was artistic and spent her leisure time making watercolour paintings. She would paint on long sheets of fine rice paper that unfolded sideways, and when dry roll them back neatly to keep in a tube. At Karuizawa she would decorate pottery with glazes, mostly depicting wild flowers of the mountain region. Her favourite was *ganpi* – a flower with four single petals in a coral colour on a thin tall stem. Sometimes she had them made in enamel for jewellery. We went for walks up the hills to pick wild flowers; back at home we would then press them and eventually mount them in notebooks of Japanese paper with covers in colourful *chiyogami*. In Tokyo she gathered her friends from school to meet periodically at Fukidecho to print *sarasa* (block printing with carved potato in natural vegetable dyes) on rice paper for making fans, and on cotton fabric which she had made into small items – boxes, bags, spectacle cases, wallets. Once while I was up at Cambridge she sent me a basket made of dried wisteria stems she had lined with a cloth dyed in *sarasa*, the subtle pattern showing through the basket weave. Yoko and Asako also joined these sarasa meetings and continued the tradition for a long time after their mother's death.

Hanako loved beautiful jewellery and designed some herself. Jewellery in Japanese culture is a little different from that in Western and other societies. Adornment of female dressing has been grounded in tradition from Cleopatra's time or even earlier. But manifestations differed slightly from one culture to another. Headdresses and bracelets were predominant in ancient

Egypt, while the Indian subcontinent went in for earrings, nose rings, bracelets and even anklets and large rings. In the West tiaras, necklaces, earrings, rings, bracelets and brooches adorned ladies for generations. In Japan, because of the style of the dress – kimono – brooches were not worn except on overcoats, nor earrings nor bracelets. In any case, any kind of piercing of ears or nose was abhorrent and considered barbaric. But Japanese ladies wore bejewelled hairpins and combs in their elaborate hairdos, as they did in China, and rings on their hands. The silk cord that tied the obi together was fastened with an *obidome* – a piece of brooch-like ornament, often bejewelled, lacquered or enamelled, worn at the front.

Until Western clothes came to predominate in the postwar period, rings with precious stones were the most important jewellery items in Japan. After the Meiji Restoration, upper-class ladies when clad in Western dress for formal occasions wore necklaces in *demi-parure* and tiaras, but they were no match for the extravagance of those sported by royalty and heiresses in the West. Precious stones such as diamonds, rubies, sapphires and emeralds were not naturally found or mined in Japan and were imported. There is a famous anecdote: when Japan's richest man, Mr Mitsui, went to visit a maharaja in India the maharaja said to him "I understand you are the richest man in Japan; how rich are you?" Mr Mitsui replied with the appropriate number of US dollars, whereupon the maharaja opened his desk drawer and brought out a ruby and held it in the palm of his hand and said "This much?" In any case, ostentation was and is considered utterly vulgar in Japanese culture; jewellery had to be discreet but fine. That means only those who understood the true worth could discern that even if small in size they signalled beauty, excellence and value. Japan will never catch up in the jewellery league of the world, as the stock of fine gems is low by any standards. Today, Japanese women are well dressed with pearl necklaces, diamond rings and beautiful brooches – but not often in the manner that 'statement' jewellery is worn in the West. Only in pearls does Japan lead the West, since Mikimoto established the international standard in pearls in the twentieth century. However, Japan has also had immediate access to fine corals, jade (from China and Burma), and ivory and tortoise-shells, which were much prized.

Hanako was always dressed in a kimono and never wore Western clothes as I knew her. But photographs show that evidently she wore beautiful 1920s outfits on her European tours when she was young. Her fine slender hands were always adorned with rings, invariably of a single stone set simply without elaborate surrounds to show off the quality of the gem that could stand on its own. Some of the fine jewellery she designed herself was made up by the leading jewellery houses of Tokyo. Her taste was for Art Nouveau and many of the decorative ornaments in the house were also in that style. One such – quintessentially 1920s – piece she designed in platinum set with diamonds and emeralds in a stylised motif of dragonflies. My mother inherited it and when I attended the state banquet at Buckingham Palace on the occasion of the state visit by Their Majesties the Emperor and Empress, she lent it to me. It was originally designed as an *obidome* but converted later to a brooch – what an amazing piece it must have been when worn on an obi. Grandmother also designed brooches set with corals in abstract design and enam-elled pieces featuring wild flowers of Karuizawa. I particularly remember her almost always wearing a bright green jade ring. When she died, Grandfather asked Yoko which she would prefer, the large single-stone emerald ring or the jade. Hanako died with the small chrysoberyl cat's eye flanked with tiny baguette diamonds in the shank, discreet and unshowy, which she wore in hospital. As Asako had looked after her in her final days, my mother told her she should have that ring. Though I had never seen her wearing it, when she died I found it in her collection of jewellery that her nieces shared: I chose it for myself as I knew of its provenance. It was just as well that my cousins thought it too sober and somewhat ageing. Grandmother would wear large tortoiseshell brooches on her winter coats. One of them was her own mother's, a very simple design but an unusually large spherical cushion shape in clear yellow tortoiseshell with no surrounds.

On important occasions there would be gifts of jewellery from my grandparents. When Jiro received an imperial decoration, identical brooches for his daughters were made specially by Mikimoto in the shape of a branch decorated with pearls. On their Ruby wedding anniversary the daughters gave Hanako an eternity ring set with tiny rubies; this came to me in her memory on her death. It was my grandmother who taught me about pearls. When I was twelve years old, on my graduation from junior school she bought me a single-string pearl necklace from Mikimoto; she taught me then how to assess the quality of pearls as to their colour, size, shape and lustre. On foreign travels too, Grandmother bought cameos in Italy and had them set to her designs back in Tokyo; she gave me a pair of unset cameos in my late teens when she came to visit us in London which I had set as a pair of earrings.

My parents too gave me jewellery from about the age of ten. One of them that I still very much treasure is a spherical gold pendant with a tiny Seiko watch embedded in it hung on a long gold chain. When I was a young child they bought me crystal necklaces to wear to parties. And there was the emerald-cut yellow topaz pendant on a fine gold chain – I wore this a lot throughout my youth.

Before she was married, her grandfather Heihachi bought Yoko beautiful Art Deco jewellery with the *pavé*-set diamonds typical of the 1920s and 1930s, in platinum, some with emeralds as the centre stone. Sadly for Yoko, during the war the Japanese government confiscated jewellery – especially platinum and diamonds – for the manufacture of essential weapons and military equipment. She was too honest to hide it; she handed in, without tears, some fine pieces. Her sense of patriotism and loyalty to her husband meant that she never complained. My mother was not able to indulge in buying jewellery on her husband's public servant salary. But she never lost her interest in it and even during the years of austerity persuaded her husband to buy her a cameo brooch on our holiday in Rome. When she came to have money of her own, some of the first things she bought for herself were pieces of jewellery. On our first visit to Tokyo after my parents returned home in 1971, she bought some proper jewellery for Sakiko and me from the family jeweller. When recovered from a bout of cancer at the age of seventy-five, she gave a dinner party at her favourite restaurant and gave each of her sisters and daughters a silver necklace – interlinked circles, handmade by an artist that she chose at a gallery in Shibuya – each one slightly different from the others, and each in a beautiful wooden box.

We have often given each other jewellery, stylish with baroque pearls or semi-precious stones but not expensive pieces, for birthdays and on our visits to Tokyo. Mother particularly likes amethysts, but is more interested in the design than in the stones. From Venice I sent her brooches and necklaces with Murano glass, but for her ninetieth birthday I gave her a small brooch with *pavé*-set diamonds in the shape of a flamingo which I bought in South Africa for her special anniversary. In her early nineties, she said she had seen a lovely necklace, a string of tiny black diamonds, and was coveting it but thought it too extravagant to buy. So I suggested that we should buy it together and I would give her my half for her next birthday. By the following afternoon she had bought it! My mother never went out without some jewellery on her; always a necklace or string of beads and a brooch and rings. Even after she became ill and in a care home she always put on some jewellery before going out to local restaurants or for a drive in the surrounding countryside – the habit of a lifetime. For her hundredth birthday present I gave her a

George Jensen crossover ring with a couple of tiny diamonds.

Hanako's love of jewellery was inherited by all her daughters. Asako was always interested in design and had a large collection, mostly of costume jewellery. Her taste was not extravagant but arty. She always wore the emerald-cut diamond ring that her father had given her and she died with it on her right hand. On a visit to London to see me, she bought an Edwardian antique pendant set with amethyst and seed pearls, and a Georg Jensen brooch to take back to my mother as a present. Years ago, I was spending an afternoon with her at her house in Akiya; she brought out an old jewelled hairpin that had belonged to her grandmother Sumiko, and suggested that we made something else with the stones – a large jade ball and another of coral. I took them back to my friend Andrew Grima, perhaps the greatest modern jeweller of our generation, and had them set on necklaces in yellow gold with *pavé*-set diamonds. Setsuko had lovely jewellery and gave some of her own rings to Sakiko and me when we visited her, as well as taking us out shopping for something we liked. She was naturally generous-hearted, giving us presents whenever we saw her. When I got engaged she asked me if I would like a long necklace of large pearls; I thought it perhaps a little ostentatious and shied away, much to my regret now. Years later she took her daughter Kinuko and me shopping together and bought us a beautiful ring each; I wore mine to the state banquet at Buckingham Palace a few months later. My mother was more than impressed with her largesse.

It may seem from all this talk of jewellery and lifestyle that Grandmother Hanako's existence was elysian. Asako once said to me nostalgically that life at Fukidecho with her parents before the war was elegant and peaceful. She might have felt that as a sheltered young woman, but when I recounted this to my mother she was not so sanguine. The political climate was deteriorating and the liberal views of the more enlightened were becoming sidelined. Looking back, life was not always so

The Imperial
University of
Tokyo, 1938

Main building.

Front gate.

Rear gate.

Tenka-no-Itohei

A stone monument inscribed by Prime Minister Ito Hirobumi – moved from Kabutocho to Mukojima in the 1980s.

Bronze statue of Itohei.

Below right: Itohei, last photograph, late 19th century.

Below left: Wedding of his granddaughter Hanako. Front, left to right: Sumiko, Kimiko, bride; back, left to right: Heihachi II, bridegroom.

Father and son as students at the Imperial University of Tokyo.

Proud graduates, 1938 – Masaru third from right.

The heiress Tanaka Hanako

Aged two or three, c. 1903.

About ten years old, c. 1910.

Below left: Ready for *omiai*, 1918; right: Bride for Jiro, 1920.

Designed by Antonin Raymond, associate of Frank Lloyd Wright; Hanako's first marital home, 1920.

On a sunny day on the terrace. Hanako in elaborate hairdo, showing off her daughter Yoko to her father Heihachi, 1921.

Photo session in the garden; left to right: Minobe Kimiko, Hanako with one-year-old Setsuko, Jiro, Yoko aged two, Sumiko, Minobe Yohji.

Grand Tour

Hanako and Jiro in Paris, circa 1925; studio on rue Royale.

'We are growing up while you are away…'; left to right: Takemi, Yoko, Setsuko, Oshige.

Rebuilding the house at 17 Fukidecho

The new house.

Drawing room with dining room beyond with Art Deco furniture and carpet.

Hanako and Jiro in their 20s in Tokyo.

Entrance hall of the new house.

Above: Hanako, Kimiko and Fukuhara relations picnic on the lawn at the Upper House, 24 Fukidecho; 5th May 1926. Little girls Yoko and Setsuko helped by the maids, with lacquerware in tiered boxes.

Left: The Tanaka family shrine in the garden; Sumiko standing, Hanako kneeling.

Below: Kimiko in the garden, circa 1920.

kind to Hanako, and by today's standards she died young at the age of sixty-six. The management of her family company got harder with the onset of the war and its aftermath, with a heavy asset tax being imposed, resulting in the sale of large sections of her estate. The family lost their interests in Manchuria and Taiwan; the gold mines in Japan had been closed by the government in 1943, never to be allowed to reopen in her lifetime. She was careful and abstemious with her daily expenditure. Her second daughter came home pregnant after a divorce; two of her daughters lived abroad with their husbands and families for long periods, depriving her of their company; and another daughter never married after a broken engagement, and died of a painful cancer. Her eldest daughter, my mother, could not be there at her death.

Fukidecho at Karuizawa: a Summer Retreat in the Hills

To escape the oppressive heat of Tokyo in the summer, many foreign prewar residents built mountain lodges in the foothills of the Japan Alps – the Chuzenji area in Nikko and Karuizawa in Nagano were their favourites. The cosmopolitan Japanese upper classes joined them with their own summer houses. Karuizawa was a sophisticated resort with an international flavour, many of the residents being missionaries from Britain or America. The Tanaka villa in Karuizawa was in an area called *Sakura-no-sawa*, not far but further up the road from the iconic Manpei Hotel, on high ground; it was bought by Great-Grandfather Heihachi from an American missionary who had built it in about 1920. We called it 'Karuizawa no Fukidecho' meaning Fukidecho at Karuizawa. ('Fukidecho' carried the connotation of being a Tanaka family estate.) It was a very lovely house, large with two and a half storeys, with a large verandah at the front with wisteria over the porch roof. It had an extension at the back where the services were, and a part of that had a corrugated iron roof and side – very similar to some houses in the Scottish Highlands.

You could see the mountains on the horizon and on fine days you could clearly see Mount Asama, which dominated the views around Karuizawa. We often went for walks in the foothills of Asama to Usui-tōgé with Grandmother carrying a parasol, pointing to wild flowers on the verges. By early September we could collect Asama berries – similar to bilberries – that were particular to the highland parts of that area. We made jam to have for breakfast. Into her old age my mother collected the berries on her sojourns at Karuizawa in the summer every year and continued to make jam at home.

The house had polished pine floors throughout with rugs. A large stone fireplace with mantelpiece above dominated the main hall; we normally spent the day at one end of this long room, where there was a dining table, sofas and armchairs in front of the fireplace, and a panelled door into the drawing room with windows on two sides. Most of the furniture was covered in white linen soft covers. A winding staircase went up past a mezzanine level with bathrooms and suchlike, to the second storey with several bedrooms. In front of the house was a garden with a tennis court beyond. There was a tea pavilion next to the house where for many years a school classmate of Aunt Setsuko, Mrs Kuroki, came to stay for the summer with her children. Her husband was Lord in Waiting to Crown Prince Akihito and could not be there for the holidays. Her daughter Nariko was in my class at school, and we played together with her young brother by the river with rocks at the bottom of the escarpment from the garden, trying not to be swept away by the current. On some weekends Uncle Yuhei with Mariko and Aunt Noriko with her husband Yasushi came; young and sophisticated, they played doubles on the tennis court, and bridge in the evenings. They seemed so happy and carefree.

Mount Asama is a live volcano: one day while we were there the atmosphere became hotter and dark clouds appeared on the horizon. Soon complete darkness fell, even though it was afternoon, and there was a tremendous shower of small grey pumice stones and ash. The large garden was covered in debris. We felt the tremors in the house. Frightened but curious we watched from the window how it unfolded. It was over in ten or twenty minutes but the air was laden with ash and dust for many hours. Ryozo, the manservant, got on with the clearing up, having gone over to the Kurokis next door to make sure they were unhurt. He collected pumice stones to be put in the bottom of plant pots for water retention – not to be wasted! Asama was often seen smoking gently and the residents were always in readiness should the mountain erupt, though it was fairly rare for it to do so. That day there had been an early warning so hill walkers and mountaineers were evacuated in time and there were no casualties.

We spent the whole of August into early September during school summer holidays at Karuizawa. For some part of it we went to stay at our Fukuda family villa some miles away at Sengataki (another part of Karuizawa), not far from the Green Hotel, where we met up with Aunt Naoko and our Nakamura cousins. It was near the Seibu shopping and amusement complex and we sometimes went skating on the man-made rink together. Aunt Naoko had the house opposite ours and she and her poet husband, together with their four daughters, spent every summer there. I never forget that in the summer of 1973, as I was leaving to go back to Tokyo, shortly before my wedding a month later in London, Naoko got up very early and came to the station to see me off, saying "This is my send-off for you; be very happy…"; for my wedding present, she gave me a roll of hand-dyed silk material in natural dyes that was the speciality of a Karuizawa store, Kusakinoya, saying "It would make a lovely evening gown."

My father sometimes joined us at weekends; Ministry of Finance officials worked day and night as their full and urgent agenda in the 1950s made holidays unthinkable. When my father was abroad in the summer of 1956 in America, we spent almost all of our summer holiday with Grandmother Hanako, Aunt Setsuko and Cousin Kinuko. Grandfather would come up in his chauffeur-driven Cadillac and stay for a few days. Occasionally he gave us a lift back to Tokyo. Mother took us to Karuizawa on the train from Ueno station in Tokyo; these were the only times that I ever went on a train in Japan. Usually Aunt Setsuko and Kinuko would go ahead of us and have the house opened and prepared for our arrival. Ryozo met us at the station. The train journey was at least two and a half hours, calling at various famous stations where they sold local delicacies in *bento* boxes. It was a tradition to buy these on the way and have picnics on the train. As we started the climb into the mountains there was a station with the famous *kamameshi*, a particular favourite. It came in an earthenware casserole with rice and stewed mountain vegetables; everyone rushed out onto the platform to buy it before the train resumed its journey. However, my mother tells me that when she was young she and her grandmother Sumiko took their own picnics containing foie gras and brioche; foie gras was Sumiko's favourite and she always took some to Karuizawa.

The memories of happy holidays we spent at Karuizawa remain dear in our hearts; Cousin Kinuko said once, when years later I was visiting Karuizawa, how much she wanted to go and visit that villa again, if just to look. That was not to be. We never went there after our grandparents' deaths when Uncle Yuhei and his family made it their holiday villa. It ultimately left their ownership and it was a sacrilege that the new owners demolished it – an example of period architecture from a well-known architect of the time. But Karuizawa has remained a place for summer holidays for my relations to this day: Aunt Mariko bought an apartment there after Yuhei died; Aunt Noriko and Yasushi had a house of their own for their family holidays near Kajima-no-Mori forest – they proudly told us about its ultra-modern technology (for the 1980s) with a remote control to turn on the central heating and hot water before their arrival. Aunt Asako too bought her own apartment and went there often in her sports car to play golf.

The Fukuda family villa called *Tsubaki-so* (Camellia Lodge), which my grandfather Koichi designed in the late 1920s with gardens and woodland around, remained in our family until my mother sold it in 2005. After my father's death she went there every summer, sometimes with friends from school who had also been widowed, but also with Eiko when she was visiting Japan. Chahchah and Francis too used it on their holidays in Japan with their young sons. It was looked after by a local caretaker, and my mother lent it to friends for their summer holidays as well. But by the time she was in her eighties, having given up driving, she felt she could not look after it any longer and keep up with the repairs essential for an old house. The land was bought by my grandmother Sada when her husband had been made redundant from the Mitsubishi shipyard; she sold the shares in Mitsubishi that her husband had held and bought two pieces of land, on either side of a lane in a lovely woodland area. On one side my grandparents built Tsubaki-so with gardens on a 300 *tsubo* (approximately 1,000 square metres) site, and on the opposite side of the lane another house for Aunt Naoko. They also bought a large woodland area adjacent to our villa, which my father sold in the 1950s to meet the asset tax that the Occupation government imposed. Sada and Koichi evacuated to Tsubaki-so towards the end of the war, leaving Masaru and his young bride in Tokyo. My mother felt that she must tell Naoko's daughters of her intention to sell our house; the Nakamura cousins instantly said they would like to buy it, and in their characteristic way insisted that they would not dream of asking for a discount. We were more than pleased that the villa has remained in Fukuda descendants' possession.

Today Karuizawa still flourishes, much expanded, with McDonald's outlets and the like. We lament the popularisation of what had been a quiet mountain resort; but then, Grandmother Hanako already in the mid-1960s was writing to my mother in Washington how much she regretted its popularisation, and looked back nostalgically to the days when Yoko and her sisters were playing on bicycles all around the wooded lanes. *Plus ça change*. I have not been back to Karuizawa; I don't want to see it in its altered state, preferring to keep my memories of the idyllic place that it once was. I am glad, however, that new people are enjoying their holidays there, in the coolness of the mountain air and with those lovely views.

Fukidecho at Akiya: Seaside Holidays

The Tanaka family also had a holiday home in Akiya. It is a small fishing village on Sagami Bay, about an hour from Tokyo. We went there in the spring and in July before the jellyfish appeared and the waves got higher. The grandparents had an enclave of several houses overlooking the beach on higher ground. The main house was built in Western style, rendered in white with a red-tiled roof, and when I was a child it was let to the Commander-in-Chief of the US naval base at nearby Yokosuka. We played on the lawn with the American children whenever we were there.

After my grandparents' deaths, Uncle Yuhei demolished this 1920s Western house, and had a lovely new replacement designed by Mariko's brother, Okada Shinichi, a leading architect in Japan (responsible for the new Supreme Court building in the 1970s). But for our holidays, while the main residence was let after the war, we stayed in a Japanese building (formerly a wing of the main house at Fukidecho) which had a direct and uninterrupted view of the bay. Next to it was another, larger, two-storey Japanese house which Grandfather let to the famous *haute-couture* designer, Hanae Mori, and her family. They stayed there every summer and seemed to have merry parties late into the night playing mah-jong. But they did not socialise with us.

Decades later, I met Hanae Mori who came as a judge in an international jewellery design competition in Vicenza that I organised as the CEO of the World Gold Council. I asked her if she remembered Akiya: she was surprised but said indeed she had spent many happy summer holidays there. Afterwards she sent me invitations to the *vernissage* of her collections. She was already in her early 80s but looked chic and stylish, in a black trouser suit and wearing large dark glasses.

Our holidays at Akiya were very relaxed and happy times. I remember that Mariko and her newborn baby came to join us, and Kinuko too. Mariko was fashionably suntanned and I tried to copy her. Occasionally Mariko's bachelor brother would come for a visit and sail his motor boat around the bay. My father too came for weekends. Grandmother came down to the beach with us sometimes but did not bathe. But in springtime she came with us to pick wild herbs on the hillside above – *zenmai* (croziers of *Osmunda japonica*), *tsukushi* (edible horsetail), and *udo* (young shoots of *Aralia cordata*). We would go down to the beach mid-morning and sit on rugs under large parasols, make sandcastles and swim in the sea, sometimes to the large rock in the middle distance. As a young girl I would be fascinated by the tiny little crabs that walked about on the sand, saying "These crabs have blue eyes; maybe they are American?" Yoko was a strong swimmer, having been taught by her father, and could dive head first from the diving board; she has nostalgically reminisced about her childhood when she went there with her parents and cousins, taking long swims to Chojagasaki along the bay, and going on the fishing boats with the fishermen from the village. As the boat would stop to take in the catch and float she said she felt dizzy and seasick; she would dive into the seas and float upright by moving her legs up and down to stay close to the boat. She said she was not at all frightened: "It's easy." Life had not changed much when we were there; the fishing boats would come in early in the mornings and late in the afternoons and we would rush down to buy freshly caught live fish, though I never went on a fishing boat offshore.

Upon her father's death, Asako inherited a piece of land opposite the compound; she designed a lovely house and garden there and it was her haven until her death. I visited her there on many of my trips to Japan, and we talked late into the night, looking over the bay and Mount Fuji on the horizon. I took some of my British friends there and they all became very fond of her. She also had a patch of land on the hillside behind and grew vegetables – a hobby inherited from her father. She was very proud of this and distributed her produce to friends and family. One of my friends, keen gardener Simon Nicholson, sent her Jerusalem artichoke tubers and she planted them out of curiosity; to her horror they took over a large area of the plot, which caused merriment amongst us all.

Osué-san was our anchor; she had been with the family looking after the Akiya property since the 1920s. She was wonderful and kept us out of mischief; she kitted us out as we went out onto the rocks in the spring to collect sea urchins, and would look after our catch. She was very fierce if we didn't obey her advice lest we managed to get hurt. She was also an accomplished cook and made our meals. Grandmother would set the menu in the morning and Osué would order the ingredients over the phone. The favoured fishmonger at the top of the lane, Uotamé, with its own fleet of fishing boats, provided almost all our seafood and delivered it to the house. For years, my mother continued to buy her favourite fish from the family she knew so well, but a decade ago the shop closed, as did many other small enterprises in the area, and she lost her friends to gossip with.

Akiya was not a fashionable resort: it was a tiny fishing village with small-time farmers on the hillside above. Before the war, Jiro's brother Masakatsu also bought a house nearby and the families congregated on the beach for swimming, collecting shells, and building sandcastles under large parasols. Aunt

Kimiko and her family also joined them in the summer. Freshly-caught fish and local lobsters were a luxury not easily available even on the tables of the rich in Tokyo. They would take some of their maids with them to help with the ladies' dressing, to set out mosquito nets in the evenings, which enveloped the whole room, and to light incense to repel moths and mosquitoes. The family had knitted woollen swimwear; both men and women were clad in these heavy swimming costumes and hats. Hanako carefully stored them in drawers with mothballs, so they kept that distinctive smell.

Sadly none of these houses remain in the family's possession, nor do they even exist, replaced by modern buildings. Osué and her husband died years ago. The beach we spent many summer holidays on has mostly been concreted over for parking for the fishermen's cars. But the seascape of rocks is an eternal reminder of our childhood days.

Recently, shortly after sunrise I was desperately looking for those rocks from the balcony of my hotel, Otowa-no-Mori, overlooking the bay of Chojagasaki and Kuruwa, trying to ascertain where Akiya was. I had rushed over to be with my mother at the height of the humid and hot summer of 2014, as she had suddenly collapsed at Misakiguchi railway station and was taken by ambulance to the Yokosuka Shimin hospital. She was critically ill in intensive care and visiting hours were in the afternoons. It was poignant to see the familiar shapes of the rocks in the distance, as in my desolate emotional state I searched for something to calm the fear that her death might be imminent. I had not seen those rocks for at least a decade, since the last time I had dined with Aunt Asako at her house, when we looked out on them shining in the sea in the early evening light, below Mount Fuji on the horizon.

Tanaka Yoko – ready for *omiai*; 1941.

5. MY MOTHER YOKO

~

O n her ninetieth birthday in 2011, my mother stood to make a speech at the dinner given in her honour by her daughters. It was a distinguished performance, using a hand-held microphone and speaking for some twenty minutes. Chahchah's two sons flew over specially from New York, as did Eiko and her husband Gus. Of her siblings, only Yuhei, her dear brother who had died a few years previously, and her sister Asako, who did not feel up to it with encroaching dementia, were not present. All my father's nieces and their husbands, as well as her Tanaka nieces and nephews and their spouses, came too. That must have been the first time that all my cousins met and dined together. It was only three weeks after the great tsunami, which had led to disaster at the Fukushima nuclear power station, and there were fears of further tremors. We chose a banqueting room in the Hotel Okura and carefully organised the seating and a celebratory menu. It was appropriate to have it at the Okura, her favourite hotel, overlooking her childhood home at Fukidecho across the road, the place most dear to her heart.

Opening her speech, Yoko said she had lived a fortunate life, and that she had not only witnessed the multitude of changes around her over nearly a century, but experienced more of life than expected at birth. She said she was born into a wealthy family where nothing could be denied; as the first child of her parents she was loved to distraction by grandparents, uncles and aunts, and all those who surrounded her; she was lucky in marriage and her mother-in-law was kind to her, as was her sister-in-law; she survived the war; she had beaten a bout of cancer; she lived in America, England and the Philippines with her own family; and brought up three daughters who all became successful in their chosen careers and lived independent lives. She also paid tribute to Minobe Junko, widow of her cousin Kokichi, saying how grateful she was that Junko had looked after, so kindly, her aunt Kimiko, whom she had loved almost as much as her own mother.

Women of her generation in Japan were brought up to obey their husbands and conform to the ways of the family they married into. Most importantly, from the day they married they were to serve the interests of the family faithfully. Yoko never strayed from that determination throughout her life, through thick and thin. Mother told me that her father advised her before her wedding that she must always rise before her husband in the morning. (Grandmother apparently didn't!) So she did. But that was the easy part: her expectations of life were dramatically altered by defeat in the war. She accepted and with her compliant nature endured hardships and unexpected changes in her way of life. Her husband's duties took her abroad, becoming used to foreign ways of life and proficient in English. She had to accept that she would be separated from her children as they married abroad. Even at the age of 100 she was able to switch to English with her sons-in-law and grandchildren.

As the eldest of five children, Yoko was in a position of respect for her younger siblings. Their parents enforced the order of priority at all times – for example, at mealtimes she would be served first after the parents. It transpired later in life that the younger sisters harboured resentment and jealousy, and complained that Yoko was arrogant because she had been prioritised and that her attitudes continued to be domineering. My mother recognised this and lamented it, but said it could not be helped. Yet during traumatic years while their parents were ill, never to recover, each of them wrote frantic letters to her, frequently saying they wished she was there. Her younger brother, Yuhei, who became head of the family, always looked up to her and respected her views. Generally, it was a close and happy family and she and her sister Setsuko, only a year younger, were particularly close. At her care home in her nineties, my mother said she would like to see Setsuko again even if she couldn't see her other sisters. Setsuko was by then in a care home herself with advanced Alzheimer's, and that could not be arranged. Kinuko said that her mother was often heard calling out to her elder sister "Oneisama, oneisama" in her dementia, half-asleep. It was not that mother was spoilt, but she had a carefree upbringing and was allowed to have an independence of mind. Though reserved, she has always been straightforward and friendly in character. She was not embarrassed about her shortcomings and never pretentious. At school, she was clever and got good marks. She made many friends who remained close all their lives.

Brother and Sisters

They were brought up together in the Western-style house at No.17 Fukidecho until it was commandeered by the US Occupation government and they moved in with their grandparents in the main house. When the siblings were young they would walk up through the garden to their grandparents daily, where their Aunt Kimiko would also be visiting. The Minobe house was next door and the gardens were adjacent. Often there would be picnics on the lawn and they rode their bicycles around the large estate, racing to score points with the Minobe and Takata cousins. They spent just as much time at the main house at No. 24 and at the Takata house beyond, where they found cousins to play with as well as their genial great-uncle. In springtime, they would collect branches of blossom in baskets and take them up to present to him. Yoko played games with her grandmother Sumiko, exchanging clothes; Mother donned her grandmother's kimono and Sumiko put on her school uniform and they had photographs taken together in the drawing room. They were looked after and accompanied by nannies and numerous maids and manservants who lived either on the estate or around the enclave in houses provided by Heihachi. When they were little, their parents went on overseas tours, leaving the children with carers at home. Portrait photographs of the children were taken by a studio to be sent abroad to enable the parents to keep up with their offspring's growth. They would not have wanted to be surprised on their return!

They learnt about plants and trees from their grandfather and father and made sketches, sat in the gardens reading together, collected loquats in the summer and acorns and ginkgo nuts in the autumn. At New Year they could fly kites in the extensive grounds and play *karuta* (a Japanese card game). A lot of their childhood was spent inventing pleasures for themselves by arranging to meet to read together, or producing a magazine together, enlisting articles from their more distant cousins, which they distributed around the estate – there were quite a few recipients – learning to ride together, taking photographs with early cameras their parents had bought for them, with the boys also learning to shoot pigeons with airguns. Amazingly, one of the magazines they produced in the early 1930s had the theme: 'Why Germany is important?' They would play *torampu* (cards) in the evenings, fanning their competitive spirit. On summer holidays they went on bicycle rides through the lanes of Karuizawa hillside, played tennis, went for hill-walks and picked Asama berries for jam making; and at Akiya got together with their cousins and organised swimming races down the coast. They went on holidays not just to Karuizawa and Akiya, but further afield to other parts of Japan for skiing and of course to the mines with Heihachi on his inspection trips; photographs show that my grandfather Jiro took Yoko in her teens to go down the mine at Tsuchihata in Iwate prefecture, wearing miners' clothes and protective hat, as well as at their Todoroki mine in Hokkaido.

It seems that their life unfolded almost entirely within the family circle, including numerous cousins and school contemporaries. Since school friends overlapped, as friends' siblings all went to the school too, they knew each other's families really well. Aunt Asako said Yuhei used to take her to concerts in Hibiya Park in her teens in the early 1940s to hear classical music. Those were the days when the colloquial phrase 'GinBura' was coined, as young people began taking strolls in the fashionable streets of Ginza. 'Gin' for Ginza while 'Bura' was short for '*bura bura*' – to stroll slowly. But as air raids intensified such outings became fewer.

My mother talks of her childhood with nostalgia and happy recollections only: she seems at her happiest then, with laughter and joyful memories. The years of her youth, the 1920s and 1930s, were carefree ones and she had little to fear. Aunt Asako too said that life at Fukidecho was peaceful and happy, but we know that dark clouds were gathering over the horizon by the early 1930s. While outside historians and observers might have been – and remain – unaware, the life of growing daughters of well-to-do families in Tokyo even then was not too remote from the 'Flapper' years of the post-First World War era.

Now it is almost as if her married years in the Fukuda family were but a temporary stage in Yoko's life: though lasting forty years, they counted as less than half the span she has lived so far. After her parents' deaths, Mother considered her brother to be her mainstay, especially after her husband's death in 1984. But ultimately, with the passing of the generations, she would find that her own home and heritage were to disintegrate.

Yuhei (雄平)*: 'Gold is the Constant'*
Yoko's younger brother Yuhei (雄平) was the only son and the third child of Jiro and Hanako. As the future heir to the dynasty,

he was much protected as a young boy as he had a fragile constitution. Still, his cheerful nature made him popular at Gakushuin. Yoko found in him a kindred spirit to avidly read novels and poetry with. Like her, Yuhei was unaffected and straightforward, but he had the knack of teasing people with inoffensive tricks and plays on words. There was always a lot of laughter around him and he was congenial company. Good at games, be it golf or tennis, enjoying concerts and the theatre but without being an insistent intellectual, he nurtured friendships easily. Inheriting the sociable character of his father he was a socialite, enjoying the company of his many friends all his life. He went on to the Imperial University of Tokyo but was conscripted into the Army on national service for a short time during the war. Though he never talked about it, he had to join the Army when Japan's fortunes were beginning to wane. Going to war without the prospect of victory must have been very hard for an idealistic youth of eighteen. Mishima Yukio, his classmate, was deeply affected when told his health was not up to military standards, and that left a lasting mark on his psyche; he wrote in one of his novels of the hatred he harboured against the man who delivered that profoundly wounding message. (That man was my great-uncle Admiral Yamanashi in his role as President of the school at the time.) His direct contemporary, Hayami Masaru, who decades later became Governor of the Bank of Japan, wrote in his memoirs that his generation was lost for direction as the world around them made a 180 degree turn from a military dictatorship to democracy as they were demobbed.

Unlike most of his contemporaries who emerged from the war having to find employment, Yuhei never had to worry about jobs or earning a living. He was expected to join the family firm and eventually to take over its management on his father's retirement. His father thought it appropriate that he should work at a major mining company first to gain experience of the real world of competition and corporate life. He joined Mitsubishi

Metal Mining Co. which was the largest gold mining company, also engaged in other non-ferrous metals extraction. He proudly showed me when I was a young girl his *meishi* (calling card), with Mitsubishi Metal Mining Company on it, that he posted at the bottom of the staircase leading up to his suite at Fukidecho. Mitsubishi sent him to a major American producer in the Midwest for several months of training. That was in the early 1950s, only a few years after the war. He became quite proficient in conversational American English then, so that in later years he would try to speak to my sisters and me in English; he would start telephone calls with "Hello, Uncle Yuhei speaking…"

He was tall, slim and handsome. He married Okada Mariko in the mid-1950s and had three daughters. Though theirs was an *omiai* marriage, they were very fond of each other and with Mariko's sociable and happy character their home was always joyful. She was the youngest child and only daughter of a former Governor of Hokkaido. Her mother, Yuriko, an elegant lady, was the daughter of Odaira Namihei, the founder of Hitachi Ltd, a company that grew to be one of the giants of postwar industrial Japan. Mariko went to Gakushuin too. Their first child, Momoko, sadly died of illness at the age of three; I will never forget the desolate cries of Yuhei beside her tiny coffin at the funeral. Their overwhelming grief left them in sorrow, but several years later they had two other daughters, Kakuko and Akiko, born while we were abroad. Aunt Mariko, who died very recently, was a very able woman: her food was always delicious and beautifully presented, her embroidery perfect in design and execution; an excellent tennis player when young and a champion golfer still playing in her late eighties. She took up photography in middle age and exhibited her work at private shows. Her home was always immaculate and beautifully decorated.

Though their life seemed always to me to be so enviably care-free, without the worries that beset most of us after the war, the burden of running the family company turned out to be far greater than anyone had ever imagined. I have come to like Uncle Yuhei a lot in more recent years. In the early years of the 1970s when I first went back on visits to my parents in Tokyo, although he was most welcoming, urging me and Chahchah most affectionately to come and stay with them, I felt that he disapproved of my living abroad and of my having a job. To him, as the prevailing convention dictated, daughters of good families should never work for a living, because it meant 'lowering one's personal status in society'. He was amazed but thought it rather impressive when I said that I was not working for money but because I believed in the philosophical objectives of the organisation. Evidently it had never crossed his mind that anyone would take into consideration the worthiness of what one was doing, an altruism which to my mind was the all-important criterion for one's work. He said to me once "Of course anyone can get a job if you are prepared to downgrade your personal status." I was tremendously hurt by this and rushed to tell Aunt Asako, who was in the midst of a feud with him at the time. But with the passage of time, as modern ways rapidly took over Japan, he seemed to accept that not only did young women in his own circle have careers but they even married foreigners, which had previously been considered 'not the done thing'.

He himself faced many unexpected trials in life. The collapse of the 'bubble' economy in 1990 that eventually took the stock market and property prices down some 75 per cent, and kicked off a decades-long recession, meant a turn for the worse in the fortunes of the family, whose wealth was largely based on property ownership and copper mines. It fell upon Yuhei to tackle these challenges almost entirely on his own and to protect his own family and his sisters' livelihoods. The old family mining company Tanaka Kogyo (田中鉱業) he had inherited and run had eventually to be closed. Mines get depleted as minerals and metals are extracted, and these become more costly to extract as mining goes deeper. The principal mines that his ancestors had opened at the end of the nineteenth century had been becoming uneconomic for some years. He had adopted modern mining techniques and developed leaching of copper and diversified into other minerals such as tungsten and pearlite. Those other minerals, alongside copper, were by the 1980s the revenue earner for the company. But by the 1990s it was all coming to the end of the road. He decided to close the mines; a complex and emotionally hard undertaking. The whole community of employees and villagers who had been in the service of the company for generations had to be looked after. The mines finally closed towards the end of the 1990s and Tanaka Kogyo was wound up. It had been the fourth largest non-ferrous metal company in Japan, after Mitsubishi, Sumitomo and Mitsui, and the only one still a private company owned entirely by members of the family. The mines were in Hokkaido, Iwate and Yamagata prefectures. In the wind-up, all his sisters and their children lost their shares in the company. He set up a new company, Itohei Kosan (糸平 興産), and turned the mountains into ski resorts and *onsen* (hot spring) hotels. Yoko and her sisters went on a nostalgic journey to Tsuchihata one summer a decade later.

The stock market crash and the associated property market collapse of 1990 took their toll in different ways. Not only did the values of securities listed on the Japanese stock exchanges continue their decline after the dramatic fall in 1990, property values across the country fell 75 per cent or more in the very first few years of the next decade. The government directed all banks to engage in asset reduction to reduce leverage in the economy; that continued for more than ten years. It established a government-owned restructuring organisation into which banks sold non-performing loans. Mergers of large city banks and absorption of smaller local banks began in the late 1990s and continued for the rest of the decade. The asset reduction by banks led to old-established customer relationships having to be reined in, with ever-increasing requirements for collateral. Old wealth built over a hundred years was thus destroyed in a matter of a decade, as the government put pressure on the banks to call in long-term loans by the early years of the twenty-first century. The century-old banking relationships which had provided the continuity and solidity of Japan's industrial infrastructure were thus broken; the Tanaka family companies were no exception. Yuhei managed and reorganised the family holdings, keeping them intact so that his sisters would not suffer any reduction in income impairing their standard of living. After all, that had been the instruction to him in his father's will.

The last twenty years of Yuhei's life were therefore difficult ones. His elder daughter Kakuko's marriage to a descendant of the Yasuda and Asano *zaibatsu* broke up. He had been so proud of his daughter having married so well and he was most tremendously excited to see his first grandson and was a devoted grandfather. Kakuko's husband had joined the company on their marriage, eventually to succeed Yuhei, but of course he then had to leave it. After his daughter's divorce Yuhei was immensely concerned for her well-being and for her children. Kakuko worked with him in the family property company. He arranged for his younger daughter Akiko's second son Daijiro to be the successor and heir to the Tanaka family, and for her husband to run the family company after his death, as Daijiro was still a child then.

He was always very close to my mother and confided in her during those difficult times. She in turn had always trusted him and believed that if ever she got into difficulties he would be there to rescue her. Since our father's death my sisters and I also much depended on his advice, especially on matters to do with our mother; when she underwent an operation for stomach cancer it was to him that we turned for advice and moral support. On her marriage he sent her a book of poems with an inscription in his own hand, beautifully moving and touching in its sentiment, saying how sorry he was to see her leave home but wishing her the greatest of happiness. He respected our father very much and they were friends; they often played golf together and practised in the golf range at Fukidecho.

Yuhei was sociable and had many close friends, with whom he and Mariko often went to restaurants and concerts, and sometimes on overseas holidays. Some of them I have myself known well, such as Chiba Kazuo, Ambassador to the UK, who was his classmate at Gakushuin, and Yamatane Tomiji (President of Yamatane Securities and Yamatane Art Gallery) who was a fellow member of a society of industrialists who were born in the same year. He also dutifully kept in touch with the large number of relatives, one of whom he visited at the Vatican as he became a cardinal (Cardinal Stephen – he was a cousin through his grandmother Sumiko, of the Fukuhara family).

Like his father, Yuhei was a gourmet and a strong drinker. Whenever I was in Tokyo I went to visit him and Mariko at their home, sometimes bringing my colleague and friend Dugald with me. They would drink together for many hours in the evening, chatting away in English. He was astonished to hear of my involvement in an African mine and intrigued to hear about the financing of the Konkola deep mine in Zambia, which I was organising in the mid-1990s. He taught me a great deal about the pricing of copper in US dollars, and what that meant for non-US producers. He was affectionate and kindly in his ways, with a benign sense of humour. He never showed any hint of malice or cynicism. He and Mariko came on a short visit to London and Paris in 2001. He so much wanted to come to see Creems and its gardens, having seen photographs, but I could not take time off mid-week as I was CEO of the World Gold Council at the time. They came to my flat in Ennismore Gardens whose classical decoration, with an Adam ceiling and antique furniture, was much to his taste, being reminiscent of the prewar Western style that he was brought up with. I took them out to dinner at the beautiful Connaught Grill Room and went back to the Dorchester where they were staying in a suite. We chatted for a couple of hours over a glass or two of brandy, during which he talked to me about his long association with gold and gold mining and told me "All you have to remember always is that gold is the central thing and that paper currencies are moving around it. Gold is the constant." I put it firmly in my mind and have never forgotten. Years later I have been telling my young colleagues at Glint Pay (a start-up digital payments platform), of which I am a non-executive director, exactly that.

Setsuko (節子)

Aunt Setsuko (節子) was only a year younger than my mother and they were brought up together, but with different nannies. Though when they were older they had frequent quarrels and Setsuko would throw tantrums at her for whatever reason, my mother has always said that they were very close. Their lives, though, could not have turned out to be more different. Setsuko attended Gakushuin and had an *omiai* marriage immediately after the war. But it failed as her in-laws were unkind to her. Grandmother Hanako, suspecting that she was unhappy, sent her most trusted servant, Takemi, to go and visit, bearing a letter saying "When Takemi leaves go with her to see her off and get on the same train and come home." So that was what she did. But she was pregnant, and in the months following gave birth to Kinuko at Higuchi Byoin. Her in-laws sent back all her possessions and had no contact thereafter. Setsuko and Kinuko lived at Fukidecho. Setsuko came to visit us at Shiroganedai very often and my father liked her very much; he would tease my mother saying Setsuko was more beautiful and spoke elegantly. Mother took no notice; they had very different looks but I think she was better-looking.

While my father was in America at Duke University, Setsuko wrote him long letters explaining that it had been arranged for her to marry a widower more than twenty years older. She wrote that she would like to have been able to consult him on this proposition. My father was shocked and wrote to my mother saying that a beautiful young woman like her should not marry a man so much older. Ono Takeshi, whom she did marry, was the son of a famous calligrapher whose first wife had died of an illness, leaving him with teenage children. She was the sister of Kajima Morinosuke, whose family owned the largest construction engineering company in Japan, Kajima Corporation. Kajima Morinosuke was the Chairman and President of the company at the time, and his brother-in-law was the Deputy President (later Deputy Chairman). The Kajima family was a dynasty in itself and dominated the top management of the company. Setsuko was thrown into a challenging situation. It is never easy for stepmothers to win acceptance on arrival; the young daughter she brought with her had to be protected; she herself had to be accepted into the Kajima corporate family and its diaspora and become a 'corporate wife' of a large public company; and maintain a large house and garden not near her parents' or sisters' homes. The marriage was arranged through an introduction by Mariko's parents.

We went to visit Setsuko soon after she married and she was excited to show us her new and grand home. Her new husband was very kind to her and to Kinuko and for many years they lived a happy life. She wrote to my mother when their father died that, after fourteen years, she now felt fully accepted. She wrote that the Kajima family were exceptionally decent and warm people. In those days there was an unfavourable undertone to the words 'second wife', so it was unsurprising she felt she had to be on her toes. She was put in a difficult position when Kajima Corporation wanted to buy the main house and garden at Fukidecho and Yuhei attached difficult conditions to the sale. When her husband fell ill with cancer, Setsuko looked after him devotedly. She made great efforts with her stepchildren, who could not have been indifferent to matters of inheritance, and she won their affection. But for many years she was burdened psychologically and emotionally and succumbed to bouts of illness. Uncle Ono walked Kinuko up the aisle at her wedding and gave her away to Namiki Takashi, an architect at Kajima Corporation, a few months before he succumbed to his fatal illness. He allowed Takashi and Kinuko to build a house adjacent to where he and Setsuko lived in the big house.

When he died I went to the house to pay my respects: Setsuko was beautifully dressed in her fine kimono and cried on my shoulder, saying "Hardship never ends…" Evidently, from her earlier letters to my mother, she seemed to have harboured feelings of self-pity in that she had drawn the short straw after Yoko married away and she spent the last of the war years evacuated to the provinces with her mother and young sister. My mother was not unsympathetic, but there was not much that could be done in retrospect to change her feelings, other than to offer sisterly consolation. Eventually they sold the houses and Takashi and Kinuko built a lovely modern four-storey building where they, their son's family and Setsuko each had a flat, not far from where they used to live.

She was always thoughtful and kind; while my father was ill she often sent him his favourite food, such as lobster, and was concerned that my mother was finding life hard looking after a difficult husband. But her insecurity made her at times over-demanding of others and she could be frightening. Setsuko was an affectionate and generous person, more demonstrative than our mother. She was also a very good cook, a talent Kinuko inherited, and whatever she did she showed great manual dexterity. She knitted sweaters a lot after the war and made dresses, as we all did. My mother admitted that Setsuko was better at these crafts than she was. She took up the *shamisen* (a traditional Japanese guitar-like musical instrument with three strings) and the *nagauta* (traditional Japanese solo singing, sung to the accompaniment of the *shamisen*) and became very proficient, especially in nagauta technique, so much so that she gave private lessons in her later years and played at public concerts. She gave me beautiful kimono fabrics so I could make dresses, bought us jewellery and took Chahchah to the sumo and kabuki. As she was living at Fukidecho with Kinuko when we were little, we were very close to her. Chahchah came back from New York especially for her funeral as she had felt particularly close.

She had a special affection for Chahchah, who is only a year younger than Kinuko; Setsuko was always entrusted with her at Fukidecho whenever our mother was unable to look after her. One such occasion was while I was in hospital aged five with a serious abdominal complication from appendicitis. Chahchah was a one-year-old baby. I was in critical condition, in a coma for two days following an emergency operation requiring a blood transfusion from my mother; she stayed with me at the hospital, sleeping beside my bed on the floor for five weeks. I remember the days I spent at the Senbai Byoin in Ninohashi; I don't remember that I was in any pain, but only that I was allowed to have chewing gum but no food. As I was never allowed chewing gum at home I was rather pleased. My kindergarten friends made 1,000 little paper origami cranes (cranes are a good omen), and strung them into a hanging ornament above my bed.

Senbai Byoin was a hospital run by the Japan Monopoly Corporation, the state-owned tobacco, salt and rice enterprise. I was taken there because my father at the Ministry was in charge of the budget allocations for state-owned corporations in the Budget Bureau at that time. My mother, in her depressed moments today, talks to me about that experience, as if to imply that I therefore have an obligation to look after her now, recalling how I would not let her go out of my room, crying "Mama, Mama…" When I was finally discharged we were told I must stay in bed for a month at home. My grandmother, who was forever protective, was still alive then and would not allow any risk to be taken. But immediately I was faced with exams to get into primary school and had to prepare. Just in case I did not pass the entrance examination to Gakushuin, I also took the exam and was interviewed at Sacred Heart School, close to our home and the next best girls' school. I was not very well prepared for this due to my illness. I hated the experience with nuns in black habits asking the questions; they seemed frightening and sinister. Fortunately I did not get into Sacred Heart. But I did pass the exam to get into Gakushuin. So all was well.

Setsuko's last years were a long sad struggle with Alzheimer's. As the disease progressed she became less and less able to remember conversations, and told my mother in desolate tones that she was losing her powers of comprehension. Having been looked after tirelessly by her daughter Kinuko for many years, she became physically too frail for Kinuko to manage and she went into a care home nearby. It was hard for Kinuko, who had devotedly cared for her for more than ten years, sacrificing her own interests. She died aged ninety-five.

Asako (朝子)

Aunt Asako was the most highly spirited of our mother's sisters, and the only one to have had a career. She was arguably the most beautiful of the four sisters; many of my friends who met her have said she resembled Princess Margaret and she indeed had a similar look and aura. She too went to Gakushuin, and she was in a group under the wing of Mrs Elizabeth Vining. Mrs Vining was a widow who came from Philadelphia and was a Quaker; she was chosen by my great-uncle, Admiral Yamanashi, while he was still the President of Gakushuin at the end of the war, to teach English to the then Crown Prince, now retired Emperor, Akihito (the Heisei Emperor). She wrote about her time in Japan in *Windows for the Crown Prince* after she went back to Philadelphia. Asako and her friends who were taught by Mrs Vining, as well as the Crown Prince himself, remained in touch with her throughout her retirement and visited her in Philadelphia. She was a thoughtful woman of high moral rectitude.

On graduating from Gakushuin, a few years after the end of the war, Asako agreed to an arranged marriage. Her fiancé was being sent to America by his employer for several months on assignment and she went to see him off at the airport. But another woman appeared, and it was clear that she was his lover. The engagement was, of course, called off immediately. Seeing Asako in deep misery, Mrs Vining suggested that she should go to a university in America, together with two other young women from Gakushuin. Mrs Vining arranged for them to take courses at women's universities on the east coast: Asako got into Bryn Mawr in Pennsylvania, another woman went to Wellesley in Massachusetts, and another to Smith College. Asako studied social sciences and stayed for four years, much longer than initially planned. America made her an independent, strongly opinionated intellectual.

The years Asako spent in America, as she told me and my sisters, were in many ways rather amazing. She worked during vacations as a waitress (quite different from the life she had been used to at home!); she was entirely on her own for those years, not once going home for holidays, which would have been unthinkable because of the cost, writing letters to her parents and sisters, visiting and staying with Mrs Vining for Christmas and Easter holidays. After all, she could not have been all that proficient in English when she first arrived. It was very brave of her to go in the first place, and brave and enlightened of her parents to allow it. The letters she wrote home that I have in my mother's archive show no signs of sadness or loneliness. Evidently she did not think of having a boyfriend. She had the self-confidence to make her own life there.

On her return to Tokyo, Asako worked temporarily with the Raymonds, the architect and his interior designer wife. But then she got a professional job at the Ministry of Science and

Technology as a civil servant. Her parents tried to find a good marriage partner for her, but by then she was getting older, in her late twenties, and her having been abroad and now working meant that it was not that easy to find a suitable match. Japanese men in those days were not used to women of independent mind like her, and yet it was quite unthinkable that she would marry outside their social circle. After many years at the Ministry, she decided to become a simultaneous interpreter and joined Simul International, using her bilingual skills. This gave her slightly more flexible working hours compared with the job at the Ministry. It had been hard for her to combine working during the day and nursing her mother at the hospital in her final days. After her mother's death, she was looking after her father inasmuch as she organised the evening meals she had with him at the 'upper house', cooked by the chef. By then she lived in her own apartment in Ginnan House just down through the garden, but dined with him every evening.

When her father died, Asako found herself suddenly all alone. Her siblings were all married and had their own families. Her home, Fukidecho, was going to have to be sold to meet estate duties. In her desolate loneliness she allowed some tensions to build up with her brother and sister-in-law, and her sisters who in turn took sides. I do not think that her siblings understood how much she was affected psychologically by her new predicament. She felt she did not receive sufficiently sympathetic emotional support. She felt isolated for some years. She designed and built a most lovely house on the beach at Akiya, on a piece of land she had inherited, and she spent a great deal of time there, driving up to Tokyo in her sports car to her apartment in Ebisu near Shibuya, and growing vegetables on her hillside plot. During the summer she went to her apartment in Karuizawa to play golf there. Some years later she bought a lovely large apartment in Hiroo, which became her principal home, and she divided her time between there and Akiya.

Asako worked on her own, still with Simul, well into her late sixties. She was a person of artistic tastes and liked both antique and modern pottery and handicrafts, dyed fabrics in *sarasa* with her mother and her group, and chose sporty and stylish clothes and jewellery for herself. She loved driving and had a succession of sports cars. She confided in me about her love affairs over dinners and drinks late into the night at Akiya. She once said that the men she went out with were not the sort of men the Tanaka family daughter would marry. She had long-lasting love affairs that ended painfully, but she was never short of suitors. She was exceptionally youthful for her age in her late sixties, and when I asked how she managed to keep her looks she replied that it was because she was in love. I doubt if anyone else knows who that was: an American – a senior executive of Texas Instruments – who fell for her when she taught him Japanese. A passionate lover, he gave her the greatest of happiness as well as sorrow. She described her intimate thoughts, self-searching, desperate sadness and loneliness – the agony of being in love – in the secret diary she kept on her relationship with him. He would stay with her whenever he was in Japan.

She said to me that it had never been in her mind that she would ever marry him, but her diary reveals that she considered him the love of her life. When he was stationed in Japan for a few years and brought his family with him, he wanted her to meet his wife: she was devastated. Asako consoled herself that she was better than his wife, and that he caught every opportunity he could find to see her. He wanted her to correspond with him in Japanese so that his wife would not understand. Towards the end of her life, with advanced Alzheimer's disease, she would only say *handotai* (semiconductors) to whatever her visitors said to her. Everyone was laughing about it; why should the word *handotai* dominate her mind? I knew why.

Asako said she was happy that we, the Fukuda family, visited her often. She wanted me to build a hillside 'log cabin' on her vegetable plot for my holiday home. She often mentioned her visit to the nursing home when I was born, bearing food for my mother, saying she was the first of the family to see me. She came to England to visit me. We spent some time at Creems and then in London where we went shopping together, went to the British Museum and to the opera. I remember she bought a fur-lined raincoat and some jewellery, and some presents to take back to my mother. As we shared an interest in growing vegetables she often sent me seeds for my garden and special fertilisers. I sent her in return seeds of kohlrabi, which were Grandfather's favourite but unavailable in Japan.

Asako's death was an emotionally difficult moment for my sisters and myself. My mother has never talked much about it with me, except to say that we have to accept that she was ill and that she lived her life as she wanted; but her thoughts must have been complex. That her sister had 'lived her life as she wanted' was in many respects in stark contrast to her own path. Asako died in June 2018 aged ninety at her care home, Sun City, in Tokyo – perhaps one of the two most luxurious care homes in Japan. Being an independently-minded and competitively-spirited woman, Asako never admitted to herself or anyone that she had begun to show symptoms of Alzheimer's disease more than ten years earlier. My mother took immense care of her from the beginning of her dementia: first persuading her and taking her to hospital each week to get her prescriptions, taking her to the bank to get money, going through her post and finding unpaid bills, organising her tax affairs with an accountant, and eventually arranging for her to buy into a retirement/care home against her wishes.

My mother tirelessly resolved many crises. My weekly calls with her became overladen with the issues surrounding Asako. But there were rewarding aspects too, in that they went out together after these errands for lunch and were able to reminisce about Fukidecho and their childhood days, which no one else would have comprehended. All past acrimonies were forgotten by then and they were comfortable in each other's company. When my mother turned ninety-two she told her sister that she too had to start considering living full-time at her retirement home at Aburatsubo and would not be able to continue looking after her. Asako just stood there and said only "Thank you for everything." By then it was clear Asako could not be left to live on her own. One day, it was arranged that she would stay in the care home for good. One of our cousins, Akiko, became her lawful guardian and my mother was freed from her daily concern for her younger sister. Mother felt that Asako was in a safe place and properly looked after and that she herself had fulfilled her duty. My sisters and I felt dreadfully sorry for her knowing how much she had been resisting it, but from a distance we could not do anything other than visit whenever we were in Tokyo. Mother said, encapsulating a characteristically Japanese concept, "Asako is a member of the Tanaka family as she never married away, it is the Tanaka family's responsibility to look after her."

On Asako's death, my mother insisted that she wanted to send flowers to the funeral. The family had decided that there should be no flowers or offerings at the simple service they had arranged. I wrote passionately to them pleading that at least our mother, the only remaining blood-sister still in health, but unable to be at the funeral herself, should be allowed to send flowers; Mother telephoned Mariko who told her flowers would not be accepted. Nevertheless, a large floral arrangement on a stand, which I arranged through a florist in Tokyo and bearing the name Yoko, was the sole floral tribute at the funeral. Chahchah and I were able to attend the interment of her ashes at the family grave, a Buddhist tradition, a month and a half later as we were in Tokyo at the same time. It was a sad day. There was a meeting of the cousins (Asako's nieces and nephews) afterwards at which we divided up her jewellery, but also discussed the division of her estate. That turned out to be unexpectedly and shockingly acrimonious. I was representing my mother who, as Japanese law prescribed, inherited one quarter of her sister's estate.

Poor Asako was, as she wrote in her diary, quite wrongly haunted throughout her life with a sense that she had not been blessed with the love of her parents or siblings, and that no one really cared how she felt. Her mother tried to convince her that every child was equally loved, but she felt left out. So much so, throughout her life Asako told herself that she must live her own life as she wished and get her own fulfilment from that. I once asked her at her care home if she was in touch with her American boyfriend; she looked surprised and said when he next came to Japan she would introduce him to me. I often wonder if he ever knew about her last years: perhaps he had tried to find her at her house in Akiya, with so many hidden, special memories.

Noriko (範子)

Aunt Noriko, the youngest of our grandparents' five children, was only nine years old when Yoko married and left home. Yet she seemed to feel quite close to her. She happened to be on a visit to England when Chahchah's son Nicholas was being baptised; she attended on behalf of our mother. She always made sure to come and see me at Creems, even on very brief visits here. When my mother went back to Tokyo for their mother's funeral it was Noriko who met her at the airport. After their mother's death, she wrote to her eldest sister often as if she was her mother's substitute, confiding in her about her own anxieties and consulting her on bringing up her children abroad.

Noriko went to Gakushuin too and married another Gakushuin alumnus, Sumiya Yasushi, son of a wealthy landowning family in Shibuya, Tokyo. His elder brother was a classmate of Yuhei at school and became a senior diplomat. Uncle Yasushi was an executive of the Bank of Tokyo and became a Senior Managing Director at the end of his career. The Bank of Tokyo, the leading foreign exchange bank, sent him on assignments to California for extended periods twice in his career. It was through his work that the First California Bank came under the Bank of Tokyo's control. Their children, our four cousins, were brought up largely in California. The eldest of them, Shigeru, who also spent much of his career abroad with Sumitomo Corporation, and his family have been particularly close to my mother. They called on her at home very often when in Tokyo. Shigeru's daughter, Reina, frequently came to confide in my mother, her great-aunt, about wanting to marry a Frenchman and how her parents might feel about her making her life abroad. Reina and her family now live near Lyon. Shigeru's sister, Reiko, is close to Eiko's age and they have become friends, sharing experiences of having been brought up abroad most of their lives. Noriko was kind, pretty, affectionate and displayed not a hint of malice or wilfulness. Sadly she fell ill with dementia at the young age of sixty-two and has spent much of the last ten years steadily declining in a care home.

Noriko was a good tennis player and she kept it up into middle age. It was her failure to turn up to one of her tennis rendezvous with her school friends that alerted them that all was not well. She was eventually diagnosed with early signs of Alzheimer's. That was the first time in their generation of the family that Alzheimer's struck. Feeling desperately sorry for her youngest sister, Yoko said "How lonely she must feel, poor Noriko…"

Yoko went to a lot of trouble to find out about Alzheimer's through her contacts and tried to find medication that would retard the progress of the disease. For some ten years, Noriko was able to live at home and Yasushi made sure she was able to continue to cook and have dinners with him; frequently, he would take her on holidays abroad so that she didn't have to attend to domestic chores; he took her shopping and bought her clothes so that she was respectably dressed at all times. Her disease progressed slowly but steadily and in twenty years she lost all her memory. When she came to Yoko's ninetieth birthday party ten years ago she was still just able to recognise us, but now she doesn't recognise even her own children. When Yasushi died she attended his funeral without knowing that it was that of her husband. In many ways, though, Noriko had a happy life blessed with a devoted husband, children and grandchildren; and now great-grandchildren.

School Friends

Alumni relationships at all schools and universities are still maintained strongly in Japan, rather more so than in Britain. Frequent alumni gatherings form the basis of networking. Yoko's class at Gakushuin met at least twice a year for lunches. They had a roster to arrange those gatherings and they took it in turns to maintain the contact list. In addition, Yoko was an enthusiastic attender of Tokiwakai, which holds annual meetings, lunches and bazaars and looked forward to them each time.

Gakushuin's teenage students were taken on excursions into the mountains to spend a week or fortnight together. Yoko wrote long letters to her grandmother and aunt as well as to her mother describing their days away, often urging them to write to her more often, as her friends received more letters from home. She appeared to be jealous of her friends and also lonely. Those letters show her acute sense of observation of nature and knowledge of flora and fauna. She does not talk about her friends or about their conversations, but more about her own response to the surroundings. But lasting friendships were formed on those school trips that Yoko retained throughout her life. Some of the women married far away in distant places such as Kyushu, but they met whenever they could and kept in touch over the telephone – often for hours at a time. When they were widowed and freed from their family commitments they went on trips together, often to their ancestral homes.

It was a lucky coincidence that when Yoko got married the Fukuda family home was only a mile away from two of her classmates' married homes. All three were within ten minutes' walking distance from each other. Those two friends had married into noble families, the Nabeshima and the Sakai; their husbands' families were the daimyo of their respective domains. I went to kindergarten and junior school with the Nabeshima children and I often went along with my mother to visit their homes; I remember, when I was about eight years old, being very jealous of them having one of the first television sets and urged my parents to get one too. In her widowhood, my mother invited them to our house in Karuizawa for summer holidays and they also went on a painting holiday in the mountains of Switzerland together. My mother was thrilled when Sakai Kiyoko invited her to visit the Sakai family ancestral temple, the renowned Eiheiji in Fukui prefecture. The Nabeshima family still live on their estate, although some parts of it have been sold for corporate entertainment venues. The site of the Sakai family house is now the Bussho Gonenkai temple (of a new form of Buddhist sect).

When Mother collapsed aged ninety-three and was recovering in the care centre in Aburatsubo, one of her classmates, Sano Tamiko, asked Mariko to take her there. Mariko said to me afterwards that she herself cried as she saw them overwhelmed with seeing and hugging each other in an emotional reunion.

While we lived abroad, if ever any friends from school came to the country, they immediately got in touch with one another: I remember the Hoshi family coming to dinner with us in Washington while Mr Hoshi was serving as Minister at the UN, and we also visited them in New York. He was in the same year at the Imperial University of Tokyo as my father, and his wife Kyoko was my mother's classmate. She was a scion of the Sengé family, who were descended from the founders of the ancient Shinto shrine in Japan, Izumo Taisha. Thus it is said that they are descended from the Shinto gods. Their son, Fumio, came to live in London in the 1980s with JEXIM; he and I became close friends and have since collaborated on business ventures. When I introduced him to Desmond Neill, an old China hand and long-term resident of Singapore, Desmond called him 'Sun God' and always referred to him as such, much to Fumio's amusement.

In London another school friend, Ikeda Masako, and her family came to live in the nearby neighbourhood of Hampstead, as her husband became head of Mitsui & Co. for Europe (he later became the company's President). Mother cooked a Japanese dish, *chirashi zushi*, and put it in a lacquered box to take to their house on their first day in London. Mrs Ikeda in her childhood was a princess, being the daughter of an imperial duke, descended from Emperor Nijo. When my parents left for Manila, leaving me alone in England, up at Cambridge in my second year, my mother felt reassured that her friend was here for me in any emergency.

The school friends with whom Yoko spent twelve years of childhood share memories of times past that form the basic understanding of life enjoyed, endured and continuing. They understand that each of them survived the transition from a life led like princesses before the war to that of commoners after the war without their titles or wealth. Yet, their conversation is never about nostalgia or regrets. They talk always about the present and the future, their animated views frankly exchanged. I consider that to be their strength and a reason for their longevity. They survived because they had the readiness to accept change and adapt to new ways. Always interested in the world around them and keeping up with current affairs; my mother surprised us all when, in the intensive care unit at the hospital only three days after she had collapsed of an aortic dissection aged ninety-three, she asked what was happening with the Russian invasion of Crimea.

Tokyo Woman's Christian University

On graduating from high school at Joshi-Gakushuin, Yoko was one of the few women from the school who went on to university outside of the Gakushuin establishment. She attended the Tokyo Woman's Christian University and studied nutrition. It was the first time that she had come into contact with people of quite different backgrounds, and her parents considered that an important preparation for life. My mother said that she had to learn to speak like ordinary people and that prepared her for life after the war; she was always rather proud of it. She has a long-lasting affection for the university, established by the educationalist Nitobe Inazo in 1918 with the collaboration of Dr A. K. Reischauer (father of Edwin Reischauer who became US Ambassador to Japan in the 1960s). There is a reason why her parents chose this particular university: Nitobe attended Sapporo Agricultural College (now Hokkaido University) in the year after Jiro's father Watase Torajiro, and they were friends. There, the students were inspired by Dr William S. Clark and many of them became Christians; Nitobe was baptised by an American Methodist missionary there. Some years later, Nitobe went to study at Johns Hopkins University in Baltimore and became a Quaker. He married an American, Mary Patterson Elkington, whom he met at the Religious Society of Friends. He became the founding President of Tokyo Woman's Christian University, and also influenced the foundation of a girls' school, Friends School, in Tokyo. These are both Quaker foundations. Nitobe knew the Watase family well and Jiro clearly felt that he wanted his daughter to be part of this progressive educational environment.

But there is another link: the architect who built the university's first building, Antonin Raymond, who was in Japan with Frank Lloyd Wright to build the Imperial Hotel. I have already mentioned Grandfather Jiro's friendship with Raymond in an earlier chapter. The campus chapel that Raymond built was probably the first building in Tokyo of perforated concrete, in the manner of Auguste Perret in Art Deco style. It is a smaller version of Perret's Notre Dame du Raincy. The Library building was clearly influenced by Frank Lloyd Wright in its horizontal planes and roof structure, as well as in the decorative motifs. They are important examples of early modernist architecture in Japan.

Yoko made many friends there, met them from time to time at reunions and has always contributed to the university's fund-raising. She liked the modernist environment and its Christian ethos. She often talked to me about the lovely chapel. And her study of nutrition came in more than useful in organising meals for her family, often telling us the nutritional content of various foods. But by the time she was graduating Japan was deeply engaged in war; with her friends from Gakushuin she joined the volunteer women's task force to help part-time at the Ministry of Finance with clerical duties. I do not think she or her friends came much into contact with the Ministry officials, and it was certainly no romantic breeding ground.

学習院々歌

一　もゆる火の　火中に死にて
　　また生るる　不死鳥の王
　　破れさびし　廃墟の上に
　　たちあがれ　新学習院

二　花は咲き　花はうつり
　　過ぎし世の　光栄をそ
　　まなかひに　世界をきらめ
　　現実を　生きてしぬべし

三　なげかいや　昔も今も
　　荒波も　狂けば狂へ
　　黒雲も　ゆく手とにらく
　　我が胸は　希望に高鳴る

四　ニノ々く　育てし我命
　　おのがしし　せとまもろとして
　　もろともに　せとまもろとし
　　常照らす　真理と平和

The gates of Gakushuin junior school. The verses begin:
'Rise again as the phoenix, consumed in the flames.'

6. The Defeat, the Occupation and a New Way of Life

~

Early Years of Marriage

The years after the war, with food scarce, were not easy for my mother. I remember going to the shopping streets near home in Sarumachi (now Takanawadai) to queue with her to buy rice with our ration coupons. She tried hard to make ends meet on Masaru's small salary; yet my father was a difficult and spoilt eater and would allow her to buy only the best cuts of beef. In those days the butchers sold whale meat disguised as beef, and we had to be ultra-careful. He would eat only white fish and only the best part, so Mother economised by eating the rest of the fish herself, saying he had left the most tasty parts. She grew some vegetables in the garden, tilling the ground herself, split wood to feed the boiler for bathwater and made clothes for us on the sewing machine at home. Her mother-in-law, though kind, was a super-efficient woman, setting high standards: perhaps not intentionally, but Mother felt the pressure. As my grandmother grew older she became frail and in the end bedridden. Although we had a qualified nurse living with us by then, Yoko had a very hard time looking after her. I know that it haunts her to this day and often she talks of that period with remorse. She had married into a family to live in an *oyashiki* (grand house) in a distinguished residential district of central Tokyo, but defeat brought quite unexpected hardships.

Yoko married my father in 1944; she hasn't talked much about those darkest years of the war but it must have been a lonely time. Her husband was at work day and night at the Ministry, she alone in a very large house. Having been used to a large household with parents, grandparents, brother and sisters, and relations all living together in an enclave, suddenly she was often on her own, her husband at work and parents-in-law evacuated to Karuizawa. Sirens would sound frequently when the American bombing started early in 1945; she would have had to rush to the shelter, only the maid with her.

The aftermath of defeat was a desolate time. It took a toll on her health; she developed pleurisy and for a while went home to Fukidecho to recover. It touched me very much to find my father's letters to her of this period in the drawer of her lacquered dressing table when I was clearing out our house; neither of my parents ever talked to me about their relationship or their feelings for one another. On the contrary, Mother had always given the impression that she had to sacrifice a lot in her married life and had never spoken of her affection for her husband. When he died, she said that she would be far more devastated if anything happened to one of us. I was surprised to hear this. In old *omiai* marriages, perhaps the couple were not so emotionally dependent as in love matches. But my mother has always struck me as being emotionally independent and self-contained.

A month or two before the surrender Masaru told Yoko that the government was moving in that direction. He told her never to mention it to anyone. Being at the heart of the government bureaucracy he knew the true situation. Mother told me that she was therefore not surprised to hear the Emperor's broadcast. Nevertheless, it was a devastatingly sad day. Yet the Army insurrection was in progress: like everyone else Yoko stayed fearfully inside the house in darkened rooms. Compounding the fear was the fact that her husband, as a government official, could be a target should the insurrection succeed.

I was born one very hot and humid summer day, two years into the marriage. My mother kept a diary of my first year, noting every small development: 'today she waved her arm,' 'today she stood up,' 'she took two steps by herself…' I was so touched when, amongst her papers, I recently found this little notebook. It was a shock of recognition, how much I had meant to her.

Four years later the US Occupation government imposed a heavy wealth tax, so that my father had to sell half of the house as well as a piece of woodland in Karuizawa, our family keeping the Western part of the house to live in. I spent a lot of time with my grandmother Sada, who lived with us. She was very protective of me and, in her old-fashioned way, didn't want to expose me to any risk while my mother had other, modern, ideas; Yoko still says I was allowed to become selfish and wilful, while Chahchah, not so much under the influence of Grandmother, or for other reasons, was a very good girl.

Whatever the case, when I was four years old I was enrolled in a kindergarten called *Shikokai*, which has now become a top kindergarten that parents try hard to get their children into. It was founded by a group of Gakushuin women who became Catholic nuns. The founder and President, Miss Tsunoda, was a cousin of my mother's friend, Nabeshima Matsuko. Mother walked me there every morning, perhaps half an hour away from home. I didn't want her to abandon me there; I was shy and frightened to be on my own; I cried and cried as she tried to leave. Moreover, I hated having to drink the milk they provided every morning. To persuade me they specially added some cocoa powder or vanilla essence to make it more palatable. Eventually my mother could sneak away without my noticing. In fact, I had a happy time at this Catholic kindergarten; I was used to praying on my knees anyway with my grandmother every morning and all the prayers, singing of hymns and crossing myself came naturally. My mother arranged that another child who lived near us would be collected in a rota with his attendant. So the little boy, Watanabe Koichi, and I went home after kindergarten together. Ko-chan, as I remember him, became a leading tailor and dressmaker in Ginza under the name Eikokuya.

When I got into Gakushuin junior school aged six, my parents amazingly allowed me to go on public transport unaccompanied. The protective grandmother was by then beginning to suffer from senility. The next-door neighbour's daughter, Kazuko, also attended the same school, so we travelled together each day. We took the tram to Akabanebashi and changed for Yotsuya. Classmates joined at other stations along the way. The journey took about an hour; in the mornings it could be crowded and we might not get a seat. We never allowed ourselves to speak to strangers, however tempting, as we were told strictly never to do so; child abduction was a common crime at the time. Children in Gakushuin uniform would be prime ransom targets. Some days I would get off at Kamiyacho and visit my grandmother; Mother would come to fetch me from Fukidecho in the late afternoon.

Winters were extremely cold and we all suffered from severe chilblains on our hands and feet. We were kitted out with knitted gloves and mufflers, but the gloves would freeze in deep winter. On rainy days we were never without umbrellas and raincoats, because the effects of the nuclear fallout from the bombing of Hiroshima and Nagasaki were thought to remain in the atmosphere and the rain would bring it down on us. Raindrops on umbrellas and raincoats burnt the material and made marks. We were afraid that it could fall on our skin. I was reminded of all this when I went to St Petersburg in 1995, ten years after the Chernobyl disaster; they were selling meat from the Chernobyl region separately at lower prices. My mother is to this day totally opposed to nuclear weapons and nuclear power stations; she had witnessed the long-lasting damage from contamination. Up to the end of the 1950s there were reports of deaths from cancer among those who were in the affected areas of Hiroshima and Nagasaki.

We economised on everything for our family to make ends meet. Even as a young child I was fully aware of the sacrifices my parents made to save money; I remember refraining from mentioning my outgrown shoes lest it put pressure on them. I always had my aunts' old school uniforms and clothes that Grandmother Hanako got out of the storage room. But it should not be thought that I was brought up in total privation. By any standards I was very spoilt; Grandmother Sada bought me a long fur cape when I was about one year old; as it was a cape I could wear it for many years as I grew up. While I was at kindergarten she also bought me a beautiful black velvet dress with a Brussels lace collar which I loved to wear to parties. My father took me to Shirokiya department store in Gotanda and bought me a handbag I liked. I proudly showed it to Grandmother Hanako but she said it was too sophisticated for a young girl. I also went with my father to Gotanda post office to collect a large case of tangerines that my mother's cousin sent us each winter from their horticultural business. We took my pram with us, loaded the heavy case and pushed it up the hill back home. We always had a lot of tangerines and we sometimes grilled them in the embers of *hibachi* (hand braziers), and also made them into a hot jelly by squeezing the juice and heating it with *kuzu* (arrowroot powder) – a very warming drink. Every Sunday my father took me on a walk to Meguro where he bought me cocoa at Kosugi, a sophisticated café with aspidistras and potted palms and ceiling fans, redolent of Edwardian times. It sold exotic fruit such as grapefruit and pineapple, as well as good coffee and cocoa. I loved these outings and would recount each visit to my mother and grandmother. When life got a little easier by the mid-1950s, on some Sundays Father took us all out to Ginza for window shopping and vanilla ice cream. On those occasions we all dressed up, my mother, Chahchah and I in our going-out outfits, and my father always in a dark suit and hat. Yoko always wore high heels; sometimes my father bought her a new pair from Washington Shoes in Ginza's main street.

Mother bought us two white bunnies with red eyes, who lived in a pen enclosed with chicken wire in the garden; Chahchah and I played with them and fed them carrots. When it snowed our mother taught us how to make ice cream; we buried in the snow a small tin of cream with vanilla essence in to freeze it. She taught me to bake sponge cakes and decorate them with candied fruit, and cream through a paper funnel with a nozzle tip. We also baked potatoes in the embers of the bonfire in the garden. Mother was always innovative about ways to entertain us. When we were a little more grown up we had a Scotch terrier in the garden. We were very fond of this dog and were sad to have to give it away when we left for Washington. In those days it was thought dangerous to eat imported fruit from Taiwan or even Hawaii, because cholera was rampant; we were therefore not allowed to eat pineapple or bananas. I longed as a child to have them and the candyfloss from street stalls, but our parents forbade us to touch anything from street vendors. Same went for *gyoza*, the Chinese dumplings that have become popular with *ramen*. Mother therefore took the initiative and made them for us herself (kept secret from our father, who detested such things). I remember thinking hers must be better than the commercial offerings.

The Allied Occupation

I did not experience the atmosphere in the immediate aftermath of the surrender in August 1945 and I was too young to remember the first few years of the Occupation. Nor have I heard my parents talk about it. But some of my family members'

196

memoirs speak of their personal experiences. I can only surmise that the initial shock, tension and fear must have been electric. The overwhelming uncertainty of what was to come over their lives could hardly have been bearable. For government officials, the implications could have been manifold. The future of the Japanese people was thrown into perpetual uncertainty. Tokyo had been devastated with air raids and bombing throughout 1945, the most famous of which was Operation Meetinghouse in March 1945, regarded as the most destructive in human history. Although my families escaped the raids on their homes unscathed, their neighbours didn't; frequent sirens sent them into air raid shelters they had built themselves in their gardens. Those who could evacuated to the countryside; my parents clearly couldn't as my father was a government official.

Tokyo at the end of the war was a scene of utter defeat and destruction. As winter set in, with the scarcity of energy and food, the extreme cold took its toll on people's health. Tuberculosis was rampant, children suffered from severe chilblains and infections. Families huddled around braziers and hand warmers and around the *kotatsu* (a low table with padded cover and a heater underneath). As a baby, born almost a year after the end of the war, I was lucky to have my mother's milk. Though food was rationed, her family had access to farms in the country and we were luckier than most. Yoko, being ingenious and having studied nutrition, cooked leaves of radishes and carrots, turnip tops and things that most people would have thrown away. In retrospect, I know that it was hard for my mother and her friends who had been brought up in very protected circumstances. Yet they all endured with untold courage the misery of the war and the reality of the aftermath in defeat. It was their commitment to survival, firm belief in hope, and their willingness to adapt that gave them a new life. They found themselves suddenly having to wield an axe for firewood, carry baskets to the fishmonger or dig small allotments to grow vegetables for the family; and somehow survived to keep a cheerful face. In the poverty-stricken, war-torn city, where extreme hunger was the norm, pilfering was rampant. I remember Aunt Naoko telling us that she had managed to grow a good-sized *daikon* (long white radish) on her allotment; she decided to give it another day to grow in size, but the next morning she went to collect it only to find that someone had stolen it overnight: she went home in tears.

The Allied Occupation of Japan was led by General Douglas MacArthur, the Supreme Commander Allied Powers (SCAP). It is the only time in the long history of Japan that a foreign power has occupied the country. The process through which MacArthur and the US Administration agreed that the Showa Emperor should remain on the imperial throne, following the Human Declaration of 1 January 1946, needs no further elaboration here. As I mentioned earlier, my great-uncle Admiral Yamanashi played a crucial role in this historic episode. The wartime Cabinet was replaced with one acceptable to the Allies and committed to implementing the terms of the Potsdam Declaration, which among other things called for the country to become a multi-party parliamentary democracy. The first postwar Prime Minister was Shidehara Kijuro, a well-known pacifist statesman before and after the war. It is interesting that the US accepted him, an aristocrat (a baron) and first cousin of the President of the Mitsubishi *zaibatsu*, Iwasaki Koyata. One of the industrial reforms that the Americans put into force was to demolish the structure of *zaibatsu* oligopoly. Shidehara was the leader of the Progressive Party and advocated closer ties with China and Russia after the war, but his conservative economic policies were unpopular with the leftist parties in Japan. He had been Ambassador to the US before the war and later became Foreign Minister and Speaker of the Diet, remaining a politician until his death. He was succeeded as Prime Minister by Yoshida Shigeru; in fact, the Americans had 'purged' Hatoyama

Ichiro just as he was chosen to succeed Shidehara, and Yoshida was appointed instead.

The Japanese government introduced sweeping social reforms and implemented economic policies that recalled America's New Deal of the 1930s under President Roosevelt. The Japanese constitution, previously modelled on the German constitution of the mid-nineteenth century, was overhauled and the Emperor's theoretical powers – based on the notion of his lineal descent from the Shinto deity who founded Japan – were removed, creating a constitutional monarchy similar to those in Britain and elsewhere. The Diet continued its bicameral system: the House of Peers was renamed the Upper House and became subject to popular elections, while the House of Commoners became the Lower House with general elections held on a constituency basis. The Americans abolished the class system and peerages were to survive only for the Emperor and his direct descendants, each of whom was given the title of Prince or Princess (but on marriage a female descendant would lose her title). For the first time women were enfranchised. Large agricultural land holdings were compulsorily broken up, with the result that farm units became small and agriculture inefficient. Agrarian incomes thereby became subject to income support policies (similar to those in the UK before it joined the EU with its Common Agricultural Policy based on price support). The New Yen was introduced, vastly devaluing the currency; in 1949 the Occupation government fixed the exchange rate at Yen 360 to $1.00, as it remained until 1972. (Until the start of the war the conversion rate was 3.6 to 1.) On its introduction all bank accounts were frozen and only limited amounts could be withdrawn to be exchanged for New Yen.

The US Occupation command headquarters were established in various locations in central Tokyo, with suitable buildings commandeered. The main headquarters was the Daiichi Seimei Building in Marunouchi, one of the few buildings not bombed out of existence in 1945. A large, imposing stone edifice that remains to this day, built in the early Edwardian period with heavily ornate bronze doors behind a tall portico, this was the centre of their governing base. One of my grandparents' houses on their estate near Toranomon was commandeered to be Occupation Headquarters 5. Itohei's last palatial residence in Yokohama was taken over to be the Occupation military's social club. In Akiya, near Yokosuka where the US naval headquarters were based, one of my grandparents' summer houses overlooking Sagami Bay became the home of the Commander-in-Chief of the US Navy at Yokosuka, whose children I played with on summer holidays.

There were GIs everywhere, looking relaxed and happy-go-lucky; I encountered them often on buses and trams on the way to school. They did not seem at all threatening to me as a young child. They had their own shops, PXs, in a street called 'Ameya-yokocho' near Ueno, where they bought American supplies of everyday items such as Palmolive soap, Colgate toothpaste, Hershey's chocolates and Westinghouse coffee, but also some good quality clothes and handbags. They rented houses for the officers but many of the soldiers lived in messes. Our next-door neighbours let their house to a middle-ranking officer who stayed on for some years after the Occupation ended. We played with the children every day and became very good friends. The Wise family were from the west coast of America and Mrs Wise made French fries for the children every afternoon; I loved visiting them to share this 'delicacy'. I remember being rather shocked to see her clean their shoes with knives from their dinner service, to get mud off the soles; to me eating equipment should not go anywhere near mud! They were kind and hospitable; Mrs Wise was astonished to find that the interior of our house was grand and sophisticated, quite unlike the one they had rented. When we left for America in 1960, as my father was posted to our Embassy in Washington DC, it was very sad for us children to say goodbye; Mrs Wise taught us to say in English "We are so sorry to say goodbye" and we chorused this endlessly across the garden fence.

The American GIs and the occupying military personnel by and large behaved quite differently from the Soviets in Europe. The Soviet Union was not involved directly in the occupation or the reconstruction of Japan. There were some 750,000 Japanese captured in the USSR and Mongolia who were sent to Siberian labour camps; the last of the ships bringing over a thousand men back returned to Japan as late as December 1956. Many of the Americans, though, took up with Japanese women and, like the story of Lt. Pinkerton in Puccini's opera *Madama Butterfly*, written half a century earlier, set up homes and had children but abandoned them when posted back home. 'Half-castes' in those days were ostracised, as Japanese basic instincts were more racialist than today; they were not regarded as proper Japanese. Though hushed and unspoken, such prejudices must have been hard for those offspring of the Occupation era. Quite a few of the GIs, however, did take their new families back to America. My Joint Chairman in the Japan Society, Lew Radbourne, who as a young Army officer had been part of the Occupation, said that the American government had a much more relaxed attitude generally towards the Japanese; the British and other Allied governments strictly forbade their military to consort with Japanese women. The British had wanted to impose a more punishing regime on Japan: direct control, with the aim of destroying all existing national institutions. However, the Occupation took the form of a US Occupation government with an Allied military presence.

There was no atmosphere of hostility: the Japanese appeared to accept the Americans and even aspired to be like them in habit and dress; wanted to learn to speak American English, and to own sophisticated goods imported from the US. America became essentially the land of dreams for the Japanese. It was not that their leaders, government officials, and the general public approached the Americans with a sense of contrition. In accepting defeat, they went about the business of rebuilding with American aid with a constructive attitude, maintained their dignity and pride, and spoke to the former enemy as equal human beings. My mother's first cousin, Kosaka Zentaro, a senior politician who happened to be in San Francisco and witnessed the signing of the Peace Treaty in 1951, wrote that Prime Minister Yoshida looked confident and forceful, hardly behaving like the leader of a defeated nation. Initially the Allies intended that the Occupation would take the form of a direct military government, the US military supported by the other Allies taking control of Japan. In a frantic attempt to avoid this humiliation, the Japanese negotiated an 'indirect' Occupation, so that Occupation policies for reform would be presented to the Japanese government for implementation through the Diet and the administration of Japan. The national government therefore functioned without interruption or loss of centralised control. The US Occupation government was merely superimposed on the existing system and institutions.

The Americans were not patronising or overly heavy-handed. In the beginning they badly misjudged the prevailing sentiment of the people and allowed the appointment of Prince Higashikuni as Prime Minister. Many Japanese could hardly believe that the former minister for the Army would become their new Prime Minister immediately on surrender. But on being presented with the memorandum on the Occupation agenda, hurriedly made immediately after the signing of the surrender, the Higashikuni Cabinet resigned *en masse*, fearing a communist insurrection. At an official level, relations were generally respectful and normally courteous once agreement had been reached, rather hurriedly in the very last days of 1945, that the imperial system of government would be continued under a new constitution, with certain individuals 'purged' from governmental and other influential jobs. (Shortly after the Occupation began in August 1945 the screening of 2.3 million Japanese citizens began and 210,000 were purged, meaning that they could not hold public or important private offices. Those removed from their jobs included some Cabinet ministers, many members of the national and local government offices, some members of the Diet, mayors of large cities, governors of all the prefectures, local government politicians, officers in the former largest 250 companies, and members of patriotic and nationalistic societies, as well as senior military personnel.) Of course, many of those who had been in commanding positions in government and the military were incarcerated in Sugamo Prison and eventually tried for war crimes. The prison in fact was run by Japanese officers and food was prepared and served by the inmates. They grew their own vegetables in the prison grounds. It was said that the wartime Prime Minister and Commander-in-Chief, General Tojo, served meals as a waiter there. I remember my mother's father occasionally saying "I went to Sugamo today to see my friend…" By and large, the general public, many of whom in any case had been against the war from the beginning, were not opposed to the purge; they were in some ways glad that the militarists who had led the country into war were being appropriately punished.

A close friend of our family, Kato Tadao (加藤匡夫), who later became Ambassador to Britain, wrote in his book of reminiscences that he came across some brash middle-ranking GHQ officers who were unnecessarily aggressive. During the Occupation the Foreign Ministry had no powers in conducting foreign relations: he and his colleagues in the Ministry were tasked to be liaison officers with GHQ, to convey the directives of GHQ to the relevant Japanese authorities. One day an American lieutenant told him to put an order into effect immediately, and should he fail he would be put in prison. Kato protested that, as a liaison officer, he was doing his best to explain GHQ policy even in the face of strong protest from the Japanese side, and that they should appreciate his efforts at mediation. He told the young officer that to threaten him with imprisonment was out of order. The officer had been told by the command that the directive needed to be passed by 7 p. m., and had even gone to the length of stopping all the clocks in the Diet at 7; he told Kato that the Diet might debate the issue for as long as it wanted into the night but it had to be passed. The officer relented and invited Kato to a tea party in his lodgings the next day, where he brought his girlfriend.

Kato was not alone in having encountered this type of high-handedness. A rather more senior Ministry of Finance official, Watanabe Takeshi, who later became Japan's first finance representative in Washington after the San Francisco Peace Treaty was signed – and a decade after that the first President of the Asian Development Bank – quotes in his memoirs a number of instances in which he engaged in severe verbal combat at GHQ during the Occupation. He too found that his opposite number would become friendly once the argument was settled.

The Allied Occupation tried to restructure the bureaucracy and remove the concentration of powers within certain ministries. The Home Ministry (内務省), which previously had overseen local administration, police, elections and public works, was broken up and redesignated the Ministry of Internal Affairs and Communications. My mother's first cousin, Kosaka Zentaro, was involved in one such restructuring attempt while he was Vice Minister (Political) at the Ministry of Finance in the Yoshida Cabinet in 1947 and was one day summoned to GHQ. He recalled in his memoirs how, speaking in a peremptory tone, they ordered him to break up the Ministry of Finance as they considered it excessively powerful. They argued that the Ministry was concerned with both sides of the national budget, the receipts as well as the disbursements. A Lieutenant-Colonel Markham spoke severely, saying "There will be opposition, to be sure; GHQ will support you fully in breaking it up. Fight with an iron rod!" He underlined his point by taking the curtain down from the window and swinging around the metal curtain rod! Kosaka responded strongly, arguing that the principal issue of the national economy was how to tackle rising inflation and that balancing the national budget was the immediate concern. That could be handled effectively only within one ministry. The GHQ never again contacted the Ministry of Finance about this matter. It survived as the most powerful ministry of the Japanese government.

A similar motive was seen in an attempt by the Americans to distance the Bank of Japan from the Ministry of Finance. GHQ evidently tried to stop the appointments of senior Ministry officials to the central bank. According to his correspondence at the time, my father challenged the rationale behind this attempt during his mission in 1951 and asserted that the Americans did not fully appreciate the culture, tradition nor the current political situation in the Japanese bureaucracy. The Bank of Japan remained under the aegis of the Ministry.

At first GHQ's policy was to emasculate Japan and, at the insistence of the other Allies – the Soviet Union, the UK and Australia – the leaders of its communist party, who had been imprisoned during the war, were set free. This resulted in them dominating the labour union general council and strengthened their hold elsewhere, especially in the national railways, teachers' and public sector workers' unions. They threw their weight about, behaving in a classically 'bolshie' manner in public, accusing the wartime government of mistaken policies, infiltrating government offices and insisting on their own version of 'reform'. The Soviet Union's aim was to turn Japan communist, and its sympathisers increased dangerously in number. A general strike was planned for February 1947, but was banned by GHQ. The Americans reversed their policy as the Korean War started in June 1950, and the labour unions were mollified into a calmer posture. But GHQ strengthened its surveillance of communist infiltration through the media. Kosaka Tokusaburo, brother of Zentaro, wrote that the influential regional newspaper company of which he was President, *Shinano Mainichi Shimbun* (信濃毎日新聞), was raided by GHQ. *Shinano Mainichi* had been founded by his grandfather in the nineteenth century and was an independent regional newspaper of renown. The communist infiltrators had put up their flag on the rooftop and started interfering in the editorial department. He said that he could tolerate neither the communists' attempt at editorial interference – let alone a takeover of the company – nor GHQ's attempt to impose its own ideology. He therefore embarked on collective bargaining; tortuous and violent negotiations followed but the communists dispersed. And GHQ was seen off too.

Tokusaburo also wrote of his stupendous effort to rebuild the family company Shin-Etsu Chemical immediately after the war. Tokusaburo started out working as a journalist after university but was persuaded by his father to join the family firm. Immediately after the war it was he who saw the company's future in silicone and, during the Occupation period, flew to New York in the hope of obtaining licences from GE and Dow Corning, which together held all the manufacturing patents, on a cross-licensing arrangement. He was rebuffed and cold-shouldered by both: faced with this unknown young man in his mid-thirties, from a recent wartime enemy, the memories and anger at the attack on Pearl Harbor were still fresh. Tokusaburo wrote in his memoirs, which he sent me on publication, that he was not going to give up and made repeated journeys, perhaps seven times. He could not find the words to express how miserable a time it was, staying in decrepit hotels and living on only five dollars a day. But his tenacity was rewarded: in the final days of 1952 as he landed back in Japan from what he thought was another unsuccessful visit, an airmail envelope arrived, as if to have been chasing after him, from GE enclosing a draft contract for a licence. Early in the New Year a contract was signed and the Deputy President of GE said to him "Your company is tiny but we were overcome by your passion. We are delighted." He did not forget to note in his book that it was 'who you know' that can swing your fortune: on that visit he had met on a Northwest Airlines flight a Vice President of Morgan Guaranty Trust, a Mr Anderson, coincidentally a friend of the President of Mitsubishi Bank, Kato Takeo. Not only was Mitsubishi Bank the main bank of Shin-Etsu Chemical, but Tokusaburo's father Junzo was well regarded by Mr Kato in another context. Anderson had put in a good word to GE. Eventually Dow Corning was also persuaded to grant a licence. It was Tokusaburo too who paved the way for Shin-Etsu to become the world's largest manufacturer of semiconductor silicon, and set up Shin-Etsu Semiconductor Ltd. There is little doubt that Shin-Etsu's continuing preeminent position in the world's chemical industry today owes much to his unfailing efforts and trustworthy character. He was persuaded in the early 1970s to stand for election to the Diet.

Zentaro's son Kosaka Kenji (小坂憲次), also a LDP politician, inherited his father's constituency and was the Minister for Education under Prime Minister Koizumi. He is still in touch with my mother.

The years after surrender were tumultuous and stormy in Japanese politics. There were six Prime Ministers in the nine years between 1945 and 1954, representing in turn Progressive, Liberal, Socialist and Democratic parties. Government officials and politicians worked furiously day and night, from crisis to crisis. They hardly saw their families. My mother's first cousin, Zentaro, could not even hold his young wife's funeral until an election was concluded in 1952, as she had died the day before the snap election was called.

It is of historical significance that the San Francisco Peace Treaty of 1951 was concluded as a bilateral treaty between the US and Japan; this allowed Japan to be an intact independent country. The other Allies were negotiating for a treaty that would have given each of them a zone under concession, in the way the occupying powers had negotiated over Germany. These negotiations were protracted through the years 1950–51. The US, as effectively the sole occupying power (the other Allies neither played any significant roles nor had much power in the Occupation), took the initiative to conclude the treaty; this was all the more urgent to them as the situation in the Korean peninsula began to threaten the US Pacific frontier. On the day that the Peace Treaty was signed, the Japan-US Security Treaty was also signed by Yoshida in an adjoining but separate building. As Kosaka Zentaro remarked, this had been a totally unexpected development, both to him and to most close observers: all the more surprising since Kosaka was one of Yoshida's closest political protégés. The Security Treaty gave the US military bases in Japan and established a close military alliance between the two nations. It was vital for the US to obtain these in the days running up to the Korean War, and it had been a condition that the US agree to a bilateral treaty. The following day the national Press in Japan was shocked and leftist sympathisers enraged, but the treaty had been signed and sealed. As my father wrote a few years later, Japan owed its independence to the US State Department and the persuasive skills of Dean Acheson there, who in overruling SCAP moved swiftly to have both treaties signed. The history of Japan since the war might have been very different had that not succeeded. Yoshida, the veteran anti-war politician who had been sidelined during the war, was more than aware of the difficult political landscape in Japan and managed to keep the talks for a Security Treaty secret.

The threat of communism remained real in the first decade after the war; the Socialist Party and the smaller communist party were more of a force to be reckoned with then than they are today. After the Occupation ended, successive Prime Ministers, notably Hatoyama and Kishi, tried to balance Japan's diplomatic alliance by closer cooperation with the Soviet Union and China, rather than relying solely on the US. In fact, the very first Prime Minister (after the debacle of the Higashikuni government) at the end of the war, Shidehara Kijuro, also shared this conviction. For sentimental reasons, rather than political, sharing a cultural heritage derived from geographical proximity, Japan continues to have a kind of love-hate relationship with China. Even in the 1970s, when China was virtually closed to foreign visitors, the Chargé d'Affaires at the Chinese Embassy in London, on encountering me at a luncheon given by Peter Tapsell MP (later Sir Peter) at James Capel where he was a partner, seeing that I was Japanese specially asked if I would visit his country. When I said I wanted to but that this did not seem possible, he advised that a transit visa would allow for some days in Peking on the way back from Japan. With the Soviet Union (now Russia) the relationship has been different; Japan has always feared the Russians invading Hokkaido as they had attempted in the mid-nineteenth century, when the Royal Navy Far East squadron saw off Russian incursions into the Japan Sea across the Sea of Okhotsk. Moreover, the Russians have resented Japan's occupation of Sakhalin and the Kurile islands and the settlement at the end of the war over these territories has not been completed to this day. Although a not insignificant number of senior Japanese politicians have espoused the notion of a 'modified capitalism' since the war, drawing lessons from Marxist writings, not many continue to maintain any attachment to communist ideology today.

Despite the fierce battles of war, cruel loss of lives, often of the nearest friends and family, the humiliation of defeat, and the Occupation Army taking over their homeland with the brashness of victors, which surely they must have resented, the Japanese took on the United States as their principal ally and adopted American ways almost unconditionally. It was all the more surprising as the effects of nuclear fallout persisted for at least the following two decades; we feared rain bringing down atmospheric nuclear fallout and always wore full-length raincoats and gloves, and carried umbrellas in the rain. Reports of deaths from cancer as a result of exposure to residual radioactive particles were common. I was shocked to find that the Americans and British had a carefree attitude to rain and often went out in it unprotected, until I realised that 'American rain' was radiation-free!

All this does not do justice to the lifelong suffering of more than 600,000 *hibakusha* (those who were exposed to and survived the atomic bomb explosions over Hiroshima and Nagasaki). The keloid scars and bodily deformities permanently inflicted on those survivors were merely the outward manifestation of the anguish, torment, and emotional suffering that marked their lives. A recently published novel by a South American writer, Andres Neuman, *Fracture*, is a masterly depiction of that human experience. In a distant corner of my memory lies what we were shown and taught about the consequences of the atomic bomb at junior school. For those of us, young children in the 1950s, it was another world.

The Americans who went to Japan on duty at the end of the war took home with them valuable memories that they recounted to their families and friends; most of all they told of the beautiful landscape and the friendships they fostered with Japanese people. At ground level, in the face of extreme food shortages, some Japanese would offer their meagre supplies of comestibles to the equally starving American soldiers they encountered in the streets; similarly, the Americans would often distribute what they had been able to obtain from their PX deliveries (that were by no means plentiful). Many also wrote affectionately to their Japanese counterparts on their return home. Some of this correspondence provides poignant reminders of the period immediately after the war in Japan at a human level. In his Christmas card of December 1951, sent to my family from Harvard University, Professor John D. Montgomery writes:

"I remember Christmas in Kofu in 1946 – unbelievably cold, and with hundreds of callers who sang carols to my piano in the wreckage of a city of hope and despair. It was a brave Christmas to see, maybe the most impressive I shall ever experience. I hope my next one in Japan is as fine. And in the hope that you may visit us again…"

Montgomery had been sent to Japan with the US Army at the end of the war to join the Occupation personnel and had just returned earlier that year.

Perhaps it was the privilege of the victors, but the Americans were fundamentally instantly-friendly people, unlike the more reserved British and Europeans. That may have been because few Americans were ever in Japanese captivity during the war as, for example, the British and the Australians were. The Americans were generally kind to young and old alike and that was reciprocated; we were brought up to be pro-American. Americans have the confidence of people who believe in their values unreservedly; the corollary of that, of course, was their uninhibited desire to extend their values to peoples of different cultures. That was a theme that my father raised with American scholars and officials during his first visit to the US on a government mission.

The First Government Mission to the US, 1951
The visit to America that my father made in March–June 1951, with two other colleagues from the Administrative Management Agency of the MoF (行政管理庁), was eventually to influence the course of his career. At the time he was Chief of the Minister's Secretariat (行政管理秘書課長) and his work centred on the US Occupation's Administrative Reform programme, which had to be passed through the Diet. He was the youngest member of that mission: it made a profound impact on him. One of his colleagues was Onogi Katsunobu, who later became President of the Long-Term Credit Bank of Japan and a friend to many British financiers. The mission focused on the study of the

structure of the US Administration and how the government worked in practice. It was arranged by the Governmental Affairs Institute in Washington DC, as an attempt by the US government to foster better understanding and form closer ties between the US and the defeated nations (there was a similar arrangement with Germany). It was called the National Leaders' Project. Japan was still under Allied Occupation, which ended the following year in April 1952 after the signing of the San Francisco Peace Treaty of September 1951. The mission, having spent time in Washington DC, then travelled to New York, Boston and Cambridge, Chicago and finally San Francisco. In each place they had a packed programme of lectures, seminars and discussion sessions with officials, political scientists and scholars.

My father was away in America for those three months in 1951. He sent me a postcard every week; almost all end with the message: "Don't say you are bored to your mother." Yoko put all the postcards in an album: I have treasured it as a lasting memory of my father from my childhood. In some ways, our family life gained an American dimension after his return, one that we were proud of. Airmail envelopes containing letters from his new friends arrived, as did American magazines – for Christmas Lorne Freeman gave him a subscription to *Time* magazine and Caroll Ford to *Vermont Life*. I decided to collect foreign stamps and loved looking at the beautiful scenery of the American countryside and the way people looked in the photographs. Some of my father's US friends even came to visit us. Professor Ralph Braibanti was one of the first of these; my father took him to play golf and to my grandparents' home. At the conclusion of their visit to Washington, the members of the mission gave a farewell luncheon for all those whom they met there; in return they received a letter of appreciation calling them the most impressive visitors they had ever had. On the personal level, lasting friendships had been formed.

Masaru continued their discussions by correspondence for years after returning to Japan, and the resultant interchange of ideas was by no means one-sided: while the Americans wanted to explain the fundamental tenets of their democracy and government to Japanese officials, and ultimately convince them of their superiority, they also had an enlightened wish to understand Japanese culture and the basis of government as practised in Japan, so that the administrative reform programme of the Occupation could benefit from insights gained from the Japanese delegates. Evidently my father strongly challenged some assertions made by the Americans, based on an inadequate understanding of Japanese culture. After the visit some of them wrote to him saying how much they appreciated his frankness and his analytical mind. Professor Ralph Braibanti wrote on 7 June 1951, on the conclusion of the mission: "I am especially appreciative of your critical analysis of the course of study. I have considered this analysis carefully, and I am making some fundamental changes in the course of study for the next group, largely as a result of your suggestions. I thank you very much for these comments." What is impressive is that those eminent scholars (who were close to the US Administration) were very ready to listen and to admit their ignorance and their wish to modify the thrust of the US Occupation's reform agenda. They wished to continue to debate through correspondence to find common ground, without any hint of patronising attitudes.

One of those scholars, Caroll W. Ford, Dean of the Babson Institute in Cambridge, Massachusetts and at times Professor at Wellesley, wrote to my father on 1 October 1951, just a few months after the end of the mission:

"I know that, during your visit here, you must at times have been disappointed at American indifference to or lack of understanding of Japanese problems. Please have patience with this. It is an ignorant attitude, not a hostile one, and arises I think from the fact that the US is just growing up into an adult among nations whereas Japan has been, necessarily, a far more internationally minded nation than the United States."

He pointed to the insularity of the Americans:

"I think it is time that college students in America became well acquainted with the USSR, British Socialism and the working class, and radical movements in different countries. It is tragic that Americans know so little about the economic systems, conditions and problems in other countries." (October 1952.)

One theme that comes through in those letters is the US desire for Japanese rearmament and a strong belief that a nation must have its own military capability as a sign of independence and sovereignty. It was of course the time of the Korean War (1950–1953) and the US very much regarded Japan as a buffer in East Asia. Caroll Ford wrote (13 December 1953.):

"As I see it Japanese function is to act as the far eastern bulwark of the Americans, Japanese and Allied defense system for a very long time. If this is to be the case Japan must never be in want of any needed financial and other support she desires to receive from the US... With all her problems Japan will continue to be a great and powerful country. It is therefore unthinkable that Japan will not in time build up and contribute to her own national defense – by rearmament – with the continued strong support of the US."

That expresses well the foundation of the US–Japan alliance that has dominated the second half of the twentieth century across the Pacific; in Japan this has been fundamental to the liberal/conservative political consensus of the Liberal Democratic Party, while the Socialist Party has opposed it. (In September 1960, for example, the visit of President Eisenhower had to be cancelled because of Socialist protests and mass demonstrations.) Half a century later, a new generation of politicians began to reconsider the degree of dependence on and allegiance to the US as being potentially inimical to Japan's national interests. But its foreign policy has in the postwar period been defined by this consensus.

Hatoyama Yukio's Democratic Party of Japan, founded in the late 1990s, challenged this orthodoxy and advocated closer relations with Russia, as Hatoyama's grandfather, Hatoyama Ichiro (leader of the Free Party), had done as Prime Minister in the early 1950s in a somewhat different context.

As I write, Japan is once again hotly debating the revision of the elements of the constitution that provide for military capability only for self-defence. Conservative elements in Europe, especially in Britain, appear to be opposed to this change. That caution seems to stem from the British experience during the war in the Far East. I have myself always felt, though, that the British and the Europeans have never understood how close Japan is to the US, nor that the US attaches cardinal importance to the Pacific frontier.

Extraordinarily enough, one of my father's friends at the Governmental Affairs Institute – Lorne Freeman, one of the young women who organised the logistics of the mission – wrote to him in 1951 asking if the newly enfranchised women in Japan were pacifists, and wondering if, ironically, this aspect of turning Japan more 'democratic' had an adverse impact on what was intended by the Americans. Her foresight appears seventy years later to be proven, as female voters seem to be more opposed to the revision of the constitution today. Professor Ralph Braibanti, writing to my father on 27 August 1951, also already foresaw this problem when advocating that the Japanese constitution should be amended to allow Japan to rearm. His suggestion was: "Some educative means must be devised by which the newly enfranchised women are sufficiently convinced of the realities of international politics so that they will see the need for maintaining an armed force." Ironically enough, Japan's suffragette movement had gained momentum in the 1920s and draft legislation was drawn up in 1927 to enfranchise women to vote in national elections, only to have been lost as militarism gained ground. It is unlikely, though, in my view that the history of

1930s Japan would have been any different with female suffrage.

The newly enfranchised women took their voting responsibilities seriously. And they understood that how they voted was their own personal decision. My mother, for example, would never tell my father how she voted, nor would my father ask her – perhaps there was no need since Mother has always been a staunch supporter of the LDP. However, it is not just women who today are hesitant about the constitutional revision; Japanese people are generally more pacifist than most, because of the experience of the nuclear devastation of Hiroshima and Nagasaki. Moreover, the younger generation, which has no memories of the war or the hardships of the postwar years, has little concern about these matters. Looking at it kindly, they are internationalists: but the older generation regrets their lack of patriotism.

How earnestly those scholars such as Professor John D. Montgomery (Harvard) and Professor Ralph Braibanti (Duke) took up the study of US–Japan relations is quite remarkable. Montgomery was writing a book on the effect the purges of 'war criminals' had on Japanese society and on the lives of those purged. My father had fierce arguments with him on a number of occasions, especially on the over-reliance on statistical analysis leading to mistaken conclusions; Montgomery carefully retorted that studies of social anthropology and social science were in their infancy and could not be relied upon. At one point, my father very much challenged Montgomery's notion of conservatism in Japan and they argued about the method of appointments in the Bank of Japan. Others, like Caroll Ford, wrote to take sides with my father, saying nothing could be done successfully by Americans in dealing with the Japanese or any other foreigners without the most thorough and intimate grasp of the culture, psychology and characteristics of the people.

Masaru studied the development of American democracy and thought deeply about the American frontier. He believed that nothing like the expanding frontiers of the previous 150 years of American history would ever again appear; that American democratic development happened under certain favourable conditions; and that in future, in the course of historical development, American expansion of the frontier would entail its modified application to other areas such as Japan and Asia. How prescient that thought turned out to be; the conflict in Asia through the 1960s in Vietnam and the more recent protest movements against 'globalisation' ('Americanisation' to many) are surely the manifestation of the limits to the American frontier. Economic necessities on the part of the US dictated that Pax Americana had to pursue a modified agenda. The economic recovery and growth of Western Europe and Japan in the postwar period were made possible by American aid, and the Bretton Woods system was based on the assumption that the overwhelming economic strength of the US would continue for the foreseeable future. The triumph of the West over the Soviet Union liberated the countries of Eastern Europe from the oppression of communism and Soviet control, but twenty-five years later Russia's increasingly hostile stance towards the West is once again creating serious geopolitical tensions. China's activities in the Pacific and most recently in Hong Kong are surely posing similar challenges in a new Cold War. Japan and major powers of the West are on the one hand questioning the extent to which America is willing to share its power and on the other the inevitable consequences of losing absolute reliance on US military strength.

Montgomery remained a close friend of Masaru's and they communicated often over many years, delving into the various issues facing each other's countries; they sent each other newly published books, discussing their conclusions and criticising methods of analysis. In one of his letters Montgomery revealed an interesting observation that is worth introducing:

"I think you are one of the few people who could intelligently discuss the question that has recently crossed my mind. It has to do with the relationship between novels and a national culture, especially in years of crisis and turmoil. You are profoundly well-read in American culture, with a range covering the extremes of popular literature and professional writing: from your readings I am sure you have derived some insight into our postwar preoccupations in both the First and Second World Wars. You may have noticed, as I did, that the First World War brought to American letters a disturbing recognition of the horror and brutalities of the battlefield, with an attendant pessimism and avoidance of values of a moral and spiritual order. In the post-Second World War novels, however, I have observed some recurrence of the 'shock-motif' with emphasis on the soldier's vocabulary and Freudian inclinations: but this has not been the dominant theme of our postwar literature. Rather, it seems to me, we have recently begun to try to recreate a sense of heroism and devotion, together with a pragmatic attentiveness to man's social behaviour.

"In Germany, on the other hand, defeat has brought a most disturbing nostalgia for Nazi greatness. In both memoirs and novels one encounters examples of frantic indignation against the Western Allies for failing to recognise the seeds of German greatness. Democracy is attacked as archaic, rationalistic, and simpleminded. The irrational elements in man have received so much more attention in recent German literature that I am convinced this seems to be a national trend. It often is brilliantly written and closely reasoned but the net effect is most disturbing.

"In Japan, I am far less familiar with the postwar writing. After the First World War, the impressionistic sketches by Akutagawa struck the Western mind as significant; but I have no way of knowing how much they were admired in Japan or whether they were in any sense typical of the postwar novel. As for Second World War novels and memoirs, I have only a general impression that the Japanese seem to show little of the unhealthy tendencies I spoke of in Germany. For example, the memoirs of people like

Shigemitsu do not seem designed to justify the militarists of the past, or even the leaders who permitted them to rise to power. In short, I have a feeling that the Japanese people themselves have repudiated militarism and nationalism (if indeed they had ever wholeheartedly accepted them). This is too profound a question for an outsider to guess, but it is of great interest to me and I would very much appreciate hearing from you about it." (John D. Montgomery to Masaru Fukuda, 6 December 1955.)

I cannot guess my father's response. There is, of course, the famous novelist of the postwar period, Mishima Yukio, who could be thought of as being profoundly within the German inclination that Montgomery postulates. He became a cult figure of the extreme right. He aroused much controversy, especially in literary circles. I remember one summer evening at Karuizawa, soon after Mishima had committed suicide, my Nakamura cousins were engaged in lively discussion with their parents about him. As they were all academics in literature studies, it had a particular relevance. There could be no doubt about his literary skills; some admired his romanticism, many disapproved of his homosexuality; some regarded his novels as containing political overtures but most regarded him as an eccentric. Henry Scott-Stokes, who knew him well, wrote in his biography that Mishima had a deeply-felt inferiority complex stemming from his youth: he was refused enlistment on national service at the age of eighteen because of frail health. His obsession with physical training and forming a private army dedicated to the Emperor were motivated not so much by political conviction as by the sense of rejection he had experienced at an impressionable age. He came from an aristocratic family and attended the Peers' School; there my great-uncle as President told him personally that, although he was academically brilliant, his health was not strong enough to join the military. Mishima held that against my great-uncle all his life and features this incident in one of his novels. Mishima's novels are redolent of the immediate prewar period's nostalgia for the lifestyle of the aristocracy. I myself share that nostalgia when reading them, as they remind me of the life of my mother's family: they were fortunate enough to continue much of the prewar lifestyle after the war, at least for a while. But Mishima and other novelists of the postwar period did not try to start a national rightist political movement of the kind that Montgomery feared in Germany. There is a small minority right-wing movement in Japan that orchestrates public demonstrations from time to time, especially in the streets near the Yasukuni Shrine, a memorial to the war dead. Their members' sentiments, though, have not been shared by the people at large.

It was astonishing for me to read that Ralph Braibanti, on the other hand, was questioning the social impact of arranged marriages in Japan. His letters were emphatic in saying that sticking to filial piety was retrograde and that free marriages were surely the way forward. From a Japanese perspective that sounds naïve. As in my parents' case, arranged marriages can provide a strong social foundation for a country, beyond any suggestion of snobbery or rigidity in society. Strong family commitment can provide a helpful framework for the young couple starting on the journey of life together. Whatever the case, the natural inclinations of the postwar generation have relegated arranged marriages to anachronisms, and Braibanti's wish has prevailed with little need for persuasion. And my parents' generation has swallowed any hidden prejudices, racial or social, with grace.

My father sent the Ministry of Finance Bulletin of Financial Statistics in English and other material periodically to those he met. Having read and analysed some recently published works by Raymond Moley (Roosevelt's principal adviser on the New Deal and the recipient of the Presidential Medal of Freedom from President Nixon in 1970) and others, my father was engaged in the study of political economy – the basis of economic policies – as he was by 1952 a Budget Director (主計局主計官) at the Ministry of Finance. The theme, so relevant at the time both in Japan and the US, was continuing inflationary momentum during the Korean War. Studying the Bulletin of Financial Statistics, one of them wrote to say "I am extremely impressed by the similarity between your methods and policies followed in government finance and ours. Your tax structure and government revenues, in categories and percentages are surprisingly similar to ours – except for payments of monopoly enterprise. However, your taxes amount to only about 15 or 16 per cent of national income whereas ours ($98 billion in 1952) are about 30 per cent of the National Product." He compliments the Japanese: "Although credit has expanded greatly since 1950, prices (retail and wholesale) have demonstrated remarkable stability since early 1951. The management of private and national finances seems excellent." America too was enjoying a benign economic environment; there were some fears that the US might be entering an economic slump and a number of my father's friends wrote to express those concerns because of the growing liquidity preference of consumers. But it was a somewhat unique condition of a high level of stability. And events proved that the US economy did not go into recession, but rather progressed to a buoyant period of prosperity through 1956. My father wrote that fiscal policy must henceforward, in all countries, be the leading instrument for stabilisation purposes. Again, his friend Caroll Ford wrote in 1953:

"The great danger that we face, however, is a continuously inflationist era ahead of us. The dice are all loaded in that direction – unlimited bank expansion, farm support policies, large wage demands and government spending with the slightest recession... Let us hope that human intelligence and enlightenment will prove sufficient to enable us to maintain reasonably stable conditions at a high level of employment."

As I write seven decades later, Western governments and central banks struggle to face the consequences of those dice continuing to roll. Caroll Ford's hope that human intelligence and enlightenment would prove sufficient to maintain reasonably stable conditions has proved a vain one; successive financial crises have been met with temporary alleviating measures, only to produce ever greater crises in turn.

In this correspondence Caroll Ford comes across as one of the finest of people; an honourable man of high intellect, compassion, and proper values. Truly a son of America, he had an uninhibited faith in God. He did not rate his younger colleague Montgomery very highly, agreeing with my father's assessment of his abilities and calling Montgomery brash and ambitious. Montgomery, though, had a great respect for Ford and sent my father a copy of Ford's retirement speech on honour, saying that "his impressive words so well exemplify his own life." Ford said that those graduating with honours received their awards not just for academic achievements but for personal qualities, of which he said "none is more important than that of personal honor and integrity." Honour to him was "a fundamental attribute of character implying loyalty and courage, truthfulness and self-respect, sincerity, justice and generosity". That to follow an honourable life, "for most people there is no finer fulfilment than their inner satisfaction which comes from following the path of honesty, truthfulness and honorable conduct." "The Price of Honor", as his speech was titled, pointed to the possibility that holding firmly to principles and ideals could cost friendships or even jobs; however, self-interest alone rarely determines 'rightness', and a course of action must be based on one's conscience. Referencing the Christian teaching to be considerate of the weaknesses and errors of others, he ends by asking the graduates: "be true to the faith that we have in you, and live honored and respected lives".

Ford resigned, aged fifty-three, from Babson of which he was Chancellor, and from teaching at universities altogether, going to live on the estate in Vermont that he inherited from his parents to write and to travel. He wrote to my father as early as in January of that year, 1955, that "Long years in many colleges leaves me pessimistic about the results of present college education in America. Education for the masses in line with Democratic thought or philosophy in the US simply has failed miserably to educate (hardly) anyone. It doesn't work. Too many are poor mentally and there is little interest in knowing anything or acquiring knowledge. I am speaking in a profound view in this matter. Education is a serious thing. Both vision and courage are lacking in our educational leaders, such as might solve the problem."

My father went back to Japan on a US Army troopship that was carrying men for combat duty in the Korean War. He wrote decades later to his former colleagues in the Navy that he was immensely impressed by the spartan conditions in which the officers lived on the ship. By comparison, Japanese officers on Japanese warships lived in luxury.

Away in America Again: Fulbright Fellowship, 1956
It was on that visit in 1951 that my father struck upon the idea of spending some time in America on a scholarship to study the US constitution and its system of public administration. He was much encouraged to do so by those scholars he had met and was given recommendations and endorsements by them. Ralph Braibanti, Robert A. Scalapino of the University of California (Berkeley), John D. Montgomery, and Caroll Ford all wrote numerous letters to have him accepted. At first my father wanted to attend the Harvard Summer Seminars Program. He passed the examination and the interview but was not allotted a place, as the programme was not open to anyone who had already been to the US. Montgomery did his best to get him into the programme and lobbied his colleague Henry Kissinger, who was involved in the selection, but could not move the intransigence of the organisers; Caroll Ford thought that Montgomery owed it to my father to get him a place, after all that he had done for him with his work. My father eventually decided to apply for the

Fulbright Research Fellowship; this entailed a research project sponsored by a university. Ralph Braibanti arranged that Duke University in North Carolina would sponsor him.

In the evenings and at weekends, Masaru was at his desk at home studying for the Fellowship exam. He bought a portable and rather elegant-looking English language typewriter. Once he was accepted he had some reservations. He would be risking his promotion prospects and would be away from his family for a long time. He sought the advice of Caroll Ford as to the wisdom of going ahead. Ford wrote to him to say that this was a unique opportunity in my father's life and that, eventually, the time away from the Ministry would work to his advantage in his career. On 7 May 1956, he wrote: "My dear friend, you can't afford to decline this award – regardless of how you feel about the opportunities which might develop to give you increased prominence in the work that you are doing for your country, but there are always such opportunities arising and the Fulbright is something which comes only once. Please remember, Masaru, too, that you are still very young and have your whole future before you." The Ministry agreed to give him a stipend while away so that he would not be totally reliant on the money from the scholarship. My father had been moved in the 1956 annual personnel reshuffle to a new posting, which he did not like. That was partly in his mind when weighing up whether to go ahead with the nine months away from the Ministry. Braibanti got him a place at Duke with the understanding that he would also visit several other universities, giving lectures, and spend some time in Washington.

My father departed on 29 August 1956 on Pan American Airways heading to San Francisco from Haneda Airport in Tokyo. I still remember in my mind's eye looking up at the night sky, watching his aircraft fly out of sight into the darkness. Mother said "He's gone away." At the Ministry Hatoyama Iichiro, who was two years senior to my father, said how much he admired his serious-minded intent and this brave decision. That decision might have been made easier as his mother had died, aged eighty-two, the year previously and he would not now have to leave my mother caring for her. She had been bedridden for the last year of her life in her room at home; Yoko looked after her tirelessly with the help of a live-in nurse. When she died, my father rushed home from the Ministry and knelt beside her bedside with all of us, and led our prayers, ending with the Lord's Prayer.

The logistics of his stay in the US were arranged by the Conference Board. He received a US Government Maintenance Grant of $9 per day for 270 days (30 August 1956 to 26 May 1957). Ralph Braibanti found a three-room apartment for him near the campus, preferable to the alternative of living in a dormitory. Masaru wrote to him to accept this apartment straightaway, saying that cost was very much less important than comfort. He arrived in San Francisco on the morning of 30 August 1956 and was met by Dee Scalapino, as her husband was away in the Far East. She arranged his programme in San Francisco over the following two days so that he could meet his friends from the previous visit and see the University of California (Berkeley) campus. Professor Scalapino, whom he had come to know well in 1951, had opened the East Asia Center for study into the government systems of China and Japan. He was a noted authority on East Asia and a frequent visitor to Japan. It was Scalapino who masterminded, from the wings, the historic US–Japan joint meeting of the respective Cabinet ministers in Hakone in 1961 (the first to take place after the war). He spoke Japanese and Chinese fluently. The Scalapino family became good friends of ours and often came to our house with their three teenage daughters. I envied the way they looked and dressed, with beautiful clothes and handbags; they seemed very grown up with their make-up and coiffure. In San Francisco too were other friends from the previous visit, notably Lorne Freeman.

Lorne was a charming American woman, intelligent and perceptive. She had attended Stanford University in her youth. Her family lived in Washington DC but in 1953 they moved to Palo Alto, California, and she followed them there. Lorne then married Donald Cantor, a Pulitzer Prize-winning journalist and a Dutchman; she had invited my parents to their wedding. Being a foreigner, as she wrote to Masaru, it was difficult for Donald to find employment in the US. She and my father corresponded for years afterwards until the end of his life, with long letters sharing views on current affairs and imparting news of mutual friends. Masaru liked and admired her very much. In one of her earlier letters she describes a holiday in the Caribbean with her father; she was appalled to see the islands being so Americanised, with the ubiquitous distribution of Coca-Cola and suchlike, so that they were losing their own culture.

From San Francisco Masaru went first to Washington DC for a few days before going on to Durham, North Carolina, to start his study at Duke. He wrote to his acquaintances at the US Treasury Department so that he could meet them en route. One was Robert W. Maxwell, the Commissioner of Accounts; he and his wife immediately invited him to their home for dinner and arranged meetings with Treasury officials. He stayed at his favourite hotel, Dupont Plaza Hotel on Dupont Circle.

Masaru soon became disenchanted with Duke University and within a month of arriving there started to think of moving to Harvard. He found Durham too provincial and the university less than academically rigorous. He appealed to his old friend Caroll Ford, asking for his help and advice, which Ford was more than willing to give. Ford thought that my father might have been somewhat spoilt by his first visit in 1951 when he was a specially invited guest, accorded courtesies and honours that he could not now expect as a simple visiting scholar, since the people he met did not know that he was a senior ranking official of the Japanese government. My father eventually wrote to John

Montgomery, who had become the Dean at the Babson Institute, asking him to make arrangements for him to spend the winter semester at Harvard. Montgomery was assiduous in enabling my father to do so, though warning him that the scholars there were not all that communicative and were engrossed in their own work at the best of times. In the event Harvard accepted him on the basis that he paid fees for attending lectures and seminars. Masaru thought this a cold invitation. Meanwhile, the President of Michigan University Graduate School wrote him out of the blue a very warm and welcoming letter, inviting him to spend some time there. Though reluctant at first, he decided to accept as he was touched by the kind and enthusiastic tone of the President's letter. He therefore spent some time in March and April of 1957 in Michigan at Ann Arbor. Montgomery had previously suggested Michigan as having a superior department of political science. He was also careful to advise that my father should be sensitive about how Braibanti might feel, as he had arranged my father's stay at Duke out of friendship. But my father's friendship with Braibanti survived and they remained in contact for decades.

He stayed at Duke till the end of the year and went to Washington for the next two months. He was much happier there and he had a number of friends he contacted at the Treasury, as well as at other government departments. Ralph Reid and John Weldon-Jones were especially kind to him; both remained life-long friends. Weldon-Jones sent us a tin of Christmas cake every year and in his will left a legacy for my mother, some years after my father's death. On Masaru's last journey from Washington in March he travelled by Southern Pacific Railroad to San Francisco via Ann Arbor – by first class as my family invariably did. The ticket folder with pictures of the trains travelling on various routes claim that they were 'America's Most Modern Trains Featuring Four Scenic Routes: Golden State Route – Los Angeles-Chicago; Sunset Route – Los Angeles-New Orleans;

Overland Route – San Francisco-Chicago; Shasta Route – San Francisco-Portland.'

Unhappy though he was at Duke, Masaru gave eight lectures there to both the men's and the women's colleges (they were separate). He was a popular speaker and often received standing ovations. He wrote to my mother about these and said that he was good at lecturing and telling stories. Indeed he was an engaging speaker, amusing and precise, never verbose nor self-assertive. I remember him talking to the assembled company at the wake after the funeral of his sister, my aunt Naoko, recalling their childhood days together. I was amazed by his erudition.

The letters written to my mother are poignant and expressive. Above all they show that Masaru was overwhelmed with lone-liness. For the first time in his life he was completely alone in a foreign country. Durham was a small provincial town miles away from the cosmopolitan centres of New York or Washington. There were no other Japanese there, which meant that he had no opportunity to speak the language, or write it except in letters home. He told Yoko to write twice a week, on Sundays and Wednesdays. With no car he was totally reliant on the facilities of the university for daily meals and for relaxation. His arrival at Duke started with an unhappy incident: the apartment that Braibanti had found him turned out to be unworkable, the landlady changing the terms of the rent and having a hostile demeanour. The room was too small and he would have had to share a bathroom with several others. So he immediately went to a hotel while looking for other accommodation. He eventually found a suite of rooms with a bathroom with the Crumb family, where he stayed to the end of the year.

At first he found Mrs Crumb aloof, but he eventually managed to get her round to being more hospitable and friendly, espe-cially as her daughter, Mary, was visiting Tokyo; Masaru ordered Yoko to entertain her and she duly took her to a tempura restau-rant. Mrs Crumb invited Masaru to tea in her rooms in return and thereafter the landlady-tenant relationship improved. At the end of the year, as he was leaving Durham for Washington, she invited him to join their Christmas dinner. My father never forgot the kindness shown by a young lecturer, whom he did not know well but who invited him during the Christmas holidays to dinner with his newly married young wife. They thought he might be lonely over the holidays; they drove some miles from the suburbs to collect him and took him back late in the evening to his lodgings.

He described to Yoko his daily activities and sent her photographs of the Duke campus, but the letters reveal his sadness at being away from home and openly speak of his loneliness. In many ways their relationship became closer, waiting more and more anxiously for their reunion.

I have never really understood how relationships within arranged marriages work. Having been educated in America and England I could not imagine ever agreeing to one. But those letters provide a vignette into one, at least in Japanese culture, with Masaru surprisingly demonstrative to his 'greatest love'. One of the letters states that he would not want his daughters to go to an American university and encounter the kind of difficulties he had. Ironically, all of his daughters were to study abroad, one of them in America (my youngest sister went to Harvard).

Those letters reveal that Yoko wrote in rather formal terms at the beginning, being assiduous in asking after his health and giving him news of the children. As was her duty, she reported on her regular visits to the Yamanashis and the family grave on the anniversary of my grandmother's death. She respectfully addressed him as 'Masaru-sama' and revealed little of her emotions. My father eventually reprimanded her for being too formal. He seemed to search for her feelings towards him, as he wrote in one of the early letters that he was touched by her sentence 'I wonder what sort of a town Durham is...' Yoko mentioned in every letter preparing Chahchah for the Gakushuin entrance examination, and my father told her to pay more attention to me as well! Chahchah was our mother's favourite. But my mother suspected that I was my father's favourite.

Yoko's tone gradually changed, until there was an emotional outburst concerning a family upset. Masaru had disagreements with one of my mother's sisters who was studying at Bryn Mawr. He regarded it as his family duty to visit her in Philadelphia, but Asako took the opportunity to criticise him audaciously for leaving his wife alone with their children at home, and for the fact that the marriage had consigned her to daily domestic routines: this was not the sort of thing her family had expected when arranging the match. Masaru was deeply wounded, as Asako suggested that there might be incompatibility between the families and referred to the divorce of one of her sisters that resulted from such disharmony. He thought that she was in an unhappy emotional state because she had just learnt of her younger sister Noriko's recent engagement; Japanese custom dictated that daughters married in order of seniority. Whether that had caused her outbursts or not, a feud between them persisted for months. She wrote to my mother and even to her own mother, who then wrote to my father to apologise. The *froideur* lasted for several years, well after their respective returns to Japan, and it became taboo to mention the name of Asako at home. Years later, she became my closest aunt and a confidante; and in fact she became very critical of her own family ways. It had all the hallmarks of a classic family melodrama, reminding one of the novels of Taniguchi Junichiro of the postwar period, most notably *The Makioka Sisters*.

It seems that this episode brought my parents closer, as they swore to one another in frantic letters that this rift would not come between them. Yoko's letters become increasingly emotionally expressive, saying she was writing in the stillness of the night after the children had gone to bed; she was most concerned that he would take it out on her but that whatever happened she would stay with him – she waited for the day she could bury her face in his chest.

Yoko was writing by then of her longing for her husband's return. Reading those letters tells one some aspects of arranged marriages that are, or sometimes are not, well managed. Children usually remain ignorant of such background noises. In recent years my mother has said that she recognised that her family was unworldly and could appear arrogant. Asako herself said in later years that her brother Yuhei could behave towards her in a way typical of the family's unfeeling arrogance. My mother was dutiful to her mother-in-law but has told me that she did not like her. I did not like her saying that, since for me she had been a wonderful grandmother and I wanted to keep my memories of her that way. I have seen my mother say tearfully to my father that she recognised that his mother was a great woman of enlightened virtues.

Family letters show that my mother's father was supportive of Masaru going to America and arranged for him to meet some of his acquaintances. Though my father was never particularly close to his father-in-law, they being very different personalities coming from different family traditions, the relationship was cordial and mutually respectful. They shared social venues in the Tokyo Club and the Tokyo Golf Club, where my grandfather was a leading figure. And my father was fond of his brother-in-law, Yuhei, who respected him very much. They often played tennis and golf together and shared many friends and acquaintances.

Soon after our father arrived in Durham, he sent us large dolls. We anxiously awaited their arrival and the excitement of opening the parcel could not have been greater. This was followed by Christmas presents of dresses. He brought back lovely things from America – more dresses and dolls for my sisters and me and a beautiful blue Samsonite hard suitcase with off-white edging for my mother, which I have kept. The interior is fully lined in light blue silk with varying sizes of pockets edged in silk ribbons. And of course in his luggage were many books on government systems and the US constitution for his library. I have kept them as they are historically important and remind me of my father's lifelong great interest.

The subject of his study during his stay as the Fulbright Research Fellow was the veto power of the President embedded in the US constitution. In particular, Masaru was interested in the ongoing debate over the desirability or otherwise of amending the constitution to allow the President to exercise an 'Item Veto', in relation to the existing Partial Veto over Appropriation Bills. Being a Ministry of Finance official in the Budget Bureau, the subject of Appropriation Bills was a natural area of interest. He had known from his visit in 1951 that one George B. Galloway had written a book, *Congress at the Crossroads*, for the Legislative Reference Service of the Library of Congress. In the spring of 1957 Masaru was fortunate enough to be able to visit Galloway at the Library of Congress in Washington to engage in extensive discussions. Galloway welcomed him, saying that even in the US there were few who researched this subject, and gave him three important works. They were Vernon Wilkinson's research paper on the 'Item Veto'; a report to the House of Representatives Commission on Constitutional Reform by Charles Zinn, who was the Constitutional Reform Officer of the Commission; and 'Reform of the Federal Budget' authored by Galloway himself and published by the Legislative Reference Service in 1950. The subject matter, as my father wrote, is not of a transient or evolutionary nature but one concerning the fundamental principle of the operation of democratic government. He put together a long paper, entitled 'Debate on the Reform of the US Federal Budgetary System', analysing the two works by Galloway and Zinn and published it in the Ministry of Finance Research Journal, *Yosan* (Budget), in 1957 on his return to Japan. It would not do justice to this important work to summarise his contribution here.

He travelled back to Japan on 30 April 1957 from San Francisco on the American President Lines' *President Cleveland*. My mother and I went to meet him at Yokohama in a hired car with a driver, while Chahchah and Eiko waited at home with Aunt Setsuko. I was mesmerised by the colourful streamers that were being thrown from the decks of departing ships to the quayside. I can still remember that scene clearly in my mind's eye.

Hokkaido: Snow-Clad Mountains
On his return to Japan, Masaru knew that he would inevitably be given one of the unfavoured 'hardship posts' at the Ministry, 'punishment' for having been away for nine months. I remember him coming home from the Ministry late one afternoon when he had gone to find out what his posting was to be; as he came through the front door he said with a chuckle "Hokkaido". He was to be the Head of the National Tax Agency of the Hokkaido region (北海道国税局長). As he wrote in his farewell message on completion of this assignment two years later in the Agency's journal, it was the first time in his sixteen-year career at the Ministry of Finance that he worked in the regions outside the Ministry headquarters and in the area of tax collection.

Hokkaido is the northernmost island of Japan, extremely cold with heavy snows in winter and at that time the most primitive part of Japan. Ainu, the indigenous people of Hokkaido and Siberia (Sakhalin and Kurile islands and the Kamchatka peninsula), with their particular culture, still lived there. The official residence of the Director-General was a large two-storey Japanese house with a garden on the main avenue in the city of Sapporo. The long wide avenue had gardens in the middle separating the lanes in opposite directions. It had handsome houses and office buildings; the Hokkaido Tax Agency headquarters were in a stone classical building on the opposite north side of the avenue from the residence. There was no question of the family relocating with him to Sapporo: we were at school in Tokyo. So father went to Sapporo and came home once a month. Our mother took us to Sapporo each summer during school holidays. It was the beginning of jet air travel for domestic flights and that was at once exciting and nerve-wracking for us children, with bumpy rides in small aircraft. It was cool in summer there compared with the punishing hot and humid months of July and August in Tokyo. Normally we would have gone to Karuizawa to escape from it. At weekends my father took us on drives to the surrounding countryside of prairies with cattle ranching and dairy farms of *Yukijirushi* ('Snow Brand') fame. He served in Hokkaido for two years. The winters were hard: there would be five feet of snow throughout the months of December to March. No such thing as central heating in those days, so the house and office too were very very cold, heated with electric radiators and hand-warming braziers. One of the better things for us was that in December, for the customary year-end *Oseibo* gifts, we were sent the delicious whole salted salmon that was a Hokkaido speciality.

The challenges that awaited my father on his arrival were Herculean. Against the background of the intensifying Cold War and Hokkaido's geographical proximity to the Soviet Union, there were concerns of communist infiltration in the agency itself as well as in the private sector. The island's poverty relative to the mainland was more than evident: much of its economy was dependent on the hard physical labour of coal mining in extreme weather conditions, as well as on fisheries in the freezing seas sharing a maritime border with the Soviet Union. The distance from metropolitan capital Tokyo made the islanders feel like 'poor cousins'. There were, too, the administrative challenges of a defeated nation. Being conscious that his arrival from the central authority could be met with hostility, due to people feeling that they had been relegated to the bottom of national priorities, or even been forgotten, Masaru embarked immediately on meeting every member of the staff of the agency, not just in Sapporo but in all the regional agency offices throughout Hokkaido – often undertaking those visits in snow blizzards under difficult logistical circumstances. His efforts were rewarded with much improved morale in the agency as he managed to negotiate a higher budget allocation with the Ministry for better working conditions and housing for the staff, both of which he had found woefully inadequate. He went to Asahikawa and single-handedly negotiated with striking agricultural workers at the picket line himself. He guided the introduction of the controversial self-assessment reporting system for income tax and achieved the highest tax receipts since the end of the war. Actions speak louder than words.

But he was not short in imparting inspiring words to the staff and the inhabitants of Hokkaido at large either. In many speeches, Press interviews and his own writings, Masaru expressed his affection for the beautiful landscape, evoking romantic thoughts and sympathy for the hardships endured in what was to him a 'new country'. In the journals of the agency he revealed his political philosophy, the essential tenets of democratic consent, and urged that the foundation of a civilised society lay in simple human gestures of kindness, love, etiquette and sincerity. He quoted passages from the German poet Friedrich Schiller on ethics and morality and from Albert Schweitzer, regretting that the war seemed to have obliterated human values once commonly held. He questioned the wisdom of the attempt in the United Nations, for example, to balance two diverging ideologies, presented in confrontational posturing, as if adherence to one or the other of their doctrines was to provide the tools for peace and happiness in human life. He emphasised that we are all human beings with instinctive moral faculties, be they allies or enemies; in all circumstances to exercise restraint, and not to forget to see the situation from opponents' point of view, always respecting the fundamental human values shared by all. Clearly he was profoundly aware of the new reality of the availability of nuclear weapons. He challenged the majority voting mandate of the UN: even if a resolution was passed with a majority the underlying issues of conflict might never actually be resolved, citing the recent movement to self-determination in Cyprus and the achievement of the Greek Cypriot leader, Archbishop Makarios. He saw that the democratic mandate was inherently fragile; a concerted effort was needed to protect it. This may sound idealistic in our modern age, but he was also a realist: quoting from an old Christian prayer he said "Ask God to teach us how to accept the impossible, but give us courage to aspire to achieve what is possible, and to teach us to know what is possible and what is not."

On the more practical aspect of the conduct of fiscal policy, he questioned the validity of a blanket imposition of bureaucratic strictures and feared that common sense and human considerations were beginning to be trampled on in Japan's administration. The fundamental tenets of equity and fairness in taxation seemed to him to be under challenge; he was particularly concerned with the dividing line between corporate taxation and individual income tax imposed on tiny companies. He believed strongly that the tax system must be equitable and, for that to carry credibility and trust, the system must be simple enough for every taxpayer to comprehend and approve. The ever-increasing complexity of the system bred mistrust, tax evasion and avoidance, as bureaucratic regulations imposed standardisation, without consideration of particular circumstances. He told his staff at the agency never to succumb to bureaucracy but to act according to their own consciences.

These thoughts came to Masaru ever more strongly in Hokkaido because he perceived that the inhabitants had a complex inner anxiety akin to that of the 'colonised', being dictated to by central government. He sympathised and tried to consider how matters could be improved for the system to be more inclusive of regional requirements. But as the farewell tribute to him by his colleagues emphasised, it was his profound humanity that moved his thinking, including on the system of taxation. He, in turn, wrote in characteristic phrasing that we must somehow develop a "gentlemanly tax system".

On leaving the post, his colleagues wrote tributes in the super-lative, regretting his departure. Decades later, on his death they wrote to my mother that his achievements in office would never be forgotten by posterity. His farewell message was as always romantic, recalling the first time he set foot in Hokkaido, seeing children with red woollen scarves wrapped around their heads walking in Wellington boots to school in the blizzards; the inspiration from seeing the snow-covered mountains in the dis-tance beyond the prairies from his window each morning, with mysterious deep lakes hidden in the distance; and that within the agency he longed to create a fine human workplace with communality of spirit. Wishing them lasting happiness and health, he bade them goodbye.

After his punishing two-year sojourn in Hokkaido, in May 1959 Masaru was appointed head of the Finance Section of the Finance Bureau (理財局資金課長) back in Tokyo.

The Family Reunited

His new appointment at the Ministry pleased Masaru, as he was now in charge of government funding in one of the principal departments of the Ministry. Our family was all together at home after nearly three years of interruptions. In April I graduated from the junior school at Gakushuin and went on to its middle school for girls; Chahchah was in her third year at the school and three-year-old Eiko was soon to go to the same Catholic kinder-garten that Chahchah and I had attended. As my father enjoyed films, he encouraged us to go to the cinema to see his favourites; one that sticks in my memory is *On the Beach* with Ava Gardner. But it was Alain Delon whom I idolised. Nouvelle Vague films were just coming in and we went to see them one after another. At home on television I watched avidly performances by popular singers of the day, such as Micky Curtis and Elvis Presley, and talked about them with my friends on the phone.

By the second half of the 1950s, Tokyo was a vibrant metropolis and the stylish streets of Ginza and Shibuya were full of *abekku* couples (a Japanese borrowing from the French '*avec*') strolling on dates, meeting at cafés and bistros. They were the young office girls and junior executives getting a first taste of freedom. My friends and I would not have been allowed out like that, but the whole city was now lit by a new sense of hope and jollity. A stylish café frequented by the sophisticates was called Café Renoir, which survives to this day. More serious encounters were held at the very posh French restaurant Crescent in Shiba Park, or Prunier in Kasumigaseki, frequented by senior officials. Crescent remains in its original early-twentieth-century brick house, with empire-style interior decoration. Glamorous theatre productions were presented in rich stage settings and some of my school friends were frequently taken by their parents. For the first time in my life I was taken to the opera – Puccini's *Madama Butterfly*. It was the time of celebrity culture. Home-grown fashion models were recruited by Parisian couture houses and crowded the pages of glossy magazines. It was back to the prewar days of European – especially French – culture, dominating a cosmopolitan society. *Seiyo-ryori* (Western cuisine) was essentially French, not the hamburgers or pizzas that came in a decade or two later to crowd the streets of Tokyo. Famous European orchestras returned to Tokyo on tour and music lovers scrambled for scarce tickets. By then people had regained the financial as well as emotional space to enjoy themselves. In sport, however, it was American baseball that caught the Japanese imagination; I was a fan of the Yomiuri Giants, and watched all their matches on television. Some evenings we had slide shows with my father's photographs of America. We set up the projector and portable screen in the drawing room and listened avidly to our father telling us the story of each and every slide.

While my father was contending with regional issues in Hokkaido, the national economy had been making strides with the postwar recovery. Much emphasis had been placed on the development of heavy industries, steel and shipbuilding in particular, but the growth of entrepreneurial enterprises made it a highly competitive economy. The Americans were complaining of 'cheap exports' of toys and other inessentials manufactured with low wages, and spoke condescendingly of their poor quality. But it was the period in which transistors were invented by Sony, in the back yard of the company's founder, and Japan doggedly climbed the international league in the manufacturing and export of steel. The Americans came to eat their patronising words by the end of the next decade.

In April that year, 1959, Crown Prince Akihito married a commoner, for the first time in the history of the Japanese imperial family. Miss Shoda Michiko was the daughter of an industrialist whose family company milled flour. Politically, it was considered a 'democratic' gesture and it was reported that he chose his consort himself at the tennis courts at the summer resort, Karuizawa. There was much excitement in the country as the lovely young princess-to-be appeared in television interviews. That was considered to be the way of modern postwar Japan. My grandmother's and my mother's generations of former peeresses and alumnae were more than disappointed that, for the first time in history, an imperial princess had not come from their school. As the engagement was announced in January, we were told at junior school by our President that we must not say she was not from our school, Gakushuin. For Princess Michiko, being surrounded at all times at Court by those who were among themselves close friends must have been alienating at first. She was educated at the Catholic school, Sacred Heart. As the imperial family is supposed to be descended from the

Shinto god, it had to be verified that she had not been baptised and that she had no Christian inclinations. The Court etiquette and language were new to her and it was rumoured that she was at times reproved by courtiers and ladies-in-waiting. Before her wedding she was tutored in the language of the imperial family. It took a toll on her health for years to come. Today, half a century later, very few would indulge in such snobbish gossip. But her journey as Crown Princess and then Empress must often have been a lonely one. She nevertheless won the hearts of the people, gaining respect and affection.

1959 was a year of turmoil in Japanese politics. The US–Japan Security Treaty, originally signed in 1951 as a condition of the agreement for the San Francisco Peace Treaty, was to be updated, putting the two countries on a more equal footing. The original treaty had no date of termination, but Prime Minister Kishi Nobusuke negotiated a ten-year renewable term. The debate continued throughout the year, culminating in the signing of the renewed treaty in January 1960. The opposition Socialist Party continued their objections with increasing ferocity for many months until Kishi resigned in October 1960. President Eisenhower's planned visit to Japan on the signing of the treaty had to be cancelled as public furore and demonstrations mounted. The Socialist Party leader, Asanuma Inejiro, was assassinated by a right-wing protester at a socialist convention. I remember that some of our school lessons centred on this subject; the master who took the social studies class was a young man of socialist inclinations. Even my grandmother and I discussed it over tea in her drawing room. She was of course, as all my family were, in favour of the treaty. The resignation of Kishi brought in a new Prime Minister in Ikeda Hayato, a former Ministry of Finance official to whom my father was close.

That was a momentous year for our family: in the autumn of 1960 Masaru was appointed to represent the Ministry of Finance in the United States at our Embassy in Washington

DC. He was very pleased with this appointment, an opportunity to go back to the country that he loved for its ethos. But I do not think that he foresaw or expected that his career would from then onwards be entirely in the international sphere and that he would spend the rest of his career abroad, never to return to serve in the Ministry in Tokyo.

'Sakura', a pastel by Fukuda Yoko – remembering the Cherry Blossom Festival on the Tidal Basin; her grandfather had sent the trees half a century before.

7. THE WASHINGTON YEARS: 'OVER THERE'

~

One day in the summer of 1960 our family life changed dramatically – the consequences were to dictate our lives forever. My father was asked to accept an appointment to represent the Ministry of Finance at the Japanese Embassy in Washington DC; he would hold the rank of a Counsellor in the Embassy, and would be the most senior Ministry of Finance official stationed in the USA. He was more than delighted to return to America, and especially to Washington, where he had many friends, having kept in touch by letter. Washington had sparked his abiding interest in how the US government actually worked.

Many things had to be decided for our family: would we leave the school or apply for temporary absence and keep our places; would we take a maid to help our mother; what were we going to do with our houses in Tokyo and Karuizawa and what would become of our dear dog? Mother had to get a driving licence; what would we have to ship over for our life there – household items including kitchen equipment, dinner service, silverware, vases, our dolls, clothes, etc. etc. – and all within the Ministry's allowance?

Our grandparents very much wanted us to take a maid with us as they thought it would be hard for our mother not to have help for the first time in her life. Mother herself was non-committal, her principal concern being not to spark envy among other Embassy staff. We children thought it better not to have one and promised we would help our mother. The cost of taking a servant was a consideration, but the burden of looking after another woman in a foreign country, who wouldn't speak the language, and who would inevitably grow lonely, outweighed the benefits of having a maid.

It was thought initially that the appointment would be for about three years and that we would return to Tokyo afterwards and to our school; we kept our places at Gakushuin and our parents paid the fees for long-term absentees. I was desperately sorry to leave my friends at school and felt I had to be able to rejoin them. We cleared up the house, locked our wardrobes and other possessions in a single room; after we left our maid, Masa-chan, remained in the house with the help of Takemi and Ryozo from Fukidecho to finish all that had to be done to clean and to provide security for the house and gardens and hand over the keys to the tenant, an official of the Japan Monopolies Public Corporation, a branch of the Ministry of Finance. Later, our cousin Michiko (Aunt Naoko's eldest daughter, who was in fact born in that house) and her husband 'borrowed' our house for part of the time we were away as they were recently married.

In the process we sold a lot of things to bric-a-brac merchants who bought everything by weight. I was distressed to see the large yellow crystal chandelier taken away as if it were rubble; all the collections of classical music records – the old 78s – went by weight too, as well as the HMV mahogany gramophone. No one in those days wanted such old-fashioned things; antiques were not fashionable. I remember talking with Grandmother at Fukidecho about clothes when she gave me a length of beautiful pale blue slightly furry material for an overcoat; mother took me to Matsuya department store in Ginza to have it tailored. We were told that since there wouldn't be school uniforms in America we had to have clothes to go to school in and that American children wore different dresses every day! Aunt Asako advised mother on what she would need in the cold winters on the east coast and said that American women wore fur coats even to supermarkets. Grandmother made sure that Mother had fine kimonos and obis so that she would be well prepared for the many diplomatic receptions and soirées. Our father asked a local lawyer friend in Karuizawa to look after our house there, and made arrangements with the florist at the cemetery to take care of our family grave, as he did with the temple where his sister is buried in Nagasaki.

At school everyone was jealous of my going away to America. My friend Kumiko, who had lived in London with her parents, gave me a lot of moral support. I wrote to my friends very often and for years I longed for their letters. At that age of fourteen, friends mattered very much as confidantes and I missed them greatly, especially in the early days before I was able to make American friends.

Our relations came to visit before departure to wish us well, regretting how long until we all would meet again. I remember Great-Uncle Yamanashi came with one of his grown-up grandsons one evening to give my father important letters of introduction to members of the US government, including to Admiral Arleigh Burke, to whom Masaru had been introduced in 1956 and who was still Chief of Naval Operations; coincidentally, he lived in Bannockburn, where we found our home. Despite my father telling him he must not come to see us off at the airport as he was in his eighties by then, he insisted on coming to Haneda airport. Aunt Naoko was there too, taking down the instructions my father gave in case of emergencies, and notes on how to communicate with us. It impressed me that she knew quite a lot of English. Saying goodbye on the last evening at home to our American neighbours next door was sorrowful; their children, whom we played with every day, were in tears as we kept saying to each other "We are so sorry to say goodbye" repeatedly across the garden fence.

From Tokyo we flew to Hawaii on a Japan Air Lines flight in first class. As we disembarked they put highly scented Hawaiian *lei* around our necks. It was a lovely early evening I will never forget with the deep pink sky at dusk. We were met by the Japanese Consul off the plane and taken in a large American limousine to the Royal Hawaiian. The iconic hotel seemed to me like a palace inside, but the pink and highly ornate exterior made it look more like a wedding cake.

The Consul invited us to his home for dinner. Next morning we breakfasted in our nice frocks in the grand dining room, where tables were separated from each other with glass screen dividers; there were white tablecloths, liveried waiters and large menu cards. I was intrigued by 'omelettes' on the menu and my father explained they were '*omuretsu*'. The breakfast menu was sumptuous with every possible kind of egg dish, cold meat, tropical fruit, fruit juice, cereal etc. – for us children it was mesmerising. We then went to look at the beach before the Consul and his wife took us around the town and shops – of course we didn't dream of buying anything. Eiko was still a little girl aged four and could get tired after a while. We stayed three nights in Hawaii before taking off for San Francisco. It seemed a challenging long journey for us as we weren't used to long-haul air travel: it had taken four and a half hours to Hawaii, but nine hours from there to San Francisco.

In San Francisco, our father had arranged to meet his friend Lorne Canter (née Freeman) and her husband. They came to dine on our first evening there at the Top of the Mark restaurant in the Mark Hopkins Hotel where we were staying. Donald Canter had just won the Pulitzer Prize for journalism. They were wonderful people and my father was in a very good mood seeing his old friend again. Lorne said to me during the dinner "Why don't you come and stay with us for a couple of months, so you can learn English and get used to America?" I was far too shy and frightened; my parents seemed quite keen on the idea and

Itohei's descendants

Takata Kamakichi (né Tanaka).

Takata Yukiko.

Tanaka Ginnosuke and Edward Bramley-Clarke with the Keio University rugby team, 1903.

Tanaka Ginnosuke.

The Great Kanto Earthquake of 1923

The headquarters building of Takata Shokai, designed by Olivier Delalande in Kojimachi, Tokyo 1914.

After the earthquake, 1923.

Below left: The grounds of 24 Fukidecho became a place of refuge for the neighbouring residents, sheltering under a large ginkgo tree and pitching tents; commemorative stone in the garden with the refuge committee members with Yoko and Setsuko.

Memories

Opposite, clockwise from top left:
The Upper House from the lawn, 1920s;

Bicycling around the estate, 1920s;

Noriko trying to swing a tennis racket in the garden of the Upper House, 1930s;

Sitting on the stone step outside the living room at the Upper House, 1952, with aunt Setsuko and cousin Kinuko. reflections of the trees in the garden on the glazed screen around the verandah;

The first class reunion of Gakushuin was held at Fukidecho;

Jiro in Yukata, 1946;

Noriko learning to ski in the drive of No.17.

Inspection of Todoroki mine, Hokkaido, 1937

Above left: Heihachi at the main lodgings.
Above: Carried in a basket-chair sedan to the mine.

Left: Yoko at the entrance to the mine.

Jiro and the foreman at the mine headquarters.

Left: Setsuko at the entrance to the mine; below: Setsuko carried by female attendants.

Yoko gets married, 1944

Engagement photograph in the garden of 24 Fukidecho, with stone pagoda in the background; left to right, seated: Jiro, Noriko, Heihachi, Sumiko, Hanako; back row, left to right: Asako, Masaru, Yoko, Yuhei, Setsuko. Below: Yoko the bride.

At Fukidecho with grandfather Jiro. Kinuko and Chahchah on his knee, with Haruko in school uniform, in the living room; c. 1953.

Haruko, one month old, with Mummy and Takemi.

Upper House in the 1960s

A drawing room complex from the east side of the lawn.

South side, bedroom complex on the right.

Garden gate into the Western house garden.

Looking towards the Western house behind the trees; grandmother's rose garden on left front.

Last time at Fukidecho – the house shuttered

Visiting Mummy's home for the last time, January 1972.

Outside the drawing room.

Chahchah and Haruko at the entrance to the Western house, 24 Fukidecho, December 1971.

my father said, smiling "Why don't you do that?" The next day he took us around the city and to see the Golden Gate Bridge which he had shown us in photographs many times at home before, and we met up with the Scalapinos who had become quite familiar to us thanks to their successive visits to our home in Tokyo. Two days later we were on the final leg of our journey to Washington.

I was extremely excited to see the Rocky Mountains on the flight from San Francisco, and took photographs from the air. To this day, that was the only time I have seen the Rockies in their entirety from west to east. We finally arrived at the National Airport in Washington beside the Tidal Basin in early November 1960. I had seen the scenery around there in many photographs, not to mention the postcards my father had sent me on his previous visits. It was now a reality before our eyes.

Washington in the Snow
A few days after we arrived, Washington was engulfed in record snow. I had never seen such a strong blizzard whirling around us; thick snow covered all roads and pavements, at least a foot deep. From that day onwards until the end of March the ice that covered the streets never disappeared. We stayed for several weeks at the Dupont Plaza Hotel on Dupont Circle. Inside, the building was as warm as a balmy summer day and static electricity sparked on touching lift buttons and door handles: something that I had never experienced before. Outside, beautiful blue sky and glistening sunshine brought happy smiling faces to everyone. Across the street was a large People's Drugstore where children went to buy ice cream cones. Racial segregation was absolute in those days with separate entrances. People of colour did not have the electoral franchise then, not until later in the decade in 1968 under President Johnson following violent protests, most notably at Kent State University. It seemed that Orientals such as ourselves were treated as perhaps

being 'honorary whites'. We were told that we should not go east of 16th Street, beyond which the majority of people were coloured and dangerous.

One of my father's friends, Weldon-Jones, took us on a drive around Washington soon after arrival. He was a senior official of the Office of the Budget Controller. Going for walks around the downtown Connecticut Avenue, it all seemed unbelievably prosperous. I was mesmerised by the shop windows and the beautiful clothes. In many ways it was the best of times in America. The atmosphere was one of confidence and hope; a new young President had just been elected, switching the leadership of the nation from the Republicans to the Democrats. It all seemed peaceful and, to our childish eyes, a spirit of harmony reigned. Yet in very little time the escalating realities of the Cold War were to descend over the nation with the Cuban crisis and the start of the Vietnam War.

Our parents embarked on finding somewhere for us to live and it was decided that we would take over the house that had been vacated by a young Ministry of Finance official who had just returned to Japan. The house was in Bethesda (Maryland) on Bannockburn Drive, in a row of small identical houses along the road with a front garden, garage and back yard. When we moved in, the very next day the next-door neighbour, Mrs Zwick, called on us in the very friendly way that the Americans have. They were a Jewish family and it seemed that they were consciously keeping themselves to themselves in the neighbourhood for that reason. I was amazed at just how much prejudice existed against the Jewish people and how self-conscious they were in America. A Jewish girl I befriended at school would be forever talking about what it meant to be Jewish and said that her brother had the ambition to become the first Jewish President of the United States. (To this day as I write sixty years later there has not been one, despite the fact that so much campaign funding is raised from predominantly Jewish Wall Street bankers.) Coming from

Japan it was an aspect of America that I had not known existed before, nor had I ever heard of kosher food.

Just down the road, the Kato family lived in a similar house; Kato Tadao was the Counsellor at the Embassy from the Foreign Ministry. (He later became Ambassador to London.) The families became close friends immediately. In the early days before we got our car, Mrs Kato drove us to the Safeway supermarket for weekly grocery shopping. We played with their children in the nearby Bannockburn swimming pool in the summer. Mrs Kato's parents had lived in New York when she was young and she was not only fluent in English but very cosmopolitan and gave American nicknames to her sons, Peter and Mike. Most Embassy people lived in Chevy Chase, a suburb just inside Washington DC. There was an elementary school within walking distance from our house and both my sisters attended it, along with Mike Kato. I was enrolled at Western Junior High School with Peter Kato. We went together on a school bus that came to collect us every morning from the top of the road.

State School: a New Experience
It was the first time that I had attended a state school and everything was novel to me. There were at first talks of our attending private schools and we visited the girls' Episcopalian school, the National Cathedral School, in Chevy Chase. But it seemed awesome. They recommended that I should go to the Americanisation School designed for foreigners to learn English before attending it. We went to see it but I very much hated the atmosphere and the person who interviewed us. So I told my parents I would not want to do this. It was decided that I should go to Western Junior High, which had an excellent academic record nationally. The school campus was sited between Massachusetts Avenue and River Road, on the dividing line between Chevy Chase and Bethesda, just on the border between the District of Columbia and Maryland. River Road is an old

Indian trail with a romantic feel, winding through woodland terrain. Each morning the whole school gathered and recited the pledge to the flag of the United States of America, followed by the singing of the national anthem. Students would then go to the classes they had chosen for that semester and move from one class to the next depending on each one's chosen programme. It was as if we were at university where one chose oneself which lectures to attend. The system of higher education from the age of twelve upwards was based on gathering a certain number of 'points' to be able to graduate from one year to the next, so that one could choose which subjects to study according to one's interests. There was a certain minimum number of points one had to achieve in certain subjects such as Maths, Science, History and English Literature. Everyone had to do PT. No one had exactly the same programme as another person, so from one lesson to another one would meet different sets of students. We would go to the school Counsellor to get advice on designing the programme at the beginning of each six-month semester.

My father was rather impressed by this progressive system, under which twelve-year-olds were expected to behave as if they were already self-determining adults. At lunch time we went to the self-service cafeteria and chose whatever we wanted for our trays and paid at the till. We would agree with friends to meet up at appointed times at the cafeteria to have lunch together. In between lessons people had assignations with their boyfriends and girlfriends to meet at certain points in the corridor as the whole school moved from one classroom to another, and more astonishingly we were able to leave the classroom during lessons by raising our hands and asking the teacher for a 'hall pass' to go to the lavatories or to meet our friends. All this was a revelation to one who came from a girls' school all in uniform with strict discipline. All girls wore make-up, carrying lipstick and eyelash curlers in their handbags. Every so often there were 'ties and heels days' when boys came in ties and jackets and girls wore high heels and their best frocks. My mother took me to the department store Lord & Taylor to buy high heels and a suitable dress. Grooming was considered an important aspect of education in those days: a far cry from the jeans, especially those artificially torn, and sweatshirt prevalence of today, a style that became fashionable with beatnik culture. Many of the girls then wore tight lace-up corsets, like Scarlett O'Hara in the film *Gone with the Wind*, to train their figure for a small waistline and uplifting brassieres; it reminded me of the Chinese parental practice of binding their young daughters' feet, as petite feet were a sign of beauty in China in the old days. Many of the girls also wore braces on their front teeth to straighten them. It seemed that American parents were particularly concerned about their daughters' looks and sexual attraction in a way that the Japanese would never have been, as it was thought vulgar to be overly concerned about such things.

My own challenge was not just that these habits were totally different from what I was used to, but that my English language comprehension was very limited. It was hard in the first six months to understand the lessons, do any homework or make close friends. Everyone was independent and leading individual lives at school; it was not an atmosphere of young teenagers sharing their emotional problems or helping each other with a difficult curriculum. I desperately wanted it understood that it was no lack of intelligence that prevented me from getting my school work right, but rather my limited English. So I often appealed to my teachers; but the Americans did not make any allowance for being foreign – once in America we were all American and must conform. I understood that that was the fundamental strength of the unity of the country. I missed Japan very much, especially my friends; I longed for their letters and wrote to them frequently. Our mother was wonderful and she helped with our homework. We bought a large illustrated encyclopae-dia set called *World Book*; armed with this and English–Japanese dictionaries we somehow managed to get through school work.

My first year at school in America was very hard, and I hated it. I could hardly understand anything that was being said in classroom teaching, especially in Science. The only subject that I could do well in was 'Maths' where language skills were not important. Mathematics had not been a subject that I was at all good at in Japan. I decided that I would do the course in algebra rather than in geometry (they were taught separately). As mathematics teaching in Japan seemed to be more advanced, I found the course relatively easy and I found myself always the best or second-best student in the class. Similarly in French and in Typing classes I was able to preserve my honour. (Typing was a compulsory part of the curriculum and we all became proficient.) Another surprise was that I was quite good at volleyball, especially in serving, and I helped win the inter-varsity tournament for our team; our PT teacher was delighted and suddenly my popularity with other girls went up. I was not at all good at games or athletics in Japan, always coming in last in running, to the embarrassment of my mother on sports days. But trying to follow lessons in Civics, mostly about current affairs, or in English Literature was difficult. I was lucky to have a very understanding teacher in Civics who was the wife of a senior Army officer; she took a special interest in me and guided me with kind attention. It was in those lessons that I met Linda Green, who became a close friend. She was the only child of a middle-class American family and was very serious-minded; after I left America she invited me with her parents' permission to come back to spend some weeks with her during the summer vacation, which my parents allowed me to do. I didn't take to the teacher in English Literature, a bespectacled Jewish woman with a hostile demeanour; the only thing that inspired me was the set text of Harper Lee's *To Kill a Mockingbird*. I was most interested in History lessons and became very familiar with American history. A young American woman taught us the very inspiring story of the progress of the new nation and I learnt a great deal about its constitution. We were told to memorise and recite the Bill of Rights. This was to give me some advantage when I arrived in London two years later, as the history of the United States was one of the papers I took for my History A-Level.

I eventually made some close friends, and by the end of the spring and summer semester, some six or seven months after arrival, I was more or less able to understand most of what was going on. Americans are friendly and kind; in the same way that they do not make any allowances for your being foreign they never hold it against you. But it is also true that the girls who immediately became close friends were those who had themselves been living abroad. One of them was Linda Galantin, youngest daughter of Vice Admiral Ignatius J. Galantin, who had served until recently at Grasse in the south of France and also at Holyhead. He was an expert on nuclear submarines and had sunk a large Japanese warship in the Pacific during the war; he recounted that experience in his book *Take Her Deep! A Submarine against Japan in World War II*. Her elder sisters had all married naval officers; Linda told me about the balls and dances that were often held for naval officers' families. Linda was born not only with a cleft palate but also with a deformed right forearm which had to be severed at birth. She had a beautiful face and showed no sadness or inferiority complex about her deformity. With a prosthetic arm she went about her life as if nothing was wrong, and made light of her incapacities. I stayed in touch with her for many years and met up with her whenever I was in Washington. Another friend was Margaret Meilly, whose family had just returned from several years in Mexico. They took an immediate interest in me and always had delicious party food – taquitos from Mexico, and meatballs on spaghetti with a piquant sauce.

I was always thrilled when school closed for snow. Quite often, as heavy snowstorms were forecast, the radio announced that all Montgomery County schools would be closed the following day. They would normally be closed for two or three days. When the storm cleared there would be beautiful blue skies and sunshine; children went out tobogganing on the streets or flew kites and we walked with friends to the drugstore in the Bannockburn Shopping Center to buy ice cream cones; mint chocolate chips were our favourite and we sometimes had Coca-Cola floats. Bannockburn was on a hillside surrounded by woodland; there were large weather-boarded mansions dotted around in the woods with driveways up to them. It was not very far from the Bethesda Country Club on Bradley Boulevard half an hour away; in the summer months we went there to swim in the pool and have lunches with the omnipresent Maryland fried chicken and hamburgers.

In those days Americans wore snow boots (more elaborate versions of galoshes, knee high for women and children) in winter, which went over the top of shoes. I had never seen these before nor have I since. They also had quilted snow jackets that were super-warm. Inside those jackets, though, they would be wearing simple summer dresses, because houses with powerful central heating were very warm. So the elegant pale blue over-coat my grandmother had made for me was not warm enough for the Washington winter and became rather redundant, hardly worn.

Diplomatic Life: New Friends, the Kennedys, the Cold War
1962 was the year of the Cuban missile crisis. As tensions mounted, there were evacuation exercises at school. A siren would ring throughout the school building and everyone had to rush to the locker rooms, face the wall and crouch. It was a frightening exercise. When city-wide evacuation exercises took place, which were not infrequent, all roads would clear and residents rushed to the nuclear shelters on the roads. At school

in various classes, such as in Civics lessons and in History, we were taught much about Cuba, the USSR, communism and the civil war then raging in the Congo. (It was, as often happens in life, a coincidence that at that time my future father-in-law, Denzil Dunnett, was the British Consul in Elizabethville and gave secret refuge to Moise Tshombe, the revolutionary leader, in his house while the UN forces fired in the streets outside. UN Secretary General Dag Hammarskjöld was killed in an air crash en route to the truce negotiations then in progress.)

Living in Washington, the reality of the Cold War was stark; I imagine that the Japanese Embassy must have been on the alert in the tense atmosphere. It was not a laughing matter for the Japanese either; the Soviet Union was Japan's 'natural' enemy, maintaining military installations on Japan's doorstep on the Kurile islands since the end of the war. But there were many happy moments and episodes during our sojourn in Washington. First and foremost, two months after we arrived, there came the inauguration of President John F. Kennedy. It was an amazing spectacle that we watched on television. Before the ceremony were many parades down Pennsylvania Avenue with colour-fully dressed majorettes and military bands; the whole city was covered in snow which made everything look stunning. In the cold of the frozen city you could see breath freeze in the air as the President delivered his inaugural address, considered one of history's most inspirational: "Ask not what your country can do for you, ask what you can do for your country." His youthful demeanour and the charming young First Lady in her elegant couture outfits symbolised the beginning of a new chapter in American history.

At school too, all the students were energised by Kennedy. No sooner had the Soviet Union successfully sent a man into space than Kennedy announced the US space programme at NASA; John Glenn, the first American in space, successfully orbited the earth the following year, enhancing national pride. There were some children of Cabinet ministers and of diplomats close to the administration at my school. It being in NW Washington, there were very few people of colour; just a few children of professional or political parents. The daughter of the Burmese diplomat who succeeded Hammarskjöld as Secretary General of the UN, U Thant, was in my year as was the son of the then Secretary of Labor, Arthur Goldberg. All that enthusiasm and hope was not to last for very long and America was soon to enter a long period of strife that could not have been imagined in the first year that I spent in Washington.

Soon after the inauguration, Aunt Setsuko and her husband came on their tour of Europe and America and spent a couple of days with us. We also had the daughter of the Prime Minister, Ikeda Hayato, come to see us at home as she was studying in America and Mr Ikeda had entrusted some things to us to take out to her. Mr Ikeda had been a colleague of my father at the Ministry of Finance before he became a politician; and in terms of political affiliation my father was close to him. There was also the visit of the Minister of Finance (later Prime Minister), Tanaka Kakuei, which kept my father busy but at the same time gave him much kudos in the Embassy as Mr Tanaka paid special attention to him. My father became closer to him after that visit and Mr Tanaka held him in high esteem to the end of his life. We had many dinner parties at home for some of my father's colleagues and friends from the US Treasury that he had known for many years.

Another visitor was the Foreign Minister, Kosaka Zentaro, my mother's first cousin. Zentaro, recently appointed to the role, came on an official visit to the US, accompanying Prime Minister Ikeda. One evening he was able to leave his entourage and come to dine with us at home. My mother was thrilled to see her cousin, Zen-chan, and we had a merry evening. Of course he was able to have useful conversations about relations with the US government with my father in private. My parents were specially invited to the official functions held in their honour, and that pleased my father. Given the traditional rivalry between the Foreign Ministry and the Ministry of Finance, the Ambassador had to take note that my father was a relation of his big boss! A historic meeting of Prime Minister Ikeda and President Kennedy took place famously on Kennedy's cruising yacht, *Honey Fitz*. No one else was allowed to be present, but Zentaro said that Ikeda came out of the meeting pleased that Kennedy had said to him that the US, Europe and Japan were the three pillars of the Western democratic world. His visit was intended to repair relations much damaged by the socialist demonstrations against President Eisenhower's visit over the renewal of the Security Treaty the previous year.

My grandmother Hanako wrote to my mother assiduously, saying how much she missed her and giving a detailed account of everyday happenings at home. She complained of difficulty in finding new maids, as Japanese women were no longer interested in jobs in domestic service; she needed more help, but still they had at least a chauffeur and two live-in maids, plus the man-servant Ryozo and the head gardener Yasu, both living on the estate. And Takemi and Oshige (who was her personal maid), though getting on in age, came in on a daily basis. Grandmother hosted garden parties for friends when her roses were in par-ticularly fine form. She went to a department store to choose some fine tea and other food to send us herself. She tells of her summer in Karuizawa, with Mariko and her very young chil-dren, sometimes going out to the hills to pick wild flowers, but said it was sad we were not there as we had been the previous summer, and that she was bored with spending all the time with babies. Karuizawa had changed; she lamented the way it had become popularised and there was Coca-Cola everywhere – a far cry from the peaceful summer resort where Mother and her sisters rode bicycles around wooded country lanes.

Meanwhile, we went on a summer holiday in our blue

Oldsmobile to tour the Blue Ridge Mountains of Pennsylvania. We had a wonderful time in a well-known resort, Pocono Manor, surrounded by wide open prairies with beautiful hills in the distance. We also went on outings to the historic towns of Williamsburg and Richmond, Virginia in the spring. I liked Richmond very much as it still had the feel of the old South, having been the capital of the Confederacy during the Civil War. Many of the houses and historic buildings had those typical wide front porches; some houses still flew the Confederate flag. The streets were lined with flowering trees. My mother particularly liked the state flower, the dogwood. Unlike Williamsburg, which had become a museum town, Richmond was a large working town, capital of Virginia, and people spoke with the charming soft Virginian accent. We also visited Annapolis, Maryland, the home of the US Navy on the Atlantic coast. There was also a driving trip to Niagara Falls; we stayed in a motel for the first and only time – a new experience!

Later that year, we moved to a similar but slightly larger house in 'rambler' style in Tone Drive near the old Indian trail of River Road. A friend of my mother's from the Tokyo Woman's Christian University, Lilly Tanaka, and her family lived nearby and she often dropped in to see us; her husband was a lawyer of Japanese-American descent and became famous in the 1970s when there were a number of trade disputes with Japanese companies. She was an amusing Japanese-American woman and was devoted to her only daughter Michelle, for whom nothing was good enough. By then, we were all speaking English quite well and enjoyed Halloween and Thanksgiving with friends. Father took us to New York with him on one of his business trips, and while he had work engagements one of the Ministry officials stationed there, Matsukawa Michiya, whom I came to know closely decades later, entertained Mother and us children in the evening. He took us to dinner in a restaurant overlooking the Rockefeller Center skating rink with fairy lights all around and to a Broadway show. New York was a metropolitan city like Tokyo and I loved the hustle and bustle in the streets with skyscrapers, in contrast to the quiet suburban feel of Washington. We met Mother's classmate from Gakushuin, Hoshi Kyoko, whose husband was Minister to the United Nations. The Hoshi family subsequently came to visit us in Washington and came to our home for dinner. When we were leaving the United States months later from New York, Mr Hoshi gave us a tour of the UN, showing us the General Assembly and giving us lunch in the guest dining room. Christmas in America was beautiful and romantic: every house was beautifully decorated with lovely door wreaths and Christmas trees on the lawn lit up in colourful lights. Though the 1962 winter was not as harsh as the previous year we still had quite a lot of snow on the ground and on rooftops, which made the Christmas scene more than apt. I loved it very much and watched television with Christmas services.

Before that in the early autumn, I went to the White House when Mrs Kennedy invited teenage diplomatic children to an afternoon entertainment of opera. The event was held in the East Room; the military ceremonial band was playing old American favourites as we arrived and walked through the red-carpeted corridor, and Mrs Kennedy together with the two teenage daughters of Vice President Lyndon Johnson received each of us in line. The opera, Mozart's *Così fan Tutte*, was performed by the New York Metropolitan Opera company. There was a mini-emergency when one of the singers' wigs caught fire and smoke started to rise, which caused a little amusement. After the opera there was a reception in the next room and President Kennedy came in to chat with us. He seemed taller than in photographs with sandy red hair while Mrs Kennedy seemed much smaller in stature than the impression photographs gave. Grandmother sent me a kimono that had been a part of her own wedding trousseau. It was in white *mon-rinzu* silk dyed with autumnal colours in a maple leaf design as the occasion was in October.

Grandmother's letter to my mother tells the story of how she decided to send me not a formal *furisode* kimono, but rather this one with its autumnal theme, which she thought more appropriate for a concert. She wrote that with a white background it would be 'up-market' and in good taste. She went up into the store room to seek it out; it was the under-kimono of her wedding attire. She also sent us the obi that would suit that kimono: one of a most formal kind in *tsuzure* weave, also in white. She advised me that I must have my manners and etiquette up to scratch, not just the clothes. As for the *furisode*, she sent it anyway by sea mail for future occasions when it might come in useful, together with the grand obi that would be worn with it. I had photographs taken in this *furisode* by Lenare at the time of my marriage; it was the one that my mother wore at her wedding reception. Chahchah got married in it. It is a treasure that I still have in my drawer.

Spring brought a wonderful cherry blossom festival around the Tidal Basin. 1962 was the fiftieth anniversary of the first planting of those Yoshino cherry trees. The wife of President Taft and the wife of the then serving Japanese Ambassador planted the first two trees in 1912. I have already written about the involvement of my great-grandfather Watase Torajiro in this endeavour. The festival was a major and elaborate affair. Every state sent a 'Cherry Blossom Princess' from whom a 'Queen' was chosen by a wheel spun by the Japanese Ambassador. The President of Mikimoto Pearl company came over with a $1,000 graduated pearl necklace for the chosen Queen. The Japanese stone lantern beside the Tidal Basin was lit to start the festival by Kosaka Mariko, the daughter of the Japanese Foreign Minister, who came over specially for this event. She herself was of course related through her grandmother to the man who sent the cherry trees in the first place. In photographs she bears an amazing family likeness to my Aunt Noriko. In the evening there was a grand ball to celebrate with all the 'Cherry Tree Princesses'; on this special occasion the

President and Mrs Kennedy, as well as Vice President Lyndon B. Johnson and his wife Lady Bird, attended. My parents were of course there, along with most of the diplomatic corps.

News from home was not so good that year: Setsuko had an operation and Grandmother suffered abdominal discomfort, later diagnosed as a stomach ulcer. This might have been the precursor to the cancer from which she died five years later. Grandmother wrote saying she was resting as much as possible and looking after her high blood pressure, and that Grandfather had rheumatism in his hip that caused him much pain. But Setsuko's stepdaughter came on a whirlwind tour of America on a Greyhound bus with a friend and visited us for a couple of days bringing reassuring news. Mariko and Noriko gave birth to a girl and a boy respectively; and Noriko was left with her three young sons in Tokyo when her husband was posted to California by the Bank of Tokyo.

Our grandparents held a special memorial service for Grandmother's parents – Great-Grandfather Heihachi II and Great-Grandmother Sumiko. According to Buddhist tradition, memorial services are held at certain intervals after death and it was the seventeenth year of Heihachi II's and seventh year of Sumiko's deaths. They had originally thought of having a garden party at home after the temple service, but in case of inclement weather they decided to hold a lunch at a new restaurant in Shiba Daimon nearby for their 150 guests. My mother sent an album she made up with pressed flowers she had worked on herself together with photographs of our family. Grandmother was particularly touched by this gesture and she put it in front of the photographs at the temple altar. She wrote that her parents so loved my mother, their first grandchild, calling after her daily for "Yo-chan, Yo-chan". She also wanted a copy of one of our family group photographs that was in the album so that she could put it in a frame at home.

As it was the first *osekku* – the girls' festival on 3 March – for

Yuhei's daughter Kakuko that year, Grandmother made the effort to bring out all the *ohinasama* dolls in the family. Ohinasama are fine dolls representing the Court of an emperor and his empress, with ladies-in-waiting, generals, Court musicians, manservants, and food offerings, all displayed on tiers. The Tanaka family had a very fine collection of several of these handed down through the generations; some of them were so large and elaborate that the tiering reached the ceiling. These dolls' faces are finely hand-painted and they are all dressed in beautifully-sewn kimonos and accoutrements. They are a part of the Japanese tradition of arts and crafts. Every girl is given a set on her birth to display on 3 March each year. Some fifty years later, at my mother's suggestion, the Tanaka family collection was given to the museum in Nagano, the birthplace of our ancestor, Tanaka Heihachi. Some pieces were given to the national doll museum. When I was born, I was given Aunt Minobe's ohinasama; this five-tiered set of very fine early-twentieth-century ohinasama is displayed at my home in Suffolk.

There was a diaspora of Ministry of Finance-related people in Washington and New York. In addition to the Embassy, where two other officials worked with my father, there were three officials in the New York Consulate. They were all my father's responsibility and his letters to the Ministry show that he took immense care of their careers, making sure that their promotion prospects and family requirements were not forgotten by Tokyo. The First Secretary at the Embassy in the Finance Section was Kashiwagi Yusuke, who later became a leading figure in the Ministry on the international scene. He and his wife and young children often came to our house. Decades later I encountered Yoriko, who was only five years old when I knew her in Washington, but was by then married to a diplomat, Fujisaki Ichiro. He was Minister at the Embassy in London as his father had been, and later became Ambassador to the USA. In addition, there were several people from the Ministry at the IMF and the World Bank. The

Executive Director representing the Japanese government there was (and is) always a senior Ministry of Finance official, and my father's predecessor at the Embassy, Suzuki Gengo, had just moved to the IMF. There were also representatives of the government-owned banks – the Bank of Japan, the Japan Development Bank, and the Long-Term Credit Bank of Japan. This group of MoF families met often in various gatherings, while wives met by themselves for luncheons and for tea, most often at the Chevy Chase Country Club. There were joint outings and picnics in the Potomac Park at weekends and the young played baseball together. On one occasion, Gyohten Toyoo, a young bachelor then, studying at university sent on training by the Ministry, came to join us and I remember him playing baseball with the boys. Toyoo and his wife Reiko, who later served in Manila at the Asian Development Bank with my parents, became close lifelong friends of the family in general and of myself in particular. Friendships fostered abroad in the early years after the Occupation had ended have survived strongly ever since, having all confronted the manifold challenges of keeping up a brave face in spite of limited resources, survived many mishaps occurring in unfamiliar circumstances, and sharing concerns over the education of children. Many from this mutual support group visited us for lunches and dinners *en famille*.

Above all, frequent family letters, from our grandparents, from Yuhei and Setsuko particularly but also from Asako and Aunt Minobe, show the intensely close-knit family relationship. They narrate an almost daily diary of happenings within the large family that we were a part of, and we in turn wrote regularly with details of what we were up to. Aunt Naoko and her daughter Michiko also kept us up to date with the Nakamura family news. Naoko had a length of crepe de chine silk specially dyed to a particularly modern and fashionable colour of mid-blue patterned in white batik that caught her eye and had it made up into a kimono and sent to my mother. Mother wore this often at receptions throughout her time abroad and after; it was so beautiful that many decades later I eventually had it made into a summer dress which I still wear.

A New Career for Masaru

For my father, the appointment at the Embassy in Washington provided the most important turning point of his career, bringing him personally into the orbit of international financial diplomacy. It was an opportunity to exercise his analytical mind regarding essential and urgent issues in the international payment system. As the most senior representative of the Japanese government in the US responsible for these matters, he gained access to the key players in the Kennedy administration to put forward the Japanese perspective and to develop a strategy for Japan itself. Early on arrival in Washington, he made the acquaintance of Professor Robert Triffin, Robert Roosa, William McChesney Martin and Henry Fowler. Their friendships were to survive beyond Masaru's tenure at Washington and gave him a foundation for his work for the next decade.

Robert Roosa and the Secret London Gold Protocol

Robert Roosa was an eminent economist who was appointed by Kennedy to serve as the Under-Secretary of the Treasury for monetary affairs. He was Masaru's counterpart at the US Treasury. His role was essentially concerned with the US balance of payments and he was the well-known author of the Roosa bond (see later in Chapter 9). A staunch defender of US dollar supremacy, he argued ferociously that no other country should hold gold in their foreign exchange reserves. His regular meetings with Masaru were cordial and they exchanged intensively their respective views on the bilateral balance of payments positions.

In 1962, however, Masaru was unexpectedly reprimanded by the Ambassador (Asakai Koichi) for overstepping the mark in

his correspondence with Roosa. My father describes this incident fully in his memoirs *Macmillan to Wilson*. He had come to
recognise early on, in the late 1950s, that the convertibility of the
US dollar into gold by governments and official holders posed
a threat to international payments as the price of gold began to
rise above the official conversion price of $35 an ounce. He was
in agreement with Robert Triffin's warning on that matter and
personally discussed it with him on arrival in Washington, but
more intensively and regularly in his own official capacity with
Robert Roosa and Henry Fowler. He was particularly watchful
of the gold market and especially the behaviour of Germany
and France. In early March 1962, he discovered that there was
a secret communications protocol between central banks of
the US and Europe on the London gold market. He contacted
Robert Roosa by letter to find out what the secret protocol was.
He had decided to write rather than to seek a meeting with
him on this subject. This letter fell into the hands of an official at the US Treasury who wrote to complain to the Japanese
Ambassador. The Ambassador, much concerned, issued a strong
reprimand which Masaru furiously rebutted. On examining the
letter the Ambassador had received, my father saw that the letter
signed by Roosa could not have been drafted by Roosa himself
because of its writing style, quite different from other communications, and immediately sought an appointment to see him.
Although Roosa did not divulge the content of the secret protocol, that meeting resulted in Roosa proposing the establishment
of a confidential bilateral financial meetings protocol between
the US and Japan. Ambassador Asakai had to eat his words.
Masaru suggested that the first of such meetings should be held
at the time of the IMF annual meetings in September 1962 in
Washington. He did not attend them as he had left Washington
by then, but his colleagues from Tokyo did; these meetings were
overtaken subsequently by the decision to hold confidential
meetings between the G10.

On arriving in London in the summer of 1962, he asked Douglas Allen in a casual conversation about the 'London gold protocol'. It was explained that there was indeed a secret gold pool to which US and European central banks contributed; it was run by the Bank of England and used for intervening in the London gold market. It was set up before Kennedy took up the presidency, when the price of gold in London went up above $40. During the 1950s there was much debate as to whether the London gold market should reopen after the war. Douglas Allen was much involved in these deliberations. It was feared that opening it could be destabilising for the dollar and invite exchange rate uncertainty, and to open it but suspend it temporarily in times of crisis or close it again would result in even further uncertainty and possible chaos. It was Charles Coombs, then head of the foreign department of the New York Federal Reserve (who later became the senior manager of the Open Market Committee of the entire Federal Reserve system) who devised this plan. Profits and losses from the interventions would be shared proportionately to each country's contributions to the gold pool. Douglas Allen said that details were confidential and he could not tell my father, but that the United States contributed approximately half of the pool.

My father reckoned that the opening of the gold market in London was important for the City to retain its status and the Bank of England not only supported but actively promoted its opening. A few years later in 1966 the Bank of England revealed the existence of this pool in its *Bulletin*. France left the pool soon after this publication. The revived London gold market was of course the London Gold Fix, held at the offices of N. M. Rothschild.

Masaru remembered his conversation with Robert Roosa the year before, when Roosa was first appointed to the US Treasury by President Kennedy. Roosa told him during an hour-long meeting that under the Bretton Woods system, the US dollar was *the* reserve currency and as it was backed by the US gold holding, effectively the United States held the gold on behalf of other countries. Therefore, it was desirable that other countries hold the dollar and not gold. The only exception was the United Kingdom, whose pound sterling was a reserve currency for the sterling area, and he recognised that the UK needed to hold gold in reserve. Germany, for example, should not hold gold in reserve, however much their balance of payments surplus might increase, but only the dollar. This made a considerable impression on Masaru, but he pointed out to Roosa that true understanding in international relations rested on full knowledge of other countries' domestic situations; he explained that the Japanese government was currently under strong pressure from the Socialist opposition in the Diet to hold more gold in its reserves. In Germany, the situation was that the more the deutschemark (DM) was revalued, the more dollars flowed into the DM, and as soon as the gold proportion of the reserves fell even slightly, the French franc appreciated against the DM.

Masaru went to see Bill Martin (William McChesney Martin), the then Chairman of the Federal Reserve, immediately after seeing Roosa on that occasion; Martin was delighted to hear from him that the Japanese government was sticking loyally to the US desire for Japan to hold dollars and not demand their exchange into gold. But, within the Ministry of Finance, there were investigations into whether and how Japan could increase its gold holdings. Masaru and immediate colleagues such as Kashiwagi were of the view that such an increase had to be approached with caution and that purchasing gold in the London market was out of the question; the only viable avenue might be to buy in the IMF disposal. Japan did not proceed to increase its gold reserves, and for short-term expediency continued to borrow in dollars in the form of short-term loans.

I digress briefly. I learnt of my father's preoccupation with gold only when I read his *Macmillan to Wilson*. He never talked about gold or his conversations with Robert Triffin, nor indeed about the decoupling of the dollar from gold in 1971. He never really discussed his work at home and although he would make some comments on the political scene he would never talk seriously about economic or financial policy matters. I suppose that he thought I would not understand and was not interested. That may well have been true in those days. In any case he was always telling me that my priority must be to dress well and be well groomed, important attributes of a lady. I now wish that he had imparted his views of gold in the monetary system. He died nearly twenty years before I came to work on gold. That was when the price of gold was at the bottom of the twenty-five-year bear market in 1999 when I was headhunted to be Chief Executive of the World Gold Council, the association of major gold producers. And today, as I write, I am working again on gold: this time to make it a universal currency for everyday use for everyone with digital technology. What would my father have thought? It seems from his writing that he recognised the inherent value of gold and in a free exchange rate system such as we have today, I do not suppose that he would object to it being used as everyday money according to the market pricing of gold exchanges.

Masaru was convinced of the crucial role of gold in the monetary system but foresaw that the Bretton Woods system of a fixed price to the dollar could not be sustained. He was constrained by the circumstances of the time and was cautious about Japan accumulating gold, even though the prevailing opinion at the time internationally was that gold holdings provided the confidence for national currencies. All countries in the world, whether they are communist regimes or free economies, hold gold bullion in reserve today. All attempts to demonetise it have so far failed.

One has to wonder what he would have thought of the cryptocurrencies that have emerged in the twenty-first century? He would certainly have studied them seriously. I suspect that he would have been impressed by the blockchain technology behind them and would have affirmed that its application and use could have revolutionary implications for the monetary system and its governance. But having been someone so deeply involved in the evolution of the international monetary system, he is likely to have seen the proliferation of cryptocurrencies as a threat to the stability of the world monetary order with wider implications for economic growth. Certainly, the 'tokens' or certificate of ownership of the 'currencies' that have purportedly been 'mined' would have raised his concern. "Who is guaranteeing the payment?" he might have asked.

Henry Fowler

Henry Fowler was a great man, a man of the utmost humanity. He had been particularly kind and warm towards Masaru. He was the Under-Secretary of the Treasury under Douglas Dillon in the Kennedy administration until Dillon resigned in 1965, when he became the Secretary of the Treasury under President Johnson. My father held regular meetings with Fowler and Assistant Secretary of the Treasury John Leddy. Indeed, it was they who solicited Masaru's advice on how to approach the historic joint meeting of the two countries' respective Cabinets, the first ever since the war, in 1961 at Hakone. Masaru told them that they should explain the US balance of payments situation frankly and in detail.

When my father mentioned to Fowler that the daughter of the Japanese Minister of Finance, Mizuta Mikio, was studying for her PhD at Yale University, he immediately asked that he and his wife be given the opportunity to invite her to their home. Mrs Fowler telephoned Masaru personally to make the arrangements for a black tie dinner party; my father remarked that many people would have made excuses of crowded diaries to avoid having to do this and he was struck by the Fowlers' sincerity.

Just as we were leaving Washington for London in the summer of 1962, staying for a few days at the Shoreham Hotel, Fowler tracked Masaru down at the hotel and asked him to lunch at the Metropolitan Club, just the two of them. Congress was in session and my father found it a particular honour that Fowler made time to do this. Fowler talked, very relaxed, about his career – of his time in the Tennessee Valley Authority during Roosevelt's New Deal, in the government of the Truman administration in various positions including being a member of the National Security Council, and his years in Britain during the war. Even more surprising for my father was that in 1965 Fowler, during a two-day visit to London, by which time he was LBJ's Secretary of the Treasury, found time to telephone him at the Embassy from his hotel, Claridge's, to suggest they meet so he could get Masaru's views on recent developments in Britain and Europe. In the short time of twenty months that they had known each other in Washington, he had adopted my father as a trusted friend.

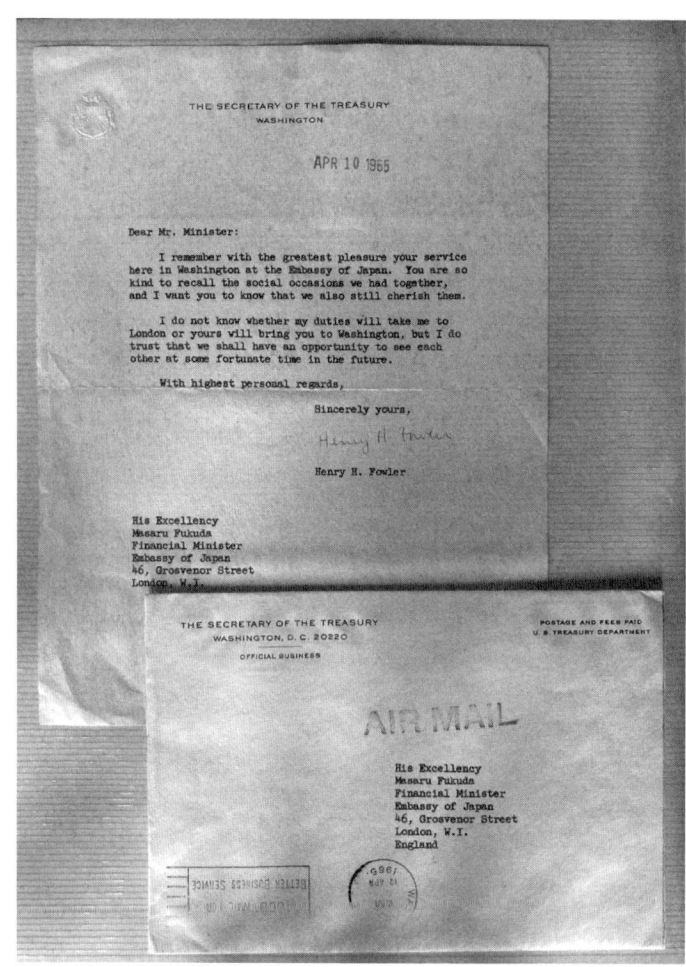

'We will meet again.'

8. Across the Atlantic: Transfer to London

~

No sooner had we comfortably settled down to our new life in Washington and begun to relish it, than my father was asked to move to the Japanese Embassy in London in the summer of 1962. It came as a surprise to us, and my father regretted leaving behind unfinished work in the US, where he had been deeply invested in several projects. Grandmother Hanako wrote to Mother, commiserating on the upheaval and the busy schedule ahead, when she would have to pack and organise our departure; there were also farewell parties to attend and to give. She remembered her visit to London on her tour of Europe with Grandfather many years before and attending dinners at the Embassy; she thought that London would give us a different perspective with its historical interest and was generally pleased about our move. As with many upper-class prewar Japanese, she liked European culture and considered Americans brash. I was sorry to say goodbye to my newly-gained friends; it was especially hard to go through all this again only two years after leaving all my friends in Japan.

My father knew his counterpart at the British Embassy in Washington, Sir David Pitblado. He was the Executive Director for the UK at the IMF as well, and on return to the Treasury in

London became Second Permanent Undersecretary and Private Secretary to Harold Wilson when Prime Minister. Sir David and his wife were more than kind, not only in giving us a lot of advice but also in writing to the Headmistress of the school where their daughters had boarded. They came to dinner one evening and Lady Pitblado wrote out where we should live and the name of the estate agent, Sturt & Tivendale in Highgate, where to shop for food (Harrods) and all the necessities of daily life.

We left Washington in the early weeks of July via New York. We stayed at the Shoreham Hotel in Woodley Park those last days in Washington, and I remember that while our parents went out to farewell receptions, my sisters and I got properly dressed and had dinner by ourselves in the dining room. We spent a couple of days in New York and met the Ministry of Finance officials stationed there who looked after us and sent us off on our journey to England from Idlewild Airport by British Overseas Airways Corporation (BOAC). My father wanted us to go to Bergdorf Goodman, the most glamorous store on Fifth Avenue, just to have a look and for the experience.

My first encounter with England was on the flight across the Atlantic; I was struck how beautifully the English steward-esses spoke in gentle tones. It was almost awesome. I realised then that English women were softer and less assertive than the Americans and that I had to get used to a new world. On landing, we were taken to the VIP lounge and met the welcoming officials from the Embassy. We went to the Chesham Hotel in Belgravia where Japanese Embassy people always stayed on arrival (this was because the Embassy was originally in Belgrave Square, before moving to Grosvenor Street); we had a set of rooms there with a kitchenette to make it easier for a long stay. It was not a success: we could not sleep because of the noise of cars stopping and starting at the road junction just below our window; British cars appeared to be almost all manual, and we were used to the purring sound of automatics in America. The hotel was old-fashioned and dilapidated and the service inadequate. It was of course much cooler than the very hot humidity of Washington in the summer. My father's secretary, Miss Lingard, helped us with all matters and we came to rely on her a great deal over the years. She had been the secretary to successive Financial Ministers at the Embassy and knew the form. All families who benefited from her enlightened advice and caring service kept in touch with her for many years after they left their posting in London. We were no exception; years later when I had already come down from Cambridge she wrote to me to say that she was getting married to a friend of Indian origin and sent me photographs of her wedding at which she wore a sari. She wanted me to meet him and invited me to her home. He was a very gentle person, a doctor, and she seemed very happy. She had organised all our family holidays on the continent, arranged sightseeing visits to Windsor and Stratford upon Avon and other notable places when we first arrived, and looked after us in every way with good humour.

Within two weeks of our arrival, Princess Chichibu made an official visit to the UK, the first by a member of the imperial family since the war. (In return HRH Princess Alexandra made a visit to Japan.) She was the widow of the Showa Emperor's younger brother Prince Chichibu, who died of tuberculosis in 1953. It was a particularly apt choice for this mission, since she had lived in London before the war, as her father Matsudaira Tsuneo was Ambassador to Britain in the early 1930s. When she called on HM The Queen for tea on this visit Her Majesty asked her "How is Ichiro?" Ichiro was her brother, who was at that time stationed in London, representing the Bank of Tokyo. While the Matsudaira parents were posted to London in the 1930s, they had played with the young princesses, daughters of the Duke of York (later King George VI). Because of Princess Chichibu's visit, my parents were fully occupied with engagements; so it was

Miss Lingard who took us to the all-important school interview.

One summer day, my sisters and I were taken to Channing School in Highgate to be interviewed. Channing had been founded in the 1880s by William Channing, the foremost theologian of Unitarianism in the US, for the education of the daughters of Unitarian ministers in Britain. It was a boarding school with a house in North Grove up the hill from the school buildings on Highgate Hill. Day girls also came from the nearby areas of Highgate and Hampstead. It was favoured by British diplomats, more convenient for putting their daughters on flights home during school holidays than boarding schools in the country. There were still some Unitarian ministers' daughters boarding there. It was not a particularly academic school but more one for educating ladies.

I was interviewed by a Miss Joan Ford, who was a teacher in English Literature. She asked me to read out a passage from a book and said "That's quite good." I was disappointed that she used the word 'quite', as in 'not very'. Whatever she thought of me, she recommended that I should be accepted to join the Upper Fifth Form. Chahchah and Eiko were similarly interviewed and accepted, Eiko in the junior school across the road in Fairseat. Miss Ford was to become an important friend and mentor, instrumental in my applying to Cambridge two years later. My parents went to visit the Headmistress, Miss Gwyneth Lloyd Thomas, afterwards. She was a distinguished scholar and a Life Fellow of Girton College, Cambridge. She lived in the Headmistress's large Victorian house, furnished and decorated in her taste of what might be classified as prewar Modern British; she had a number of paintings by Edward Bawden, a friend of hers, and some Bloomsbury artists. Her study at the school was also decorated in that style. Her academic interest was the seventeenth-century poets Andrew Marvell and John Milton.

The school was in three large connected buildings: one large Victorian, one Georgian brick and one modern. There was also a separate Georgian brick hall where we had morning prayers and some PT lessons, including contra-dancing. There were two honours boards with the names of all those who were given scholarships by the school in gilt lettering. When I left I was given the Rosslyn Hill Leaving Scholarship, so my name is listed there.

We had to order our school uniforms from Peter Jones and mother took us there to have them made. It was an extensive outlay: Harris tweed suit, consisting of a single-breasted jacket with box-pleated skirt in mid-brown; double-breasted overcoat in the same tweed; dark brown mackintosh in gabardine; dark brown beret; dark brown gloves; games skirt in the same tweed; fawn knee socks for games; light brown aertex games shirts; dark brown merino wool V-neck sweater and cardigan; cream-coloured Viyella button-down shirts; and brown lace-up shoes for outdoor wear and brown loafers for inside the school buildings. It was all rather amazing. The uniform was very stylish in classical tailoring and I could wear the overcoat, for example, quite fashionably when I was up at Cambridge. Having come from the progressive atmosphere of an American school where girls wore different dresses each day, it was now back to wearing uniforms and a discipline more akin to our school back in Japan.

My father looked for a house, now that our school was arranged. The Ambassador (Ohno Katsumi) strongly recommended that we should live in Kensington or Belgravia. The official residence was in Kensington Palace Gardens, the Embassy was in Grosvenor Street, and all Embassy staff were encouraged to live nearby. Father went to look at some recommended places but he very much wanted a house with a garden rather than a flat. He did not like the fact that most of those flats shown to him were in dark Victorian or Edwardian buildings. A Foreign Office official who was going abroad on tour suggested we rented his Georgian house in Richmond and we went to look at it; but not only would it have been too far from the school in Highgate (though we could have boarded), the Embassy chauffeur advised against it, being south of the river. He said the traffic across the bridge could cause problems and it was too far for him when my parents had daily evening engagements. Eventually we found a modest house with a garden in Hendon. That was not far from the school and although not a special building or location it was not expensive to rent and was well furnished, with parquet floors and wall-to-wall carpeting in the living quarters. It had a garden behind (where my father liked to mow the lawn), a comfortably-sized drawing room with French windows onto the garden, a dining room with a bay window, and four bedrooms. The kitchen had a dining area separated by a screen of cupboards from the cooking area. We had our family meals there each day. We lived there for four years and were by and large happy. But the location invited some slightly sarcastic, comical enquires to my mother on occasion from Mme Shima, the wife of Mr Ohno's successor: "How is it in the countryside?" And generally the Embassy people thought we lived in a rather way-out and outlandish area, not smart enough.

My father was collected every morning by Mr Hunt the chauffeur in an Embassy car, a Humber. For our family car he decided to buy a Mercedes Benz despite the Ambassador's stipulation that all his staff must buy a British car. This Ambassador was exceptionally assiduous in 'buying British' in deference to his host country – part of his diplomatic effort to get Japan accepted in the face of residual hostile attitudes. He was not pleased with my father exercising his independence as a Ministry of Finance representative, not needing to accede to his every diktat. But many of his colleagues at the Embassy were rather envious of my father's decision as they admired our car; and indeed one of them bought it from us when my parents left London.

Soon after we moved into our house, my mother had to return to Japan for a few weeks to her parents as she developed gynaecological problems. In that time, domestic chores became my responsibility, including preparing meals and cleaning the house. As it was August, school holiday time, I found myself quite free to attend to them. I wrote to my mother each day describing what I had bought from the local shops to cook and which suppliers were preferable. My father was quick to comment on my cooking and I stuck to what he liked, but it was quite hard to please him. After navigating the move from America to London, being met with a busy schedule on arrival, and contending with his wife's illness, he was exhausted. I wrote to complain to Mother how reluctant my sisters were to help with the hoovering and the like, asking her to come home soon. I had just turned sixteen then. In moments of angst at her care home in recent years, she said to me, "I was a bad Mama, I was too often ill and I left you to look after the family … it must have been hard for you…" No amount of consoling that I had forgotten it all would allay her regret.

We started school in the autumn, travelling by train to Golders Green, then getting on the 210 bus to Highgate, which stopped right outside our school. Channing was primarily a boarding school, and we day girls were considered somewhat peripheral. By October of that year London was shrouded in smog. It was a particularly bad year for freezing fog and smog that reduced visibility to nearly zero. It was a frightening experience, as people went about with gas masks and public transport came to a near-standstill. One evening my father was nearly not able to return home. School closed of course, and we were locked inside our home; the smog crept in through the window frames in a weird and threatening way. When I was a little girl at home in Japan I read in Japanese translation *Little Lord Fauntleroy* by Frances Hodgson-Burnett and romanticised about England. The strong impression it made on me, with the thick fog engulfing soot-encrusted stone buildings in London, was now a reality in front of my eyes.

My father bought me André Maurois' *History of England* soon after our arrival. I read it many times as a reference during my study of history, both while at school and at Cambridge. It was an enlightened choice of my father to get me into understanding Britain.

England after America: a Different Culture
We had no particular expectation of what England would be like. Although my father had been to London before on a brief business trip, he didn't know the country at all well, in contrast to his familiarity with America. It was unavoidable that we should compare every aspect of the two countries every day and make assessments of which we preferred. We arrived in what was a new country to us and we found few if any similarities with America. We grew to like England very much, but in the beginning it was a challenge.

In stark contrast to the Americans, who accepted no excuses for us being foreign and expected us to conform in every aspect of life, the British were forever making excuses for us not being natives. "We imagine you wouldn't understand this because you are not British…" That could be taken as politeness towards foreigners or even kindness; but it also meant that it was more difficult to integrate quickly. Moreover many people, especially the young at school, had no idea even where Japan was and we were often asked if it was part of Hong Kong. In America there were the *Nisei* (second generation Japanese–Americans who had emigrated before the war) and there was some familiarity and recognition. But in Britain, there were very few resident Japanese: only two hundred in London, fifty of whom were in the Embassy and the rest mostly on secondment from their companies. At times it seemed that we were regarded as real strangers, their lack of experience of Japanese people causing the British to seem aloof to us.

Wartime Memories and Reconciliation

Among the many people who had fought in the Pacific, there was considerable residual hostility towards the Japanese; it was only fifteen years after the end of the war and memories of hard fighting and POW camps in Changi (Singapore) and more importantly in Burma were still fresh. Some even referred to their experiences in the Nanking massacre. Even very pro-Japanese diplomats in the Foreign Office would never let us forget it. Embassy personnel were at all times prepared to encounter hostility everywhere. It was not unknown for a Japanese official attending a dinner function, for example, to be attacked verbally and sometimes physically in the gentlemen's cloakrooms by a hostile local. There was more than one such incident when a Japanese colleague excused himself from the table to go to the cloakroom and did not return for a long time; they had to go to see if he was all right, but might find him pinned to the wall by someone who had evidently been in a Japanese camp in Burma, shouting violently. The person who went to the rescue on one of those occasions was a senior British journalist (Reginald Cudlipp) who had suspected something might be wrong and insisted on going himself. Often Japanese diplomats were glared at in the streets: in a comical account a young officer of the Embassy was accosted in the street and asked if he was Japanese; he immediately replied "No, no, Malaysian…" as he thought he could get away with it with his dark complexion and slightly wavy hair! Such quick-wittedness won him the appointment as Ambassador to the Court of St James's thirty-five years later.

For decades to come efforts at 'reconciliation' continued in many forms. In the 1980s and 1990s I myself occasionally felt that the excessive amount of effort on this front was somewhat counterproductive and actually perpetuated hostile attitudes. But it was real enough that anti-Japanese demonstrations by former prisoners of war filled the streets of London during the state visit of the Emperor and Empress as late as 1998 – more than half a century after the end of the war. The Japanese government was more than prepared for this, and made sure that the Emperor's suite included a top diplomat used to being in combative situations, the former Ambassador Chiba Kazuo. The Japanese Embassy's diplomatic efforts relied heavily on cultural dissemination, education of the young (the grandchildren of those who fought in the war), and youth exchange programmes throughout the 1970s, 1980s and 1990s. I called it 'Origami diplomacy' with a hint of sarcasm – as I felt that by then economic relations between the two countries were extremely well advanced, with massive direct investment in Britain by Japanese industry. There were some admirable initiatives by private individuals on both sides – most notably Hirakubo Masao – who had fought in the war in Burma, that led to the visit by the British Burma veterans to Japan and the Japanese Burma veterans to York Minster in the 1990s and 2000s. Keiko Holmes has also for a long time arranged reconciliation venues and events for Far East prisoners of war.

Many British veterans of Burma too formed associations that fostered the spirit of reconciliation; in the mid-1990s I was suddenly and quite unexpectedly invited to a meeting of one of these by John Nunnerley, a Burma veteran, at the Royal Overseas League. It was not clear to me why, and I was initially apprehensive. At the time I was Joint Chairman of the Japan Society, the principal bilateral society between Britain and Japan, but my fellow Chairman, a Brit, had not received an invitation. There seemed to be no other guests at this meeting, though some members' wives were there. It was a cordial and happy occasion; I had to explain that I have little connection to the war, inasmuch as none of my immediate family fought in it and I was born after it, but in any case no one seemed to be talking about their war experiences. They, nevertheless, said they were happy to meet me and that they wanted me to come to future occasions too. And I did so for a number of years. John Nunnerley was a delightful man; his hobby was gliding and evidently he was an expert, having been an RAF pilot. We never talked about the war. By contrast, though, the members of the Burma Star Association were the hardcore that could not forgive or forget. I was of the view by the late 1980s and 1990s that Britain and Japan had developed a particularly close industrial as well as financial relationship (in which I myself played a part) and that that momentum needed to be maintained.

There was a close circle of personalities surrounding the Embassy, who from the end of the war dedicated much work to political and economic reconciliation. The aforementioned Reginald Cudlipp (brother of Lord Cudlipp of Mirror group fame), a well-known journalist and economist, established an economic research establishment, The Anglo-Japanese Economic Institute. He was a major contributor to disseminating information on the Japanese economy in Britain via its bulletins. When I first joined Vickers, da Costa as an economist on Japan, these bulletins provided rare and much-needed insight into the Japanese economy. Sir Julian Ridsdale MP devoted much of his political life to relations with Japan for decades, visiting the country frequently, entertaining visiting Japanese politicians at his grand home in London, intervening to resolve misunderstandings, giving a London home to his Japanese friends' children while in Britain; the role he played cannot be underestimated. He was the nephew of Rudyard Kipling and of Stanley Baldwin, three times Prime Minister during the 1920s and 1930s. His family were all involved in these endeavours and not only were his wife and daughter frequent visitors to Embassy functions, his son-in-law, Sir Paul Newall, on becoming Lord Mayor of London, made Japan the destination of his first overseas visit. He wrote a book on relations between the City of London and Japan. In the 1950s and 1960s, Sir Esler Dening and Sir Oscar Morland, both British Ambassadors at Tokyo, were friends of Japan and frequent visitors at the Embassy. In Westminster, Lady Gammans

MP and Julian Snow MP ran the Anglo-Japanese Parliamentary Group. In the City there were Edmund and Leo de Rothschild, Sir Siegmund Warburg, Lord Jellicoe (S. G. Warburg), Andrew Carnwath (Baring Bros), Robert Craigie (Panmure Gordon; son of Sir Robert Craigie, the British Ambassador at the outbreak of war), Ralph Vickers (Vickers, da Costa), Charles Wainwright (Foreign & Colonial), William Clarke (City journalist, founder of the Committee for Invisible Exports) and others, who took an interest in Japan as potential business partners. By the 1980s, Sir Peter Parker, who became Chairman of British Rail and who had been in Intelligence with the British Army during the war, launched an initiative to foster better relations through language teaching (The Sir Peter Parker Awards for Spoken Business Japanese); he led the Japan Festival initiative in 1990.

My Father, Whitehall and the City

Being concerned with financial matters between the two countries, my father formed particularly close relationships in the City. That was to lead to one of the most important achievements of his career: issuing the first Japanese government bond denominated in sterling in 1963, the first overseas issue in over three decades. His counterparts at the Treasury, Sir Douglas Allen (later Lord Croham), David Hubback, Nicholas Jordan-Moss, Hester Boothroyd, Henry Jenkins and Sir Derek Mitchell became good personal friends and stayed in contact well after his and their retirements. David Hubback's daughter, Camilla, was at New Hall, Cambridge when I went up. They were a particularly intellectual family, and Camilla and I both read History. They seemed frighteningly intelligent whenever we went to dinner at their house in Hampstead Garden Suburb. Henry Jenkins invited us to his family home in Oxted, Surrey and his family were most welcoming, showing us around their house and garden. Hester Boothroyd (Under-Secretary at HM Treasury) was a regular luncheon guest of my father's and after my parents left London for Manila, she invited me to her home in Chelsea to meet her daughters and her husband, Francis Boothroyd, who ran a research institute.

As often happens in life, I found when I bought my house in Suffolk a coincidence in that both Francis (by then widowed) and Hester's brother, Colin Benham, lived in the village too. Colin's family had lived in Colchester for generations and he and his first wife, Marion, were great supporters and friends of Suffolk artists – Peter Coker, John Nash, Cedric Morris, Lett Haines *et al.* For a time Colin ran the Minories Gallery in Colchester. With my interest in art, I was more than happy to meet him. This happened quite by accident: I went to the church art show in Nayland one Saturday afternoon and, as the organiser of the exhibition, he was attending to the visitors; I showed some interest in a painting by a local artist, John Ridgewell, and Colin engaged me in conversation, saying that was the best painting in the show. John Ridgewell was a more than competent painter – known amongst the cognoscenti for his surrealist landscapes – and I got to know him soon afterwards and bought another painting by him. Colin told me that Hester had died of cancer a couple of years previously and that her daughter also died of cancer a year later. He had asked me how I came to be in England and, when I explained that my father was a Ministry of Finance official, he asked about any possible connection with his sister. He pointed to his face and asked if I could recognise facial similarities with Hester, and immediately invited me to dinner at his house in Nayland with his recently married new wife, Margaret, a horticulturist. Margaret designed a large border for me and became a good friend. The house was full of Colin and Marion's collection of modern art, which was an inspiration.

Perhaps the friendship that survived the longest was with Sir Derek Mitchell. He had been private secretary to Chancellor of the Exchequer Reginald Maudling and then at Downing Street as private secretary to Sir Alec Douglas-Home and Harold

Wilson. He visited my parents in Tokyo on a number of occasions after retirement and corresponded with my father for many years. When I went to work at the World Bank in Washington he was the head of the UK Treasury delegation, Executive Director for the UK at the Bank and the IMF. He immediately asked me to one of his dinner parties at his home in Kalorama and I was able to meet a number of senior personalities in Washington there, some of whom became important friends. I benefited greatly from the relationships my father fostered in London: Edmund de Rothschild always invited me to his annual luncheon parties at Exbury in the rhododendron season and with his wife, Anne, came often to my dinner parties; Lord Jellicoe and Bill Clarke tried to find me a job when I came down from Cambridge; Andrew Carnwath introduced me to his son who was also up at Cambridge then and invited me out to dinners and took me to meet his parents at their house in Ugley. Nicky Kaldor (later Lord Kaldor) and his wife Clarissa invited me to their home in Adams Road often for Sunday lunches when the eminent Cambridge economists gathered – Joan Robinson, Richard Kahn, Robert Neild *et al*. I felt completely out of my depth as their conversations turned to economic theories. He gave me his book translated into Japanese and signed it in Japanese!

One early encounter that my father particularly appreciated was that with Lord Jellicoe, who was at Warburgs. On hearing that Admiral Yamanashi was my father's uncle he found in his father's archives the photograph and the seating plan of the victory banquet that Yamanashi had attended on HMS *Iron Duke* at Scapa Flow a week after the Battle of Jutland, together with some correspondence between the two men. He gave them to my father to take to Yamanashi. The old admiral was more than moved to receive them, but my father had to explain to Jellicoe that he was too ill to write to thank him. Of all those who my father came to know at Warburgs, Lord Jellicoe was his best friend and closest contact.

We settled down in London during the summer and autumn of 1962. My parents were out virtually every evening at diplomatic functions; there were Embassy receptions and dinners at least once or twice a week for visiting Japanese dignitaries as well as for British government and industry personalities. And there were the cocktail parties and dinners hosted by British counterparts. One of the more colourful such hosts was Mr Nubar Gulbenkian. The well-known son of the oil magnate Calouste Gulbenkian, Nubar was a member of the Iranian Embassy in London, having taken Iranian nationality. Japan being a major export market for Iranian oil, he kept closely in touch with its Embassy. For some reason, he took a liking to my father and invited my parents quite often to dinner at his home in Arlington House off Piccadilly. Yoko, seated next to him at table, would comment on the excellent cuisine, as Nubar Gulbenkian was a gourmet. On one occasion she expressed delight at the delicious huge asparagus; lo and behold, the next morning a large bunch of asparagus was delivered to our home by his chauffeur. On another, as she liked the new season grouse that was served, the very next morning two brace of grouse in their feathers arrived. As we were just leaving for north Wales to stay with my school friend, Libet Williams, we took the grouse with us. That met with merriment but Lady Williams was not entirely amused at having to pluck and draw the birds. Nor did they like the bitter taste of grouse; our present was not a success. My parents, on returning from those dinner parties at the Gulbenkians', regaled us with entertaining stories of what went on and the flamboyant host. His monocle, the long beard, orchid in his buttonhole, extravagant lifestyle and gourmet dinner parties were legendary; he had a built-to-order Austin, looking much like the black cabs of London, but uniquely with the doors patterned with basket work in gold. He was evidently a witty conversationalist as my father told us of many amusing remarks that he made at table.

My father was also an active participant in the Association

of Economic Representatives in London. One of the friends he made here was his Italian counterpart, Antonino Zecchi, a charismatic official with a beautiful, elegantly-dressed wife. I remember him talking about the Zecchis often, and my parents dined with them on numerous occasions. Sadly, Antonino died while my parents were still in London. My father was elected to succeed him as the Association's Chairman in the latter half of his stay in England.

A Diplomat's Wife

My mother was busy with ladies' luncheon parties and attending various Anglo-Japanese societies for the ladies: the Ikebana International, Otomodachi-kai, and the Japanese women's society. As one of the ministers' wives, she had to take on the roles of Chairman of the Japanese women's society and deputy Chairman of Ikebana International. She had never had to play such roles before and found it a burden. Ikebana International was a group founded by an English woman, Stella Coe, who was devoted to the art of flower-arranging, *ikebana*. I believe it was funded mostly by herself. All the Embassy ladies and wives of the Japanese banks and companies almost automatically belonged to it. They held periodic exhibitions and meetings to learn the art, occasionally inviting from Japan the leading ikebana artists to teach the British enthusiasts. Yoko found that many of the Embassy wives were expert at ikebana (which she wasn't) and was amazed at what those ladies created with limited resources in England. She went to the woods at Kenwood to collect desiccated logs to put in her arrangements; she tried to find wild flowers in the meadows that could be used, as florists were extremely expensive; but then she found that one of the ladies had covered the ground of her arrangement with frozen peas – what an innovative idea!

The Otomodachi-kai was an initiative of the British Foreign Office wives who had been on postings in Tokyo; it was organised on the basis that one British wife would be an *otomodachi* – a friend – of a Japanese wife in the Embassy in London. Others with Japanese interests, such as wives of Japanese scholars, were also members, as were the wives of some Japanese company representatives. The British *otomodachi* would arrange to meet her Japanese *otomodachi* to go to exhibitions or museums or other places of cultural interest, or just for tea. There were also general meetings of the society. Its aim was to foster friendship and to make sure the Japanese wives were not lost or lonely, overwhelmed by the pressures of diplomatic life in a foreign country. Yoko's 'friend' was Hazel Beasley, the wife of the historian of modern Japan, Professor W. G. Beasley. She enjoyed Hazel's company very much and they met quite frequently. Hazel also came to Japan after my parents' retirement and Yoko was able to renew her friendship.

Diplomatic life was perhaps somewhat different from what it may be now. Wives very much 'served' with their husbands, and they had another dimension of diplomacy to attend to. It was unthinkable that spouses should have other jobs or interests; my late mother-in-law, wife of a British diplomat, was an artist and it was thought she did not participate adequately in the Embassy wives' agenda, for which she was criticised. Some wives found it hard to cope and their mental health could suffer. Diplomats represent their countries and governments in foreign countries; their reputation and behaviour have knock-on effects on international relations. They may have little time for personal friendships or family concerns; their children's education has to be arranged back at home; they are separated from their children most of the time, relying on support from close relatives; being away from their home countries most of their working lives means few friends could be made at home, and on retirement they can suddenly find themselves lonely. It is different from normal civilian life, and far from the glamorous lifestyle portrayed in some quarters. Daily commitments to entertaining official guests and attending receptions and dinners are mentally and physically exhausting duties, not just 'going to parties'. So much so, Lady Williams – Libet's mother – founded the Diplomatic Wives Association at the Foreign Office.

Yoko quickly got used to a different kind of formality: wearing hats and gloves to luncheons and tea gatherings, new clothes for the numerous cocktail parties and dinners each week. She grouped together with other ladies of the Embassy to collect Japanese ingredients from the monthly shipments from home; discovered good-quality fishmongers in Soho with friends where they could get *hard* cod's roe – a Japanese delicacy (Soho was in those days a dangerous area where daylight murders were frequent); and rose to the more demanding schedule of social life that was the duty of a senior diplomatic wife. The Ambassador's wife set a strict high standard in dress and manners; I remember the Embassy ladies being instructed that the petticoat must be the same colour as the dress. Royal occasions were numerous, with banquets and soirées at the Palace, garden parties, the Royal Box at Ascot and Wimbledon. As her husband was from the Ministry of Finance, Yoko also had to attend to the welfare of the families of the finance circle; there were many gatherings of the wives of those representing the banks and securities and insurance companies. With no help in the house it was a busy life for her. There was also a cohort of friends at Gakushuin's London Tokiwakai society, including a classmate and others who were close to her age. It gave her a haven at their periodic gatherings of kindred spirits, away from her duties; she would never miss them.

From time to time there were family outings of the financial community. I remember one, not long after we had arrived in London, when they hired a pleasure boat to sail up the Thames to Windsor, with lunch on board. The youngest member of the delegation in London from the Development Bank of Japan (a government-owned bank under the aegis of the Ministry of

Finance) who had just arrived recently was Ogata Shijuro (緒方 四十郎), with his bride Sadako. She had recently been awarded her PhD from the University of California (Berkeley) under the tutelage of Professor Robert Scalapino, a close friend of ours, as mentioned earlier. Decades later she became UNHCR (United Nations High Commissioner for Refugees) and more famous than her husband. She took my sister Sakiko under her wing as a fellow Japanese woman in the UN orbit. Shijuro later joined the Bank of Japan in its foreign relations department, and became a well-known figure in the international central banking community. I saw him every year at the IMF annual meetings; he would forever tell everyone how frightening my father was and that the only way to get him to smile was to mention his 'brilliant' eldest daughter's name. I am sure he meant it kindly but I found it rather irritating, especially as, as Masaru's archive shows, Shijuro was much helped by my father with very senior introductions in Europe and America throughout his career.

Another person on that boat was Hayami Masaru (速水優), a representative of the Bank of Japan. After retirement from the central bank he joined his wife's family company, Nissho-Iwai Corporation, one of the largest general trading companies, and became its Chairman and President; he was called back in 1998 to become Governor of the Bank of Japan. He was a most delightful man, cultured and well-read – often quoting Rupert Brooke; a devout Protestant, very straight-talking (which won him many enemies, but he would quote the Bible at them!). It was he who as Governor insisted that Japanese politicians had to bring in legislation to disallow monopolistic practices and liberalise Japan's industrial and economic structure, so that the Japanese economy could emerge from the deflationary cycle of the 1990s. He was adamant that monetary policy, of which he was in charge, had to work in tandem with fiscal policy, which was the responsibility of the Ministry of Finance. That irritated MoF officials, resulting in policy disharmony. He knew my father well of course, and his wife my mother; soon after the boat trip he was relocated to New York, but as my father's work was transatlantic they kept up frequent contact.

I came to know Hayami well when he was at Nissho-Iwai and subsequently at the Bank of Japan, where I called on him on my visits to Japan. In his memoirs, which he sent to me after he retired, he writes most touchingly about the visit of the Showa Emperor to London in 1971. As the Chief Representative in Europe for Japan's central bank, he was included in all state occasions, and he was one of the few who went in his morning coat to welcome the Emperor on his arrival at Victoria Station. He wrote that seeing the Emperor in London brought tears to his eyes. Born ten years later than my father, he was conscripted into the Army while at university near the end of the war, when the future seemed all too uncertain. Hayami had another connection with my parents in that he became Chairman of the trustees of Tokyo Woman's Christian University, my mother's alma mater.

Vice Minister of Finance Ishino signing the first postwar
government bond issue in London, July 1963. Masaru making
sure (centre behind); Westminster Bank headquarters.

9. International Financial Diplomacy: Japan is Back

~

In the summer of 1962, new developments in international finance were unfolding in the City of London. Concerns over international financial liquidity and balance of payments difficulties in the US were gathering momentum for policymakers at HM Treasury and the government. Prime Minister Macmillan took a particular interest in the issues, as he saw threats to democracy should any remedial measures taken by the US result in economic contraction in the West. Meanwhile, the Bank of England and the City were eager to capture the opportunity to regain their status in international financial markets, with the imminent advent of the Eurobond market in external dollars. The sudden imposition the following year of the US Interest Equalisation Tax, which took transaction flows away from the supremacy of New York, provided that crucial opportunity. This development produced potentially vast opportunities for borrowers as well as for intermediaries. For the policymakers the abrupt move by the Kennedy administration crystallised their concerns, even aside from the immediate impact that the new measures might have on interest rates and flow of funds across waters.

I do not intend to write an essay in economic history here, but the threat of shortage of international liquidity was the subject that concerned my father most in his work – in his own words what he "worked on passionately day and night". He engaged in constant direct discussions with Treasury and central bank officials in the UK, Germany, Switzerland and the US. He wrote expounding his own thoughts on the issue and events in which he was directly involved. For Japan, which he represented, it was the first time after the war that it endeavoured to join the international negotiating table of leading nations. The following section is based largely on my father's memoirs. It is a vignette of the international financial diplomacy of that time. Though his memoirs covered a wider area of these issues and included a profound analysis of them, including the events leading up to the sterling devaluation of 1967 and the policies followed by the Wilson government after its election in the autumn of 1964, I am limiting this account to what involved my father directly.

Threats to International Liquidity

'International liquidity' refers to the official means of accommodating imbalances in international payments. It comprises the gold and foreign exchange holdings of monetary authorities (the central banks and treasuries), plus additional means of payment available to them through international and bilateral credit facilities such as those provided by the IMF. Credit facilities of the IMF, accompanied by increasing the quotas of the industrial countries, have allowed the phenomenal expansion of world trade and economic growth in the postwar period. Britain and Canada drew on the stabilisation credit in 1961 and 1962 in defence of their currencies, and the United States itself entered into a standby agreement with the IMF in 1963. The question of liquidity shortage began seriously to concern policymakers in 1960 (the year my father arrived in Washington), when the price of gold in the London market rose well above the Bretton Woods agreement of $35.20 per ounce, greatly increasing incentives for central banks to exchange surplus dollar reserves for gold with the US Treasury. The US had run balance of payments deficits throughout the 1950s as it provided international finance for reconstruction efforts in Japan and Europe. By August 1960 *total* outstanding dollar liabilities to foreign countries began to exceed US gold stock, and by the end of 1965 the outstanding dollar liabilities to official institutions (central banks and treasuries) which could be exchanged directly with the US Treasury exceeded the US gold stock. Professor Robert Triffin famously testified before Congress in 1960, warning that the ever-mounting accumulation of US dollars outside the country threatened the continuing viability of the Bretton Woods system based on the convertibility of the dollar into gold. The rise in the market price of gold indicated the underlying fear that the US might devalue the dollar. 'Triffin's dilemma', as his theory came to be known, predicted that the system would not be able to maintain both liquidity and confidence in the fixed exchange rate system. This came home to roost in 1971 when President Nixon suspended convertibility of the US dollar into gold by official holders. Masaru wrote in his memoirs that logic dictated that what Triffin foresaw was an inevitable consequence of the US policy of continuing dollar supremacy. They knew each other well and Triffin kept my father informed with behind-the-scenes commentary in detail in letters to London and Manila.

For policymakers the issue of international liquidity was not an academic debating point but was a political matter that affected the relative strengths of leading nations. Alongside military superiority it is at the heart of Western capitalism. Masaru's interest was not just intellectual; he stood at the centre of building Japan's international credibility at a time it was making every effort to be accepted by the Western powers as one of them. Prime Minister Ikeda Hayato, having been a career MoF official and Minister of Finance before becoming Prime Minister in 1960, placed primary importance on raising Japan's position in international financial markets; he and Masaru, well known to each other, were therefore on the same wavelength. My father prepared the ground for Ikeda's visits to Washington and London at the highest levels of both administrations. That produced outstanding results for Japan. One of them was the country joining the OECD in July 1963, ahead of Australia, and the other, in the same month, was the historic issue of the Japanese government bond in pounds sterling for the first time in more than thirty years. The process of how this happened is described in the next section of this book.

Before embarking on that, a brief background on how the international liquidity issue came to the fore of international debate is in order. Necessarily, this is a simplified and simplistic exposition of more complex history. Although President Kennedy's inauguration in January 1961 was hailed in triumphant terms, he had won the election by a small margin and his reelection in 1964 was uncertain. That was mostly because the economic performance of the US during the early years of that decade was less than stellar; there was the mounting balance of payments deficit, the poor performance of the stock market, rising unemployment at 6 per cent that could not be stemmed, and increasing capital outflows, with both foreign dollar borrowing in the US markets and American companies' investment overseas in both portfolio and direct investment. If they were to tackle the balance of payments deficit, the administration was faced with having to choose between tax cuts and expanded fiscal spending for growth on the one hand and a tighter monetary policy with higher interest rates and less fiscal spending (domestically as well as overseas in military and development aid) on the other. America was not alone in facing a large and growing balance of payments deficit; the UK (the other, though much smaller, reserve currency with the sterling balances held in London) was in a similar position. President Kennedy spoke of his commitment to the defence of freedom against communist oppression and the status of the United States in the world in his characteristically powerful and inspiring speeches, and dismissed any rumours of austerity measures. It was urgent that confidence in the US dollar be restored as the market price of gold was rising in the face of increasing US dollar foreign liabilities.

In the first instance, in 1961 the US secretly negotiated with the IMF the General Agreements to Borrow (GAB), which the Managing Director of the IMF, Per Jacobson, presented at the annual meetings of the IMF in September 1961 in Vienna as a *fait accompli* requiring no votes. It came into effect in January 1962; the GAB was established when ten industrial countries (the G10) agreed to make funds available to the IMF with an additional $6 billion to increase its lending resources. Those countries were: the US, Belgium, Canada, France, Italy, Japan, the Netherlands, the UK, Germany and Sweden. It was joined by Switzerland two years later. The GAB enabled the IMF to borrow specified amounts of currencies from those countries under certain conditions. The G10 became a forum for governmental negotiations on these issues in certain circumstances, but not always. In addition to the GAB, the United States introduced in March 1962 the Federal Reserve Reciprocal Currency Arrangement – a network of swap lines with foreign central banks – specifically to forestall any official run on the US gold stock. This became the first line of defence of the dollar, as the Exchange Stabilization Fund of the US Treasury, set up the year before, which allowed interventions in the foreign exchange forward markets, was constrained by lack of available resources and subject to Congressional approval. Over the following years the swap lines were expanded widely to fourteen central banks and one with the Bank of International Settlements. Swap lines were drawn for temporary expediency to cover for foreign exchange risk and protect the US gold position. But that rested on the assumption that the US balance of payments deficit was of a temporary nature that could be restored to health in due course. Yet some others thought a more permanent solution to the fundamental disequilibrium of international payments had to be worked out.

There were several proposals emerging by the summer of 1962, but the starting shot to challenge the continuing viability of the Bretton Woods system was fired by Britain with the Maudling Plan.

The Macmillan–Ikeda Summit

My father was reading the British newspapers on the plane on our way to London from America on 14 July 1962 and learnt that there had been a major Cabinet reshuffle – 'the night of the long knives' – in which Reginald Maudling had replaced Selwyn Lloyd as Chancellor of the Exchequer. The *Daily Mail* had carried an article on 12 July, as did the *Evening Standard* of the same day, that should the Conservatives badly lose the by-election in Leicester, a Cabinet reshuffle involving changing the Chancellor could not be avoided. Masaru was impressed with the powerful influence of the national Press in Britain, but the reality was the waning popularity of the government as the tight fiscal policy following the sterling crisis of 1961 was weighing on the voters. He had been much impressed with the style and statesmanship of Selwyn Lloyd at the Vienna IMF meeting the previous autumn, when in the concluding remarks of the conference he had manoeuvred the divided meeting into passing the GAB without a vote. My father was therefore initially disappointed to hear the news. He recorded in his memoirs some years later that he saw Rab Butler being interviewed on television when he retired from politics, and he said that in appointing Maudling to be Chancellor, Macmillan had been influenced by the youthful image of President Kennedy, giving rise to the infectious atmosphere of a new era dawning. (Butler had in fact leaked the information on the reshuffle, originally planned for the autumn, to the owner of the *Daily Mail* on 11 July, and as the newspaper reports came in the following morning the Prime Minister went ahead with the reshuffle immediately.) Macmillan was deeply concerned about the international liquidity issue; it might have been that a fundamental reappraisal of the international monetary system by a new and younger Chancellor of the Exchequer was thought to provide the necessary impetus, although the immediate reason was a difference of opinion with Selwyn Lloyd on incomes policy and reflation.

Within a few weeks of arrival in London, Masaru heard Macmillan make a somewhat mysterious comment to the House of Commons at the end of a speech on the economy: he referred to the proposal by the IMF Managing Director, Per Jacobson, on GAB, and said that it provided a source of additional capital in times of need but that he believed it did not provide a solution and a new internationally agreed system should be sought as the US was experiencing pressure on the dollar; his words were typically shrouded in extensive allusions to the need for international cooperation, mutuality of economic dependence, and Britain's readiness not to stand in the way of an agreement amongst nations. His speech seemed to be critical of the way that the GAB resolution had been passed without a vote at the IMF, an international institution in which international dialogue and decision-making had to be guaranteed, but it also made clear Britain was seeking a more far-reaching solution to the fundamental problem.

Sensing that behind these enigmatic remarks was a plan being hatched within the British government, Masaru sought an immediate meeting with the US finance representative, a Mr Bean at the American Embassy, to whom he had been introduced by a mutual friend in Washington. Bean said that it was possible Britain was considering a revision of the IMF agreement, but he had not been consulted even with any kind of a hint before Macmillan made his comment, nor had the American Embassy enquired thus far with the Treasury nor the Bank of England; he appeared to be greatly interested in the matter brought to him and said he would speak with his friend at the Treasury. Masaru then went to see Mr Douglas Allen (later Sir Douglas, later still Lord Croham), who was the head of the international finance department of the Treasury.

Douglas Allen explained quietly and in a charming manner with a smile what lay behind Macmillan's comment. Masaru recalled that he looked up at the grey sky from time to time through the window of his large office. From that day onwards Douglas Allen became a lifelong trusted friend, and they were able to help one another in the diplomacy of finance for many years. When I went to visit him some years later, when he was Permanent Secretary of the Treasury, he courteously said "We miss your father in London." Decades later at his memorial service Lady Croham immediately said to me that she knew who I was because her husband used to talk a lot about my father at home.

Douglas Allen told Masaru that Britain knew that the GAB was not an adequate solution, but that, at the point at which the US government had already made an understanding with Jacobson, for Britain to criticise would have embarrassed the US. Therefore at the Vienna IMF meeting Britain had agreed unconditionally. He further elaborated that unless the fixed price of gold could be raised there would be a dead-end to international liquidity. But he thought it virtually impossible to raise the gold price without causing other major issues to arise. If so, 'a piece of international paper' would be required to supplement gold. It had been for a long time considered in Britain that continuing adherence to the Bretton Woods system would cause a shortage of international liquidity that could lead to contraction of world trade, as countries tried to defend their balance of payments with tight economic policies which in turn could cause the world economy to fall into depression. European countries holding surplus dollars were currently beginning to refuse to hold dollars in their foreign exchange reserves. Therefore it was felt that a mutually-owned account at the IMF could be established with some agreed ceiling on the amounts, and it would have to be guaranteed with gold. He then said that hammering out this sort of approach was not the initiative of the Treasury nor of the Chancellor, but was the conviction of Macmillan himself at the heart of his strategy against the spread of communism; that for democratic countries to continue to prosper everything had to be done to avoid contraction of world trade or, even worse, economic depression.

What came to be known as the Maudling Plan, Mutual Currency Account, was worked out and drafted by Lucius Thompson-McCausland, then adviser to the Governor at the Bank of England. Thompson-McCausland was Keynes' long-serving associate, working closely with him on the Bretton Woods system, attending the conference itself. Douglas Allen appeared to be a close friend of his. It was planned that Maudling would present the plan at the forthcoming IMF Annual Meetings in Washington in September. It was not yet decided at which venue discussions should continue after announcement to progress the Plan – whether the OECD Working Party 3, the G10 or a special committee formed inside the IMF. Douglas Allen did not favour the WP3 route; of course he would go to Washington beforehand to consult with the United States.

Masaru immediately informed the Ministry in Tokyo; but his dispatch was not circulated to the Japanese delegation attending the IMF meeting. My father felt sidelined. His efforts were, however, not unrewarded. His dispatch had caught the eye of the Prime Minister's private secretary, who showed it to Prime Minister Ikeda. On the way to London to sign the Commercial Treaty (a revival of the old Anglo-Japanese Treaty of Commerce and Navigation that lapsed in 1920) the following month, Ikeda was calling in on European capitals. He summoned Ambassador Ohno Katsumi (大野勝己) in London to Paris for a pre-visit briefing, and told him to give an order to Masaru that in preparing for the summit meeting with Macmillan he should explain to the British that the Japanese Prime Minister had a deep interest in the Maudling Plan and was supportive of it. A key issue in the background prompted Ikeda to play *realpolitik* with Macmillan: while he had been working hard to get Japan into the OECD, given that Australia was waiting in the wings and the British Foreign Office either reserving its position or paying mere lip service to Japan's joining, Ikeda now seized the opportunity to turn that into committed support for membership at his meeting with Macmillan. Japan would support the Maudling Plan at the IMF; the quid pro quo was that Britain should support Japan joining the OECD.

Macmillan and Ikeda got on well: having previously been Chancellor and Minister of Finance respectively, they shared common understandings. Indeed, Macmillan said at the meeting that having had similar experiences with the finance portfolios there were many areas of true agreement between them, which was both a coincidence and a pleasure. Licking his pencil, he took the already-prepared joint communiqué and replaced the sentence on Japan's entry into the OECD: 'We will bear it in mind with a sympathetic attitude' with 'proactively support it'. The end result of this was that Japan was accepted to join the OECD less than a year later, in early July of 1963 (formally acceding in 1964), well ahead of Australia.

Moreover, there was an initiative in the communiqué in which Masaru also had a hand. Given Ikeda's interest in international finance, he felt that the Prime Minister would want something of lasting significance to mark his visit to the UK. It was not likely, and in any case possibly not desirable, that Japan should make a significant sterling deposit with the Bank of England (she had done so on the occasion of Prime Minister Kishi's visit a few years previously, but sterling was now under pressure). He had to think of something else. Even if a deposit was to be made, it would necessarily be a small amount. Masaru hit upon the idea that there should be formed a new bilateral discussion forum that would meet from time to time to exchange views on international finance matters for mutual benefit. The text of the joint communiqué had already been drafted by the Foreign Office. He went to see David Hubback at the Treasury, who had been private secretary to Chancellor Selwyn Lloyd and had just become head of the international finance department, succeeding Douglas Allen who was now heading National Planning at the Treasury. Hubback and his deputy, Nicholas Jordan-Moss, listened to Masaru's proposal and agreed at once that such an initiative would be welcomed by the Treasury. They also understood Masaru's position that inserting this proposal into the joint communiqué had to be at the initiative of the British Foreign Office. Jordan-Moss wrote out the required text for the communiqué then and there and telephoned the head of the Far East Desk at the Foreign Office, Arthur de la Mare (later knighted), who was well known to Jordan-Moss as they had served in Washington together previously (the de la Mares became close friends of my parents during their time in London). The very next day the Foreign Office contacted the Japanese delegation expressing its desire to put into the joint communiqué that henceforth both countries would follow a closer protocol on financial relations and that they shared an interest in the problem of international liquidity.

Prime Minister Ikeda was more than pleased: my father knew that he had said the original version of the communiqué was too weak and wanted it to include something along the lines of Japan being ready to offer assistance to the UK in times of need. Standing in the receiving line next to Macmillan at the Admiralty House reception on 13 November 1962, as my father approached he called out to him to say "Hey Fukuda, that new text of the communiqué is all right, isn't it?" My father replied "Yes, it is fine, Prime Minister," though he was nervous as to whether the new text was definitely there until it was published.

Readers may think all this is trivial, but joint communiqués by heads of government used to be examined with a fine-tooth comb by all serious political observers, trying to discern what lay behind the text, until Twitter, YouTube and other internet-driven media took over in the twenty-first century. Moreover, the efforts of Masaru and others, including the Prime Minister, must be seen in the context of Japanese aspirations in the international arena at that time. Postwar reconstruction efforts were bearing fruit, with the emergence of both large and small industries. Japan was beginning to gain international competitiveness by the beginning of the 1960s. It is clear from my father's writing that he saw his own role as one which brought Japan into the discussion of major issues, the most important of which were those of international liquidity and exchange rate stability. He was particularly adept at gaining access to the leading policy-makers and winning their personal confidence. Indeed, when I met Sir Douglas Allen years later, he made the point that my father had enabled a confidential exchange of views with Japan.

On return from the IMF meeting in Washington in 1962, Douglas Allen told him that despite an objection from the Secretary of the US Treasury (Douglas Dillon), Maudling had gone ahead and presented the plan. Masaru was told by Nicholas Jordan-Moss several months later that Macmillan and Kennedy, being related by marriage, had a private correspondence line 10 Downing Street to the White House – and Macmillan had warned Kennedy that if the shortage of liquidity continued, not only might world trade shrink but President de Gaulle would continue to convert dollars into gold and the United States might end up unable to cope with similar demands from other European countries; he sought a direct personal decision by Kennedy himself. JFK held meetings of advisers who were sworn to secrecy; all papers at the meetings were destroyed, as his biographer, Theodore Sorensen, confirmed after Kennedy's assassination. Macmillan and Maudling were confident that Maudling should defy the Executive branch of the US government. The Plan was much criticised in the United States, including publicly by Robert Roosa, then the Under-Secretary of the US Treasury. Douglas Allen continued to explain to Masaru that the central objection of the US to the Maudling Plan concerned the requirement for the dollar in the Mutual Currency Account to carry the gold guarantee. From the British point of view, having already had to accept the 'Roosa Bond' (a scheme by which countries with surplus dollars should purchase a long-term bond in US dollars instead of converting to gold, the bonds to be repaid in Swiss francs), and with the European governments' reluctance to hold any further dollars, they could not yield on this essential point. No conclusion was reached but discussions were to continue with IMF officials and in the unofficial meetings of the WP3. Douglas Allen also said Sir Denis Rickett, the Permanent Secretary of the Treasury, learnt in the corridors of the meetings that the European countries of the EEC were considering a joint initiative to revise the international exchange rate system, and did not show much reaction to the Maudling Plan.

In the background, despite official representations, both Japan and Germany were doing their best to accommodate the US position. It was Germany that originally extended the swap line to the US in 1961, as Japan did too with Masaru's valiant efforts to give a government guarantee to Kansai Electric Power's dollar borrowing from the US EXIM despite constitutional difficulties – my father said it was one of his proudest moments of negotiation, even though he had been privately convinced of the folly of increasing public sector borrowing in dollars.

Following Maudling's speech at the IMF in September 1962, HM Treasury prepared a full exposition of the plan and delivered it to the governments of the US, Japan (through my father at the Embassy), Australia, and the major countries of Europe. My father was told that a confidential executive committee was being established with one representative each from HM Treasury, the Bank of England, the US Treasury and the Federal Reserve to pursue the negotiations. Meanwhile, the European countries were suggesting that foreign exchange reserves of countries other than the US should allow for one third in gold (Germany's position) or even two-thirds in gold (the French position), and that their gold holdings acquired through official conversion were not returnable. While Bonn was more cooperative with the US monetary authorities in exchange for tangible advantages, this was not the case with Paris; the French government was openly critical of the dollar exchange system, converting a large part of its dollar holdings and advocating further conversion to other EEC countries. This gold diplomacy was one of the French (de Gaulle's) strategies to gain political leverage during the 1960s. De Gaulle's ambition to build the European Economic Community into 'a third power' (via a political union) was of course a part of this. All of that is a subject close to my heart, having spent a long time in my working career on it, but it is outside the scope of this book to go further into it.

The negotiations between the US and the UK through the confidential executive committee continued over six months. During that time Britain's application to join the EEC had met with the famous 'Non' from de Gaulle in January 1963. But the US Treasury position was also one of intransigence as postulated by Roosa to Masaru in 1961 and at the IMF meeting of 1962. Although the Maudling Plan was abandoned, Masaru commented that it had achieved one important objective. That was finally to turn the US Treasury's adamant stance of sticking to the existing exchange rate system towards discussing positively with other countries the possibility of revising the system going forward.

They abandoned the Maudling Plan with no regrets and went ahead with increasing IMF capital by 25 per cent, with acrimonious discussions over the proportions of contributions and the burden of gold cover to prevent an excess burden being borne by the US dollar. At the very beginning of July 1963 Masaru read an editorial in the *Guardian* newspaper hinting that there was a change in the US policy stance and immediately went to see David Hubback: although Hubback denied that there were any inferences to be drawn from the *Guardian*, his body language alerted Masaru that something was up. He immediately informed Tokyo. His instinct was right: literally within a few days came a dramatic announcement by President Kennedy: the United States would impose an Interest Equalisation Tax, and while it engaged in discussions with other countries in search of a revision of the international payment system, the United States would follow an expansionary policy.

Masaru was told by Samuel Goldman at HM Treasury, then Third Permanent Secretary, that all countries had to recognise that although the Press was reporting the US Treasury's residual reservations about the government's commitment to start talks on the revision of the international exchange rate system, the decision was made personally by President Kennedy. He emphasised that everything in the future depended on that fact. It seems, therefore, that Kennedy heeded Macmillan's strong advice. Masaru learnt from Bean at the US Embassy in confidence that the forum for those discussions was to be the G10 but that there would be a meeting of the G10 representatives chaired by Roosa ahead of the IMF annual meeting so that that could be confirmed at the meeting of finance ministers. The Interest Equalization Tax came into force on 18 July 1963, and it was to have a preponderant influence on the course of international financial markets – namely the advent of the Eurobond market.

With much happening on the broad front, Masaru was exceptionally busy that month on a major project he had initiated immediately after arriving in London a year earlier and which was just about to reach a successful conclusion. This was the issue of a Japanese government bond in sterling in London, for the first time in over thirty years.

Japanese Government Sterling Bond Issue 1963: the Inside Story
It may seem to today's readers that this particular bond issue was a parochial event of minor significance, but it was, and not just for Japan, an important milestone that merits a full account. It was a breakthrough event for City bankers in that, for the first time since the war, a foreign government outside the Commonwealth issued a bond in London in sterling; until then such issues had been forbidden by law. The day after the bond was issued all British national newspapers hailed it as such. My father thus played a principal role in reopening the London market as a primary international financial centre; the negotiations were conducted with tenacity against the background of an obstinate British government stance of the day.

On arriving in London Masaru's predecessor, Mr Inada, who went back to head up a bureau at the Ministry, had left very little in the way of a handover. He just said that Masaru would enjoy London because he had a good political sense and that he should concentrate on reading the British Press, such as *The Times*. My father in fact liked reading the *Daily Mail* most; as he said to me, he liked to read the gossip columns and enjoyed seeing the photographs of glamorous women.

In looking through a drawer of the desk in the office he came across some correspondence that intrigued him. There he discovered in a letter from the then President of Nomura Securities, Okumura Tsunao, to Ambassador Ohno that Okumura was trying to arrange a visit to Japan by a group of senior financiers from the City of London, and that Okumura was keeping in close touch on this plan with Prime Minister Ikeda. Masaru immediately called on all the members of this mission: Schroders (The Hon. Alexander Hood); Rothschilds (Edmund de Rothschild); Warburgs (Siegmund Warburg); Barings (Andrew Carnwath);

those in charge of Japanese relations at Westminster Bank; and M. Samuel (later Hill Samuel). He was most impressed by the old building of Rothschilds, where the partners shared a large room and all correspondence was shared between them, as he was fully knowledgeable about the role the bank had played in history. He wanted to make sure that the mission would not be disappointed, but of course it was incumbent on him to lay the ground for their meeting with the Prime Minister.

He therefore made sure that Ikeda referred to the speech by the Governor of the Bank of England, Lord Cromer, given at the annual Mansion House dinner a few weeks previously. From my father's perspective, it was an important and significant speech. Cromer said openly that he was fundamentally opposed to the government managing foreign exchange rates and controls, and investments overseas; recalling that it was the private sector, the merchant banks, that had developed the City of London as the global financial centre; that the golden age of the City was founded on the long experience of specialist financial expertise which must now be revived to play the central role. Pre-empting any countering view from Whitehall that anything that could lead to an outflow of capital would be inimical to Britain's balance of payments, he advocated that the role of a capital market should be as an *entrepôt*, where money would flow in and flow out, and it need not itself have a large capital base. Money would flow to the global capital market naturally from other countries, the essential condition being that there existed superior financial techniques that were the prerogatives of the merchant bankers. Britain's future lay in activating these sleeping talents to allow the City once again to become the centre of international finance.

Although other countries' finance ministry officials were barred from having contacts with the Bank of England, and Treasury officials particularly discouraged it, Masaru managed to see Eric Haslam (in charge of the Far East) at the Bank. Haslam said that the Governor's position was a view widely held inside the Bank, and foreign exchange control should be abolished. On his enquiring casually with Douglas Allen at the Treasury, Allen said that Cromer's speech was an expression of his personal view and it was out of his jurisdiction; such fundamental policy matters would require Treasury authorisation. Nevertheless Masaru reported it to Tokyo and it caught the eye of the Prime Minister, who instructed him to make sure that his views were known to the relevant authorities in Britain. When the City bankers' mission paid a courtesy call on the Prime Minister it had been pre-scripted that he approved highly of the speech by Cromer and that he much hoped that his views would come to pass.

This was a part of 'scenario building'. Masaru had in mind to somehow soften the then prevailing stance of the British government and the Treasury and allow Japan to raise capital in London. He was aware that Britain disallowed, constitutionally, foreign countries from doing so, except the nations of the Commonwealth. Soon after Prime Minister Ikeda's successful visit to the UK, Masaru went to see John Stevens (later Sir John), a Director of the Bank of England, and asked if there had been any developments since Lord Cromer's speech: Stevens confirmed the constitutional position and said a bond issue by the Japanese government would not be possible; the recent issue by Iceland, not a member of the Commonwealth, was enabled only by using the postwar Uniscan agreement with Scandinavian countries. But Masaru was not to be deterred, and called on various banks with which some funds were deposited by the Japanese government to mark Ikeda's visit. He was frustrated to be met by a somewhat nonchalant response from the bankers who thought the gesture was that of the Bank of Japan (through which the funds were routed to them) and no amount of explanation by my father and his colleague, Okura Masataka (his deputy at the Embassy as First Secretary from the Ministry of Finance, later President of the Bank of Yokohama) about the overwhelming effort made by the Ministry of Finance to push this through seemed to result in their comprehension. But at one of these banks he unexpectedly gained an opening.

At the Hongkong & Shanghai Banking Corporation, the head of the London branch and Manager for Europe, George Stewart, said in response to Masaru asking for cooperation in exchanging information, even if a bond issue could not be allowed, that he was surprised by the lack of developments since the Governor made that speech; indeed, if nothing was going to be done he should *not* have made such a speech. Masaru mentioned, I am sure tactically, that if a bond issue in London was not possible Japan would explore issuing in continental European markets. Stewart replied that he was lunching with Sir Edward Reid of Baring Bros the following day and would speak to him about it. He thought that Reid might lend a sympathetic ear, as he knew quite a lot about Japan from his uncle Lord Revelstoke, who had arranged many of the prewar Japanese government bonds. Masaru knew that Reid was then Chairman of the Accepting Houses Committee and of his connection with the Baring family, his mother having been a Baring, and of course Lord Cromer was therefore his cousin. He always researched meticulously the personal background of whoever he was to meet – that was a part of his skill in diplomacy – but he had not heard of Lord Revelstoke.

Within a few days, my father received a letter from Reid asking to meet. He immediately reckoned that if he was to say that, although the Japanese government had the desire to issue in London it had no particular definitive design, the meeting would end in a mere exchange of generalities and no progress would be made. On the way to Barings in the car, he decided with Okura that he would advance the proposition of a refinancing of the Japanese government sterling bond of 1899, which was soon to mature. That was an idea that Okumura of Nomura and the Ambassador had already suggested several months previously to

Chancellor Selwyn Lloyd, but which had been firmly rejected by him; HM Treasury through Derek Mitchell had written to Okura confirming that rejection. Though Okura was eager to capture this renewed opportunity through Sir Edward Reid, he therefore remained sceptical and nervous. Masaru remembered the words of wisdom imparted to him by Edmund de Rothschild shortly before; in the very first days of January 1963, de Gaulle had delivered his 'Non' to Britain's application to join the EEC: Eddy de Rothschild said to him then that Britain had suffered many defeats and unfortunate turns of events in its long history but it happens often in life that another misfortune would arrive to upset the outcome of the previous misfortune; British people would not be deterred.

Masaru, with the courage for which he was well known, went ahead with his approach and it was in fact successful. As expected, Sir Edward asked him directly if he had a definitive proposal. Masaru explained that whatever might be possible would have to be within the confines of the constitutional provisions and not impact Britain's balance of payments adversely; and that the refinancing of the 1899 Japanese government bond in sterling could be the appropriate opportunity. He said this was his personal view but that on hearing the British reaction he would exchange views with Tokyo. He told Reid that this matter of capital raising in London had been broached by Prime Minister Ikeda during his London visit in November to Chancellor Reginald Maudling, and was of course the thrust of Cromer's Mansion House speech.

Baring Brothers had a long history of association with the Japanese government; it was the lead underwriter for the issue of the Japanese government bond in London in 1902, the year that marked the signing of the Treaty of Anglo-Japanese Alliance. Japan had joined the gold standard five years earlier in 1897, thereby increasing its creditworthiness in the eyes of foreign investors. That bond was the fourth Japanese government bond issued in London; the very first had come in 1870, the proceeds of which financed the construction of the railway between Tokyo and Yokohama. The third such issue in London was the 4% sterling loan of 1899: this was to mature on 1 January 1964.

My father's proposition was to refinance this loan with a new issue in 1963. There had been sixteen Japanese government bond issues in London before the Second World War: the last one being the 5.5% sterling loan of 1930. Japan had never defaulted on any of its bonds.

I digress briefly: years later I encountered by chance the Baring Brothers' Archivist at a reception at the Bank of England Museum to mark the publication of a book by the National Voice Archive on 'City Lives'. I was featured in this book and the Archivist sought me out amongst the guests to say that they had in the Barings Archive some original correspondence between my father and the partners of Barings at the time of the 1963 issue: would I like to have copies? He sent me some internal memoranda of the meetings held between my father and the senior members of Barings, and numerous letters. He also pointed to an exhibit: the cheque presented by the imperial government of Russia in payment of war reparations to Japan at the end of the Russo-Japanese War. What I write below is based on what I learnt from the papers he sent me.

In mid-January 1963 Sir Edward Reid, following the meeting with my father, wrote to say he was now putting forward a request to HM Treasury through the Bank of England for permission for a Japanese government loan to be issued in London. A little while later he wrote again saying he had heard from Lord Cromer by telephone that the Treasury had indicated it would take two months to give a response. Sir Edward asked my father to keep this reply confidential.

Masaru reckoned that since the Bank would naturally be discussing this with the Treasury, it would be wise to inform David Hubback at the Treasury of the background circumstances, also

Frederick Atkinson, at that time seconded from the Treasury to the Foreign Office, as the matter concerned policies towards non-Commonwealth countries. Hester Boothroyd, who was the Assistant Under-Secretary under Hubback, immediately said she would stay late that evening to write a memorandum. To Frederick Atkinson, Masaru carefully explained that if it was to be a *refinancing* bond it need not affect the constitutional issue. He recorded in his memoirs that it was Roland Williams of Rothschilds who gave him a strong hint that the refinancing of the 1899 bond would be the most appropriate in making approaches to City bankers. That was far-sighted advice, in that the consortium which supported the Japanese bond issue to finance the Russo-Japanese War (1904–1905) was immediately revived – as my father wrote, "It awoke from sleep over 30 years" – and it was instantly ready to underwrite this new issue.

On 25 April, the Governor of the Bank of England telephoned Reid confidentially to say that the Treasury was willing in principle to give permission; Sir Edward wrote to inform Masaru at once on the same day, saying that the 'consortium' would be meeting within a week, although no details were yet available from the authorities.

Masaru told Barings that the Japanese government was not in any hurry to settle details or to commit itself to a refunding of the loan. He further indicated that it was likely Japan would be effecting a new issue in New York in September and his colleagues at the Ministry in Tokyo would be preoccupied with it during August; in any case as it was not clear what type of consent would be granted by the Bank of England – in certain situations an issue to refinance the 1899 loan would require Japanese parliamentary approval – and he would not want to embarrass the Bank of England through it issuing a public statement which subsequently would have to be retracted or amended. According to my father's memoirs there was substantial opposition to a refinancing bond in Tokyo where a fresh new one was being favoured and some factions in the Ministry tried to bring forward a bond in Switzerland or one in DM in Germany. My father in fact persuaded the Treasury that it need not be a refinancing bond but an *investment bond* in the same style as the one issued in New York the year before and got this permission in writing; yet the Ministry made a 180-degree turn and ended up saying it preferred a *refinancing* bond after all. Sir Edward Reid was determined to make it happen whichever type of bond it was. My father attributes the success of these tricky and sensitive negotiations with the Treasury to the skilful efforts of Nicholas Jordan-Moss. The Treasury wanted to issue a Press Release to prevent speculation and to issue a statement before the annual Marlborough House Commonwealth heads of government meeting to pre-empt opposition from them. But Masaru dissuaded them, as there remained technical issues that had to be ironed out, including the fact that the amount to be issued exceeded the outstanding loan amount. The current session of the Diet was ending in early July. This was now early June; while he and the Japanese government would do everything in their power to expedite matters if the underwriting consortium felt it was essential to complete this operation before the summer holidays, he thought it better to leave it to the autumn from a practical point of view. Furthermore, the British Treasury wrote to him to say that it preferred the timing of the issue to be close enough to the maturity date of the old loan (1 January 1964) to show the link between them – not more than approximately three months before the end of the year.

Barings and the consortium, though, lost no time. They reiterated that their desire was to try and achieve whatever the Japanese government wanted and emphasised that in negotiating the terms they were on the same side of the table. Masaru asked Barings to seek guidance from the Bank of England regarding the 'condition' on the timing of the issue from the Treasury. Meanwhile he continued his discussions with the Treasury on the amount of issue, explaining that the Japanese government had already bought some of the outstanding issue during the previous two years, leaving only approximately 60 per cent held by British nationals, and that the repayment on 1 January 1964 was already in the national budget that had been approved in the Diet. He further explained that the government had recently converted some US dollars into sterling in the interest of promoting good relations with Britain. The amount proposed was £5m (close to £100m in today's money) and the Treasury agreed this amount with the Chancellor of the Exchequer. Nicholas Jordan-Moss wrote from the Treasury to Masaru on 2 July 1963 that "… we recognise that purchases by your Government during the last two years or so have provided a receipt to our own balance of payments." The Treasury also indicated that they would prefer the length of maturity to be 20 or 30 years (it was agreed at 25 years). During June, meetings with Barings focused on the interest rate: Masaru at first intimated that the current interest rate in London might be too high to be acceptable to the Japanese parliament, compared with the rates prevailing in Tokyo and in New York. Barings and the consortium had taken some confidential soundings from institutions in London and it very quickly came down to what Masaru indicated would likely be accepted – 6 per cent. Meanwhile Sir Edward Reid at Barings had discussed the matter of timing with the Governor of the Bank of England as Masaru had requested; and on 17 July wrote to my father quoting from a letter received from the Governor: "We have had a word with the Treasury and it has been agreed that the loan may be brought any time between now and the end of the year. Will you please take this letter as formal authority to that effect."

With that official confirmation and all terms agreed already with the underwriting consortium, they lost no time and went ahead with impressive speed. Within two weeks, on 1 August 1963, the Japanese government's bond was signed and issued. It was twenty-eight times oversubscribed and immediately went to a premium. The *Times* editorial hailed the issue as signifying the return of the City of London to the international financial markets. The *FT* and the *Guardian* also wrote laudatory commentaries. Masaru wrote that it was to George Stewart of the Hongkong Bank that the City was in debt. And he arranged for Sir Edward Reid to be honoured in Japan with the award of the Order of the Rising Sun 2nd Class, which Reid received in person in Japan several months later.

The then Vice Minister of Finance of Japan (head of the Ministry of Finance) Ishino Shinichi came to London to sign the bond. Immediately after the signing ceremony Westminster Bank, the lead manager of the issue, gave a luncheon in his honour. Mr Ishino gave a fine and heartfelt speech, remarking that it was a historic event in the long relationship between the two countries and that it was not simply an economic transaction but that Japan had in its motives the importance of reestablishing good relations with Britain after the war. He reminded those present of the history of Japanese government bond issues in London since the Meiji Restoration and that it was the first time in thirty-three years that Japan had returned to the London capital market. It was poignant when he spoke of his two happy years in the Financial Commissioner's office in Bishopsgate as a young officer of the Ministry of Finance, twenty-five years before in 1938.

The General Manager of the Westminster Bank was Arthur Chesterfield, who was concerned with the consortium discussions throughout. It was the consortium that had always been involved in every Japanese government issue: Westminster Bank, Baring Brothers, N. M. Rothschild, J. Henry Schroder Wagg & Co., Morgan Grenfell & Co., and the Hongkong & Shanghai Banking Corporation. Panmure Gordon were the brokers to the issue, and the Bank of Tokyo the paying agent. Slaughter & May and Freshfields were the legal advisers. White & Cheeseman were the jobbers that made a market in the bonds on the Stock Exchange floor. In 1982 I was able to show the then Crown Prince (now Reiwa Emperor) the bond still listed on their pitch.

The day before, on 31 July, the British government gave a luncheon at Lancaster House which was hosted by Sir Edward du Cann MP, the Economic Secretary to the Treasury; the day before that, the Japanese Ambassador gave a major luncheon party at Claridge's Hotel in Mr Ishino's honour. It is worth noting that the sense of rising momentum for Japan to rejoin the leading nations of the world was heightened by it joining the OECD earlier in that month. My father gave me the black Parker pen that was used to sign the bond. I used it for my entrance exams for New Hall, Cambridge, and have always treasured it. (Unfortunately, it now cannot be serviced for continued use.)

On 31 July Mr Ishino visited both the Treasury (Reginald Maudling, the Chancellor of the Exchequer, Sir William Armstrong, Permanent Secretary) and the Bank of England (Sir Humphrey Mynors, Deputy Governor, Sir John Stevens, a Director) and had exchanges of views on a confidential basis, particularly with respect to the United States' position. It was barely a fortnight since the Interest Equalisation Tax had come into effect. On completing the loan agreement Mr Ishino went on to the continent. Amongst others, in Germany he held meetings with the President of the Deutsche Bundesbank, Karl Blessing, and the President of Deutsche Bank, Hermann Abs; in France with the Deputy Governor of the Banque de France, Pierre-Paul Schweitzer; in Switzerland the Director General of the Swiss National Bank, Walter Schwegler. The notes of the meetings and subsequent correspondence reveal the keenness of the European financial community to develop relations with Japan; Hermann Abs even wrote to Prime Minister Ikeda following Ishino's visit urging that Japan should come to the German capital market, indicating the readiness of Deutsche Bank.

A Sterling Achievement

The success of this issue signified perhaps that Masaru was at the zenith of his career. His personal qualities as a senior official of Japan's Ministry of Finance were immediately recognised by leading figures of the City at the time. Mr Ishino, who came to sign the bond, wrote in his own hand a personal letter saying that as he was nearing retirement he would make sure to tell both his successor and the Minister himself of Masaru's exceptional abilities so that his career was suitably well promoted.

Ambassador Ohno Katsumi, one of the greatest postwar Japanese ambassadors, regarded this issue as a milestone in the restoration of good relations with Britain and became a lifelong friend and supporter. He particularly recognised Masaru's political skills and negotiating abilities and wrote to him frequently after his own retirement saying working with him provided one of the few 'oases' during his term in London and that the bond issue was a high point of his own career. The night before he left London the following year he wrote to say on return to Tokyo he would immediately go to see the Minister of Finance.

Masaru wrote in his memoirs that even had the bond issue failed, he would have comforted himself that at least he had turned the dogged attitude of the British government around to adopt a more open approach to international financial diplomacy. It was to prove a triumph for Britain as well as for Japan.

Historical connections surviving into the postwar era speak volumes for human sentiments. The broker to the issue of the 1963 bond was Panmure Gordon, which had also been involved in the prewar issues, and senior partner Mr Twining wrote particularly to remind my father of his delight at his firm reestablishing the connection. Panmures had been the broker to the Japanese government in London; it is perhaps not surprising that the son of the British Ambassador at Tokyo at the outbreak of war, Sir Robert Craigie, had joined Panmures (Bobby Craigie). It was not a coincidence of history that an Allan Shand of Parr's

Bank (Parr & Co.) went to Japan in the 1860s and became a special adviser to the Japanese government; Parr's Bank later became part of the Westminster Bank, which played a leading role in the consortium throughout the twentieth century, ever since the legendary Minister of Finance Takahashi Korekiyo skilfully organised the London consortium to raise funding for the war with Russia. In writing this book, I discovered quite incidentally that Parr's Bank was owned by my sister Sakiko's husband Francis Parr's family.

Masaru was responsible for one more *tour de force* soon after the historic bond issue. That was when the Minister of Finance, Tanaka Kakuei, wanted to hold a bilateral meeting with Maudling during the IMF annual meetings of September 1963 in Washington. This was at the time an unheard-of, unprecedented event. But, fortunately for Masaru on a personal level, he was allowed to attend the IMF meetings as a delegate of Japan and able to go to his beloved Washington in September. He masterminded the staging of this meeting by contacting his recent acquaintance, Derek Mitchell, who had become private secretary to Maudling. To find a mutually convenient time for the two finance ministers during the IMF conference was extremely tricky; but with Derek Mitchell's kind efforts, Tanaka's desire was fulfilled. Masaru of course provided all the briefing. Tanaka invited Maudling to visit Japan and Maudling replied that he had heard there were good golf courses in Japan. In the event, the following year, when the IMF annual meetings were held in Tokyo, his wife and daughters were specially entertained and stayed longer to visit Kyoto and for shopping, while Maudling himself rushed back to fight the general election.

A vignette of that year soon after the bond issue: Lord Home as Foreign Secretary invited Ohira Masayoshi, Japan's Foreign Minister, and his entourage to his home in Scotland for grouse shooting and lunch. I doubt if the Japanese actually carried guns, but the cover of *Private Eye* carried an amusing take on the occasion on the moors. My father told me afterwards how impressed he was that Lord Home with some panache quickly shovelled up peas that had escaped from Mr Ohira's plate and put them in his mouth. My father was also much impressed with Lord Home's modesty: after a dinner at the Embassy the following year when Lord Home (by then Sir Alec) was no longer Prime Minister, while all other dignitaries were being ushered into their official chauffeur-driven cars my father asked if he might find his car for him: Sir Alec replied that he was driving himself home in his own small car.

During the four years he served in London my father was promoted in rank; from arriving first as Financial Counsellor at the Embassy to Financial Minister and then to Envoy Extraordinary and Minister Plenipotentiary. The last of these is an imperial appointment and he was sent the grand citation from Japan. My father was the last Ministry of Finance representative in London to hold this position; none of his successors has been promoted to that rank. He was immensely proud of this appointment and it meant a great deal to him, given his original loyalty to the Emperor when he joined the Ministry. MoF officials in those days owed their allegiance to the Emperor and no one else. The President of Nomura Securities, Mr Okumura, sent a telegram of congratulations, among numerous letters from others.

Japan and Emerging Eurobond Markets

While Masaru was busy negotiating with the Treasury on the government bond issue, a major breakthrough was being made in the Eurodollar market: on 3 July 1963 Autostrade of Italy issued the world's first Eurobond. It was to mark the 'rebirth' of London as Europe's and the world's financial centre, as Lord Cromer had advocated so powerfully at Mansion House in the autumn of the previous year. It was a coup by S. G. Warburg, highlighted by Cromer for their innovative skills. The Autostrade bond in Eurodollars was guaranteed unconditionally by an

Italian government-owned public corporation and the syndicate consisted of banks from several European countries. It was listed simultaneously in London and Luxembourg, in what came to be known as the London–Luxembourg method. The Bank of England had made clear just a little earlier that it would allow an issue of a foreign bond denominated in currencies other than sterling if it was to be listed simultaneously on a stock exchange other than London. A simple definition of a Eurobond is an international bond that is denominated in a currency that is not native to the country where it was issued. Part of the motivation for inventing this type of bond was tax arbitrage. The Autostrade bond was issued at Schiphol airport in Amsterdam to avoid stamp duty in Britain, with the coupon payable in Luxembourg to avoid British income tax. Eurodollars (US dollars held outside the US in Europe) existed before 1963 and through the 1950s the amount rose substantially. But those were in short-term instruments and deposits, and the environment of international banking was heavy with restrictive regulation and controls. The more regulations in place, the more clever mechanisms were thought up by bankers to dodge them. Eurodollars provided the essential liquidity to finance trade at a time that the Bretton Woods system constrained the creation of the required liquidity, as discussed earlier.

Masaru wrote in his memoirs that although he had chosen to issue the Japanese government bond in sterling in the orthodox manner as a UK domestic bond, given the balance of payments pressures on Britain he had always felt that it should not be repeated and that Eurodollar bonds should become the mainstream mechanism in long-term finance. Essentially, the creation of Eurobonds and their structure made it possible to use Eurodollars for the purposes of long-term finance. Britain was supportive of this initiative, so long as it did not impact long-term interest rates, but rather allowed an expansionary economic policy, to avoid deflation. Japan similarly supported it, with the view that it was probably the 'least harmful' alternative, and considered the stability of the US dollar of utmost importance. This was not without controversy. Within Europe there was also a move to create a 'unit of account' to avoid fluctuations between the different currencies of Europe by having a universal coupon rate, while leading German bankers such as Hermann Abs of Deutsche Bank told my father that Germany preferred to have bonds issued in its own currency and not in Eurodollars.

My father was deeply involved in the issues of subsequent Japanese government bonds in 1964 and 1965, as well as for the public sector corporations, in Germany and Switzerland, travelling across Europe from Paris to Bonn, Frankfurt, Zurich, Basle and Bern, meeting and negotiating with the respective central bankers, Treasury officials and senior bankers in the leading banks. He played a decisive role in the negotiations leading up to the issue of the Japanese government bond in Swiss francs in Zurich and managed to obtain for Japan very fine terms. The Ministry of Finance representative in Switzerland, Mr Takiguchi, had for years dedicated his time to realise this government bond in Swiss francs, with tortuous discussions with Swiss bankers, and he asked Masaru specially to come to Switzerland to help him negotiate the final stage. My father paid a special tribute to him for his determination.

The situation with the DM issue was rather different, as the Ministry's representative, Mr Sagami, saw Masaru as a rival and seemed to engage in lobbying in the Ministry. My father respected Mr Sagami and said that he was impressed with his wide reading and commended the outcome of the DM issue. But they had different views on the euro capital markets: my father foresaw that the future lay squarely in the expansion of the Eurodollar markets, while Mr Sagami believed firmly that Japan should follow the DM. In the immediate aftermath of the Autostrade issue, for at least the first year, Masaru was of the opinion (which was shared by many of the London bankers) that the Eurobond market was new and untested, and that it was not the venue for government bond issues, but could be used in the first instance in government-guaranteed bonds – for example the Tokyo Metropolitan Government or the Japan Development Bank. That the Tokyo Metropolitan Government bond was issued by the New York–Luxembourg method before the government bond in DM aggravated Mr Sagami, who felt he lost face with the German government. When finally the DM government bond was being signed, Masaru was told by Tokyo to attend the ceremony; he duly went to Frankfurt for this but found too hostile an atmosphere to stay and returned to London early. He wrote that, as often happens, a misfortune turned to luck: in the hotel lobby Robert Roosa approached him for a chat, as did the President of the Bundesbank, Karl Blessing, with whom he maintained contact over many years.

Some people consider that the birth of the Eurobond was an inevitable outcome of the prevailing market forces dictating the flow of finance, and it was in the City of London that innovative financing techniques resided in abundance. Certainly the punitive extra tax of 15 per cent that the IET collected from an American holding foreign bonds was a catalyst in the immediate and rapid expansion of the Eurobond market. IET was a domestic tax in the US to make it less profitable for Americans to invest overseas by taxing the purchase of foreign securities. It was designed to reduce the US balance of payments deficit.

The imposition of IET and the development of the Eurobond market alienated the US investment banks, which found themselves disadvantaged in the new issue business. They therefore in turn tried to join the Eurobond market by invoking a clause in the Glass-Steagall Act of 1933 that allowed them to raise funding for foreign entities overseas provided that the bonds were not offered to US residents. Using this method they managed to lead and join the syndicates in Eurodollar bonds, in some cases listing them in New York and Luxembourg simultaneously. This came to be known as the 'New York–Luxembourg method'.

As far as Japanese issues (corporate or government guaranteed) were concerned, those previously under negotiation in New York to issue as domestic bonds were moved to London for better terms (the first of these was for the Tokyo Metropolitan Government) and the American investment banks involved insisted on continuing their roles in what were now Eurodollar bonds. British merchant banks, which until then operated in a partnership with US banks, sensed increasing competition on their home ground and in some cases (e.g. S. G. Warburg and Kuhn Loeb) severed their previous links and set up their own outlets in New York. The competitive spirit of the London bankers was exemplified by Lord Harcourt of Morgan Grenfell – as he said to Masaru "It is the American policy that has increased issuance in Europe and suppressed those in New York; so the Japanese need not feel any obligation or be embarrassed with the American banks who had nurtured Japanese issuers in New York. A large proportion of DM bonds are placed in European countries outside Germany and in that sense they are international bonds but they suffer from the decisive weakness against Eurodollar bonds that they cannot be placed in places such as Hong Kong."

The Eurobond market expanded phenomenally, and even within three years by 1966 it grew to $1 billion, reaching $4.5 trillion by 2009 and over $12 trillion by 2020 (nominal value).

Japanese Corporate Issues

Major Japanese industrial companies were planning on capital raising overseas, predominantly in New York before the imposition of the IET. But with the situation changing, Japan's securities companies were by the autumn of 1963 already preparing to bring Japanese corporate borrowers to London. British merchant banks were vying for lead management and underwriting positions in those offerings, as the strong economic performance of Japan made them attractive. Most notably, S. G. Warburg was perhaps the most aggressive in seeking to establish a leading position in these; as of course were Barings, Schroders, Morgan Grenfell and Rothschilds, which had been part of the Japan consortium.

The very first Japanese company to raise capital in London was Takeda Chemical: Nikko Securities arranged together with Morgan Grenfell a Eurodollar convertible in the London–Luxembourg formula. This was immediately followed by Yamaichi Securities together with Fuji Bank and M. Samuel (later Hill Samuel) bringing another Eurodollar convertible according to the same London–Luxembourg formula for Canon. My father said that Canon held a sumptuous celebration in London. Soon afterwards there followed one for Teijin in the same format, led by Nomura, Banque Lambert Bruxelles, and M. Samuel. By early 1964 there was another, for C. Itoh in the same formula arranged by Nikko with Burnham of New York and Hambros. Meanwhile Taisho Marine & Fire issued EDRs (European Depository Receipts – the first ever) with Hambros in London.

Masaru was amazed to find that the Frankfurt office of the Industrial Bank of Japan (IBJ) had secretly arranged for Hitachi to issue its convertibles in London on the same London–Luxembourg formula with Yamaichi and Dillon Read with Rothschilds leading. As with most of the other issues, Hitachi was originally planning an issue in New York – hence the involvement of Dillon Read. He was particularly impressed with the way the partners of Rothschilds worked together on every detail of each transaction, without leaving it to the partner in charge of the transaction. IBJ from Frankfurt enlisted Rothschilds to make this issue possible and Philip Shelbourne made particular mention of their role in his speech at the completion dinner in London. At that dinner, held at the Dorchester Hotel, Masaru was asked to give the key speech of the evening. He made a characteristically romantic oration that many people referred to for many years afterwards.

Another major issue came from Toray, which Nomura Securities organised with S. G. Warburg; Mr Okumura, the President of Nomura, came personally to London to oversee the placing, saying "Toray is the bluest of blue chips"; much expectation followed. In the event it was, while not a failure, not as successful as hoped; Henry Grunfeld, co-founder of S. G. Warburg, said to Masaru with a hint of sarcasm that Warburgs found that Japan issued its government's DM bond in large size in Germany almost at the same time and they found their client base disappearing. On the fifth day after launch there was massive selling pressure from Germany and the price of the Toray bond fell sharply.

There were of course Eurobond issues by other countries – Denmark, Norway etc. – but the spate of new issues by Japanese entities was notable and Japan was seen as the engine of growth for the European capital markets at the time. Moreover, this continued unabated into the 1970s and 1980s and beyond. While I was in the City, the competition between the merchant banks and also between the Japanese securities companies was immense, trying to capture the next mandate.

The top management of those companies came to London to negotiate, to agree the terms and for the signing ceremonies. The Ambassador hosted numerous dinners for them at the Embassy residence. The large securities companies – the Big Four as they were known: Yamaichi, Nikko, Nomura, and Daiwa – opened their representative offices in London in 1963 and 1964 under Ministry of Finance direction, and my father was of course the principal regulator overseeing their activities in London.

All corporate capital raising, whether domestically or internationally, as well as the opening of any offices, required Ministry of Finance approval. Representatives of banks and securities companies called on Masaru regularly to bow deeply to 'God', as the MoF officials were colloquially called. Years later, when I worked in stockbroking, involved with Japanese equity securities, some of those who knew my father then joked with me that he had been much feared. Yet his charisma won the affection of even those who had been shouted at and his intellect and leadership skills inspired them to hold him in high respect. Every month he addressed the Japanese financial community in London at the Palmerston Club dinners. Many of them became very senior figures in the Japanese financial world and they extended their friendship to me as I developed my career in finance. I owe my father a lot in this respect, although he never interfered in my career.

For one of the new issues at the time, after the signing of the convertible bond, the chief representative of C. Itoh & Co. in London invited my parents and me to the ballet at Covent Garden, followed by dinner at Prunier in St James's Street. Prunier was one of the best restaurants in London at the time and Ted Heath told me years later that it was his favourite. It was a royal gala performance for the retirement of Dame Ninette de Valois as the Director of the Royal Ballet. I was more than thrilled to be included in the party and told my friends at school who were much impressed. Afterwards the Chairman of the company sent my father an inscribed silver salver in commemoration of the issue.

The leading industrialists who visited London at the time were quite different from the sombre bankers and bureaucratic diplomats that my parents had hitherto been used to. Some were tycoons who dominated the Japanese industrial scene in the postwar period. One in particular remains much in my memory: Mr Oya of Teijin Ltd, a giant of corporate Japan. Small in stature, genial, but exuding an air of authority and independence, he presided over this most successful of companies for nearly a quarter of a century. In the earlier decades of postwar Japan there were such inspirational personalities who gave the dynamism to the economy, resulting in the phenomenal growth rate and the country's meteoric rise as an industrial power. Morita Akio who founded Sony, Matsushita Konosuke of Panasonic and Honda Soichiro, to name but a few. Mr Oya's wife was a notoriously colourful personality; she would arrive in London with at least twenty large suitcases and trunks which required a separate van to transport to their hotel – I once saw her arrival at Heathrow airport, dressed in pink chiffon, giving instructions to her entourage. She was flamboyant to a T, attending Embassy dinners dressed in the most colourful attire. As the company made polyester fabrics she had to show off all dresses and kimonos made of those materials. Her conversation too was uninhibited in a way that shocked the more demure diplomatic wives. On one hilarious occasion, seated next to Masaru, she addressed him saying "Minister, you have very long eyelashes…"; it was lucky he could handle graciously such audacious remarks. The Oyas' largesse was notable, distributing polyester kimonos to every member of the Embassy on each visit. My mother gave them to me to make dresses out of, as they were not wearable as kimonos, being synthetic. She caused a lot of merriment at those Embassy functions and provided us with many amusing conversation points afterwards.

New Hall, Cambridge, 1965 – an unexpected turn of events.

10. HOME IN LONDON

~

The four years we spent in England were the last time that our family was all together. Though diplomatic life meant that our parents were out most evenings and we did not see much of them, there were weekends and holidays. With our father in America for nearly a year in 1956, followed by two years in Hokkaido, our family life had been somewhat interrupted in my youth.

Initially, school was a bit of a challenge coming from America, especially for me: the language was different, the curriculum was different, even games were different. The culture was one of strict discipline in manners and presentation: deportment was worthy of being awarded badges; a hierarchy of prefects; no talking in the corridors or in Hall during morning prayers; never taking the stairs two at a time… Misdemeanours would result in being given 'Order Marks'. As in other girls' schools, 'Order Marks' meant having to stay after school in a room and write out 'lines' – 'I must not talk in corridors' etc. – thirty or forty times. In the worst cases girls were told to stand outside the Headmistress's study until she called them in one at a time and gently reprimanded them. Before lunch senior girls on sentry duty would stand outside the dining room to inspect every student, to check whether she had washed her hands and combed her hair before sitting at table. Each table of eight was 'taken' by a prefect who led the conversation, and made sure of table manners. Every girl was given a table number as she entered the dining room and it was pot luck whether she got the table number of a 'kind and nice' prefect. No one wanted to be seated at the Head Girl's table. In my first year at school the Head Girl was particularly clever and I remember she once told the table that on that day they were to talk in Latin! When I became a prefect and took tables, I was popular with the younger girls: I was on the side of the rebels.

I arrived in the year that my form (Upper Fifth) sat GCE O-Levels. The other girls had already done one year of the curriculum and I had to catch up on the missed time. The school arranged extra lessons in Maths, History and English Literature. I found all this hard work and generally speaking did not enjoy school at all. I found a sympathetic soul in an American girl, whose father was a journalist stationed in London. She highlighted the differences from America and helped me settle in. But there was a kindred spirit in a British diplomat's daughter. That was Libet Williams, who was to become my lifelong best friend. Her father Alan was the Consul General in New York at the time; her mother, who was White Russian, had many relations spread across the US and Libet spent a lot of time there during the holidays – in New York City, Long Island and Florida. Her father was then posted to Panama as Ambassador and was knighted. It was a difficult post with political and civil strife in the country; the British Embassy was stormed on one occasion. The Headmistress would call Libet to her study and tell her that her parents were safe. In the same way Libet learnt that her mother was now Lady Williams. After a year or two, her father became Ambassador to Spain. Libet was and is an avid reader; she would hide a book under her jacket everywhere she went and even during morning prayers she would be surreptitiously reading Georgette Heyer or Morris West under the hymn book! She never did get caught.

Libet and I wrote to each other frequently during the school holidays as she would go home to her parents in those faraway places. The trials and tribulations of being diplomatic children were the unspoken bond between us. I went to spend long holidays with her and her family both in Spain and in north Wales, where they went for their leave in the summer. After my parents left England, her family adopted me as if I were part of them, and indeed they then provided my 'home' in Hampstead, which I frequently visited after Sir Alan's retirement.

I had never before played hockey or netball, though I had been good at volleyball in America. They made me play left wing in hockey – not a great success. We went in a coach to the school hockey field about ten minutes away; they would never take girls in games outfits onto the street. We had to learn contra-dancing or Scottish reels as well as some ballroom dancing. I wasn't much good at them either. Mostly because of my language deficiencies – British English being very different from American English – I found lessons in Biology, Scripture and English Language tricky. They did not teach domestic science as their mission was to educate 'ladies', but we could choose between embroidery and art. I chose art, and that was the only subject that I was recognised as being moderately good at. During the morning break we went up the hill to a bakery called Rances and bought doughnuts and rolls. Sometimes they took us out in the evening to the West End to see plays.

Somehow I scraped through my O-Levels and went on to the Lower Sixth Form, by which time we only had to concentrate on three subjects for A-Levels; I chose English Literature, History and French. Familiarity allowed me to be a little more relaxed in my second year. To my astonishment they made me a prefect – sooner than many other girls in my year. They might have thought that would instil more confidence. On my part I felt a little embarrassed and almost guilty should my friends feel envious. Moreover, in the second term the form elected me Form Captain. I was very reluctant to take this on and protested, but to no avail. One of the duties of being Form Captain in

Sixth Form was to choose and read the Lessons for the morning prayers in Hall. Scripture was not my strong point; I dreaded it. I had to choose a theme for the week and select passages from the Bible and consult the Headmistress on the choice. I consulted the Concordance and had a go. Miss Lloyd Thomas approved my selection and said they were good choices and interesting, something of a relief. Being a prefect meant that, amongst other privileges such as being able to wear 'mufti' on certain days at the end of term, I could be in the Prefects' Common Room, which had a fireplace with a mantelpiece and overmantel mirror above and French windows opening onto the garden opposite the eighteenth-century Hall. We chatted there on all manner of subjects, including our aspirations for the future after school and the possibility of getting boyfriends as well as the frustrations of being at school. Most of the others were in the year above mine and busy preparing for what they wanted to do after leaving school. In my school work I fared not much better than the previous year and struggled to pass exams.

The only way I could pass the year-end exams (and later the A-Levels) was to memorise everything the night before. I therefore memorised all the set books in English Literature – Chaucer, Shakespeare, Keats, Browning, Fielding's *Tom Jones* etc. – and in History I memorised my own notes from our lessons. I dreaded the French Oral but somehow muddled through. The day after the exams I would forget it all.

Unlike me, my youngest sister Eiko loved exams. She always excelled and she thought the time around exams was wonderful, with no homework being set. She made very close friends with her classmates, one of whom was Ingrid Bleichroeder, daughter of the then Chairman of Samuel Montagu merchant bank, who was much loved in the City for driving his own Rolls-Royce to work wearing a chauffeur's cap. Ingrid and Eiko would spend hours on the telephone and play in each other's homes during the school holidays. Chahchah too was not bad at school and she might even have been commended for some of her work, which would be announced before all the school. She went riding with a close friend at stables in north London. My father very much liked and encouraged her equestrian interests.

A big break came in the early autumn of my final year at Channing. I had been circling in a state of anxiety about what would happen after school: all my friends in Japan were going up to university, but there was no chance I would get into any university in England, let alone in Japan. I confided in my mother that if I couldn't go to university no one would even marry me, as in our society we were expected to have a university education, as well as tuition in the arts of flower-arranging and the tea ceremony. Mother was even threatening that I had better go back to live with my grandparents. One day at the very beginning of term in October, Miss Ford, the English Literature mistress, came to me and said "My dear, don't you want to go to university?" I said "Oh yes, but how can I? There is no chance that I would get into a university in England because my English is inadequate, and even less in Japan. After all I haven't been at school in Japan for the last five years. I have been much distressed about it…" She smiled and said "Why don't you try Cambridge? I think you have a good chance of getting in." I could not believe my ears. I just looked bewildered and said "How do I do that??"

Miss Ford had been discussing and 'plotting' this during the summer with Miss Lloyd Thomas, who had in fact retired that year; we now had a new Headmistress. LT, as we all called her, had agreed with Miss Ford and would help with letters of recommendation. Miss Ford thought that I should go for New Hall, Cambridge, which at the time had a particular form of entrance examinations, consisting of writing three essays in three hours on general philosophical subjects, rather than a series of papers on matters we learnt at school. The college stated in its prospectus that they were looking for young women who had 'originality of ideas and logical expression'. Well, I didn't think

I had either! New Hall set their entrance exams ahead of other Oxbridge women's colleges.

So it was that I sat the exam in mid-October, which required no preparation. I did not think that there was any chance at all that I would get a place, but there was no harm in trying. Miss Ford advised that I should apply to other Oxbridge colleges as well: Lady Margaret Hall at Oxford, her alma mater, Somerville, and Newnham, Cambridge. I remember that the paper set twenty-five essay subjects, all of which were of a general nature; the very first one was 'Why do you believe that the sun will rise tomorrow?'

I wrote one about poetry, another on European history about the conflict of conviction and self-interest, and another about characterisation in novels. A few weeks later I was called for interview: that was a complete surprise since it happened to only about six per cent of those who took the exam. My mother bought me a royal blue double-breasted suit from Jaeger and I went by train as arranged by the school. Miss Ford also arranged that I should be looked after for lunch by our old girls who were up at New Hall. All went well with the interviews with the President of the college (Miss Murray, later Dame Rosemary) and the Senior Tutor (Miss Hope Hammond): I was surprised to be asked by both of them why I didn't read English rather than History which I had applied for, but was told that I could change subjects once I was up; that gave me a glint of hope about my prospects! But then I made a terrible *faux pas*. After lunch with the Channing old girls in one of their rooms they suggested I borrow a bicycle to get to the next interview in the afternoon with the Director of Studies in History. One of them said she would come with me on her bicycle to show me the way to her house. I found that I could not ride the bicycle as my skirt was too narrow to get onto the bike. So we had to walk and I was late arriving at the interview by twenty minutes. The girl who was supposed to be interviewed after me took my place and I waited for her to finish. The girl came out saying "Don't worry, she is very nice." (This girl did not get into New Hall but went to Somerville, Oxford.) I went in apologising profusely and in a hyper-nervous state. But Mrs Clover – the Director of Studies in History – took little notice and carried on with the interview. She was complimentary about my essays, saying I gave "very good instances". She talked for a long time about her interpretation of Roman history, which I knew nothing about. It seemed that she talked for longer than myself: it felt like a long interview. She was a historian of mediaeval Europe, specialising in Archbishop Lanfranc. But she said at the end "I so much enjoyed talking with you." My hope was restored. When I was up at Cambridge I referred to my late arrival at the interview; Mrs Clover said "No one would be late for an interview at Cambridge – so I presumed that there must have been a very good reason." She taught me the correct scale of values.

For the following few weeks back at school all the mistresses were going around with their fingers crossed. One day in late November I received a telegram. In those days the telegrams were first phoned through by the post office and then physically delivered. It read: 'New Hall offers you a place. Congratulations. New Hall, Cambridge.' As it happened it was I who answered the phone late one afternoon at home. I told my parents, who were incredulous, and my father in his usual way just said he did not believe it and it could not be true. But then when the telegram was delivered he was deeply moved.

At school everyone rejoiced and there was not a hint of jealousy from my classmates, even though I was the first to get a place at university. For several days I received many congratulations from various mistresses, including some whose favoured student I had not been before, who nonetheless kindly said they were so proud. Miss Ford was of course more than delighted. Years later she said to me that in all the long years she had been a teacher my getting into Cambridge was her happiest moment. The most welcome outcome of it all was that I no longer had to worry about school and exams. Cambridge required only that I passed two A-Levels, whatever the grade. So I could just enjoy myself at school and not worry. I accepted my place at New Hall at once and had the cheeky satisfaction of declining invitations to interviews at Somerville and other Oxbridge colleges to which I had applied.

My parents' friends sent me congratulatory presents, mostly of jewellery. The Japanese community rejoiced that a Japanese girl had been accepted as an undergraduate without having previously been at another university in Japan; my parents could bask in my glory wherever they went for a while. I toyed with the idea of reading Economics rather than History, but my father decisively forbade me to do so, saying "I won't pay for you to read Economics which is not a proper subject." He considered it an unbelievable feat and an honour that I should have been accepted at Cambridge. When we first arrived in England we had gone for a drive there, and seeing the soot-encrusted mediaeval buildings of ancient colleges he had remarked that undergraduates must get depressed living in such an environment, but this no longer seemed to worry him. He kept saying to me "You nearly died when you were five years old, so you don't have to excel at Cambridge but just don't fail the exams."

Life at home was peaceful and happy. My father took us on holidays to Scotland where we visited Edinburgh and Gleneagles as well as driving along Loch Lomond and stopping by at Stirling Castle. I liked Scotland very much on my first visit and unexpectedly came to know it well later. Miss Lingard arranged for us to visit Europe and stay in lovely hotels – to Paris, Rome, Versailles, Nice, Naples, Pompeii, Turin, Bergen and Oslo, Le Touquet, Majorca – and on seaside holidays in Torquay and Bournemouth. In many ways they were extravagant holidays: grand hotels and staying in suites; chauffeur-driven cars; caviar and fillet steaks at dinner each day. We visited the famous museums and galleries and strolled in the streets. My father bought us dresses if he saw one he liked and mother asked him to buy her a cameo brooch in Rome which she treasured. There is no doubt that my father had extravagant tastes, though spending infrequently and on the best things. 'Value for money' was never a part of his vocabulary. He liked being addressed as 'Your Excellency' wherever we went on the continent. All of us were at all times properly dressed; casual clothes or jeans were never part of our holiday wardrobe.

That first summer after we arrived in England, my friend in America, Linda Green, invited me to stay with her and her parents in Washington. I was miserable at school and we all longed to go back to the US as life seemed easier there than in London. Much to my surprise my father said I could go. So I went to stay with Linda for about a month in August of 1963. Her parents were very kind and met me at the airport and took me out to the theatre. They also arranged for me to meet up with other friends. Having been told of my visit, my parents' friends at the Japanese Embassy invited me to their homes for lunch or tea and gave me presents; I still have a beautiful set of towels one of them gave me. Linda and I went to the movies and met up with mutual friends to go shopping in F Street, down-town Washington, and visited our old haunts. On my return, my father thought it audacious of me to have spent all the money he gave me for the holiday. But in some ways he was impressed with my daring. I had a wonderful trip on my own for the first time in my life. While I was in America, my family went to Germany, visiting Cologne, Heidelberg and Frankfurt. I heard that my father was able to speak some German, which he had mostly forgotten. I wrote to my parents every few days.

Soon after I got into Cambridge my grandparents came for a visit. I had to vacate my bedroom, a large double room with a washbasin (as many houses were equipped with in those days) overlooking the garden and sleep in the same room as Chahchah. I took them to the opera and to dinner afterwards in a posh French restaurant. My parents entertained them and various of their friends invited them to their homes too, including the Ambassador. The abiding memory of their visit was that my grandmother, rather than being happy at my having got into Cambridge, said to me "Please do not become a 'bluestocking'; you will never have to get a job or work; don't forget your heritage – be always a lady." I burst into tears and was highly upset: mother gave me an aspirin to calm me down. Why Grandmother said this when her own daughter Asako had gone to an American university and had embarked on a career is a mystery; but she presumably had entertained an ideal for her granddaughter and feared I would not live up to it. Some family letters show, though, that back in Tokyo she was bragging about my success to her friends and relations. Grandmother went shopping with my mother in Bond Street and bought an evening bag for her daughter-in-law at Asprey's. But for others she was rather abstemious with her souvenirs to take home. She asked me what precious stones in jewellery I liked best: "emeralds" was the answer, and she said she and my mother liked them too.

I went up to Cambridge in the autumn of 1965, my parents' final year in London. My mother kitted me out with clothes and other things that I was expected to take up with me in my trunk, though we had no idea what I really should be taking. I asked Lady Williams with whom I had just spent a lot of the summer holidays. She had been up at Oxford before the war. Mother took me to Norman Hartnell in Bruton Street and bought me some key things, such as a party dress, a coat, a suit. I don't suppose anybody else went to the Queen's dressmaker for student life. I didn't know that this was *haute couture*; we just thought it was a high-class dressmaker. She then took me to Jaeger for everyday clothes – a twinset and a skirt, an informal dress, sweaters. We had a trunk into which we put all the clothes, with some crockery, tea cups and saucers, plates and glasses and suchlike. In college, I found them redundant; my fellow students

'Daddy sent us a doll from America.'

Osoroi – matching clothes.

In the garden: 'Daddy is going away to America', 1956.

Our dog Putti in the garden.

Fukuda ancestral stone lantern, donated to Kotokuji temple in 2010.

Childhood days

Shichigosan – Haruko seven and
Sakiko three, 1953.

On the swing in the
garden with Mummy,
c. 1953.

'Going to school soon' – graduation from my Catholic kindergarten in my velvet dress with lace collar.

Misakicho Baptist church, 1908–1916.

Rebuilt after a fire in 1916: 'grandmother took me there to worship…'

Haruko at school

First year at Gakushuin junior school 1953; Haruko 7th from left, back row.

Art class outing – sketching outside the Akasaka Detached Palace.

School outing to the Unesco Village.

Akiya

Hunting for sea urchins in spring low tide with Osué, 1950s.

Asako's retreat, 'Kashinoki Lodge'.

View from Kashinoki Lodge, late afternoon sunset.

At Westminster Bank headquarters, 31 July 1963

Clockwise from top left:
A last-minute tête-à-tête. Masaru with Vice Minister Ishino.

Still waiting…

'That was a good piece of business…'

Drinks after the signing; 'congratulations!'

Aspirations for Japan's role;
NHK TV roundtable interview
for Masaru, December 1966.

Moving to Manila soon; in the drawing room of
uncle Yuhei's house.

Whisky and
soda in the
tropics.

Nakamura Kusatao, the haiku master.

Masaru visiting his sister and her family from London, 1960s.

Haruko at the White House, received by Jacqueline Kennedy, Lynda Bird and Lucy Baines Johnson, 1961.

drank out of mugs. I had never encountered a mug and wondered where to get them. I found a lovely shop in King's Parade
called Primavera which sold artistic craft items and decided to
buy the things that I wanted there. I wrote to my father asking
if I could have a little more pocket money. It was all a mystery
and nerve-racking. The first weekend I was up, one of the girls
reading History asked me to tea in her room as her parents were
visiting; I found that they were serving things that I had never
seen before – something that her mother called 'curlicues', and
pieces of pork pie. I did not know that people had anything for
tea other than cucumber sandwiches and little teacakes.

All the other women at New Hall seemed awfully 'brainy' and
I felt totally inadequate. They seemed to be sophisticated and
efficient, knowing their way around the libraries and university
societies. New Hall women were very independent, and some
rather individualistic, most of them having been at grammar
schools. In those days it had an excellent academic record; being
a recent establishment (1954) and having fewer students a year
– forty-five in my year but twenty-five in previous years – we
were sent to have supervisions with dons in other colleges. Like
everybody else I went everywhere on a bicycle: to lectures, to the
libraries and to meet friends. It was compulsory in those days to
wear a gown to lectures or to supervisions and it was forbidden
for women to wear trousers with gowns.

Compared with others, New Hall was a relatively free and
liberal college; we had to dine in Hall only four nights a week
and many women went out on non-Hall nights to dine in other
colleges as guests or to restaurants with boyfriends. We were
known to have the shortest Grace amongst Oxbridge colleges.
We all made friends through other friends and at libraries and
university societies: though my recollection is that I was socially
inept and spent many evenings on my own in my room feeling
inadequate, letters to my parents reveal that I had a busy social life
and had my share of invitations to go out from unlikely suitors,

many of whom I was telling my parents I had 'fended off'! Once in my first term I was 'stood up', though at least I was trumped by Miss World! I had been looking forward to going out with a handsome man I had met at the History Library, the Seeley, but that afternoon there came a knock on the door and the chap said "I am terribly sorry but I have been asked to escort Miss Denmark this evening at the Union." The Union was staging a debate on the motion 'Beauty is Skin Deep' the following week, and all the Miss World contestants were in Cambridge. Lo and behold, she was then chosen to be the Miss World that year.

I wrote to my parents at least once a week, telling them of my activities, and sometimes they phoned me. They did not come to visit, though other women had their parents come occasionally during term time, and this meant that I met some of my friends' parents. There were many parties and dances every week and we got our *exeats* to stay out after 'gate-hours'. I bought a long evening dress from a shop called Vogue; we also lent and borrowed evening gowns as none of us had so many dresses: "I'll lend you this, it's a lucky dress for me." Going to tea with friends in their rooms, toasting crumpets on the electric bar heaters and spreading butter and Gentleman's Relish, or asking people to drop in for sherry before Hall were daily features of life at Cambridge then, and in the mid-morning we often went for coffee at the Whim in Trinity Lane. In the afternoons a fellow historian from New Hall, Priscilla Grasby (now Truss) and I often had tea at the Copper Kettle in King's Parade, famed for good buns and sandwiches. She and many people I met that first term in Cambridge have remained lifelong friends. If our supervisions were in the early evening the dons offered us sherry or gin and tonic as we discussed our essays. Mrs Clover said that supervisions were meant to be a 'meeting of the finer minds'. We read out our essays at supervision and discussed them. She said to me on one occasion, when I was confessing that I found mediaeval history very difficult, "Your essays are poetic; you have aesthetic sense." It was a kind and consoling remark to a hope-less student. She also said on another occasion "Don't worry, no one will ask you what class your degree was afterwards; you must enjoy life at Cambridge – that is as important as getting a degree…"

I bought a gramophone and listened to music in my room every day – the symphonies and piano concertos of Beethoven, Haydn and Mozart that we always listened to at home, but also more modern compositions such as Fauré's piano concertos, and I developed a new interest in jazz. I remember playing Miles Davis's *Kind of Blue* endlessly. Though I am not particularly musical, and not good at singing or playing any instruments, a girl who lived in the same house in our first term, Nadia, who had been in the National Youth Orchestra playing the viola before she came up, introduced me to her erstwhile colleagues in the orchestra. She took me to a house at the bottom of a rural lane off Trumpington Street – 23 Chaucer Road – where they 'hung out' all day and night. It was a large Victorian house open all the time and people came and went, lounging on sofas, just chatting or playing pieces of music together, and I loved going there. They adopted me into their milieu even though I could not hold a candle to their musical talents. Amongst them were some who became nationally famous musicians – David Atherton, Antony Pay, Christopher van Kampen to name a few. They introduced me to the music of Schoenberg and Stravinsky and other modern composers new to my ear.

As soon as term ended everyone rushed home, as did I that year. For the Christmas 1965 I went to stay with Libet Williams at the British Embassy in Madrid, as I did in later years and for summer holidays also. The Embassy was then a handsome nineteenth-century residence on the corner of Serrano and Castiglione streets in the centre of Madrid. Libet and I, accom-panied by her younger brother Lawrence, went shopping in the fashionable street of Serrano to buy beautiful leather clothes and hand-crafted jewellery. Opening our large parcels, carried in by Lawrence, with Lady Williams back at the residence always provided a lot of merriment, with her demanding to see them on immediately; there would be a mini fashion show in her bedroom before lunch. The Williamses gave a Christmas party each year with dancing in the Hall after dinner; they had met in Vienna just after the war and were expert in the Viennese waltz, and so the dancing always began with Alan and Masha leading the waltz. They were beautiful occasions with all the Embassy staff and their families as well as the leading British community in Madrid; we would go to the hairdresser earlier in the evening to have our coiffure perfected. I wrote to my mother saying I would buy her a black evening bag she was wanting at the time so not to get it before I returned, as such things were less expensive in Madrid. Unfortunately the bag I bought her in black suede with enamel decoration shed the dye on one's hands and was useless. Mother, though, kept it in her cupboard all her life. Libet got up early in the morning and went riding in the cold, often with snow on the ground.

It was a time of tension over Gibraltar. Whenever Spanish government ministers came to lunch or dinner at the Embassy, conversations at table would focus on the issue. Lady Williams was proficient in Spanish and would conduct erudite conversations; she had read modern languages at Oxford and was fluent in French and German as well as in Russian (her native language) and had been quick to pick up Spanish on arrival. Her interest in international politics ran deep and her conversations were always interesting and perceptive. Her paternal ancestor was a Decembrist revolutionary who had been exiled to Siberia. She went to visit his grave when the Soviets invited her to visit her ancestral country in the last years of the Soviet regime in the late 1980s. She took me on sightseeing tours around Madrid on the first few days after my arrival; on occasion the ambassadorial Rolls-Royce would get eggs thrown at it. When we entered the cathedral in Plaza Mayor together, seeing the great number of relics displayed all round in the side chapels I exclaimed: "Thank God for the Reformation!" – she never let me forget it. At weekends Alan took us in his private car for picnics in the Valle de los Caidos and to the Escorial. The cook, Maria, made wonderful picnics in baskets. Those places of historical interest meant a lot to me as I had studied the Habsburgs. I remember thinking that the Escorial was a historical museum – something to look *at* – but in contrast historical monuments in Italy – Rome for example – seemed more integrated into contemporary living. History was alive in Italy, and nowhere else quite matches that. The realisation excited my interest in the study of history, and Italy has become my favourite holiday destination.

Our life at home for the four years that we spent in London together was perhaps the happiest time for our family. We were well settled and got used to our routines. All of us made agreeable friends and we all got over our initial scepticism about England; we came to love Britain more than America. My father bought me a little blue Renault when I got a driving licence. I went off in this car to explore London, often on my own. It was one of the very first automatic transmission cars of that size. By 1964 I was included in the London Diplomatic List and invited to the Palace on some diplomatic occasions. There were the summer garden parties at Buckingham Palace: mother bought me a special dress from Hartnell and a hat and long white gloves to wear – we were told that we must not wear a lighter colour than the Queen who would be in pastels – and with my father in morning coat and my mother in kimono we were taken there by Mr Hunt, the Embassy chauffeur. I thought it was very smart that the police stopped the traffic outside the side entrance to the Palace so diplomats could sweep in. There was a separate tent in the garden where all the diplomatic corps had tea.

More special was the formal evening soirée inside the Palace in the autumn for diplomats. All Japanese wives wore their best kimonos, as did I. We stood in long lines and Her Majesty the Queen, the Duke of Edinburgh and other members of the royal family walked past us, stopping briefly with each guest to whom they addressed inconsequential remarks. Prince Philip characteristically made jokes with some of the Japanese ladies asking what they carried in their *obis* – "What do you hide in that bag on your back?" They mingled with the guests over drinks and finger food. My father introduced me to Lord Butler ('Rab') who had just become Master of Trinity College, Cambridge. Hearing that I had just gone up to New Hall, he said "You must come and see us." I was amazed that a little while later he had remembered this and sent me an invitation to drinks at the Master's Lodge saying there would be a small number of students. There was a real politician!

For those royal invitations I got special permission from the college to go up to London. There was also Ascot, when we were invited to the Royal Enclosure; that fell in the middle of May Week when colleges held their May Balls. I went to one ball, and having danced all night went up to London for Ascot, then went back again to another ball. The first year that my parents went to Ascot, Mother bet on a horse which was her namesake, *Oceana* (her name Yoko means 'child of the ocean'); it came in at long odds. She gave me the winnings, with which I bought a piece of pottery sculpture by my pottery teacher, Ian Godfrey.

On one of my explorations of London in my Renault, I had come upon a pottery studio in Chelsea, a fashionably bohemian area then. It was in a narrow side street and I went in to have a look. A potter accosted me and said I could come and try throwing pots if I wanted. I was much taken by this suggestion. I asked my mother to come with me to have a look and she agreed that I could do this during the school holidays. There were three or four potters working there and one of them took me under his wing: that was Ian Godfrey. He was not only a wonderful teacher who taught me much about the art of pottery and firing with glazes, but was also a kind and friendly person with no airs and graces. He took me out to have coffee in the nearby Picasso café, a haunt of artists at the time. He had developed a particular style and made pieces which were more sculptures than pots; the piece that I bought with my mother's racing winnings was a chariot with little figures mounted on it. In fact, a larger version of this was in the Victoria & Albert Museum. I had no idea that he was an established and well-known potter. Recently, when visiting the National Museum in Taipei I saw very similar ideas in the pottery of the Sung dynasty; no doubt the source of Ian's inspiration. His work always carried a lofty and joyful feel. Ian Godfrey taught me that in pottery the clay had to 'live'. Sadly he died young of an illness. I have kept up an interest in pottery all my life and have a small collection, including works by John Ward, John Maltby, Janet Leach and others. Bernard Leach's inspiration was Japan and Shoji Hamada; I could not afford to buy the masters such as Lucie Rie or Michael Cardew, who was Bernard Leach's student and whom I admired very much. But I also share my mother's enthusiasm for Bizen ware and other Japanese ceramics. She made some pots herself after retirement, but painting has been her more important interest.

During summer holidays, when the Williamses came back on leave, I went to spend a few weeks with them in north Wales. They had a large house and extensive gardens; we made jelly from medlar and crab apple and went on walks along the beaches as well as in the Snowdonia hills. While the men went to climb Snowdon, we often went shopping for Welsh weave at the mills in Trefrew and Betws-y-Coed. There were driving trips further afield and sometimes to watch sheepdog trials. Libet loved going to the neighbouring farm to help them in the pigsty. Lady Williams's mother, Mamou, was still alive then and she would cook meals for us. She was a Russian aristocrat who had escaped the revolution in 1917; an amazing person who overcame unexpected hardships as a refugee in England

– having brought up her five children, some of whom went to live in America, she spent her later life going to and fro between New York and London staying with each of her daughters. She told me how, looking out of the window of a millinery shop in St Petersburg one day, she saw the Bolshevik army advancing in the street below; immediately her husband – a minister in the Duma – was on the telephone telling her to rush home, and they left Russia forever on the instant. Her father had been a well-known poet who lived next door to Alexander Pushkin, a close friend. I was very fond of her. She was strong and lived on well into her nineties.

In London, I sometimes went to the libraries of London University to do some one-off research. I got a special pass to do this, as I wanted to do better in the English Constitutional History paper in Part I of the Tripos. The sixteenth and seventeenth centuries were my strong interest as I had done a lot of work on them at school as well as at Cambridge in my first year. It was also an area of particular specialisation by the then leading scholars in history at both Oxford and Cambridge: the Reformation, the Elizabethan parliaments, the causes of the Civil War. Geoffrey Elton was giving lectures which I attended avidly: 'The Tudor Revolution in Government'. At Oxford, R. H. Tawney's controversial thesis on the rise of the middle classes and Trevor-Roper's decline of the aristocracy were hotly debated topics for historians of the period. I wrote up the result of my research on 'the alignment of forces on the eve of the Civil War'; my supervisor, Patrick Cosgrave, was more than encouraged to say that I should be well up on the list to get a First on that paper. (But I didn't.) For leisure, I went to the municipal library in Hendon to borrow books; my father was horrified to find one day that I had overdue books – he was very angry with me and said that if I continued to behave this way he would ban me from the library.

We bought patterns to make dresses with material from

Liberty's, as we loved their designs. Mother got very interested in tapestry embroidery. She loved going to The Needlewoman Shop in Regent Street to get patterns; soon our home filled with her output. She was in her element – sometimes she would draw out the design herself and make wall panels and rugs. I have kept many of these to decorate my own house and I marvel at her skill. I also learnt to do drawn-thread work on table linen; Chahchah stitched a view of our garden and I had it framed to hang on the wall in my room at Cambridge. In those days we did a lot of needlework; after I went up to Cambridge I often made my own dresses entirely by hand as I had no access to a sewing machine.

My father liked mowing the lawn. On Sundays he would spend a lot of time tidying the garden and making bonfires. If he didn't like the look of something we were wearing, he would threaten to burn it on the bonfire. He went to play golf some-times with colleagues at well-known golf clubs, Wentworth or Leatherhead, but often he headed off on his own to Mill Hill and nearby courses. He was a good golfer, sporting a handicap in the lower teens. He also liked watching television, especially current affairs. I remember him saying that the forthright way in which the legendary broadcaster Robin Day questioned the then Prime Minister, Sir Alec Douglas-Home, would never happen in Japan. He was both amazed and impressed by it – an aspect of British democracy that allows full debate. While the British media have become even more direct with their interviewees today, Japan's NHK and other media remain pretty deferential and polite to their guests.

An Unexpected Move: Au Revoir
During the summer of 1966 a colleague of my father's from the Ministry came for a visit. My mother told me later that she sus-pected then that Father would end up being asked to be the first Executive Director for Japan at the soon-to-be founded Asian

Development Bank. It transpired that this colleague had himself refused to undertake this assignment and sought to persuade my father. There was initially a debate amongst the founding countries' governments as to the location of the Bank. The first possibility was Tokyo, but for political reasons it finally landed on Manila, in the Philippines. Mother's fears were justified. The Ministry persuaded my father to take this position despite his strong reluctance; he had been fully expecting to return to the Ministry as Director-General of a mainstream Bureau. Had he felt able to refuse, our lives would have been very different. Watanabe Takeshi, who was to be the first President of the Asian Development Bank, wrote impassioned letters to Masaru asking him to represent the Japanese government under his presidency. Masaru's sense of loyalty in the service of his country meant he had to accept this appointment. So it was that the family was going to move to Manila. I was just starting my second year at Cambridge when in mid-October of that year they left London. The return to Tokyo involved a short holiday in various places, from Athens to Hong Kong. They went to stay at Fukidecho with our grandparents for a couple of months before the Bank was officially opened in early 1967.

There was no question but that I would continue at Cambridge and get my degree, and I never worried for a moment about being left alone. My parents' colleagues and friends promised them that they would keep in touch with me and that in any time of need I should contact them for help. None of us was particularly emotional about being separated. I don't remember that we even discussed it. It never occurred to me that I would never again live with my family or that I would not even see them for five years.

That may seem inexplicable today, when the cost of air travel and communication has been drastically reduced. But at that time air fares were unaffordable for private individuals to travel across the globe, and even telephone calls were virtually impossible. No internet, emails nor even faxes, let alone WhatsApp or Zoom. So we wrote letters to each other frequently, at least once a week. When the British Post Office went on strike for weeks and we could not send letters I resorted to asking the Foreign Office in London to put my letter to my parents in the Diplomatic Bag c/o the Ambassador at the British Embassy in Manila, Sir Roger du Boulay.

I saw my family off from Heathrow. A party of Embassy officials, some with their wives, and various senior members of the Japanese community all came to the VIP suite to wish them well for their journey. A close friend of my mother from school, Ikeda Masako, came with another friend of hers, a Mrs Tanaka. (As it happened, a year or two later, after the Ikedas left London, the Tanaka family, with a daughter of similar age to myself, gave me a home in London during the vac and were enormously kind to me and to my sister Sakiko.) They stayed with me to the end as we watched the plane take off. I suddenly felt close to tears as they disappeared into the sky. I was surprised by my own emotions in that moment. They suggested we had tea together in the terminal. Afterwards they took me to King's Cross to catch the train back to Cambridge.

Getting ready to go – December 1966.

II. MANILA: ONLY
DEMI-PARADISE

~

Launch of the Asian Development Bank

The two months my family stayed in Tokyo before going to Manila were spent at Fukidecho. Retrieving household possessions sent back from England, making preparations for the move to a developing country, where daily necessities might be scarce, getting tropical clothes: hectic days. They were summoned to engagements at the Imperial Palace and other official government receptions, dinners and lunches, all to mark the inauguration of the Asian Development Bank (ADB), throughout that November. The Board of Governors of the newly established Bank came to Tokyo and were hosted by Their Imperial Majesties, the Prime Minister, the Minister of Finance and the Governor of the Bank of Japan.

Another notable invitation came from Eugene Black, Special Advisor to President Lyndon B. Johnson on South East Asian Social and Economic Development. He issued a somewhat modest invitation card, certainly in comparison with the large gilded formal invitations from the governments. But his role in the establishment of the Asian Development Bank must be recorded here. My father knew him well and respected him very much. He became President of the World Bank immediately after the war in 1949, an assignment he undertook reluctantly.

He was originally a commercial banker with Chase Manhattan Bank. But his name and influence certainly lived on for decades, as I found when I myself went to work at the World Bank in the early 1970s. He remained there for thirteen years thanks to his strong commitment to the objectives of that institution; with the force of his personality and his strong engagement with the staff, the World Bank was nicknamed 'Black's Bank'. Though he did not take part in the anti-communist fervour of McCarthyism in the 1950s, he feared the global spread of communism, believing firmly that economic prosperity achieved through capitalism was an essential prerequisite for political freedom. In 1966 while he was Chairman of the Brookings Institution in Washington, President Johnson asked him to be his Special Advisor. Black was quite hesitant to take on this position but the President would not take no for an answer. Though the US had previously opposed what was originally a Japanese proposal in the 1950s, for President Johnson the creation of the ADB was an important step in securing the support of south-east Asian countries for the Vietnam War. Eugene Black was charged with organising and establishing the ADB. So, he must be credited as the 'Father of the ADB': and it was fitting that he should have issued the invitation card in his own name, with no accreditations of titles or positions.

The inauguration of the ADB was a landmark event in Japan; Masaru as the first Executive Director representing the Japanese government was interviewed many times in the newspapers and on television. He expressed his hopes and aspirations for the Bank and his vision for future Japanese policies in the region. It was the first time that he worked on issues relating to the development of south-east Asian economies. For Japan it was the first time since the war that it took the reins to play an active part in the development of the region that it had fought hard over, in equal partnership with the United States. For the initial capital of the Bank was provided in equal measure by the two countries, each contributing over 20 per cent of the capital ($200m) with 17 per cent voting rights. The President of the Bank was to be Japanese. Surely it was a major turning point for the country in recovering its reputation on the international stage.

At an international conference held in Hawaii in the very early years of the Bank's foundation, Masaru was one of the plenary session speakers, on the subject of 'The Role of the Asian Development Bank in Economic Development in Asia'. Professors Robert Triffin and Harry G. Johnson were among those to respond. In the speech he discussed the introduction of the Special Resources Fund and its funding. The Special Resources Fund was a project that my father worked hard on both in its formulation and in its implementation. He speculated on the funding mechanism which in the early stages would have to raise the capital in New York or European markets, since there were no international markets in the developed nations of the Asia Pacific (Australia, New Zealand and Japan). Japan hoped to develop the bond market in Tokyo, but at that time it was not adequately structured to provide a liquid market; even Japanese government bonds were at the time largely 'placed' with institutions. The Japanese government donated $100m to the Agricultural Special Resources Fund in 1968.

During his five-year tenure Masaru wrote several important published papers. One concerned policies relating to agricultural development and social impact. It is remarkable for its grasp of detail. At the Bank he was known for his forthright views. On the tenth anniversary of its foundation, a senior staff member, Suma Kazuaki, wrote a monograph on the people who could not be forgotten; he devoted a long tribute to Masaru. Amongst other things, he wrote that everyone waited with bated breath for Director Fukuda to speak at Board meetings of the executive directors; as he started to speak, silence fell, everyone hanging on every word. Suma wrote that his comments were always not only constructive but wholly encouraging of the staff who were presenting. They were deeply inspirational. His eventual departure was much regretted by the staff of the Bank, who wrote their heartfelt appreciation for his contribution to this new international organisation.

Meanwhile Masaru continued his regular correspondence with friends in London, both in the City and in Whitehall. Much of this correspondence remains; on one occasion Sir Siegmund Warburg was so taken by one of his letters that he circulated it to colleagues. (This letter was later given to me by Sir Siegmund's then colleague, Sir Ronald Grierson.) This correspondence was not just inconsequential chatter: for my father it was vital to bring Asia into the mainstream arena of international finance while for the City bankers it was important to seek opportunities for funding in the emerging Asian countries in the area of sovereign debt. Most importantly, they were vying for a position in the funding of this newly established international organisation. On arriving in Manila, that was the most urgent matter for Masaru. ADB would have to raise capital in international markets; he communicated, in confidence, with his friends in the City on how the land lay as to which venue was likely to be chosen for the first funding of the Bank: the orthodox New York issue; a Eurodollar issue; an orthodox DM issue; an orthodox Swiss franc issue; or some combination of these? Could it precede the next World Bank issue in New York? Complex relationships, personal or otherwise, in the line-up of the syndicate affected this decision. Any time that they were in Manila, these people called on their old friend Masaru.

Life in the Tropics
The country my family arrived in, in late December 1966, was in a state of emergency under President Marcos with martial law in operation. Gunfire was frequently heard in the streets of the capital. My father rented a large house with a swimming pool in the garden from the Minister of Finance of the Philippines

in a fenced and guarded suburb of North Forbes Park in Makati. Most of the Japanese staff at the ADB including the President lived in this enclave. My sisters went to the American school within it. They had live-in maids and a gardener. All the Japanese living in the Philippines at the time had to be exceptionally careful with the staff they employed, as many Filipinos felt a residual hostility due to their experiences in the war. The Philippines had been invaded by Japan at the very start of the Pacific War in December 1941 and was occupied until the 1945 surrender. It was one of the most gruelling theatres of the war. The Filipinos remained loyal to the US as the latter kept their promise of independence for the country.

Yoko's weekly letters to me talked of a relentless and oppressive tropical heat. She found the lack of change of seasons exhausting. Power cuts were frequent; food in fridges could not be rescued and she had to cook it immediately. Though there were happier aspects of living in a country with a plentiful supply of avocados and artichokes, which she loved, and other exotica, my parents found life there challenging. They had never expected that they would live in the Third World, with all the attendant inconveniences and unexpected difficulties. Confronting them was bewildering. On one occasion the children of a Japanese colleague were kidnapped. Everyone had to be resourceful and imaginative in daily living.

Chahchah and Eiko did well in their school, acting in school plays and taking part in other activities with students of various nationalities. My parents were clearly nervous and worried about me alone in England. "Stop worrying about me, Mummy!" I wrote repeatedly. A few months after they had left, I became stricken with a series of minor illnesses: my father sent a telegram to his former colleague at the Embassy, Ibuki Bunmei, to find out if I was all right; Mother expressed distrust of British doctors and sent me chloromycetin, an antibiotic. Frequently my father sent me money as he was worried that I might not have enough in times of extra need; I feel sure that he believed it was the only practical thing he could do.

My parents were fortunate in having people they knew amongst the Japanese community in the Philippines. The wives of both the Ambassador (Yasukawa Takeshi) and of the President of the ADB (Watanabe Takeshi) were both at school with my mother, only a year or two older. The Yasukawas had daughters of a similar age to my sisters, and they became lifelong friends of Eiko. Mrs Watanabe and her sisters were all at school with my mother; the whole family was well known to us. Their eldest daughter, Hiroko, was studying at Smith College while we were in Washington and had come to see us. She later married a distinguished Japanese banker of the Industrial Bank of Japan who came to head up the Bank in London and whom I got to know well. Mr Watanabe's official private secretary was a young Ministry of Finance official, Gyohten Toyoo, about whom I have already written.

One of the senior executives at the ADB was Takagaki Tasuku, seconded from the Bank of Tokyo, well known to Aunt Noriko and her husband. The Takagaki family became close friends of my parents and on their return to Tokyo asked to register their grandson at our address in order to be able to get into a school in our catchment area. On one of his business trips to London he brought some money and messages from our father. Chahchah was also up at Cambridge then; he invited us to dinner at the Hyde Park Hotel in Knightsbridge (now the Mandarin Oriental) and we were more than happy to hear news of our family first-hand. Decades later, Mr Takagaki (by then President of the Mitsubishi Financial Group) contacted me while I was at Lazard's on a confidential financing deal on the property development of Paternoster Square by his bank. He brought the Chairman of Mitsubishi Estate with him to meet me; this gentlemanly Chairman was a Mr Fukuzawa, the grandson of the famous author and entrepreneur, Fukuzawa Yukichi.

It was the first time that the family came into regular contact with people of other Asian countries; the wives of directors often gathered for lunches or tea parties and showed each other aspects of their particular cultures. Mother was asked to show techniques of flower-arranging, tea ceremonies and the like. She wrote to me how she improvised on those occasions without the necessary equipment, and of the amusing comments received from those foreign ladies. She was interested to learn about Indian cuisine and the sari as well as hand-block printing techniques. Years later, when I was asking her advice on what to give as a wedding present to an Indian bride, she was more than helpful in pointing out what she might prefer; she recommended either pearls or a length of traditional Japanese woven Tatsumura (龍村) silk.

My mother sent interesting Filipino handicrafts to me at Cambridge. The Filipinos made fine dress material from pineapple or banana skin fibres, embroidered beautifully. Some were very much like translucent organza. I made blouses and dresses by hand and wore them for many years afterwards. There were lizard-skin handbags, which I liked, hardwood trays inlaid in ivory and raffia work baskets. My parents furnished the house with tropical hardwood furniture which they brought back to Japan on retirement for our house in Tokyo. They were very well made by any standards.

A couple of months after they left England, Michaelmas Term at Cambridge ended and I was in a bit of a panic as to what to do for the vac; seeing everybody else preparing to go home, the reality of being left alone in England suddenly dawned on me. My new boyfriend whom I had recently met invited me and an American girl, Dianne Hunter, who was in the same plight, to his home in Lincolnshire for Christmas. (His mother was an unenlightened provincial and said I must be pagan, so wouldn't allow me to ring my parents while she said Dianne could: I thought that was mean.) But what would I do for the rest of the holidays? Dianne and I decided to look for a flat together in London, but could not find a suitable one. Exceptionally kind friends of my parents from the Embassy, the Akiyamas, invited us both to stay with them at their house in Wimbledon. They welcomed us with fantastic meals. When we returned from Lincolnshire, two other Embassy people said we could borrow their homes while they went away on New Year holidays. It was not so easy for the Easter vac two months later; Dianne decided to stay in her room at New Hall, even though it was rather lonely without many students there. Again, I borrowed the house of a Ministry of Finance official, Dan Hirosuke, in St John's Wood while they were away for two weeks; amazingly they said that I could bring my friends, Nadia Gawadi and her boyfriend Antony Pay (who became a famous clarinettist) from Cambridge. That was wonderful; but then, just as I had to leave that house and find somewhere else to spend the following two weeks, I contracted German measles. I could not find anybody who was able to have me to stay, either for fear of being infected or because they had other guests. Eventually I went to stay in the attic room in the Nippon Club on Chelsea Embankment. It was suggested to me by Elizabeth Wright, who was the personal assistant to the Ambassador. Early on our arrival in London, my father had introduced us; she was young and beautiful, the daughter of the British High Commissioner in Kuala Lumpur during the Malayan Emergency. I felt pretty depressed at that time; not lonely as many people, including Elizabeth, came to visit me and sent me food and flowers but still somewhat helpless. My parents wrote desperately anxious letters, as I had been somewhat under the weather for the whole of that winter. I did, however, manage some triumphant moments like organising the Valentine Ball and acting as its Chairman, for the university's United Nations Association (CUUNA), of which I was an active member. I recruited Pink Floyd, with their beautiful psychedelic lighting, to headline the ball; that was a month before they released their first record. I remember that to advertise the ball we hired a helicopter and showered the whole city of Cambridge with small pieces of pink paper printed with 'Who are the Pink Floyd?'

Reading my letters, my parents got the idea that I was living life to the full, going to parties and dances, engaging in extracurricular activities and making lots of friends. Lizzie Barker Bennett, a year younger at school, came up to New Hall that year and we often gave dinner parties together, cooking complicated dishes on a single Belling cooker. She and I became very close friends and I often went to stay with her family in Oxted. They made delicious meals with home-grown vegetables and we would go bramble picking in the autumn. Lizzie and I made batik cloths with melted candle wax, and other handicrafts. I learnt to cook with her and learnt a little about gardening from her too. She is my closest friend and anchor, often providing the essential reference point. Attending several parties in one evening at Cambridge was not rare and balls, dances, cocktail parties, and twenty-first birthday celebrations were on the weekly agenda; we often spent hours discussing philosophical and political subjects deep into the night. I wrote in my letters how much I was enjoying this, opening my eyes to new ideas. I was trying also to engage my father in discussing political developments, writing to him about the 'shocked' reactions of my Cambridge friends to the devaluation of the pound sterling followed by that of the French franc. My mother kept urging me not to forget to do some work as well!

Mother's Sorrow

The five years that my family spent in Manila were marred by the deaths of both my maternal grandparents within three years of each other. For Yoko to have been away from home for both her parents' last days must have been more than hard to bear. Taking family duties as her priority, as she had pledged the day she married, she remained always loyal to her husband and endured her sadness bravely, as was expected of her. In those days Japanese diplomats were prepared not to be at their parents' or even their children's deaths, nor at their children's weddings, as they put their duty first. She had been living abroad for seven years and had seen her parents only three times in that period; but that was more than most of her fellow diplomatic wives. Letters from her family to Yoko from this period are highly poignant; they would provide ample material for the script of a period melodrama of the pre-internet age.

Soon after my parents left for Manila, Grandmother Hanako began to complain of abdominal discomfort. Before they had settled down properly, letters from Yoko's brother and sisters described repeated tests and investigations at hospitals and doctors' opinions. Their great anxiety and frantic efforts to relieve their mother's discomfort are spelt out vividly in almost daily communications. Various prescribed medications did not alleviate her condition. The initial optimism of the doctors that it was benign stomach ulcers proved false; by May of that year the cancer had already spread and Grandmother was hospitalised, unable to eat and in great pain. The true nature of her illness was kept from her, as was customary with cancer in those days, but there was little hope of recovery. Yoko's letter to her lying in hospital was read out by Aunt Asako, who could not hold back her tears and had to ask Noriko to finish reading it; Grandmother too was in tears as she listened to Mother's words. Yoko sent her cards she made herself with pressed flowers from her garden and almost daily letters that were placed beside Grandmother's pillow. To make matters worse Grandfather Jiro, fearing that he might have a similar condition developing, asked for an investigation and was found to have a very early stage of stomach cancer; he immediately asked to be operated on and stayed in the same hospital as his wife. He recovered well in a few weeks but was in a frail condition on a soft diet for some time. From the end of May to the beginning of June, Yoko went back to see her mother for the last time. It was not long before she died, in early August when Yoko arrived back just a few hours too late. Aunt Noriko, who was living in Tokyo with her young children while her husband was posted to California by his bank, went to the airport to meet her eldest sister and had to break the news of their mother's death. Mother wrote to me saying that in the coffin at home in Fukidecho, Grandmother Hanako looked serene and at peace, unlike the emaciated figure, struggling with pain, she had seen for the last time in hospital a few weeks before. Her father led her in and said "Poor Hanako, she suffered so much…" After the funeral, he gave her a large single stone emerald ring of Hanako's, saying "You are the eldest, you must have this ring in her memory."

Yoko had to go back to a steaming Manila after the funeral; my sisters said that she was sorrowful for several days but that she regained her composure quickly. I wrote to her in total shock, saying I had loved my grandmother very much even though I had said some rude things. I was very upset when I learnt of her imminent death after my mother's first visit. It was quite unthinkable; after all, only two years earlier she had come to visit us in London. It was at the end of my second year at Cambridge, after the May Balls, with my boyfriend about to take up a two-year stint with VSO in Kenya to teach English in the bush. His mother was unsympathetic when she saw my sorrowful state: "You are not crying about your grandmother dying; you are crying about the end of good times," she said. All that contributed to my distress.

Letters show that my mother became introspective, self-critical and depressed for many months. I wrote attempting to console her with my youthful philosophy of life and death, saying that Grandmother had been allowed to be nearer God but that her spirit lived on and would stay with me through my mother. She regretted that she was weak-minded and naively honest;

I responded that, were it true, those qualities were actually part of her strength and charm. Seeing her at the age of 102, as I write today, those characteristics are no longer predominant; her determination to live has been astonishing – perhaps she gained it in her widowhood, alone with all her daughters abroad. She made her own life according to her predilections; far from those self-critical thoughts, her paintings show her ability to develop skills and portray her perceptions of the world on her own terms.

With Grandmother gone, Aunt Asako wrote melancholy letters about days spent tidying away her mother's possessions with her aunt Kimiko; she kept some important kimonos for Yoko, which Grandfather urged her to send so that she could wear them at official functions. Aunt Asako was working at the Ministry of Science and Technology during the day but had dinner with her lonely father each evening. It was a particularly busy time at work and she had found daily visits, while taking turns with her sisters to stay overnight with their mother in hospital, particularly hard. The emptiness of Fukidecho with Grandmother gone was astonishing. Osué, the housekeeper at Akiya, was brought over to look after Grandfather and the vast house. On the 4th of every month (as Grandmother died on 4 August) the whole family gathered at Fukidecho to dine together with Grandfather Jiro. Until the first anniversary of her death, the family was in mourning.

For the first Buddhist anniversary memorial service at the family temple – Seishoji in Shiba – a service was held jointly for Grandmother and her parents, to mark the thirteen years since Great-Grandmother's death, and the twenty-three years since Great-Grandfather's. That put an end to the year of mourning. Then came another scare less than a year later, causing much anxiety in the family, with Aunt Setsuko finding a lump and undergoing a mastectomy, though thankfully it turned out to be benign.

Aunt Noriko wrote to my mother asking for advice on whether

she and her children should join her husband in Los Angeles, leaving her father in Tokyo with Asako. Marriage could not be sustained with long-term absences; she was lonely coping with all domestic challenges on her own; her young sons were growing up without their father. Yoko, speaking from her own experience of the 1950s, with her husband away in America and in Hokkaido, recommended going to California, even though Noriko was anxious about her sons' education. After her mother's death it seemed that Noriko found in her eldest sister, fourteen years her senior, a mother substitute and wrote to her often about personal concerns, saying she looked forward to Yoko's return to Tokyo so that she could talk to her about matters that she could only have talked about previously with their mother. Noriko left for California in the early autumn, a few months after Grandmother's death; Grandfather found this a blow. He planned to visit them for Christmas 1969 and take in a visit to a friend in Mexico on the way back. He asked his granddaughter Kinuko to accompany him. The business at the mines was going well then, with strong copper prices, and he could easily take time off and leave it in the hands of his son, Yuhei. But his health began to deteriorate in late autumn and the visit was cancelled.

A Happier Interlude

The two years after Grandmother Hanako's death were generally a happier time for our family: Chahchah got into Cambridge, taking the exam in Manila by post, and went up in October 1968 to the same college I had graduated from; I myself came down from Cambridge in June that year and got a job in policy research with the Atlantic Trade Study, thinking that this would be temporary – a year or two at most, before being reunited with my parents.

I went to Africa to see my boyfriend – the first time any member of my family visited that continent. The trip to Kenya during the

Christmas vac of 1967 was more than an eye-opener; it was an experience which profoundly affected my outlook and ignited an interest in the economic development of Third World countries. I wrote long letters to my parents about what I experienced and saw – the extreme poverty and sickness (leprosy), life in the bush with no water or electricity, the aspirations of young politicians, the courage of all those who lived there against natural adversities, the wildlife, and above all the sensationally beautiful wide expanse of landscape. The smell of Africa as soon as one landed on its soil has remained a permanent reminder of my love for the continent all my life. It was the first of many visits; coincidences took me back to central Africa on business and years later I developed a working relationship with South Africa as a non-executive director of one of its banks for more than eighteen years. Looking back, it was surprising that my parents allowed me to go on that trip in the face of their constant worry for my health and safety. But they would not have known that we had to scare off deadly small green snakes at night on the path to the 'hole in the ground' where tarantulas lurked!

During my third and last year at Cambridge, I was writing to my parents about my plans to visit for the summer after graduation in June and spend four months with them before returning to London to start my 'temporary' job. I had refused to go back to live with my grandfather at Fukidecho, which was what my mother would have preferred, but that seemed to me like being incarcerated in a fortress. My father thought it would be a waste of my time to join them in Manila and that a temporary job for a year, until they moved back to Tokyo, would be the answer. I spent a long time looking for work that year, not knowing what I really wanted to do but applying for jobs in journalism and PR, none of which materialised. During one of the interviews I was granted by a major advertising and PR firm, for the first and only time I came across sexual discrimination: the director interviewing me said "You might be quite good at this, but you, a woman, wouldn't be able to take a client out for a drink in a pub. So no, I can't offer you a job." Contrary to his expectation, in fact I went on to take clients out to pubs, bars and restaurants throughout my stockbroking career.

My father was immensely worried about his own financial position and even thought that Chahchah would have to win a scholarship somewhere, preferably in the United States. After much worry, especially for Chahchah herself, she got into Cambridge. My letters to my parents over this period were fraught, telling them I was most tremendously grateful for what they had given me already and talking of my concern for their unhappy state of mind. I even resorted to lecturing them that they should stop complaining about their predicament in a disagreeable environment and think of interesting new things to do. This didn't go down well. Father's high blood pressure got worse and his worries were compounded. I promised that I would be abstemious and live within my salary, while getting a room of my own so that Chahchah had somewhere to come during the vac. No amount of reassuring messages would assuage their concerns. "I am after all your daughter: have faith!"

I was most tremendously happy that Chahchah was in England from the autumn of 1968, and we met often and talked on the phone even though we wrote letters to each other every week; during vacs she came to stay with me in the flats I shared with friends. It gave comfort to our parents that we were together. She and I became very close, confiding in each other in a way we had never done before. She is independently-minded and brave, perhaps taking after our mother in that way. Though I was always concerned about her, by the time she was in her second year up at Cambridge she started resenting my attitudes and went her own way, avoiding 'being stuck with elder sister'! – but often in some chaos trying greedily to fit in too many activities. Even when she was a little girl, just learning to speak, she said proudly "I am a tiger, so I am strong!" (She was born in the

Year of the Tiger according to the old Chinese/Japanese calendar.) Like all younger sisters she was competitively-minded and would always try to do the same as me or better. She wanted to have the same dresses as me and would refuse to be dressed in more childlike clothes. Her competitiveness has done her a lot of good as she built her career. The uninhibited way in which I wrote to my parents revealing details of my 'grouse' with her caused them even more worry and on occasion Father would write to his Ministry colleagues in London to find out what was going on; I would then inform him that this was an overreaction that wreaked havoc with the Embassy officials. His colleagues meanwhile were immensely kind, making sure that we had somewhere to stay during the vac and often inviting us to dinner in London – sometimes at their homes and sometimes at top restaurants such as the Coq d'Or and L'Écu de France – giving us the background feeling of security that we needed.

When Chahchah first arrived from Manila and I was taking her up to Cambridge for the first time, we rented a car to take her and her luggage there: it was promptly stolen from the street in Hampstead. We had to quickly rush around buying some clothes for her, and I was terribly worried that she would find herself feeling insecure being separated from her familiar possessions. But as Miss Hammond, our tutor, said, Chahchah is like a Russian doll that immediately springs back up when pushed down. She went on a long hitchhiking and camping tour of Turkey with Francis (her future husband) during the summer vac; no sooner had they arrived in Greece than their wallets with their passports were stolen. They came back finally in early September laden with wonderful things they found in local markets, including an Ottoman embroidered gown in red velvet for me, but Francis had contracted jaundice and was taken to St George's Hospital at Hyde Park Corner on arrival. I had postponed my summer holiday while they were away, so concerned I was as there was no way of getting in touch with them on their journey. Francis was a year ahead of Chahchah, at Magdalene, and on graduating he went on a Henry Knox scholarship to study for a doctorate in Control Engineering at Harvard. He later made his career at IBM in America.

When I came down from Cambridge my father sent back to me the little Renault they had taken to Manila. I was considering buying a car by doing some temporary translation work when I graduated, but he thought it more economical to send one across the globe! It arrived at the London docks after a long sea journey and off I went to collect it. It was wonderful to have my car in London and I went everywhere in it, incurring large parking fines. But it made it possible to head off to the country at weekends and to visit friends who lived in the suburbs.

Most memorably, I went on a month-long holiday in it with David to France and Italy in the summer of 1969. We were waiting for Chahchah and Francis to get back safely from Turkey, but there were no signs that they would do so in a hurry, as indicated in their occasional postcards. I asked if Chahchah could stay with the Tanakas on their return, and they kindly agreed; so we set off with maps and a Michelin Guide in hand. As we both read History at Cambridge, we sought out the places of historical significance in mediaeval Europe. I described in my letter to my parents at the end of the trip in the happiest terms each and every place that we visited, with elaborate explanations of their historical importance. On arriving back we found that Chahchah had not awaited our return but gone off to a dance in Berkshire, leaving a note saying she was then off to France for three days. Big sister was not amused.

Haruko's First Job

While my parents were contending with life in tropical Manila, I graduated from Cambridge and as agreed with my father I found a job, initially for a year. It was hard, despite going to some interviews at large advertising and PR companies in my third year; although I would have preferred to get a job in something art-related such as the Arts Council or a museum or gallery, public sector jobs were not open to me as a foreigner – it was similar in policy research institutions such as Chatham House. During the summer months my father asked some of his friends to help me find a suitable opportunity. They were all immensely kind. Lord Jellicoe invited me to lunch at the House of Lords together with Lady Violet Bonham Carter, whose son Raymond was also well known to my father as he was at Warburgs. He asked me if I wanted after lunch to sit in the Gallery of the House and watch the debate; I had to decline as I was meeting a girlfriend with whom I was flat-hunting, whereupon he offered to help me to find a flat. He wrote to various merchant banks asking if there was an opening for me, including his own, Warburgs. He also introduced me to Brian Beedham, deputy editor of *The Economist*, who said that if I could write an article for the magazine on any subject of my choosing, they might ask me for occasional contributions.

But my break came when I went to see a senior journalist my father knew well in London on the *Financial Times*, William Clarke, who was then running the Committee for Invisible Exports that he had just founded. Bill Clarke sent me to see Charles Pulay, then editor of the business section of *The Times*. Pulay said I should see Hugh Corbet, who had just left *The Times* and was establishing an institute on international trade policy called The Atlantic Trade Study. I went to see him immediately at his flat in Cornwall Gardens and he told me of his plan to set up a research-based political lobby on international trade policy. The Kennedy Round of GATT negotiations had just been concluded and there were concerns that momentum for trade liberalisation might be lost. A number of economists and former Foreign Office officials amongst others were taking the initiative to form a group; the Chairman of the Atlantic Trade Study was to be Sir Michael Wright, who was Britain's negotiator at the Geneva Disarmament Conference and Ambassador to Norway, and the Hon. Treasurer was to be Sir Douglas Busk, former Ambassador to Finland and Venezuela. Hugh explained that there were nascent proposals to form a North Atlantic Free Trade Area (NAFTA) and on the other side of the globe a Pacific Free Trade Area (PAFTA). Those proposals were being worked on by eminent economists and like-minded thinkers and opinion formers on both sides of the Atlantic, as well as in Japan (by Professor Kojima Kiyoshi). He thought I could find it interesting and my instincts if not knowledge of Japan would be useful. He could pay me only a small salary but I could give it a go. It sounded intriguing and I accepted.

I worked with Hugh and a secretary in a small office in Buckingham Street near the Adelphi off the Strand for two years. It was a wonderful job for a fresh graduate embarking on a career in London. I was in constant touch with some of the world's most famous economists and opinion formers: Professor Harry G. Johnson, who at the time held chairs simultaneously at Chicago and at the LSE, was our Director of Studies. There was a Board that contained Leonard Beaton (columnist on *The Times*), Douglas Jay MP, Maxwell Stamp, Hans Liesner and others. The institute was funded by contributions from British industry that saw its interest as lying with the Commonwealth rather than the EEC. My job entailed putting together and editing our research publications and sometimes organising seminars and conference papers. There were frequent visitors from the US, including Harald Malmgren who worked closely with us. I learnt a huge amount about trade policy, international politics and most importantly the issues in Britain's negotiations to join the EEC. As a group, we were opposed to joining the EEC with its customs union approach to economic integration, and we were concerned that the world might fragment into regional trading blocs – a concern shared by the newly-elected Nixon administration in the United States. Hugh also ran a very senior dining club called the Foreign Affairs Club which was chaired by the Shadow Foreign Secretary – during my time first Patrick Gordon Walker, succeeded by Lord Home. The Club had a membership of over a hundred, by invitation only, and met once a month in the Waldorf Hotel ballroom. It invited as the guest speaker a senior politician from America or Europe – Hubert Humphrey, Dean Rusk, Helmut Schmidt, and many others. I met and dined with the very top of the international political establishment – an amazing experience which I could never repeat.

I wrote many articles for publication in journals and newspapers and contributed a chapter to a book we were publishing on EFTA. That was the first time that I was published in a book. I was fortunate to find that Hugh and I got on well and we were on the same wavelength on every dimension of international politics. We remained friends for many years even after I was invited to join the Overseas Development Institute (ODI), on a better salary which I badly needed. As my parents were still in Manila, I continued with my career, which now focused on the developed countries' trade policies towards the less-developed countries and in particular on the impact that Britain joining the EEC would have on the Third World. The Director of Studies at the ODI who asked me to join was a wonderful man, Dr Tom Soper, who has remained a lifelong friend despite his being a committed supporter of the EEC and EU. Unfortunately, soon after I joined, he left the ODI to join Barclays Bank. I made some interesting friends there amongst the fellow research officers – one of whom was Sunetra Bandaranaike, daughter of the then Prime Minister of Ceylon (now Sri Lanka); it was a very international place, with an Iranian secretary, Polish economist, Yugoslav receptionist and German librarian.

My father had visited Tokyo for a few days in September 1969 and was able to dine with Grandfather at Fukidecho; he informed his wife's father that he expected he would be returning to the Ministry in the spring of 1970. In fact, the much-awaited return home was postponed until the following year. He had been to see Watanabe, the President of the Bank, on that visit as they were both in Tokyo at the same time, to ask for his support for relocation back to the Ministry but Watanabe was unsympathetic and obdurate. My father was very unhappy about having to remain in Manila for another year, and it proved fatal to his career. The stress of the long posting in Manila took a toll on his health and in the last year of their stay he contracted shingles and had to be hospitalised. But for my mother it had another fateful consequence.

Grandfather's Death

Yoko's father had been recovering his strength and his penchant for gourmet meals and whisky, playing golf, and holidaying in Karuizawa in the summer. But over the winter of 1970, his health began to worsen and his other children began to raise the alarm. Yuhei wrote that he "shuddered to think of the repeat of two years ago". These fears were justified. With only a few months of respite at home, Jiro's health progressively deteriorated, with two long stays in hospital including another operation for cancer which proved to be too late. The doctors initially warned Yuhei that his father might not have much more than a month left. Again, Grandfather was not to be told and those in the know had difficulty keeping to the agreed script. My parents had expected to return to Japan in May that year and had started the preparations. How disappointed Yoko must have been when those plans were aborted. During the spring months of April and May her father's condition remained relatively stable and he was able to lead a quiet life at home, occasionally going out to the Tokyo Club for lunch with friends. He had taken up writing letters to Yoko quite frequently since Hanako's death, with news from home. Unlike my father's letters to myself, they were in a chatty mode, giving accounts of daily activities. Yoko went back for a fortnight in May to see him; Grandfather was elated, asking her to stay at Fukidecho and sending a car to meet her at the airport. He touchingly wrote that he might not be able to entertain her adequately with fewer servants around now and asked her also to apologise to Masaru for inconveniencing him with her absence. But towards the end of June his condition started to decline rapidly and once again Mother rushed home. Grandfather died in early July within a few days of her arrival, aged seventy-three. Yoko sent a telegram to her husband: "Father has gone." Eiko had to write to me with the devastating news. I was shocked and saddened and wrote a formal letter to Mother in Japanese (I normally wrote in English). In it I not only attempted to comfort her in her deepest sorrow but also expressed my first realisation that Fukidecho had provided the backdrop of security in the farthest recess of my psyche, and that without grandparents nothing but emptiness remained.

The months that followed their father's death were tumultuous for Yoko and her siblings. As often happens in many cultures, when parents go the bond that kept the family together weakens. In the immediate aftermath of heightened emotions, selfishness comes to the fore: festering resentments return, hitherto hidden feelings resurface, and endless acrimonious exchanges ensue at family meetings to discuss inheritance. Aunt Asako, much regretting that her eldest sister was not there to provide a calming influence, wrote long and tormented letters relating the disputes between Yuhei and Setsuko on all matters relating to the estate, the house and its contents, eventually concluding that even between siblings people are different and we were each ultimately alone. It was a very hard time for her, bearing the brunt of clearing out the house with a monumental number of possessions. Again, Osué and Ryozo helped her daily to sort things but a few months later Osué became unwell and had to return home to Akiya. Fukidecho was still Asako's home as she had not married, and suddenly not just her home but all that provided an anchor for her had disappeared. She suddenly felt alone. Ryozo and his wife lived in the house for some time to keep it secure, presumably on Uncle Yuhei's instructions. There had to be a division of the contents between the siblings; important works of art had to be valued. Asako went to America for a month at the end of that year only to return to yet more clearing up and family disputes.

Yoko characteristically suggested that she would make a patchwork from her father's enormous collection of neckties. Asako sent them to her, and mother made several cushion covers with them, giving one to each of her sisters. In some ways she was lucky to have been spared many of the disputes in person, at least until returning to Tokyo nine months later, when she had to join the clearing up. By nature, and also being the eldest, she was not ever inclined to compete for material possessions. She said that the only thing that mattered was having a memento of her old home. I myself share this attitude, believing that I should buy with my own money whatever I want and not fight over inherited possessions. Apart from her share of the art works, Mother brought back several tin trunks of fabric remnants that my grandmother and great-grandmother had kept. I took quite a lot of these, as they were from beautiful old kimonos, to make patchwork with – they are now my quilt covers.

Yoko continued to have close relationships with her siblings. Yuhei took the reins of the family business. He led the family and kept it intact, always faithfully continuing gatherings on various occasions, be it someone's birthday or just to go out for a good meal. The five siblings dined together in a *fugu* (blowfish) restaurant on Grandmother's birthday each year. He also kept up contact with the wide-reaching diaspora of Tanaka, Watase and Fukuhara relations.

Crossing an Ocean

My parents and Eiko finally went back to Tokyo in April 1971, to our old home in Imazatocho (now Shiroganedai). Eiko, having left Japan aged four, was now fifteen. But for myself the winter of that year was a turbulent time. I got engaged to David the previous summer, as he was going to America for two years to do a postgraduate degree at Fletcher School of Law and Diplomacy. I had agonised for some years about marrying a foreigner and what that meant; I knew that my mother would be deeply saddened to have me living abroad, forever making it difficult to meet often. I wrote to my parents about my equivocations very openly – about the possibility of dislocation from my home country in every respect. We eventually decided to get engaged – as even his parents were by then encouraging us to do – and planned on marrying once David had completed his studies and got a job. My father was much in agreement that we should not embark on our marriage before David had a means of living. I was much moved when recently, in his files, I came upon a copy of a most touching letter he wrote to me in August that year, concerning the £1,000 (in 2023 equivalent to £18,000 adjusted for inflation) he was sending me, equal to more than two months of his salary, saying that I was not to spend it on daily living, but rather as a 'special fund' to prepare for my wedding or to visit David in Boston if our wedding was to come later.

I wrote literally hundreds of letters to institutions in America in search of a job so that we could see each other during that time, mostly in vain. I went to Boston for Christmas, when Chahchah came also to see Francis at Harvard; we celebrated Christmas together in Boston, singing carols in Louisburg Square, and went on a driving holiday in snowy upstate Massachusetts. I went on to Washington for four days to do some research for my work at the ODI and to see some people who might be able to help in my job search. One of them was Harald Malmgren.

Harald was the US Trade Representative for the GATT Kennedy Round, a convinced free trader and a brilliant neoclassical economist. He sent me to see Professor David Henderson, the Director of Economics at the World Bank. He was looking for someone to organise the work of the department, and he much liked my Oxbridge background, himself having been an Oxford don. The following month, he arranged for me to be offered a job at the Bank: I was the youngest professional and one of only three women professionals at the Bank at the time. He was to become a lifelong friend. Still, I hesitated in accepting an administrative job, in contrast to research and writing in which I had been increasingly involved. However, my relationship with a new Director of Studies at the ODI had grown tense, as we held diametrically opposed views on the trade and development research I was working on, concerning the impact on developing countries of Britain joining the EEC. It was not tenable, from my perspective, to have published a book in my name with opinions that I did not hold. So in early 1971 I moved to the US to work at the World Bank.

Thanks to the long postal strike in Britain, I had to resort to asking the Foreign Office to use the Diplomatic Bag to Manila; nevertheless I was already in Washington by the time my parents learnt of my transatlantic move. A stormy exchange of letters ensued. We had not seen each other for five years by then, during which time we relied on our correspondence to maintain a mutual emotional understanding. Reading my letters of this period is painful and appalling. While I took their sympathy and unfailing support for granted, their anxiety was clearly far greater than I appreciated. They both thought my attitude to work was too casual and selfish. I was young and idealistic, but as my father pointed out, "the world was a rude and hard place." He was happy that I landed a job at the World Bank, but he thought my complaints about the nature of the job too naïve. He urged that I stick to the Bank, which would give me a pension for life! The word 'pension' had not yet entered my psyche.

Arriving in Washington, I found life less than agreeable. While assuring my parents that I was all right, my letters are full of descriptions of the dangers of living as a single woman and how much I hated the way of life. Washington had changed almost out of recognition from the place we had left in 1962; downtown was now a ghetto and buildings had become dilapidated or even abandoned. It had the highest crime rate in the whole country; one could never go out alone and we confined ourselves to the perimeter of Georgetown or the suburbs of Virginia or Maryland. It was hard to find an apartment I could afford and furnish (there were no furnished rentals) while American banks did not have the system of overdrafts that I had been used to in London. I eventually found a little apartment in an old colonial house in Georgetown, but the tenants downstairs threatened to shoot me whenever my floorboards creaked; people carried guns in their pockets, and even at the cinema I found I was sitting next to a gun. It was humid and hot, with ancient air-conditioning in the window of my bedroom; I often went to the office at weekends where it was more comfortable. I was lucky to find that my old friend from school, Linda Galantin, was working as a statistical assistant at the IMF and we quickly picked up on our old friendship. But she lived miles away in Silver Springs and we could not meet outside of the office very often. The prevailing political mood was tense as the opposition to the ongoing Vietnam War was gathering momentum with violent demonstrations; every car that crossed the 14th Street Bridge was photographed by the Pentagon that lay adjacent. One day the centre of Washington was surrounded by troops carrying rifles and bayonets lining every street, and armoured tanks located at every major intersection, as the Vietnam veterans staged their most violent demonstrations yet. They declared that they were going to stop the Federal government from working; but in defiance all government departments and the World Bank and the IMF ordered all personnel to attend work. I woke up at 4 a. m. to the sound of an exploding car under my window. The whole of downtown Washington was covered in the smoke from tear gas as the demonstrators marched down every road, set fire to parked cars, and threw water balloons down from the tops of buildings. I escaped one such as someone swept me into a nearby building, saying "Get out, you will be killed."

During my first week, the luxury hotel in Georgetown I was staying at was held up by gunmen in mid-afternoon. The Seven-Eleven store diagonally opposite my apartment was held up three times in the week after I moved in. Taxi drivers would not take one across the more insalubrious parts of the capital to get to the other side of Washington; they would always stay outside my front door until they were sure I had got inside. I rented a Volkswagen 'Beetle' to go and find furniture in a second-hand warehouse in Arlington called The Thieves Market, but I found that petrol stations would not accept cash; no shop kept cash – you had to have a credit card which I could not get as a new arrival.

Some people said I would soon get used to it; but I wondered if I *wanted* to get used to a life of being stuck in my apartment in the evenings, unable to go out alone and accepting almost any invitations that came my way. Though some friends from London visited, and a Cambridge friend, Rosemary McKinnon, and her husband John, lived not far away and could come to dinner sometimes, I was lonely. One special visitor was my schoolmistress Miss Ford, newly married to the Rt Rev Richard Rutt; he was the Anglican Bishop in Korea, and, later, Bishop of Leicester. It was an unexpected and enchanting moment. During my lunch break I often walked up the road to the Phillips Collection to look at paintings to lift my spirits. David was in Boston, a long way away. My observations of American society seem in many ways perceptive even in retrospect; it appears today, as I write, that not much has changed over the last half-century – or perhaps it has, but for the worse. Young Americans then were appalled by and abhorred the increasingly dominant influence of corporate political funding; they felt helpless as it seemed to them to threaten the integrity of the democratic electoral system.

I did, however, witness the dramatic events of August that year, the 'Nixon shock'. One of my new friends was the top official responsible for international monetary affairs at the US Treasury: Will Cates was appointed by Nixon, to work with Secretary Connolly and Under-secretary Paul Volcker. He rang me on that historic day and said bluntly "Watch television tonight. I am just leaving for Camp David." He told me in no uncertain terms that the days of multilateral negotiations were over; from now on America was going to make bilateral deals, ending the postwar commitment to multilateralism of the GATT – the foundation on which the phenomenal growth of international trade and economic prosperity depended. Japan and West Germany were the principal targets: they must revalue their currencies against the dollar and remove import restrictions against US products. He impressed upon me the seriousness of that intent. Moreover, the Americans found Japan's use of interpreters in the negotiations frustrating as the translation was often less than accurate or the interpreters' command of the English language wanting. I passed this on to my father; he took these observations seriously and immediately telephoned Gyohten about them.

As I made some new friends and settled down in my little flat in Georgetown, I grew more contented, but I certainly didn't want to stay there for long. Most of all I found the work at the Bank boring and, as David Henderson kindly said, I was "under-exploited for my talents". I hated the large bureaucracy and the institutional strictures. In any case, the Bank was reorganising departments in the autumn and my job was going to disappear. An opportunity appeared when Macmillan, the publishers, wrote to me to ask if they could publish the work I had abandoned at the ODI. John Wood of the Institute for Economic Affairs, who had read my manuscript, had recommended it to an editor at Macmillan. Had I stayed at the World Bank this would not have been possible, as employees were not allowed to publish books of their own. So I left Washington. Though my book was squarely on the side of a multilateral approach to international trade negotiations, Will Cates remained a special friend until his death. When I left he said "We will correspond", and he came to visit me in London as well as at Creems.

I returned to Cambridge as a research student in October 1971 in order to get the book into shape, having saved enough money to live for a year in England. (One of the better side-effects of working at the Bank was a good salary in comparison with Britain – and it was tax-free.) My parents' anxieties increased even more. But I thought it good to have a break from working and find time for reflection; I read widely, went to the theatre and opera, art galleries and museums, and published some articles. I continued in my letters to discuss at length my views of politics in the United States and in Britain with its move towards joining the EEC, something which I had worked so vigorously to oppose at the Atlantic Trade Study. I missed Chahchah a great deal, as she had become my confidante; she wanted to do a postgraduate degree but my father said he could not afford it. I offered to stay at the Bank for another couple of years to pay for her tuition and living expenses. But in the end Father relented and Chahchah went to Fletcher when she graduated from Cambridge. She was happy there, with Francis in nearby Cambridge, Massachusetts and went on to get a job at the World Bank's Young Professional programme. While my links with Africa were sub-Saharan, her job took her to Algeria and Morocco.

The venerable Sengakuji temple, near Shiroganedai, famed in literature and kabuki as the burial site of the 47 ronin (masterless samurai), whose killing of a tyrannical shogunate superior led to their mass suicide there.

12. BACK TO NEAR NORMAL?

~

L
ife never turns out as one expects, let alone plans. That could not be more true than for my parents and for myself. They never expected to live abroad continuously for eleven years, in three different parts of the globe, nor that they would be separated from their children for much of that time – after we said farewell at Heathrow that October in 1966 I was not to see my parents for five long years. Nor did we daughters expect that our lives overseas would continue for the rest of our days. Nor do I suppose they ever expected that the international life we embarked on in 1960, when we went to Washington, proved irreversible, with the near-inevitable consequence that all three of us would marry foreigners and make our lives abroad. It was never expected that I would even have a career.

Living so many years separated from parents and in foreign countries, Chahchah and I began to feel a sense of alienation from our own country. We had spent our adolescent years being educated abroad and then making our lives by ourselves. Our Japanese language deteriorated fast; as we did not meet Japanese people we barely spoke or read it for years; we were writing to our parents in English, and we as sisters spoke in English, though we continued to converse in Japanese with our parents. Mother's weekly letters were in Japanese, but my father's were in English. It was the reverse of the inferiority complex we suffered when we first arrived in America. We could not identify ourselves as Japanese people; we knew little about the country and no longer had close friends there. These issues were not particular to our family, as all diplomatic children wrestled with some similar sense of estrangement. They felt more at home 'as foreigners' in foreign countries. Though my sister-in-law, Ursula, went to school and university in England, she was essentially happier abroad as a foreigner speaking the language – French and Spanish in her case – wherever she found herself. She struggled to settle down back in England when her father retired and resorted to trying to find a job abroad. For Japanese children the issues of integrating back into Japan's education system on returning home was harder: some mothers went to school with their children to take notes and go over their lessons with them back at home each day. Most Japanese diplomats insisted on their children, especially boys, going back to Japan to get their secondary education at home for the sake of their future careers. My parents never expected that their daughters would have to get jobs in Japan and never gave thought to us keeping up our Japanese. It seemed to be enough that we were doing well in England. But for Chahchah and me, returning to Japan started to feel as if we were visiting a foreign country – that was psychologically traumatic, throwing us into an identity crisis. We could appear like foreigners there, not speaking the language, yet looking Japanese. Taxi drivers could not make us out, hearing our conversations in the back seat; some were even rude, presumably because they thought we must be Korean or Chinese. We couldn't read the street signs or notices at stations, nor menus in restaurants. We couldn't understand some of the things our relations said. In short, we couldn't communicate; it was very frustrating. I therefore looked for a job (finding one at the stockbroker Vickers, da Costa) which had something to do with Japan. Eventually it would involve business trips back there so that I could visit my parents and also relearn the language on the job. Poor Chahchah never had that opportunity and to this day she cannot write in or read Japanese. We both have to be grateful to Google: Chahchah uses Google Translate and gets a rough sense of short Japanese texts. I cannot write in Japanese, but recent software allows one to enter phonetic roman text, which is then converted to Japanese characters. At least that now allows me to communicate with my mother's care home staff using email.

Home at Last

My parents arrived back in Tokyo as the blossom was in its full glory. Our house had been lived in latterly by our Nakamura cousin Michiko and her nuclear physicist husband, Tsutomu, a descendant of the samurai clan chief of Matsuyama. Michiko had in fact been born in that house, when it was much larger before the war. They had done their best to look after an old property that was becoming dilapidated with age; at least my parents were able to move back in immediately. In July of that year the first anniversary of Grandfather Jiro's death was commemorated with a garden party at Fukidecho. My father made a point of telling me that it was a grand and fine occasion but lamented that it would be the last time the family would gather at that unique estate at Fukidecho; the house and immediate garden were to be sold soon after. I wrote to my mother saying how sad I was that I could not be there, and how much I felt for her sorrow. Yoko sometimes went to the gardens to pick flowers and branches of blossom; seeing the house totally shuttered and closed would have been shattering; she missed her parents very much and I saw her sobbing before their photographs. With two daughters abroad, and her parents no longer waiting to greet her, it was not the joyful homecoming Yoko would have wanted.

The next decade of her life was mentally trying – as Aunt Setsuko said to me "It seems she is finding life very hard." Retiring from the Ministry, my father had to find an equilibrium in a new phase of life, and was suffering from depression and melancholia. I was most concerned about him and wrote frequently, wishing him better and making suggestions that he might write books on international finance (but not memoirs, as I considered them self-indulgent and he too young) as well as getting a new job. Eiko's school had to be arranged: not ever having been to a Japanese school, her desire to attend a Japanese high school was impractical. She went instead to the American School in Tokyo. Enterprising as she always was, she learnt Japanese at night school, starting from scratch as if she were a foreigner, and became proficient in it. She also taught English privately. She cultivated a great interest in the culture of Japanese tea ceremonies and attended masterclasses. Mother was pleased and encouraging. For a while, Eiko flirted with the idea of becoming an actress, which met with strong opposition from our father. A brilliant student, she eventually enrolled at Radcliffe College, Harvard; Masaru was deeply pleased, and more than proud of her academic achievement. She graduated with a Magna Cum Laude in History.

For Christmas 1971, Chahchah and I went home to see our parents – at long last a family reunion! My parents and Eiko came to the airport to meet me and I still remember them looking very happy as I emerged into the arrivals hall at Haneda. It was the last time that I saw our old house, the one that my grandfather Koichi had built and where I grew up, because my parents decided to rebuild it soon afterwards. I much regretted their decision, but Mother explained that the house was too old and not suitable for retirement. They wanted modern amenities like central heating. Chahchah was pleased to be reunited with their white poodle, brought back from Manila. We delved into the tin trunks from Fukidecho with old fabrics and remnants and made scarves and blouses – it was just like old times.

Our father suggested that Chahchah and I take a short trip to Kyushu or Kyoto to see some impressive parts of Japan. We went to Kyoto on one very cold winter day on the by then famous 'bullet train' in the first-class 'Green Car'. We also went to have a look at Fukidecho, and Ryozo greeted us nostalgically. That was the last time that I saw the main house at Fukidecho, where I was born and had spent so much of my childhood. Our aunts and uncle were delighted to see us and Yuhei insisted that we came to stay with them for a night. At first, I hesitated and said that I was not sure if I could take a Japanese bath – I was used to washing in the bathtub! Yuhei was very proud of the new beautiful *hinoki* (cedar wood) bath and didn't want soap in it; but good-natured as he was, he said "OK, you can soap in the bath and so you *will* come and stay?"

The three weeks that I spent at home were a wonderful holiday for me, as I had been mentally stressed for a few years; I remember my father commenting on the sophisticated colour of my velvet trousers; Mother took us shopping and Mrs Tanaka, who had been so kind to us after my parents left London, was thrilled to see us and took us out to dinner at Mon Cher Ton Ton in Roppongi – that was the first time ever that I had *teppanyaki* which was introduced into Japanese cuisine (probably from Hawaii) while we were away. Her daughter, Teru, who had become a close friend of mine when we spent many weeks together during the long vacs from Cambridge, was working as a nanny for British Ambassador Sir Fred Warner and his wife Simone. She, too, having been away in her late teens could not go to university back in Japan and was worried about getting married. It was a happy trip and I was sad to leave – the first of many such farewells, coming with a pang every time.

Back in England, I wrote to my parents about my impressions of Japan after an absence of eleven years. I wrote that Tokyo seemed shambolic both physically, with huge amounts of building work, and mentally, people confused as to their values. Britain was stable by comparison; there was a better framework for living, even though the pace of change might be slower.

Japan was at the beginning of the high growth era – a meteoric rise that was to be the envy of the world, in stark contrast to the 'British disease' that beleaguered the country through the 1970s. It seemed that in Japan everything was happening at once and new ideas were taking over at speed. I expressed scepticism about where Japan would end up.

Debut in the Private Sector
It was not the happiest time for our parents. Masaru, being past the Ministry's prescribed retirement age and having to find a new job, was visibly distressed, having lost a lot of weight and looking drawn. His inner mental struggle was all too visible, and Yoko found it hard, coping with his complaints and distressing temper. He had never been an easy person at home, with his domineering personality, but in his depression he grew even more difficult. Yoko also joined the discussions on the settlement of her father's estate. Masaru, being meticulous in financial matters as a MoF official, told her she was to inherit only government bonds and not any shares. She wrote to me about all these 'goings-on' as if I were a friend, a confidante. She did exactly as her husband told her. And she was not prepared to get involved in wrangling over money; she believed that Yuhei would be fair. Her inheritance, though, gave her financial security for the rest of her life and she never forgot her gratitude to her parents, often bowing deeply in front of their photographs.

Masaru eventually accepted the position of Senior Advisor at Burnham & Co. (later Drexel Burnham Lambert) which was opening a representative office in Tokyo. Just as many people feel on retirement that their life has been a failure, he too felt it a 'come-down' in no longer being a government official; in his case, for the first time in his life he was working in the private sector and in the investment banking and broking industry, which previously he had looked down upon. He considered banking would be more respectable. In the old days, senior Ministry of Finance officials on retirement were 'placed' to head up quasi-public institutions. That was the quintessentially Japanese tradition of 'Amakudari' – *descent from heaven*. Some went on to become governor of the central bank or the national tax agency; others to head government-owned banks such as the Export-Import Bank of Japan or the Japan Development Bank. My father told me, in his hospital bed before he died, of the jealousies and rivalries that intervened at the end of his career; he never forgot nor forgave. His principal rival, at the time in a position to influence those placements, happened to be a distant relation of my mother's and claimed that Masaru did not need the Ministry's assistance since his wife was wealthy. When at his funeral, the long queue of worshippers coming to pay their respects stretched for miles, Mother said to me "It serves them [his rivals] right…"

On his return to Japan in the early spring of 1971, Andries Woudhuysen, a senior partner of Burnham & Co., had written to the Ministry of Finance asking how he could contact Masaru Fukuda. Woudhuysen had met and known him since the early 1960s and had been much impressed. His letter to my father was followed with more from Maurits Edersheim, a general partner, and from the Chairman, I. W. Burnham II himself. It was thus on the initiative of Burnham that my father was persuaded to become its Senior Advisor in Tokyo. For some years he angled for an advisory position with a British merchant bank, which he considered to be more distinguished. But that was not to be.

Masaru worked immensely hard with his usual commitment, including close negotiations to get all clearances from the Ministry to have the representative office established in Tokyo for Burnham, and even helping with opening bank accounts and finding the office space in Marunouchi. He introduced them to senior personalities, the presidents of the major broking houses such as Nomura Securities, so that Burnham could be accepted and included in the capital market there, and it was able to participate in some major issues as underwriters.

Numerous letters over the ten-year period Masaru stayed with Burnham, from Edersheim and Woudhuysen, express their supreme appreciation for his contribution as well as confiding in him on confidential matters of company strategy; they persuaded him to stay for far longer than he intended. His numerous attempts to resign were in vain, as he was in fact persuaded to stay until his health seriously declined. They always wrote to him respectfully as "Dear Mr Fukuda", and never understood that he meant what he said when characterising commercial profits from trading activities as 'ill-gotten gains'. He lunched daily with influential senior personalities, normally at the Tokyo Club. It became a legend that he almost always had smoked salmon and an omelette. The first thing that he complained of in his letters to me was that he no longer had the use of a personal secretary and he had to go to the post office, which he had not done for a long time. It was hard for him to take these small reminders of his change in personal status. The Chief Representative in Tokyo whom he worked with first was Alexander Neuwirth, followed by Itoh Takeshi, known to us as Peter, the son of the Chairman of C. Itoh & Co. Coincidentally, I had known him well at Cambridge where he was studying after graduating from a Japanese university, and Chahchah later found that his sister Keiko worked at the United Nations when she herself took a job there. My father liked and respected him very much and the whole family became close friends. To give an idea of how socially restrictive Japan still was in the 1970s, Peter, despite being the scion of a family that owned one of the major Japanese companies, could not be issued with a credit card from a Japanese bank because his employer Burnham was not known in Japan. My father spoke to the President of the Fuji Bank to get him one. I was shocked to hear from my aunt Asako that she similarly had difficulties getting a credit card because she was not married; single women, however rich, were regarded as second-class citizens.

Macmillan to Wilson

On Masaru's return to Tokyo the editor of the journal of the Ministry of Finance asked if he would contribute an article, reflecting on his overseas posting. In the *Finance* magazine of March 1972 was published the first of a three-part series of recollections entitled '*Macmillan to Wilson*'. Parts two and three followed. They represent a memoir of his time in London, and I have referred to some sections in Chapters 8 and 9. My father considered these recollections some of his best writing. Shortly before his death, knowing that he had a short time left, having suffered two major heart attacks, he had these three articles copied and bound into a volume and sent it to his close friends. In his handwritten covering letter he said that he was going to translate it into English but as he was approaching the end of his life it was urgent, and asked that they receive it as his final farewell gift in gratitude for their long friendship. The last time that I saw him in hospital he said he wanted me to translate it into English after his death. This has always been on my mind and I regret that I have not been able to keep my promise so far. Any translation of this *magnum opus* would seem banal; it would take a literary genius to capture the poetry of it, yet it requires close technical knowledge of finance, plus a detailed knowledge of the history of British politics.

   There are many messages of tributes to colleagues, particularising the lasting contributions they made and their moments of triumph. He is gracious towards his adversaries but totally open about conflicts of opinion or even suspected hostile acts within the Ministry against him. Above all it displays his negotiating skill, behind which lay his grasp of the essentials from deep analysis, curiosity about motivation and ability to see the other side of the coin. His gift for presenting the Japanese government's position with clarity and precision was often commented on and appreciated by his counterparts in America and Europe; it paved the way to breaking many an impasse.

Those whom Masaru met were able to gain confidence in him, I am sure, as he was a good and witty conversationalist, displaying deep knowledge of history. He read very widely: political memoirs and biographies interested him the most, as he was always seeking to learn how things happened. He read very slowly, digesting every page with care – not like myself skipping over pages, rapidly looking for what interested me (that was partly out of necessity, having to read some ten books a week to write an essay at Cambridge). I belatedly in my third year learnt from a great historian, John Vincent, that reading one important book or article carefully and thoroughly, ignoring other voluminous tomes, was better. I forget what I read soon afterwards, but my father retained everything.

He gives a detailed historical analysis of the background to the sterling devaluation of 1967, with behind-the-scenes insights, and the economic policies followed by the Wilson government after it came into power in October 1964. His acquaintance with its advisers, Professors Thomas Balogh and Nicholas Kaldor, the discussions he held with his friends in Whitehall, Sir Douglas Allen heading the Treasury and Sir Derek Mitchell, Principal Private Secretary to Prime Ministers Douglas-Home and Wilson, and the frequent meetings with senior personalities in the City and the Bank of England are incisively described. His detailed knowledge of the British political system and its history come into focus in discussing the transition of power from the Conservatives to the Labour Party during this period. He devotes paragraphs to the personalities and the political fortunes (or misfortunes) of Macmillan, Home, Butler and Wilson. It is remarkable in its confident style.

One or two reminiscences that come into this series of articles are worth recounting. First was the conversation Masaru had with Ralph Vickers, the Senior Partner of Vickers, da Costa, stockbrokers. In 1965 the Japanese stock market went into a deep and prolonged bear phase, following a crisis in the country's largest firm of stockbrokers, Yamaichi Securities. This was when my father encountered Ralph at a reception and said how sorry he was that the equity market in Tokyo was falling, knowing that Vickers was the only active broker in the City in Japanese securities. Ralph replied "We have been making a lot of money in the last few years; just because the market is going down now, we cannot complain." Masaru thought this a truly entrepreneurial response. Vickers, da Costa was the only British firm active in Japanese shares during the 1960s and together with the Foreign & Colonial Investment Trust, which was the first British institution to invest in the Japanese market after the war, was the pioneer in Japanese investments. In 1972, some months after he wrote these articles, I coincidentally went to work at Vickers, da Costa on a part-time basis while I wrote my first book. I was somewhat apprehensive telling my father about it, as I knew of his fundamental dislike of equities and his contempt for stockbrokers who made money out of 'trading' and 'dealing', which he regarded as downmarket activities. However, he did not say anything about it, other than that he was glad I had got a job. And in fact he never mentioned that he knew Ralph Vickers. Ralph continued to send Christmas cards, and wrote to him to say how sorry he was that I was leaving the firm when I departed two years later, yet claiming he thought I would be better suited to a more academic type of work – sour grapes! He would have regretted saying that had he but known how successful I then became at the largest London stockbrokers (though admittedly I did also have two slightly academic books on policy issues published at that time).

Another happy reminiscence was in 1965 during the Wilson administration. Masaru describes the drama of de Gaulle's thrusting diplomacy, first against the United States over the exchange rate system and opposing the capital increase of the IMF; secondly leaving NATO; and thirdly within the EEC over its Common Agricultural Policy. The United States did not lose time in taking the opportunity of seeing a divided Europe to announce that henceforth discussions on the future of the payments system would not be confined to the G10 but would be held in a wider forum, such as the IMF, rejecting the French insistence on using the BIS. Immediately on announcing this, the Secretary of the Treasury, Henry Fowler, toured European capitals. After visiting the continent, he came to London; it seemed that he had been sussing out views in Europe about the weakness of the pound sterling and Wilson's Prices and Incomes policy before he arrived. It was then, as mentioned, that much to Masaru's surprise, despite what must have been a very full schedule, Fowler telephoned him at the Embassy from his suite at Claridge's to hear his views and possibly meet at short notice.

Masaru starts these series of articles with an assertion that the present is already the past, and that what happened in the past guides the present and the future. He writes that these articles are the result of deep study. True to form, the epilogue at the end of these articles was romantic: quoting from Reginald Bevins' *The Greasy Pole*, when he wrote of the ephemeral nature of political success and achievement. Sophisticated and great statesmen though they had been, the big names of twentieth-century British politics – Lloyd George, MacDonald, Baldwin, Chamberlain, Eden – were by then forgotten in the minds of the British people. Yet Aneurin Bevan, who never became Prime Minister, was one of the few that remained in the people's hearts. Masaru admired him very much as a true conviction politician and a father of the welfare state. It is characteristic that he was drawn to Bevan; he often teased my mother, saying he would stand as a Socialist whenever he flirted with the idea of going into politics.

New House, New Job, New Routine
The next time I went back to Tokyo, eighteen months later, our old home was no more. The new house was built in a simple style, partly in prefabricated material. Nothing grand, but with

the high ceilings my father wanted, carpeted throughout, with lots of built-in cupboards and easy to maintain. They planned the layout as they wanted. Mother insisted on having at least one tatami room, where she could manage her kimonos. The new house was sited where the large garden had been, and the garden was now laid out in front; there was a new wall and new gates, and a covered car port; but the old ornamental stones, the tall stone lantern and the trees were still there. Yoko planted the flowering dogwood that came from Fukidecho by the car port and hung the lantern from the house she grew up in in the porch. The large antique Chinese basin from the gardens of Fukidecho was placed under the window next to the front porch. The drawing room furniture was mostly what they brought back from the Philippines, but Yoko's lacquered dressing table and other small pieces of furniture that she brought in her trousseau, old chests of drawers and some of the Edwardian inlaid mahogany furniture and the glazed bookcase in maple from the old house were upstairs in the large and sunny bedrooms. Mother brought the large oak dining table and set of chairs from our grandparents' house.

It was nostalgic to see the familiar furniture and paintings that I grew up with. The painting of the Ponte Vecchio in Florence by a well-known early-twentieth-century Japanese painter, Kobayashi Mango, that was the centrepiece in our old beautiful drawing room was given a new place in the new large drawing room. Nothing brings back memories of my childhood home better than this painting. I have it now in my own home, Creems.

Though I did spend a lot of time there on my visits, chatting with my parents and having meals, this new house was never my home. I stayed there on very few occasions and never lived there. The first time that I went on a business trip to Tokyo was in 1974, the year of the big bear market, and I had to go on a long and circuitous cheap package tour flight across south-east Asia. I of course stayed with my parents. But it was quite clear that my mother found it more than tiring, as Japanese brokers kept telephoning me and she had to take endless messages while I worked during the day visiting companies and going to meetings. Moreover, she had to do all my laundry. It also irritated my father that I was being picked up in a car by Japanese brokers to go to meetings every morning. So, from then on I always stayed in a hotel at my mother's request. Hotel Okura was only fifteen minutes away by taxi, so I could easily go to see them in the evenings. And my mother liked coming to see me at weekends as the Okura was just next door to her old home, Fukidecho, and she liked the elegant and sedate atmosphere there; we often went shopping together or went out to lunch in Ginza, before she rushed home in the late afternoon to cook dinner for my father. Sometimes Aunt Setsuko joined us for lunch, and I often went to visit Uncle Yuhei at his home, just a stone's throw away, for breakfast or dinner. I also had dinner with Asako in Tokyo at least once on every visit, and at weekends went to visit her beautiful home at Akiya, sometimes taking my British friends who were travelling with me.

Back in Japan, Yoko reignited her interest in painting. She joined the *sumie* (Japanese brush and ink paintings) group where some of her friends painted. At class reunions she reconnected with friends from school whom she hadn't seen for more than ten years. She did a lot of gardening. My parents also bought a small flat in Hayama in a newly-built mansion block, an hour's drive from Tokyo, so that they could holiday by the sea. They liked going there for weekends and for a drive along Sagami Bay, buying lobster and their favourite tilefish (a kind of sea bream) from her favourite fisherman in Akiya. Yoko went there often on her own in her widowhood and invited some of her similarly widowed friends from Tokyo for the day. She was able to reconnect with her life before she went abroad, even though sadly she could not go to Akiya any longer, as she used to so often, since the houses there were now in Yuhei's possession.

Masaru eventually recovered from his melancholia and settled into his own routine. He went to his office in Marunouchi and continued his association with former colleagues in the Ministry, as well as senior management in banking and securities. He lunched most days at the Tokyo Club in Kasumigaseki, his old haunt where he would encounter his old friends, played golf at the Tokyo Golf Club, went for walks at weekends in the neighbourhood, subscribed to the *Wall Street Journal*, ordered recently published political biographies – Roy Jenkins, Macmillan *et al* – from London, mowed the lawn, watched television and listened to classical music in the evenings. With the advent of computers, I found him studying mathematical theories of semiconductors. In the summer, my parents and Eiko went to our house in Karuizawa. A few years later, Eiko went to university in America: my parents were then on their own. Father's files show his extensive reading, the detailed notes he kept of any changes to legislation concerning finance, press cuttings on developments in the international monetary system about which he corresponded with his peers, many exchanges of letters with Robert Scalapino at Berkeley, and letters from his friends in the Navy with their news. Prime Ministers Tanaka, Ohira and Fukuda always sent him New Year greetings. He was actively engaged in various new issues with regulators at the highest level for Drexel Burnham. He had regained his equilibrium.

During the 1970s the world was opening up apace and it became possible for us to telephone each other in emergencies. International calls were still expensive and we used them only very occasionally, continuing to rely on weekly letters. But international travel became somewhat more common with greater availability of cheaper flights, and increased frequency. Our family was able to meet more often than over the previous decade, and our parents could look forward to each of us visiting about once a year. Yoko went to see Eiko at Harvard and Chahchah in Washington. Masaru, never having had to cater for himself, had to learn how to boil the kettle and make coffee. We always had Maxwell House ground coffee made in a percolator and he was virtually addicted to it. Yoko wrote to him almost daily while she was away; in one letter she talks of going to a concert in Boston with Eiko and how hearing a Mozart concerto she thought of him as it was a piece he so often listened to in the evenings.

Eiko came to London for visits every year or two and I looked forward to having her to stay. She spent hours on the telephone talking to her friends. When she was at Creems I was astonished to find that she befriended the old farmer down the road and borrowed his horse to go riding around the country lanes. The rather 'rough' farmer seemed to have taken to her and kept asking after her for years afterwards, saying she would be welcome to ride his horse anytime. Sometimes she came with her friend from Harvard, Jenny Oleansis, whom I liked a great deal. They went on a tour of Europe together with their backpacks.

When she came down from Harvard and went back to Japan, Eiko decided to get a flat of her own. I remember that my father, seeing a pretty enamelled red saucepan in the Georg Jensen shop near his office, got it for her to start her life in her own apartment. I thought at the time how characteristic it was of him to buy such an expensive utensil and how it showed his tender feelings and affection.

At the end of 1973 my first book was published on the impact that Britain's membership of the EEC would have on less-developed countries. It was about policy implications, not an economic statistical analysis. I had worked immensely hard on this book and consider it the greatest achievement of my career. My father was most proud of this. He considered that it was worthy of praise just for having such an internationally renowned publisher as Macmillan. I don't know if he ever read it; he never commented on the content. This was followed by another book in 1974, on Japan and its policies in world trade, with an American academic publisher. My father approved of my pursuing an intellectual career, which he considered respectable, while I worked in stockbroking to earn a living. Although he never much talked about it, he understood how intensely competitive an industry stockbroking was and said that the intensity with which we had to work was of a quite different order of magnitude to working in international organisations or in other industries. He warned me that men in my firm might harbour hidden hostile feelings towards me. I was totally unconscious of such attitudes and, in many ways, those were the happiest years of my working life, but in retrospect he was probably partly right.

He was shocked to hear me say one evening at home that "Money CAN buy happiness!" "Oh, really? Do you think so?" he said and chuckled. Though it is an old universal debating point, families like ours firmly believed otherwise. In our society it was still vulgar to talk about money, let alone ask for it. I, for one, could never request a rise at work; a far cry from the remuneration-driven culture that the City has fallen into in the last thirty years. My father despised those who were motivated by money and, indeed, he was ready to point out to his colleagues at Burnham all too frequently that stockbroking and investment banking were parasitical activities, employing his oft-used term 'ill-gotten gains'. He had respect for the value of money and was ultra-careful with it, whilst never being miserly. He always advised that we should never lend money to friends. He concluded for himself from our conversation that commercial life could change one's perceptions, but from my perspective I was thinking of the things that one could do with money that one couldn't do without it. I have never been motivated by money for its own sake, and have been all too ready to spend what I had in order to enjoy life.

With my work on the Japanese market, I was able to fly over twice each year from the second half of the 1970s and see my parents. Sometimes I would tell my father which companies I was visiting; he was very disapproving of the consumer finance companies. He considered them high risk and not respectable. His caution was borne out less than a decade later, with major bankruptcies. In those days 'respectability' counted for a lot in the Japanese 'Establishment'. My mother said to me that while he was pleased with my successes he was also irritated, with a hint of jealousy. So, I must not brag about it all!

Japanese Male Chauvinism

On one of my visits my father said "You know nothing about what Japanese men are about." I cannot remember what prompted him to make this remark. It was intended to be some kind of a warning. He probably meant to say that I should not be taken in by their flattery; Japanese men might give the impression of being outwardly deferential, but the inner reality might be much harder, with a hidden resentment stemming from male ego. Japanese men were and probably still are far more misogynistic than Western men. Male ego would not allow women to walk through the door before them; I would forever be bumping into men barging through as I instinctively went first. When I was telling this to my cousin Yumiko, a professor at a leading university, she told me that she always had to wait until all men, including her juniors, had gone through the door before she did, so she could never be in a hurry! When I visited Japanese companies some of the executives found it embarrassing that a woman was coming as a guest, looking puzzled and insisting on addressing the young Japanese broker who accompanied me. The broker would afterwards bow several times to apologise to me on behalf of the man whom we had just met. At a steel company the Managing Director hesitated: "I am not sure if I can be talking to a lady about a blast furnace…" To this day, I have no idea 'what Japanese men are about': are they any different really from English men? But then I probably don't know what English men are about either…! Outwardly at least, modern Japanese men behave more like their Western male counterparts, muttering "Ladies first, isn't it?" with a smile.

Certainly my father was chauvinistic, believing entirely in the superiority of men over women. Though he was always respectful and courteous to women generally, there was no question but that men had to be served first; women existed for the service of men, but men had to protect women because they were stronger. Women were objects of desire, but women with superior intellect were something of a different species; those he would allow to have views, but to express them only after the men. A Japanese woman friend of mine, who had achieved the rare distinction of becoming a Professor of Engineering – generally considered a very masculine subject – at a major university, said that if a woman proved she could do something that a male counterpart could not he would treat her as an equal. When a *Times* journalist visited Japan and wrote an article about me on her return, she wrote that "When Haruko Fukuda goes to Japan she is treated as an honorary man." This prompted Geoffrey Wheatcroft to write in the *Sunday Telegraph* colour supplement that I must be lacking a chromosome!

'Women's Lib' and throwing away brassieres was not strong in Japan in the 1970s, as it was in the West, but in the twenty-first century sexual discrimination in jobs has become taboo even in Japan. I remember Ambassador Chiba Kazuo saying to me, though, that he could not possibly fully understand the British psyche since he had never had a love affair with an English woman. It was an amazing thought, let alone admission, by a very senior diplomat. Yet it was characteristically an original remark of his; Kazuo was one of the greatest Japanese ambassadors of the postwar era, known to be combative, and I feel privileged that he became a close friend. In that spirit of mutual support between friends he also said to me "You are a woman, so you can carry on making strident remarks in your articles in public with your properly held views on Europe; men cannot do that. Please carry on doing it." That was at the time I was asked to write some articles about what the effects might be of Britain joining the euro on Japan's direct investments into Britain. Some Japanese and also, disgracefully, British companies' top management complained to my boss at Nikko Securities that my political views were unhelpful to them. Kazuo did mean it, but of course one can interpret that as unconsciously exhibiting the most condescending male attitude about women. (On every visit to London after retirement he called on me and we dined together. When the Heisei Emperor made his state visit to Britain, the Japanese government, knowing that there would be protests from wartime victims, sent him as the official spokesman in the emperor's suite. He was brought back from retirement to field the Press in London.)

On reading letters from my files as I wrote this book, I have been more than touched to find true friends – older Japanese men, even in the stockbroking world, who died years ago. And I can count several more today who I trust will always be real friends. So Japanese men are not that different from those of other nationalities after all!

The Deaths of Naoko and Kusatao

One sad occurrence was the sudden death of Aunt Naoko. In 1977, while I was visiting Tokyo on business, she suddenly collapsed during a haiku retreat. Her husband Kusatao, the haiku poet, would take his group on an annual retreat, normally into the hills, and that year they were staying at the Koyasan temple. She had said before departure that she wondered if she could go, as she was not feeling well. Her married life had been one of total support to an unworldly husband, with a classic artistic temperament. She arranged all her husband's affairs, and his pupils and colleagues in the circle also relied on her loyal support, so she felt compelled to go. On the second day there she felt unwell and went upstairs to her room to rest. There she collapsed with a stroke, never to regain consciousness. She was taken to the nearby hospital in an ambulance and her daughters rushed to her bedside. She remained unconscious for several days; the doctors considered taking her to a major hospital in Tokyo for an operation but it was too risky to move her. Kusatao went back to Tokyo and the daughters took it in turns to look after him. They asked their uncle Masaru if they should tell their father of his wife's true condition: he said without hesitation that of course they must. Contrary to the daughters' concern for his frail emotions, Masaru said that Kusatao was her husband and men understand death as they get older. Shock and sorrow enveloped the family and the members of the diaspora of the haiku world; they published a volume of tributes and haiku written for her on her death. She was only sixty-four years old.

The funeral was held at the Catholic church in Kichijoji, which Naoko had helped to build and where she was a leading figure. The large church was packed with mourners. My father came in full morning dress and Mother in her black funeral kimono. Surrounded by innumerable floral tributes, the open coffin received a carnation placed beside Naoko from every mourner to say a last farewell. She looked beautiful as she always had done. Kusatao, thought by his daughters to be a man detached from the real world, could not contain his sorrow. After the service, while we waited for her ashes at the crematorium (in Japan burials are not allowed even for Catholics: every dead body must be cremated) my father gave a spontaneous talk to the relations who remained. I shall never forget the fluency and directness with which he spoke. He said although she was his elder sister, she was a *nakama* (comrade) to him, recalling childhood memories. All his first cousins were there and reminisced with him. He talked of her life dedicated to her husband and his haiku, giving up her piano, and to her strong Catholic faith. When it was all over, he said to my mother and me "Let's go to my parents' grave and report to them that Naoko has died." So we went on to the

Fukuda family grave and said our private prayers. Naoko's ashes were eventually interred in a Catholic cemetery.

Kusatao lived for another six years, into his mid-eighties. Moments before his death, his daughters arranged for him to be baptised and receive the last rites. His death was announced on the national television news. Befitting a great poet, he was embalmed, and a death mask made. Cousin Yumiko, a professor in French Literature at Ochanomizu University, set about putting his complete works together into several volumes and had them published.

Weddings in London
Although Masaru started to have mild angina attacks and suffer from high blood pressure by the end of the 1970s, family life continued as normal – except that Masaru and Yoko's two elder daughters had married abroad and left Japan forever.

For years I agonised about marrying a foreigner and wrote to my parents about my anguish. Emotionally confused, I longed to find peace with myself. Cross-border mixed marriages were not common in those days and there were challenges that one had to be prepared to face. My friends were tremendously long-suffering, listening to my indecision, and giving me moral support. I much enjoyed seeing my sisters when they came to visit during this period and longed to see them for many heart-to-hearts into the late evenings.

Those anxieties were partly the cause of the break-up of my first engagement; then in 1973 I decided to marry Jimmy Dunnett, an architect. My mother was sad at the prospect of my living abroad for good and long explanatory letters followed. I went back to see my family in the summer before the September wedding. We went to Karuizawa together too and that was the last time that I saw our summer holiday home. Aunt Naoko and all our Nakamura cousins were there and Naoko gave me a great send-off, saying "marriage is the most important thing in a woman's life." My mother came to the wedding and was able to meet Jimmy and his family. His parents were about to leave for Dakar in Senegal, where his father had been appointed Ambassador, in early October and the wedding was organised before their departure. Yoko invited them to dinner at Prunier in St James's Street, and Jimmy's aunt, Aunt Mike (Denzil Dunnett's elder sister) invited us to her home just outside Crowborough with outstanding views of the South Downs. She took me shopping and bought me some special new dresses from Christian Dior Couture in Bruton Street, dressy suits from Norman Hartnell, and new handbags.

I had to find a flat for us to live in; that was very hard with our meagre resources, and the one I found in a mews in South Kensington was in such a tatty state that Mother burst into tears when she saw it. Jimmy's family background was somewhat similar to mine in that his father was a diplomat and both his uncles were Whitehall knights. His grandfather had been a senior member of the Indian Civil Service and Reform Commissioner in Delhi prior to India's independence. His mother was a painter, and her family all lived in Lancashire; Jimmy and I visited them often. She was a person of immense artistic taste and I liked her enormously. When we got engaged she wrote a wonderfully affectionate letter to my parents, as she also did to Masha Williams. It was through the Williamses that I met Jimmy in the first place; the Dunnetts had served in Madrid while Sir Alan was Ambassador there. Ruth Dunnett had suffered a major heart attack in their previous posting in Mexico City and was frail but an ambassadorial post at sea level in Dakar was specially found to provide for her health. Sadly, she died only a few months after they arrived and Denzil had to complete his service there with his daughter Ursula. Having been in the diplomatic service, they had no problem with their son marrying a foreigner; indeed, as Jimmy said at the time, they would almost have expected that. The Dunnetts were Edinburgh

Scots and they liked to go during their leave to various parts of
Scotland for fishing and painting holidays.

We got married in St Columba's Church in Pont Street, with
the reception at the Williamses' house in Hampstead. Jimmy
and I shared an interest in art, and we would go to exhibitions
and galleries most weekends and regularly had friends to lunches
and dinners at our flat. He bought a single lily stem every week
for the flat; I later bought a beautiful painting of one lily in a
vase by Patrick Procktor. We hung on our walls many watercolours and pastels by his mother, mostly of Spain, France and
Argentina, and an oil painting by Leslie Hunter in the dining
room which was his parents' wedding present to us. Denzil's
father collected the Scottish colourists after his retirement to
Edinburgh and they had a number of very good paintings of
that genre. Jimmy played music every day in the flat – the piano
and the oboe – made sculpture at St Martin's School of Art,
went to life drawing classes, and of course painted in watercolour all the time. He worked with the well-known architect Ernö
Goldfinger. Ernö and his wife, Ursula, became close friends and
we often visited them at their beautiful modern house which
he had designed. Ursula was a painter and they had been part
of the circle of Beaux Arts in Paris during the 1930s. They had
a wonderful collection of modern art, much of which was given
to them by the artists – Henry Moore, Amédée Ozenfant,
Max Ernst, William Hayter, Bridget Riley, to name a few. The
house and the collection were given to the National Trust on
their death. After Jimmy and I separated, Ernö would ring me
often, saying "Bad girl, why haven't you come to see me? Come
now, right now!" On one such occasion I found on arrival André
Kertész, the great photographer, sipping Ernö's dry martini in
the drawing room. Kertész gave me a signed catalogue of the
exhibition he had just opened the previous day. I went to work
each day in the City; Dugald gave me a lift and often had breakfast with us. There was a lot of merriment as to how porridge

had to be eaten standing up according to the Scottish protocol and certainly with cold cream in a separate bowl.

The following year Chahchah and Francis got married. A few months before the wedding my father visited me in London. It was the one and only time after he retired from the Ministry that he went abroad. Due to his precarious health it took a determined effort on his part to undertake this journey. He disagreed with Jimmy about architecture and touched a raw nerve; my father said not to worry because he and his father-in-law didn't agree on most things, but they could keep a cordial relationship. He thought that architecture should not have political dimensions while Jimmy had idealistic convictions about social housing and the beliefs of Le Corbusier *et al*; of course, the architectural scene in Britain at the time was all about social housing. My father, though, sent Jimmy articles on Tange Kenzo which he translated for him and other architectural publications over the years. He was interested in going to see Summer Fields prep school in Oxford whence many British Prime Ministers had sprung and where Jimmy had also been. He tried to get in touch with his old friends from Whitehall and the City, but it being Whitsun weekend most of them were away and, to his disappointment, not available to meet. He was appalled to see our flat and started looking for another one for us to live in. No amount of protesting would stop him; he was searching for estate agents and looking at advertisements in the newspapers. He was not going to allow my romantic idea of a slightly bohemian and 'arty' life in a mews to enter into his considerations; as it turned out he knew me better than I did myself. He invited Francis's parents to dinner, but they too said they were in the country for the weekend and could only come briefly for a drink at my flat. He was perplexed by their refusal to dine with him and told me to ask again as he was not likely to come again. Francis was in America and couldn't meet him either. It was not altogether a totally successful trip for him, but he said he was satisfied that he came to see me.

Francis, having gained his doctorate, started working as a lecturer at Imperial College, London. Chahchah was in Washington at the World Bank; they had decided to get married but live separately, meeting only every few months. Eventually Chahchah decided to take a year off to do (yet another!) postgraduate degree – in agricultural development economics at Sussex University – and they were at least in the same country. It was very nice for me to have Chahchah and Francis living in England for a couple of years as we could meet often. Their home was a basement flat on the Cromwell Road, not far from our mews. When Denzil came back from Africa, Jimmy's sister Ursula bought this flat.

After returning to America, Chahchah decided to get a job in New York; Francis decided that he had to get a job in the United States so that, as he said jokingly, they could "live in the manner to which Sakiko was accustomed". He eventually found work with IBM at their research centre in Yorktown Heights, New York, while Chahchah eventually found a position at the UNDP. They both enjoyed very successful careers in their respective organisations, while bringing up their two sons in New York.

On retirement from the UN, my sister became a professor at the New School in New York, where she is still. Initially she commuted to Manhattan each day from her house in Croton-on-Hudson, adjacent to the Teatown Reservation. Whenever she or Francis planted any vegetables or flowers in the garden, wild deer would sneak in from the reservation and eat them. I went to visit sometimes, skating on the pond in winter and going for drives in the lovely New England forests in the autumn. When Chahchah broke her leg skiing, I went over to look after her for a couple of weeks. They eventually also bought a flat on the West Side of Manhattan.

Chahchah decided to get married in a Unitarian church in Rosslyn Hill, Hampstead, because of our old connection with Unitarianism from the Channing days. Francis, being a Catholic, found it a novel experience; certainly, his parents must have found it strange. Whatever the case, I had to organise the wedding reception. We decided to have the party after the wedding at the Dorchester in a lovely room with a roof terrace, overlooking Hyde Park. It was a lot of work liaising with the banqueting team and I financed it with the money that Father had sent me a couple of years previously for my own use. I wanted to make it an extra special occasion for them. Moyses Stevens graced the duck-egg blue room with floral arrangements on stands and bouquets on tables. The roses climbing on the pergolas on the terrace were in full bloom. Fortunately, the sun shone and it was a lovely day. Our mother came over and she was happy. Francis and Chahchah went to stay at a pub at Yattendon in Berkshire so that on the day after the wedding, we could all have a picnic with the newlyweds. It was a beautiful summer day and I remember wearing my mother's old dress from the prewar days of crepe de chine in brown with white polka dots and a black straw hat with colourful fruit around the crown. For the wedding Chahchah wore our mother's *furisode* kimono; it was the one in which, just before I married, I had photographs taken by Lenare, the society photographer. Francis wore his Eton tailcoat and stiff collar. I wore my *tomesode* kimono – a black wedding kimono with family crests and a colourful design towards the hem. It had been my mother's, passed on to me.

Fukuda Masaru, 1914–1984.

13. THE DEATH OF A SAMURAI

~

My father, Fukuda Masaru, lived his whole life, subconsciously, within the tenets of the samurai. Directly descended from long lineages of samurai on both sides of his family, he upheld the moral virtues of that life; those qualities were, as he said just before his death, what he admired most in his mother and his uncle Yamanashi. He remained true to his sense of obligation as a member of the governing class all his life. He was an internationalist, often described by his colleagues as a colossus of a man – not given to hubris, but a man of wide vision and one who appreciated the true meaning of forgiveness. Always loyal, direct and open, honest and sincere, his humanity expressed itself in a true consideration for others. He died of heart failure at home, aged seventy, on 12 January 1984.

He had started to feel mild angina symptoms from the late 1970s, and was being careful with his activities and attending regular medical check-ups. All seemed reasonably well for a while. Family news, with the birth of Chahchah's first child, Nicholas, was cheering and they were able to go home to see our parents. Eiko got a job as a journalist, and eventually came to work in London and then in Paris for Reuters. I was very happy to be able to see her often. In 1980 when I was elected a partner of James Capel, I had had to borrow some money from my mother to buy the partnership shares; my father wrote me a heartfelt letter that he would like to have been able to give me the money himself, but couldn't – yet he still sent me a contribution towards it. The following year I bought a house in the country to have more space for weekends and holidays with my own money and a mortgage. On my next visit, my father wanted to see photographs of it and the garden; he said they looked beautiful, with a satisfied nod. For the ten years after I got married my letters settled down to regular reports of daily activities, often mentioning encounters with Masaru's acquaintances in London, and commenting on current political developments in Britain and Japan – no more anxious-making correspondence. But Eiko told me later that our father had sensed from my letters that I was unhappy and told her so.

In April 1983, while he was at one of the regular check-ups at hospital, my father suffered his first heart attack. In some ways it was lucky that he was on the spot and able to be given immediate medical attention. He was put in the CCU (Computer Controlled Unit) at the Red Cross Hospital in Hiroo, Tokyo, not far from home. My mother phoned me to say that the heart attack was not major and the doctors felt confident he would recover. I had been in Tokyo the previous month and had not detected any health concerns, but in retrospect the area around his eyes was slightly swollen – I was told later that that was a tell-tale sign. But more alarmingly my mother said that a small moment of altercation that had passed between us during my visit had upset him greatly and that could have significantly worsened his heart condition. Being domineering at home, he was not given to being contradicted by his daughters; we always obeyed. I wrote to him immediately, pouring out sympathy about his plight, being stuck in hospital with an array of medical monitoring equipment around him, and also apologising profusely for any arrogance on my part. I hastened back to visit him.

As I arrived, one day in late April, and approached the CCU

room in which he lay, a nurse told me that absolute stillness was
required and that his heart was a broken china bowl to be cradled
with care. She said that they had told him I was coming to see
him that day: Masaru said he could not meet his eldest daughter
unshaven; the nurses had responded that shaving would not be
allowed, as it would make him tense, but he insisted. The nurse
said in that case they would give him a shave lying down. Then
he demanded that he must sit up: he could not have his daughter
visit him lying flat on the bed. So, the nurses tilted the bed ever
so slightly. When I went in, he was obviously greatly pleased
to see me. For a number of days Mother and I took turns to
visit, and she brought food that he could eat – jellied consommé
featured frequently, with grapes, omelettes and other things he
liked. Eventually he was able to walk, then go up and down the
stairs and his spirits lifted. Before leaving the hospital, he said he
wanted to stay in a VIP private room there for a couple of weeks
to recover rather than go straight home. This was arranged and
we were able to visit him freely there. Word got round that he
was ill and many letters, flowers and books arrived from his close
friends from the Ministry and the Bank of Japan as well as from
the finance industry.

As my father's condition began to improve, and having lost
his interest in watching television or reading the newspapers
which were previously his passion, he decided to write to his
friends. Writing letters put less stress on his heart than receiving
visitors. He wrote in English because writing in Japanese characters was harder after the heart attack, and his handwriting,
which used to look as if it were printed, became disarrayed. He
wrote at the hospital a short volume of his memories from his
visits to America in the 1950s. I now realise why he wrote this
in English: he wanted his daughters to be able to read it. He
said in the Preface "I decided to write my Memory to keep on
record, whatever worth it may have, for my children and some
of my friends." It is entitled 'A Private Report to Members of

Satsukikai'. Satsukikai (五月会) is the alumni association of the officer intake of his year in the Navy. He asked me to get the photocopies of his handwritten monograph bound for sending, and I went to Itoya in Ginza to organise it; he was much pleased with this outcome and with the swiftness with which I managed to get it done. It is significant he addressed this to his friends from the Navy; they were the ones who had shared an important and arduous experience with him in his youth, none of whom could betray his friendship or were in any way rivals.

The monograph contained memories of significant encounters Masaru had in America in the early 1950s, when he had been a young officer of the Ministry, and an essay on the Fifth Amendment of the US constitution. He said that those memories made him happy and rested. They indicate his strong commitment to American democracy and are his tribute to the American people who lived the spirit of democracy that was the foundation of their country since the days of the Founding Fathers. His incidental meeting on the economy-class-only flight from Chicago to Washington in 1951 with President Truman (then in office), and the kindnesses shown to him by strangers, are particularly recorded.

But more substantively Masaru writes of meetings with several leading personalities of the time in the United States. He was introduced in 1951 to the former Secretary of State (1949–1953) Dean Acheson, by the Japanese Ambassador to the United States, Iguchi Sadao (井口貞夫). Masaru recorded that "The impact he gave me by his towering attitude – but not arrogant – was unforgettable." He reminds the reader that, as was explained in Acheson's own book *Present at The Creation*, it was Acheson, not, as portrayed by the mass media, Yoshida Shigeru (吉田茂) who brought independence to Japan against the opposition and obstructive approach of the Soviet Union and other countries at San Francisco in 1951. Masaru, thinking that he could not waste Acheson's time on his visit, decided that he would ask him just two things: first, why was Congress dominated by lawyers; and second, what was the essence of 'right' judgement – how to make a decision?

With John D. Rockefeller, to whom he was introduced by his old Ministry boss, Ihara Takashi (伊原隆), he had a happy meeting, exchanging cordialities in the Rockefeller Center, which he was excited to visit. Of Dean Rusk, who was at the time (1951) Assistant Secretary of State for the Far East while Japan was still under Allied Occupation, he came away with a disappointing impression. Rusk asked him to put pressure on the Japanese tax authorities to give the privilege of tax-exempt status to the benefactors of the Rockefeller Foundation – he was on the Board there. Masaru changed the subject to US–Japanese relations, saying that information on Japan in the US was scarce, and public knowledge or understanding of Japan meagre. He made the point that, without a more broad-based understanding at a grassroots level, progress in bilateral relations might be difficult. Rusk disagreed, saying that professional contact between diplomats or specialists would be the right approach. Masaru remembered Professor Ralph Braibanti, on that same trip, telling him that America was a vast country and without changing the education system from kindergarten up it would take a long time for the Americans to become familiar with Asia.

Ambassador Iguchi also introduced him to the young Senator Mike Mansfield; Masaru got the impression that Mansfield was an intellectual and a scholar. He was critical of the US policy on nuclear tests in competition with the Soviet Union. Mansfield arranged for him to get a free access pass to the Senate Floor Gallery. As he became more prominent in the Senate, though, my father was unable to continue their exchanges.

In 1956 Masaru's uncle, Admiral Yamanashi, had written to Admiral Arleigh Burke, Chief of Naval Operations at the Pentagon. Admiral Burke took the initiative to write to Masaru at Duke enclosing some reference material on Leadership, which was one of his research projects, and told him to visit when in Washington, giving him his telephone number and the names of his aides. Masaru was more than surprised by this kind gesture, but at that time his financial resources (living on the Fulbright Fellowship stipend of $9 per day) were limited. He saved enough money – he says "somehow" – and went to Washington. He managed to find a long-stay hotel there through Robert Maxwell, a friend he made in 1951, who was Commissioner of the Bureau of Accounts in the US Treasury. Masaru telephoned the Pentagon from that hotel and got an appointment; on arriving he found that one of the two aides sitting outside the Admiral's office was friendly but the other expressed scepticism, given the Admiral's heavy schedule. Masaru asked the difficult aide to convey his appreciation for the Admiral's kindness and said that he did not have to see him as it was quite understandable his time was precious. But within ten minutes, he was asked to go in, and found the Admiral eating a sandwich with a glass of milk. Burke explained to Masaru that he knew Admiral Yamanashi extremely well and also Vice-Admiral Hoshina Zenshiro, who had been the Captain of the battleship HIJMS *Chōkai* that Masaru served on. He talked about leadership with my father. Admiral Burke is remembered to this day as a brilliant naval officer with a stellar career record, and the main class of US Navy destroyers carries his name.

As this monograph was addressed to his naval colleagues, Masaru wrote about the Japanese Navy and its organisation, its culture as he remembered it, about Vice-Admiral Hoshina, and paid tribute to the senior officers of the *Chōkai* and those who were his instructors there. In the final chapter of this monograph he recounts the history of the trial and execution of General Yamashita Tomoyuki (山下奉文), who was commander-in-chief of the Japanese Imperial Army in the Philippines at the end of the war. Yamashita asserted that the atrocities committed by the Japanese Army were conducted without his knowledge or orders and hence he was not in a position to prevent or stop them. When he appealed for judicial review by *habeas corpus* through his defence lawyers, provided by the US Army, this was disallowed by MacArthur and it eventually went to the US Supreme Court. Masaru quotes the impassioned speech of the dissenting judges in the minority – Justices W. B. Rutledge and Frank Murphy. They strongly argued the tenets of the Fifth Amendment of the US constitution. He writes that he is moved by them every time he reads them. He was of course speaking with the knowledge that so many Japanese had opposed the war from the beginning but had no choice but to join it.

He wrote that America was changing, so that the old spirit of legal justice seemed to be disappearing there, judging by the Abscam or Lockheed trials, dealing with major corruption scandals. He also laments the general deterioration of standards on Wall Street. He attributes some of the reasons for these to increased immigration and a dilution of a strong Protestant faith. When the Japanese were considering revising their constitution, they should try to understand what the ideals of freedom and democracy meant to the Founding Fathers of America; he felt that reality in Japan remained distant from the ideals of 'free world', 'democratic world', 'the West' – words proudly espoused by Japanese politicians. Those ideals are engraved in stone on the pediment of the Supreme Court building in Washington DC in four simple words: 'Equal Justice Under Law'.

In conclusion, my father wrote that we in the West must take the initiative to save human society from a nuclear catastrophe; a direct nuclear exchange between the US and the Soviet Union would result in neither side winning but in an end to human civilisation. The anti-nuclear movement should not be the monopoly of those on the left of the political spectrum.

He enjoyed receiving letters from his old Navy colleagues. He had said in a letter at the beginning of the monograph that he had had a heart attack and was recovering, but he could not now live up to what he had been taught at school in German: '*Der Wille zum Leben tut viel.*' He said that vital spirit for living was now missing from his mind.

He was told to go for walks each day and try not to eat too much cholesterol-forming food such as soups and eggs, which were his favourites. My mother wrote to me saying how much he was pleased with my visit; any hurt from my previous visit seemed to have evaporated.

On one of his daily walks around the neighbourhood in the late summer of 1983, however, Masaru had an unexpected fall – he had not fallen in a long time – and it shocked him. He injured his knee and could not continue with his perambulations. He himself later identified that fall as a fatal moment. In November he suffered a second major heart attack at night at home and had to be taken to hospital in an ambulance. It had already been planned that I would go to Japan in November on a business trip, taking a client with me to visit companies. I therefore went ahead of schedule and stayed for five weeks. During the day – and into the evening over dinners with clients and brokers – I worked; then I went to the hospital, often staying late into the night beside his bed. There were one or two crisis moments when we were called during the night and we rushed to the hospital as his condition became critical. He was in the CCU at the Red Cross Hospital again, by now a familiar place, the nurses and doctors well known to us.

On the very first day I was there, my father, lying flat on his bed as instructed, said to me "You must separate and get a formal divorce." I instantly said not to talk about it now. But he ordered me to write down what he dictated: he wanted to ask Lady Williams to intervene and to give me support, as he himself was stricken by a grave illness. He dictated the letter and told me to send it by telegram straight away. He told me that I must leave everything in the flat to Jimmy and not quarrel about possessions or money. It was all right for me to get divorced, as

I was an established career woman and had my own life to lead. Having done that and confirmed that I had sent the letter, he said he could now die in peace knowing that I would be all right.

This time, the doctors said that it was serious as the second artery had now been damaged. The next attack would be fatal. They suggested that he should undergo open heart surgery. My father refused. My mother and Eiko tried to persuade him to have the operation. He would not hear of it; he said to me when I was alone with him in his room at night, "You will be on my side; they want me to have this operation but I don't and only you, you alone, will be my ally." He then said "How strange it is, human beings become like this; I am not afraid of death."

One evening, he told me that he did not want a Christian funeral. He said that although he was brought up a Christian, he had thought about it a lot recently and decided that he no longer believed in it; he wanted a Buddhist funeral. To this end he had written to the temple in Nagasaki where his eldest sister is buried and asked them to conduct his funeral service in Tokyo. He then told me about our close relationship with the Shimazu family. He had never talked about his family background before to his children.

He kept up his humour and teased the poor naïve nurses who were not used to patients in his condition making jokes about their own illnesses. Some of them thought he must be losing his marbles and started reporting to the doctors who took them seriously! On one occasion, having been told that he should lose some weight (though he was by no means obese), he said to a nurse "I am going to become skin and bone." The young nurse couldn't understand the irony. I had to explain that it was his kind of joke. But he was very impressed by the dedication and skill of the nurses; he said to me "Those nurses are angels, like Florence Nightingale; women must always have a smile: don't forget, you must do that too." I have never forgotten this, and often hear him saying it to me.

By mid-December, Masaru was sent home; he had again wanted to have a couple of weeks to recover in a VIP room, but they were all occupied and he could not have his way. Yoko looked after him constantly at home; he was by then in a frail condition. She had a daily maid to help, as she could not have coped on her own. I had left when he was still in hospital, in a small private room, sitting in a chair as I said goodbye for the last time. I can still see him in my mind's eye. I suspect it was hard for him to see me leave as well: he said almost angrily "Hurry up and go" while I lingered to catch the doctor to have a word. I was in tears most of the twelve-hour flight back to London the next day, realising that I might never see him again; I wrote a long letter to him on the plane. I went to spend Christmas with Eiko in Paris where she was working for Reuters. Jenny Oleansis came too. Eiko lived in a nice flat in the Marais and we had a happy time, going to Christmas mass at Notre-Dame.

Once at home, realising that his days were numbered, Masaru decided to organise a memorial service for his own father, who had died only a few months after the war; it had not been possible to have a proper funeral service. He wrote a short monograph about his father and had it properly printed with a cover and sent to his Fukuda relations, including the Shimazu family with whom he had not been in touch for a long time, and Grandfather's other nieces. He wrote a covering letter in his own hand and included with it a loaf of Castella (a Nagasaki speciality, a rich sponge cake that Grandfather was fond of) from the well-known bakery in Nagasaki. The service with a Protestant minister from the nearby church was arranged to take place at the end of January on the date of Grandfather's death by our family grave where his remains are buried in the vault. Masaru died just two weeks before this service was to take place. We went ahead with it as planned, barely a week after his funeral when the urn containing his ashes had just been interred there. Singing by the graveside a hymn we always sang at home, most of us were in tears.

My father wrote to friends, saying that before he died he wanted to put together some of his more recent writings, the result of years of private study. He sent them copies of an article published in 1979, four years previously, on the US Presidential veto power in federal appropriation bills. As I have noted earlier in this book, the US constitution and the Federal budgetary system (about which he published long articles in the Ministry of Finance journal in 1957) were his particular research subjects. As his letters were received by friends, some of them immediately wrote back saying how prescient he had been, recognising the significance of his work, as President Reagan was just then facing a budget appropriation crisis.

A few days before he died at home, he told my mother what to do, who to contact to have his will effected and who she had to notify. He had everything prepared; nothing was left uncertain upon his death. My mother said that a few days before he died, he asked to see the family albums with photographs of our childhood, and dwelling on every page he wept, saying "They were adorable…"

Frantic telephone calls came at night several times from Yoko, saying he was very unwell but refusing to let her call the doctor. "Should I call the doctor or the ambulance – I should, don't you think?" "Yes, call the ambulance! Call the doctor! I will come on the next flight." I got up early, packing my suitcase with some black clothes just in case. I remember waiting for the train on the windswept platform at Colchester on a freezing cold morning, feeling worse than desolate. Soon after I arrived at my desk at the office, the telephone rang: it was Aunt Mariko. I knew at once. She said, without referring to death, that my father was now resting in the morgue at the hospital: "Very disappointing, wasn't it…"

God did not spare him the agony of death. My mother told

me later that to die is a difficult thing; the human body does not succumb peacefully. He suffered enormously at the end until he was taken to hospital and sedated.

Arriving at home the next evening, the house was full of relations; my cousin Kinuko rushed out to the gate to help me with my suitcase; Aunt Setsuko immediately hugged me in tears. The paulownia coffin had already been brought home and candles were lit. Chahchah arrived soon afterwards, and she and I sat with the coffin, as is customary, through the night in vigil. We had reflective conversations to help each other in our sorrow. The following days were busy with visitors calling to pay their respects, and we had to organise the funeral details. Yoko was very composed throughout. She took us to Ginza to buy formal black outfits to wear at the funeral, as she said our father would like us to look elegant and smart. She chose for me a lovely Ferragamo suit in black cashmere that I wore for many years afterwards. As is the Japanese custom, on the eve of the funeral came a ceremony when close family and friends paid their respects. I wore my mother's black funeral kimono for this occasion and sat in line with her and my sisters, as the mourners offered incense to the departed. The head priest from the Shuntokuji Temple in Nagasaki came to chant through the whole ceremonial evening. It was snowing outside all day and evening, as if to shower the earth with God's sorrow.

Yoko had a hard time organising the funeral, as we were unfamiliar with Buddhist traditions. She contacted a friend of hers who had become a Buddhist nun to find out what to do and choose the chants, while Yuhei helped her with how to entertain the priests. As the announcement had run in the newspapers, floral tributes started to arrive, a large number of telegrams were delivered throughout the day and the telephone never stopped ringing. The Ministry of Finance, on the instruction of its head, sent half a dozen officials to man the reception and act as ushers and many of the arrangements on the day were put in place by them. They recorded every mourner's name and address and what they had brought as offerings. The snow had cleared during the night and it was a cold brilliant sunny day. It is said in Japan that God weeps the day before, but when the sun shines the following day for the funeral the departed goes to heaven. The vast number of floral tributes, many of them on high stands, were placed around the altar and against the two long walls of our garden. Famous names – Prime Ministers, leading politicians, presidents of leading financial institutions and banks, governors of the Bank of Japan, ambassadors, senior officials of the Ministry of Finance, alumni associations of the Navy and the Ministry, relations and many many friends – graced those tributes. And they all came in person to the funeral in the freezing cold. The queue of mourners and their cars stretched for miles in every direction up the main road, causing congestion even on the Sakurada-dori. The three priests sat before the altar and chanted prayers in for several hours into the mid-afternoon. All of those Ministry of Finance officials who had served under my father abroad and their wives waited in the garden until the end, when the coffin left for the crematorium. One of them said to me "We are all here; no one is missing." Masaru could not have wished for a greater send-off. Yoko made a short speech in front of them, standing on the steps of the front porch of our house, thanking them for their attendance and saying that without waiting for the customary period to lapse, according to Buddhist teaching, we would be taking the ashes to be interred in the grave immediately afterwards because the children had to return to their homes abroad. We then left in a convoy of cars following the hearse, driven with the priests in one car and the family members in several others.

At the crematorium in Kirigaya, as the coffin disappeared into the furnace Yoko lost her composure for the first time, covering her face in tears. Her siblings and our Nakamura cousins were all there and came with us to the grave. She had asked the advice of the Protestant minister if his ashes could be put in the same vault as his parents, who were Christians. The minister advised that his name could be engraved on the side of the tombstone with his Buddhist name given at death (*kaimyō*). He was given the name *FukujuinShodoTaisenKojiRei* for his soul. The priest said to me "Please call out to him from time to time in that name."

The day after the funeral, a long-term colleague of my father's at the Ministry, Gyohten Toyoo, wrote an article in the *Nikkei* newspaper paying tribute – "Mr Fukuda was so frightening, yet so overwhelmingly kind." He recalled many instances of my father's working life that he had shared, especially in foreign countries, and that he was a giant amongst Ministry officials, a great patriot.

The days after the funeral were a busy time for us. I stayed with my mother for another fortnight. We had to send letters to all those who attended the funeral, eight hundred or more, some of which had to be handwritten. Many people also wrote to us from the provinces and from overseas and they had to be answered. Some people who had not been able to come on the day of the funeral came to visit.

One day a very special visitor arrived: Tsuchida Masatsugu (土田正嗣) of the Ministry of Finance. He was then Private Secretary to the Minister of Finance. He came to convey the official message of condolence from the Ministry. Moreover, most importantly, he came to present the citation and badge of the posthumous award of a promotion in the government decoration my father had held. He told us that my father's writings have been placed in the government official archive together with a tribute from the Ministry stating that he was a giant among officials, referred to in the Ministry as 'emperor'. He suggested that we might want to call on Mr Matsushita, the head of the Ministry. We did so at his office. Matsushita Yasuo, who became Governor of the Bank of Japan a few years later on retirement from the Ministry (a well-trodden route for its officials), had of course been at my father's funeral in person as well as Tsuchida himself. I had known Mr Tsuchida well in London, as he had been posted as First Secretary at the Embassy there a few years previously. He was a very impressive official and later went on to become the head of the Banking Bureau during the Japanese banking crisis of the mid-1990s, when I re-encountered him. I was in the lobby of the Pierre Hotel in New York when a lone figure approached and asked "Fukuda Haruko-san?" It was Mr Tsuchida. Despite his holding a high-ranking position, he was deferential and courteous to the daughter of a Ministry official who had been senior to him. He was an honourable man. His elder brother was also a distinguished figure as the head of the National Police Agency and was responsible for security during HM The Queen's state visit to Japan in 1975.

On the anniversary of his death a year later, Ibuki Bunmei (伊吹文明), then a newly-elected member of the Diet, wrote an article in the *Nikkei* newspaper in tribute to Masaru. Ibuki was a career Ministry of Finance official and served under my father at the Embassy in London. After my parents left the UK, he was exceptionally kind to me and my sister, often inviting us to dinner with him and other Ministry families. When my parents returned to Japan from Manila, he came to call on my father at home every New Year, and my father entertained him to lunch regularly at his club. As he wrote in this article, when he was elected to the Diet in January 1984 Masaru wrote to congratulate him in his dishevelled handwriting (because of his advanced illness): "I am truly pleased. I am too weak to write long." A few days later he died. Years later, Ibuki became Secretary-General of the LDP, held several Cabinet posts and became Speaker of the Lower House of the Diet, presiding over the inauguration of Abe Shinzo as Prime Minister. In that article, he wrote that of all those many who had helped and taught him in his over twenty-year career at the Ministry, he remembered Masaru the best.

As a very young official, he had been told off, shouted at – he thought Mr Fukuda was a very frightening boss. Yet strangely, there are no unpleasant memories of him. Perhaps it was because there was a hint of shyness about him. Convictions built on serious study, unwavering belief in protecting the national interest, a straightforwardness that appealed to the British, yet elaborate but apt expressions in English conversation, sticking to the essential truth in all matters – some of Masaru's characteristics mentioned in his dedication. Ibuki recognised that my father did not rate consensus-builders, such as those who tend to dominate modern Japan. Reading his article again today, I appreciate the affection in which he held my father, who was twenty-five years older than him.

Though it is true that Masaru was grounded in a hierarchical society, he was a democrat. And it would be wrong to say that he was a man of the past or of a lost world; his writings and his observations, as well as the values he held deeply, were the product of an acute sense of the political and social changes around. Indeed, he had foresight and was driven by it. I have thought sometimes that I was glad he did not live to see the sleaze and scandals of Japanese bureaucrats or the severe social tensions in modern America, a country which he loved and had a passionate interest in. But he had lived through the tumultuous years of postwar Japan with his vision, which he so tirelessly imparted to younger colleagues. Letters of condolence we received from them universally praised him for his wider perspective and his humanity. And no doubt, had he lived longer he would have had wise contributions to make in a rapidly changing world.

I found it strange that I could accept his death without trauma. It seemed that the progress of his illness followed a natural path of physical decay leading to death. I could accept his loss in those terms. Many people asked how come he died so young: modern medical science should have prolonged his life. He was a difficult patient, stubborn and determinedly in control of himself; the doctors found him hard to relate to. I went to visit his principal physician one evening at his home, hoping to explain my father's attitudes and psychology to him, but to no avail; the doctor did not give me a sympathetic hearing, just repeating that if Masaru would not accept his advice and that of his colleagues in the hospital then he could do no more. I cried on my own on the way back, and from then on consoled myself by resorting to secretly disliking him. Japanese doctors are notoriously arrogant; he was one of the worst examples. They pride themselves in being addressed as 'sensei' (teacher).

Having been brought up not to show spontaneous emotion in public I kept my tears under control; my mother was the same. My respect for my father was magnified by the way he prepared for his death. Before I left him for the last time, he said to me "You must not have any regrets … you have been able to come and nurse me in my final illness." He made sure that my memories of him were not unrequited. Ever since I saw my family off on the plane when I was just twenty I have lived my life alone, separated from my parents. Communication with them happened mostly by letters and infrequent meetings. My parents really lived in my mind rather than by physical close-ness. After his death it was not much different; I thought of him as I had always done. He was a samurai, always disciplined, not given to showing overt expressions of emotion even within the family. He had imparted his affection towards his children only by occasional cryptic messages. It was not as if he wrote us chatty letters. So in some ways nothing had changed. Six months after his death I suddenly found myself in floods of tears when alone at my house one summer day, as if I realised only then the enormity of what had happened.

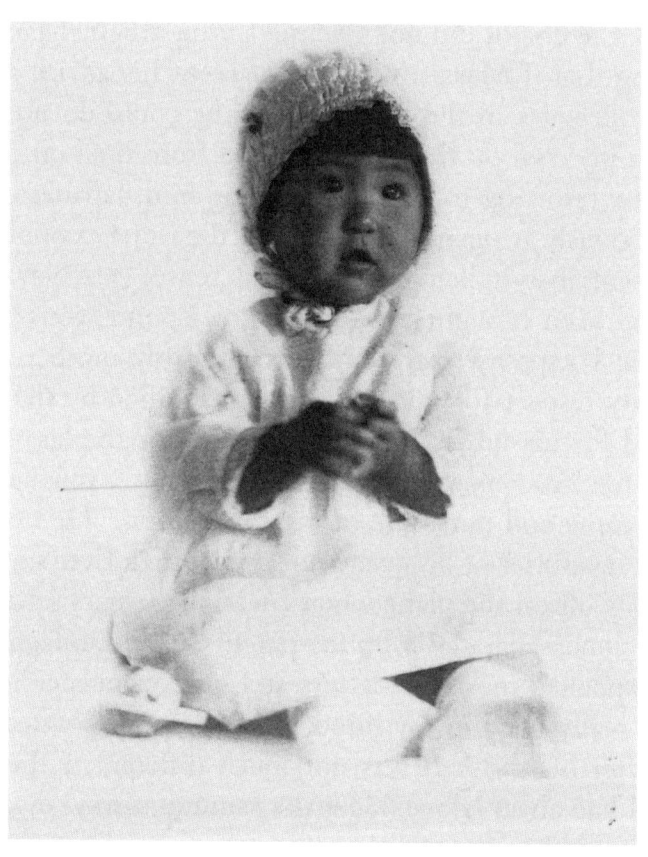

'I am going to live to 100, don't you believe me?'
June 1922, aged 1.

14. THE CENTENARIAN HEIRESS

~

Anew chapter began for Yoko. I have always thought that her strength lay in an ability to accept her fate. Having been brought up never to show emotion in public, she appeared poised. We were not there in the early months of her widowhood to know how much physical and mental exhaustion she had to overcome. It was touching to find, many years later in a drawer, a piece of paper on which she had written her prayer to God.

She had always obeyed her husband and his wishes, however much she protested in disagreement; arguments and rows were not infrequent at home. She was in that sense an old-fashioned Japanese wife who followed her husband, but unlike most she was not one to suffer in silence; she was vocal in her views and would spontaneously express them with emotion. But with her mother-in-law, she knew not to answer back, never showing any grudge. She had pledged on her marriage to serve and protect the Fukuda family and she continued to do so in her widowhood. What I didn't realise until then was how much emotional independence and inner strength of self-determination she possessed.

We worried that Yoko would find it lonely to live by herself for the first time in her life and urged her to get a live-in maid or at least a daily housekeeper. She was adamant that she wanted to live without worrying about other people in the house. It was as if, or so at least it seemed, not only had a whole burden been lifted from her shoulders, but she realised she was free – now she could live her life as she wanted. And she did not become more dependent, emotionally or otherwise, on her children. She set about clearing out our father's wardrobe, giving away his ceremonial clothes to younger relations, and attending dutifully to letters and to dealing with the matters of inheritance and estate duties. She made all decisions by herself and paid taxes and dues on our behalf. None of her children could read the documents in Japanese, let alone understand the laws on inheritance. She kept meticulous records of these and organised her life in such a way that she would be prepared for every emergency. In a locked drawer she had put everything that would be needed in the event of her death: money for the funeral, her bank books, seals, life insurance policies, her will. She always had a small suitcase packed ready in case she had to evacuate quickly from an earthquake, with cash, credit card, bottle of water, aspirin and medicines, plasters, etc. It was not long before she began to look better and happier, as she was able to set her own routine. She could go out at will, joining some groups, travelling, going to Karuizawa in the summer with friends, and eating whatever she felt like. She genuinely enjoyed her freedom and seemed not to be afraid. She was only sixty-two years old when our father died.

She joined the Tsuta Club, founded by my cousin Kinuko's husband, Namiki Takashi, to explore traditional Japanese culture; the group often went on trips outside Tokyo to visit famous potters or musicians. She relished these gatherings; she would meet her sister Setsuko and niece Kinuko there as well as a classmate from school and made new friends. Her innate curiosity and fearless ability to get involved in new things and new societies allowed her to find fresh interests and pleasures. She even went with some of those artists she met to *karaoke* bars, a novel experience – she had never been inside a bar or a nightclub, let alone one with karaoke, and she was much liked by those new friends for her unaffected ways; they celebrated her ninetieth birthday in style for her at one of those bars, with a gift of a set of *Bizen* cups from a master potter. She painted every day at home and said it was her principal pleasure and interest. Her painting group gave her a social circle she enjoyed. She read avidly her favourite authors' historical novels and detective stories. With her siblings she went out frequently in the evenings to restaurants. She walked to the luxury supermarket The Garden in Shiroganedai, half an hour away, several times a week, as well as to the local fishmonger and butcher carrying her shopping basket. The garden was her passion; she weeded and planted by herself even in her nineties, bringing in tree surgeons to prune the ornamental trees each year. Buying a small scanner and printer, she took pleasure in making her own Christmas and New Year cards with her own paintings.

Yoko never forgot our father; every day she would refresh the offering on the *butsudan* (the cabinet containing the altar) with water and cooked rice and light the candle and incense and say a short prayer. She was dutiful in following the Buddhist tradition of having memorial services at certain intervals. On the first anniversary of our father's death and on subsequent occasions every few years, she asked the same priest who had conducted the funeral to come to the house and chant prayers. Close family relations were invited, and she hosted a dinner in a restaurant afterwards. They were good occasions, with the amusing priest who was very partial to whisky. He told us that in Buddhist temples whisky is called 'medicine'. She decided about ten years ago to donate the large Fukuda family stone lantern that had stood in our garden to his temple, Kotokuji (広徳寺) in Tokyo. There it stands beside the path leading to this impressive temple complex.

Travels and Outings

Now free to travel at will without worrying about our father at home, Yoko went abroad to visit her daughters and her friends. Two years after our father died, Chahchah was posted by UNDP to serve as its representative in Burundi. She invited Mother to go and stay with her and her son, aged four. Burundi is a primitive country by any standards, landlocked in central Africa and French-speaking. Mother jumped at the opportunity and went to spend a few months in Bujumbura, looking after her grandson with an African nanny/housekeeper. She came to stay with me on the way back, bearing presents of Burundi handicrafts. Her sister Setsuko, also widowed, invited her to go to Taiwan. She said that her father used to go there often and brought back *karasumi* (bottarga), which remains one of her favourite dishes. They also went to South Korea, famous for amethyst cutting, and she bought pieces of amethyst jewellery as it was her favourite stone.

She of course went to America to attend Eiko's wedding to Gus. It was a beautiful day in the New England forest. The ceremony was held outside in the autumn sunshine. She dressed Eiko in the *furisode* that was originally hers and was the same one that Chahchah got married in. Mother was happy with Eiko's marriage and bought the couple a small apartment in Brooklyn. Eiko had decided that she wanted to live in New York where her friends were and do a doctorate at Columbia. She started teaching at universities and is now a professor.

Back in Japan, Yoko went to Okinawa with her classmate, who had been a Princess of Okinawa before the war, and was grandly entertained by former retainers; she was also thrilled to visit the famous Eiheiji temple (永平寺) in Fukui prefecture with one of her closest classmates, Sakai Kiyoko, whose family owned it. She said that it was one place she had always wanted to go to. Sakai Kiyoko and Nabeshima Matsuko were the two classmates who also lived in the neighbourhood of Shiroganedai after their marriages during the war when Yoko married into the Fukuda family there, and the three of them remained very close, often encountering each other at local hairdressers and grocery shops. Nabeshima-san went with them to Eiheiji and there they were together again as a threesome. With all her sisters, she went on the train to their family's old copper mine, Tsuchihata in Iwate prefecture, now converted to a mountain resort; that was a pilgrimage to remember. She went there again some years later with Eiko and to Sendai, where the Fukuda grandmother came from. With Chahchah she travelled to the mountains of Kiso and to Kyoto.

She came to England to see me many times, as she did to America to see my sisters, and to attend her grandson's graduation. She loved Creems and the garden, and my gardeners liked talking to her as she was very knowledgeable about flowers. On her first visit, she rowed a small boat on the river (the Stour) in my meadows, while the swans chased us. She painted watercolours and pastels of the garden and the meadows; we cooked dinners together and went to visit friends in the area. She would ask how I had made some particular dish: she would copy it when she got home. We went to Mersea to buy fish: when I asked if she would like herring she looked worried and said "How do you eat it; herring is horse food?!" So I decided to buy Dover sole instead; she wanted it *meunière*. We bought live lobsters and she made *sashimi* with them. She also went to stay with our friends from the London days, the Akiyamas; he was at that time Ambassador at the Hague. His wife Natsuko, affectionate and hospitable, had become a close friend and invited Mother to spend holidays with them wherever they were posted.

In 2008, Dugald suggested she came to his summer home at Machrihanish at the bottom of Kintyre. We told her seals came to sunbathe on his beach. She enthusiastically agreed and packed her painting things. She didn't mind the long journey either, from Tokyo to London, then flying Stansted to Edinburgh, and then driving from Edinburgh to Machrihanish. On the way we stopped for lunch at Loch Fyne seafood restaurant; she wanted to buy Arbroath smokies which she had never had before. The next morning, she said they were "quite good". On the first day at Machrihanish we were going to go painting at Southend with Dugald's artist friend, Ronald Togneri. At an ironmonger in Campbeltown she saw a plastic chair for children outside the shop; I wondered why she wanted to buy it – she sat on it herself on the beach and painted. All three of them painted the same scenery on the beach, looking towards Ailsa Craig and Sanda Island. Yoko made pastel paintings of rocks with sea flora. She gave one to Dugald to hang in his house at Machrihanish, but Dugald's and Ronald's paintings are in my drawing room; Ronald put in Dugald and Mother painting on the beach. They are a joyful reminder of that very happy day. She was tireless and would stride along on rocky and uneven terrain to the Gauldrons bay for miles while I tottered along behind asking them to wait for me. We visited Ronald and Helen's house in Campbeltown; she admired his paintings, selecting the one she wanted to buy. We drove along the east side of Kintyre to Torrisdale Castle where she bought local woollen sweaters and rugs from the Crafty Sheep shop, and saw beautiful scenery around West Loch Tarbert. At the end of the holiday, on the way back we stopped at Inveraray to buy some tartan and bumped into our friend Iona, Duchess of Argyll. Dugald was keen for us to get his Ancient Maclachlan tartan and I bought a length to have a suit made.

Two years before that we decided to spend Christmas in Rome. We rented a flat in Parioli and Mother came to join us. Libet Williams also came for the New Year. We cooked breakfast and some evening meals at the flat, but generally went out to restaurants. Mother loved delicious Italian dishes and fresh fish and oysters that were abundantly on offer. We went to many of the old haunts of the gourmets, Tullio, Rosetta, Giovanni's,

Sabatini in Trastevere, to name but a few. Every day we went out to see art in museums and churches; being very knowledgeable about paintings of the Renaissance, Yoko was in her element and wanted to see everything. I was very impressed by her artistic knowledge and appreciation; I learnt a lot from her myself looking at paintings with her then. She particularly wanted to see the Raphaels – Rome is of course the place to see them. Long queues in the rain outside the Sistine Chapel wouldn't deter her. Again, she would stride ahead while I tottered on behind. At Christmas she took us to dine at the top of the Hotel Eden, whence you can see the seven hills of Rome. We went shopping too in the Via Condotti and the Corso and remembered our family visit there with my father half a century earlier. She went around in her new hat acquired at Borsalino in Piazza del Popolo. I remember her buying silk-lined kid gloves and she particularly wanted to see the new Fendi shop where she bought some perfume. Ever since I was a young girl we were interested in perfume – finding new scent, trying different ones, exchanging presents. Mother had recently come across a new Fendi scent and she thought of buying it there. In my youth, Givenchy's *L'Interdit*, Dior's *Diorissimo*, and Nina Ricci's *L'Air du Temps* were the old-time favourites that she liked.

In 1988 I had moved from James Capel to Nikko Securities in London. With that move, paradoxically, my visits to Japan became less frequent; there was not so much need for me to go there as Nikko had a huge headquarters operation in Tokyo. After 'Big Bang', Japanese and American banks and brokers were eager to enter the London market by acquiring British broking houses. Indeed, we at James Capel sold our shares to the Hongkong & Shanghai Banking Corporation, just as most other brokers also became part of major international banks that were busy building universal banking operations. Successful players were sought after and I myself was also offered several positions in both American and British firms. I eventually decided to take up the offer from Nikko, mostly because I wanted to see what the inside of a Japanese company looked like. Never having worked for a Japanese firm, I was curious.

Nikko went to see the top people at the Ministry of Finance as a matter of courtesy, because I knew many of the senior officials there. Like all other securities firms, Nikko was closely regulated by the Ministry. Gyohten Toyoo, by then Vice-Minister for International Affairs, was shocked to hear about my move. He immediately phoned me to say that he thought it was appalling; as with my father, the Ministry officials had a pretty poor opinion of Japanese brokers. He said "I am concerned that you should get into the murky world of Japanese brokers; please promise me that you will only stay for a maximum of two years." I could hear Masaru in those words, though my father would have either said nothing or forbidden it altogether. I did promise Gyohten that it would be for two years only, but crises in the securities industry two years on prevented me from leaving Nikko and I stayed for eleven years. In fact, as Gyohten feared, the Japanese financial industry fell into a mammoth crisis when the 'bubble' bull market collapsed in 1990, mired in scandals. To protect its integrity and reputation, the senior management of Nikko repeatedly asked me not to leave. That is a subject for another book.

My mother was not so concerned about my moving to Nikko; though unlike her sisters, who liked speculating on the markets, she never herself invested in stocks and shares as her husband would not contemplate engaging in such 'downmarket' activities, yet she did not harbour any contempt for stockbrokers – after all her great-grandfather had founded the market! In fact, she went and opened an account with Nikko's branch near home and put some of her money in investment trusts. It was her way of showing support, just as she had opened an account with the Bank of Tokyo when her youngest sister married one of its executives. I was astonished to find three decades later that

Pilgrimage to the mines

Now a big hole… Tsuchihata mine in Iwate prefecture.

Four sisters before the commemorative stone.

Wild flowers and the hills.

Fugu evening: Yuhei, Yoko, Asako, 1990s.

Noriko and Yasushi, newly married, playing tennis at Karuizawa country club, late 1950s.

'… let's have a pint…' Asako and Noriko, 1980s.

Tsubakiso Karuizawa

Above: As it was designed and built by Koichi, mid-1920s.

Above right: Tsubakiso in recent years.

Right: With the Nakamura cousins, 1980s.

Right: Verandah as was.

Below: The road outside.

Bottom right: The house as was.

Emperor's state visit 1998; Empress signing the book with Haruko (joint chairman of the Japan Society); left to right, standing: Ambassador Hayashi, Captain Robert Guy RN (Executive Director of the Japan Society), Emperor Akihito, Lew Radbourne (joint chairman of the Japan Society).

Left: Mummy at the Creems garden, west border, 1990s.

Above: She sketched it like this…

Painting by Ronald Togneri of a lovely day.

Yoko on a tiny plastic chair, with Ronald looking across to Sanda Island.

Having fun
visiting the
Akiyama
family in the
Netherlands,
1990s.

Visiting Holland
in the early spring
flowering time.

Going out
with sisters
one summer
evening, 1985.

Ukiyo-e of pilgrimage to the stone monument of Tenka-no-Itohei, late nineteenth century.

Yuhei making a pilgrimage to the stone monument erected in honour of his ancestor Tenka-no-Itohei at his birthplace in Nagano hillside. Shinto priest conducting a commemorative ceremony.

At cousin Kakuko's wedding, early 1980s. Left to right: Noriko, Asako, Haruko, Yoko, Kinuko.

Last Years

Going out to lunch with Haruko, 2018; Yoko aged 97.

Sonorous Court garden.

Aburatsubo Bay sunset at Christmas.

she had also diversified her investments into foreign currencies, including the Australian dollar and the euro. When I was complaining to her that I was hard up, she said "Why not speculate on the stock market and make some money?" That was the last thing I was going to do – evidently, I have inherited my father's ultra-cautious samurai character, while Mother had hers from her grandfather and entrepreneurial great-grandfather.

Opportunities to go home diminished through the 1990s and 2000s, as my work had relatively little to do with Japan; I panicked when I decided to give up full-time jobs and became a non-executive director of various companies: how am I going to see my mother with no business trips to Japan? Fortunately, she was not the conventional 'clinging mother'; she was extremely independent and was not going to compromise her own schedule even if I had just arrived on one of my infrequent visits. She would cook dinner for me with my favourite salted salmon or bring back live lobsters from Akiya. On every visit we went out together to look at shops in Ginza and enjoyed days out at art galleries and exhibitions at weekends. As she got older she preferred to go out to restaurants. I phoned her every Saturday wherever I was; she said that she rushed home in time for my call each week. Having written innumerable letters to three daughters and to her parents and siblings for over twenty years, she said she didn't want to write letters any more. International calls had become more affordable and we relied on frequent telephone calls.

Painting

From her youth, Yoko was always good at painting. As her mother and grandmother were accomplished watercolourists she was encouraged to learn the skill. Before she married she painted in oils and pastels with a well-known painter whose wife was her mother's cousin. Her early works from that period are fresh but virtuose. She painted still lifes in oil but landscapes, mostly of Karuizawa, in pastel. Aunt Asako always had her large pastel of Mount Asama hanging in her drawing room. I wonder where that painting has gone. After she married there was no time or space for her to continue painting as it was during the war and thereafter she had a family to look after during the difficult years of postwar austerity. My father said that one of the reasons he decided to marry her was that she was good at painting and had an interest in art. But his career took her to a diplomatic life stretching over eleven years, during which it was not possible for her to spend time painting. When they went back to Tokyo in 1971 she determined to take up painting again.

She decided to try out Japanese brush painting, *sumi-e*, for the first time and joined a ladies' painting group run by a well-known Japanese artist, Ohta Shoko, to which some of her friends belonged. They included the wives of Finance Ministry officials who served with us in Washington and Manila, the Gyohtens and the Sakatanis. The *sumi-e* class gave her an important social milieu as well as an interest in perfecting her painting skills. At Sonorous Court she joined first the watercolour group and then the pastel class; she was already very proficient in painting and became a leading light there. She painted every day and it gave her pleasure and meaning in life. She painted in black and white and in colour in Japanese brush painting, some of which she put onto eight-fold screens. She painted large pastels that she had framed. On her ninetieth birthday she gave each guest at the dinner a coloured Japanese brush painting as a memento. Her paintings show that she has a strong sense of colour combined with skilful and well-practised technique and composition. Her favourite painter is Cézanne. On seeing one of Dugald's oil paintings of Aburatsubo she immediately said "He is very good; how can he paint like that…" He is a good painter, but so is my mother.

Planning for the Future

When Yoko learnt that there was a retirement home with a care complex opening in Aburatsubo, a beautiful yachting harbour near the Misaki fishing port at the bottom of the Miura peninsula on Sagami Bay that she knew so well and loved, she went to see it. It was run by an American company: a large complex of newly-built apartment blocks connected to a care centre with a clinic attached. The residents were over sixty years old, and if and when needed they could move to the care centre with twenty-four-hour nursing. Yoko thought she should buy into one of these in preparation for her old age. "You won't come back to Japan to look after me; I have to take care of myself," she said. She insisted on my going with her to see it. I would hate to be in an institutional environment, but she didn't seem so averse. And in any case, I was sceptical of her buying an expensive retirement home with high service charges and I couldn't see that she needed to do this yet; she was only seventy years old then. But she was determined: "Illness strikes suddenly; by then it would be too late to find a suitable carer to look after me at home." Without hesitation, she sold her apartment in Hayama and bought Aburatsubo. She was proud of having sold her apartment at the top of the market in 1991.

There, at Sonorous Court, Yoko started another new chapter in her life. She went there for a couple of days each week to make new friends and get used to life there for the future. She chose the rooms so that she could see Mount Fuji on clear days from her balcony and decorated her apartment with furniture from Hayama. She embroidered all the cushions and soft furnishings. She joined the chorus group and the painting group and made new agreeable friends. It being a luxury establishment, many of the residents were from well-to-do families and some had experience of living abroad. On occasion, she said cheekily, she dared to go swimming in the sea by herself. She invited her friends from Tokyo for summer barbecue parties in the garden and to special dinner evenings. For ten years she could still drive there but when she gave up driving aged eighty, she went on the train from Shinagawa station not far from our home, carrying her painting material in a shopping trolley, getting on and off the escalators at the stations with ease.

Years went by with her new life, to-ing and fro-ing from Tokyo. More than a decade after our father had died, on one of her annual medical check-ups, it was discovered that she had very early cancer of the stomach. Her mother had died of it and her family had a history of cancers; it could not be taken lightly. There were urgent telephone calls with Yuhei as to whether she should have an operation to have it removed or opt for other treatments. Yoko, in her usual determined way, said she was going to have the operation and insisted that she had it at St Luke's Hospital in Tokyo. She has always liked this hospital, known to be very progressive and American as well as being a Christian foundation. She was not afraid of operations: as Mariko said, "Mama is very *modern*."

St Luke's was a beautiful modern hospital with every patient in a private room. I asked Yuhei to come to the hospital during the operation because I was nervous and didn't want to face the meeting with the surgeon afterwards on my own. All went well; her cancer was tiny – only the size of a grain of rice – and had not metastasised at all. Keyhole surgery had not been developed by then, so it was a major abdominal operation. Their system was impressively 'No-Pain and Quick Recovery'. With the epidural it didn't hurt, and she was made to walk a long distance each day around the ward and go in the lift by herself to have X-rays taken. I was amazed. Yuhei and her sisters all visited daily, so there was a merry party around her bed throughout the day. I took my tapestry embroidery to do sitting in the corner. Yuhei was surprised that I could sew! She was not able to eat for several days but was fed intravenously; by the tenth day they were giving her *sashimi* and soft rice. She was discharged by the end of the second week. Yuhei sent a car to take her to Sonorous Court where she could have specially prepared meals brought to her apartment. Eiko came over to look after her and stayed in a guest room at Sonorous. Her foresight in buying into Sonorous paid huge dividends.

Yoko made a complete recovery and in time she was eating more than I was. Delicious food is one of her pleasures; she would cook it herself even just to eat on her own. She is proud of eating everything that is put before her and not being picky – perhaps that is the secret of her longevity. She picked up her routine, going to and from the retirement apartment to home in Tokyo, and resumed her social life.

Her sister Asako slowly started suffering from dementia about ten years before she died, eventually forgetting her appointments, looking sallow and depressed and finally not making much sense at all. Yoko used cunning ploys to take her to the doctor and get her medication and looked after her every week for many years, as no other sibling could give her that attention, Yoko naturally took it as her duty as an elder sister. Though they were never particularly close, Yoko said that these visits to the doctors gave her an opportunity to reminisce about Fukidecho; there was no one else left who knew it as she had. They laughed together, recalling amusing moments from childhood. But emotionally and physically it exhausted her. When Asako was put in a care centre, Yoko said that it was the Tanaka family responsibility to take care of her. She was completely clear in her mind about the traditional Japanese social mores of family units defining the boundaries of responsibility. She herself became a part of the Fukuda family when she married, no longer Tanaka. Yuhei had died a few years earlier: it was my cousin Akiko who became her legal guardian.

The death of Yuhei came as a blow to Yoko. They were close and he was her anchor; Yuhei in turn was loyal to his eldest sister and protected her. When he fell ill with pancreatic cancer, she was shocked that he seemed to be so frail in mind as well as in body. The burden of organising the family business was heavy and at times he seemed to be exhausted by it all. He had a family party at home when he came out of hospital the first time, bringing in the chef from his favourite sushi restaurant. It was almost the same as it had always been. But we all knew that his time was limited. He attended the family temple, Seishoji, to prepare for his death. One autumn day several months later, while I was visiting Tokyo on business, my mother phoned to say that Yuhei was in a critical condition in hospital and asked that we went together to visit him immediately. That was the last time I saw him, lying in a hospital bed in a tiny private room in the not-yet renovated old Toranomon Hospital. Breathing heavily, he was hardly conscious. A few days later he died. I was able to attend the family *Tsuuya* (通夜) at home. All the close family were there; Yuhei looked serene and handsome as he always had been. Candles were lit and mirrors were covered as is the Buddhist tradition. Mariko had some Chinese food brought in from her favourite restaurant, Chugoku Hanten in Mita. Mother thought the only black outfit I had with me was hardly suitable for mourning. She let me wear it nevertheless. I was not able to attend the funeral a week later as I had returned to London by then. It was a very grand event with the large circle of friends and family that Yuhei had around him. With his death, a chapter in the Tanaka family history closed. Yoko tried to be supportive of Mariko and to continue periodic dinners with her and Yasushi. By then none of her siblings, Setsuko, Asako nor Noriko, were in any state to go out.

Yoko has always claimed that she was weak-minded, but she was brave and attended to her own personal problems uncomplainingly: she went for cataract operations on her own, arranging to stay overnight in a hotel adjacent to the hospital; she went repeatedly to have her painful hip and back examined and got orthopaedic corsets; and got hearing aids as she grew hard of hearing. Aunt Mariko and Yasushi were of the view, as she entered her ninth decade, that she should not be left alone and that we should go back to Japan to live with her. Mariko made a rare telephone call to me, asking me to consider it carefully; I assured her that we would be there when needed. I was not very pleased that she should put this pressure on us, but then she presumably felt the burden of responsibility on herself.

Yoko was an avid reader of the *Nikkei* newspaper. While we lived abroad she always longed for the arrival of the *Nikkei*, via courier from Japan. When she was ninety-two years old she thought it extravagant to subscribe at her home in Tokyo as well as at her retirement home by the seaside. When she mentioned this to one of her nephews, he told her that he read the *Nikkei* on his smartphone. She immediately wanted to do this herself. So I took her to the Bic Camera store in Yurakucho and together we bought a mini-iPad. The young salesman was astonished to hear her age. I set it up for her so she could use it on the train going to the retirement home apartment and in the apartment itself with a wi-fi dongle. She managed to use it for a couple of years until she suddenly collapsed and had to go into the care section.

A Change of Life

One very hot summer day in July 2014, when Yoko was ninety-three, she was on her weekly visit to Aburatsubo. She got off the train and was about to board the shuttle bus for Sonorous when she felt an agonising pain: it was an aortic dissection on her heart. The owner of the FamilyMart convenience store rushed out and called an ambulance. She was taken to the Yokosuka Shimin Byoin, a public hospital twenty minutes away. A midnight call from my cousin Kakuko revealed that the doctors feared she might not survive the next twenty-four hours; she wanted me to speak with the doctor. The doctor asked me if they could use morphine as she was in extreme pain but that there could be side-effects. I said immediately that they should not hesitate. He then asked, should she be operated on with open heart surgery lasting ten hours? Without an operation the chances of her surviving were very slim, but again there were severe risks. I said firmly that they must ask her as she had always made her own decisions; he responded angrily that she was not in a condition to make any sensible decisions, and that as she had been brought into the A&E he knew nothing about her. I thought it an unfriendly remark and was not very impressed; I explained again that she was totally used to making her own decisions and insisted that she must be told and asked to decide herself. Mariko, who had rushed over with Kakuko, said that if it were herself she would want to be out of pain and that was the most important thing. I agreed with her. I immediately phoned Chahchah and asked her to tell Eiko. All three of us packed our suitcases, made hotel reservations and rushed back to be at her bedside. She was in the ICU for about a week, under the care of an excellent young physician who spoke a little bit of English. She was then moved to a private room, before relapsing a week later and having to be moved to the Hayama Heart Centre, one of the top hospitals specialising in heart surgery at that time, again in an ambulance accompanied by the young doctor. An extremely able heart specialist there asked her if she would like to have the risky operation; Yoko replied that she would not object if that was the curative option. She was always a believer in modern medicine, and was not afraid of medical procedures. After a series of tests the doctor decided that it was better to see if she could recover without an operation as she was quite strong and the dissection seemed to be healing. She survived and stayed at the Hayama Heart Centre for two months; by the time she was discharged she could walk for 40 metres.

Chahchah and I made detailed arrangements for her funeral in case she died while we were not in Japan. We met a Mr Sengé, a cousin of mother's school friend Mrs Hoshi mentioned earlier: an old-fashioned gentleman who spoke in Gakushuin language that seemed almost comical in this modern age. He runs a company that arranges funerals, a Gakushuin network that could be trusted. I said that some of the arrangements could be similar to what he had arranged for Mrs Hoshi, who had died a year earlier. When I was telling her son, Fumio, about this conversation Fumio said we should change to a Shinto funeral because it would be much cheaper than a Buddhist one! (Anyone in Japan can have a Shinto funeral while Buddhist funerals are very expensive.) A very kind and dear friend, Furuno Akihisa, who lives in Hayama agreed to be on standby should anything happen. We also went to see the care centre arrangement at Sonorous to make sure of its readiness, if she was to go back there on leaving the hospital. We did consider a rehabilitation centre, but none suitable could be found near Tokyo. So it was decided that on leaving the hospital she would go to the care centre at Sonorous in a private room; as her recovery progressed she would be able to go back and forth to her own retirement apartment there. During those two months Eiko and her husband Gus came over, as did Chahchah's younger son, Henry. It was wonderful to have Henry with us for a while after his mother went back. People at the hospital kept gazing at him admiringly, saying he looked like a film star, handsome and tall. Eiko stayed on till nearly the end of September when Chahchah went over again to take Mother out of the hospital and install her at the care centre. It was hard for me to leave her in hospital after a month, promising to return in another month's time. As I said goodbye, she could hardly hold back her tears and looked at me with a fierce gaze, while I kept saying Eiko would still be there.

Mother was overjoyed to be out of hospital and she was welcomed by all her friends and the staff she knew so well at Sonorous. Her bright smiles were wonderful and rewarding to see. She was well looked after by the experienced carers and nurses. But in the early days after hospital she was physically frail, as her muscles had weakened lying in bed for two months, and mentally she was slightly confused and in a panic.

Home in Tokyo No More
It was during that time of panic that Yoko decided we should sell our home in Tokyo. It was a momentous decision: it had been her home ever since she married in 1944 and she had never expected that she would lose it. The first house there had been built by my grandfather in the late 1920s and had been the Fukuda family home for three generations; the land and the house were left to us by our father. In her panicky moments she imagined many different options in her mind: sell the house to someone who would build an apartment block and she could live in one of the flats, which would be easier to manage than a whole house, with a carer; move to another care home that was more accessible in Tokyo; or come to England or America to live with a daughter. As she was in a very frail condition, with the doctors warning that another aortic dissection could occur at any time, it seemed to us that the safest place for her was in the care centre. Mother longed to go to Tokyo and kept asking if she could. But the care centre people were very protective and cautious. In those days she was surrounded by friends whom she had known for years; those who were already in the care centre sat at the same table for meals, engaging in merry conversations; they came to her room to share the chocolates and biscuits sent by their own relations. The kind and friendly carers would often drop in for a chat. She liked talking with them and she was happy. I would tell my friends in England proudly of the excellent old age care that existed in Japan, at minimal cost compared to the system in Britain. We arranged our visits so that one of us would be there almost every month and told ourselves that our international family life could continue seamlessly.

But we were, as it proved, simple-minded and over-optimistic. Time does not stand still and unforeseen developments destabilise even the best-laid plans. The challenges of keeping up an international family life were to multiply, not least thanks to the Coronavirus pandemic that enveloped the world in early 2020, making international travel virtually impossible. Yoko's friends all aged and some have died. We never foresaw the possibility of a change of ownership at Sonorous that altered the lifestyle and the routine, resulting in most of the familiar carers leaving and new residents arriving from different backgrounds, changing the atmosphere. Should we have given more thought to keeping our house so that at least for a while she could live there with a carer and one of us alongside?

My sisters and I debated the wisdom or otherwise of selling the house. Even though my sisters stayed there when in Tokyo, for much of the year we would somehow have to keep the house secure from burglary and fire and maintain the garden; managing an agent to look after it from abroad would be a challenge in itself. It had never occurred to me that we would sell the house during Mother's lifetime; I had never given thought to what we would do once she became unable to look after it. It was not as if she needed the money to pay for her care home. I asked Uncle Yasushi, the only remaining close male relative of that generation, what he thought of it; ever practical and unsentimental he said there was no question but that we should sell, just as he and his family had sold their parents' and other homes they owned. Modern life in Tokyo was all about smart apartments with 24-hour concierges: big houses with large gardens were an anachronism. Urged on by my sisters I set about the process of selling the house. The negotiations for the sale turned out to be arduous and having to conduct them from London for much of the time was less than satisfactory. I was warned the real estate market in Tokyo was murky and often corrupt. I relied on an old friend of many years' standing from my James Capel days who had hugely benefited from our commissions when he had been a minor Japanese stockbroker but was now much involved in property. He did not turn out to be a trusted friend after all. I was disappointed with myself, an experienced financial negotiator (!), and thought it a less than totally satisfactory outcome. It all took a toll on my health and I developed a severe case of shingles.

It also involved clearing out the house, a far greater task than we had ever imagined; after all there were nearly a hundred years of family possessions within. The house had been built with deep cupboards and even underfloor storage; organising the disposal of unwanted possessions was a complex affair with the local authority. Japan has been fanatical about recycling for decades, separating every kind of waste collected on different days of the week. Dugald, Chahchah and Francis came to help. Chahchah worked at JAICA and Francis at the Tokyo office of IBM during the day while I worked in the house. I went there for several weeks to sort out the house and the garden. The purchaser of the house was planning to demolish and level the garden in order to build a large apartment block on the site; they wanted us to clear the site before taking possession. The cynical way in which he came to buy our house more than upset me. He left a note through the letterbox long before we had decided to sell, saying he wondered if Mrs Fukuda was ever going to come back to live there; she had been so kind to his children looking after them when he and his wife were out; they loved to see our garden from their windows; if ever we wanted to sell our house they would certainly keep the garden as it was and look after it... He never showed his face and sent a representative to sign the contract – an ugly side of Japan that I had not expected to encounter. It would have been customary in Japanese culture even today at least to have made a courtesy call; after all he lived next door in a grand luxury apartment block he had built on the land that originally belonged to the Fukuda family.

I found a contractor through a friend who came to remove all the outbuildings. But I also wanted to rescue some of the fine trees and shrubs. I could not bring myself to see those beautiful trees just being cut down; my friends in Japan thought I was crazy. That again proved less than straightforward: I was told that camellias and daphnes are prone to hairy caterpillars and they could not be planted in public places! I tried to give some trees to public gardens but that eventually proved impossible; I was particularly sad to see our fine old *sarusuberi* (crepe myrtle) tree felled. It had been in our garden since I was little and I played on it, climbing up the branches to sit on one and jump off. Even more disappointing from Mother's perspective was the tall *hanamizuki* (dogwood) at the front of the house which had been struck from seed from the one at Fukidecho. The municipal authority wanted it, but apparently if the tree was ever going to be moved the roots had to have been wrapped around the root ball from time to time! But some shrubs were taken to the few friends who had outdoor space. Some roses were given to the garden at Sonorous to be planted there. Chahchah arranged to Skype with Eiko in New York, showing her from room to room things that Eiko might want; we spent hours going through the kimonos and valuable items deciding how to share them between us. There were no arguments or disputes; whatever someone wanted went to that person. I found an antique dealer who showed interest in some items and he came over on a Sunday to negotiate, Chahchah saying "Ring him now straight away, never mind it's Sunday, just tell him to come!" Vast quantities of books had to be collected and virtually given away to a second-hand book dealer who said there were too many; he had to come back several times. It was difficult to find a home for second-hand furniture or household items, however good a condition they might be in; Japanese people are not interested in used items. To somehow dispose of them posed yet another challenge. I was lucky to find a local courier with a van to take some items to mother's apartment in Sonorous, but more importantly I engaged a shipping company to transport what we wanted to

New York and London. Large removal lorries came with huge wooden crates over three days to pack. It was lucky that we had a big enough carport. One of the more difficult things for me to do was to cope with Japanese bureaucracy on terminating utility contracts for electricity, gas, telephone, etc. But for the kindness of my friend Furuno Akihisa, who came over to help me, I would not have coped.

When the sale was agreed, I so wanted my mother to return just once more to the house. The care centre people had said that she could not go as far as Tokyo, because even in a car there would be too much vibration which could cause another emergency to her heart. But from experience I knew that Rolls-Royces produce very little vibration, so hired a chauffeur-driven Rolls-Royce and a carer. It was a beautiful early summer day in Tokyo. I went to collect her and she was excited with the journey. She chatted all the way, going past some familiar places that were dear to her around Akiya and Hayama. I had asked my school friend Inoue Takako, who is very fond of my mother, to come to the house with sushi for lunch. We gathered around our dining table and had a wonderful lunch together; Mother kept saying to Takako that she should take away any of our china that she could use. After lunch we sat in the garden that was her creation, tended by her for forty years, and had tea and cakes. We got her to rest on a sofa bed for a while before she was driven back in the Rolls with Chahchah in the late afternoon. That was the last time that she saw her home. She was in good spirits all day and showed no sign of regret.

Yoko knows deep down that we have sold our house but occasionally she talks of going back there with a live-in carer; on being reminded that the house is no longer, a flash of sadness comes across her face as she nods silently; that is painful for me to see.

At the Care Centre: Hopes and Disappointments

The panic may have subsided, but our mother's tremendous mental struggle to figure out where her future lay continued, between trying somehow to persuade us that she should come to live with us either in England or New York or perhaps move to another care home in Tokyo so that she could be visited more easily than in Aburatsubo. She desperately wanted to be able to walk better and be independent. In the first few years she even thought it possible that she would be able to go to Tokyo on the train again and kept asking the doctor if that would be all right; she would stay in a hotel overnight. She wanted to attend the regular reunions of her classmates and always asked me to accept those invitations. Amazingly, at least half of her class was still alive and many of them very active in their mid-nineties. The news of close friends succumbing to dementia or going into care homes did not surprise her; she thought it inevitable. In the first few years some of them wrote to her and very occasionally she would ring them to have a chat. Though she resented being addressed as 'Yoko-san' by the carers, which she considered con-descending – at least Yoko-sama if not Mrs Fukuda please! – she participated in activities organised for the residents of the care centre – quizzes, floor games, singing, skits – at all of which she excelled. There were the Special Dinner evenings each month with elaborate menus which she always looked forward to and wanted to invite guests to. In the early years some friends and relations did make the journey to please her but it became more and more difficult to find anyone who could easily accept her invitation. In any case those occasions became dumbed-down in recent years with the new management.

Chahchah and Francis went to spend almost every New Year's Day with her together with their children, combining it with a short skiing holiday in Hokkaido. She has been assiduous in visiting our family grave every year on the memorial day of our father's death in January, just as our mother has always done.

Dugald and I have gone to spend Christmases and New Years with her too; the first Christmas at the care centre we had our friend Hamish Aird with us and Yoko was very much on the ball, trying to make sure Hamish had enough to eat and more wine. Quite remarkably, she switches to speaking English easily even now. At the care centre they arranged elaborate dinner parties for Christmas and New Year for the residents and their guests. Eiko has also managed between her jobs to spend several weeks at a time with her, often around their birthdays in March; she has even contemplated over the years going to live near there and start a horticultural business or get a job in Tokyo. I never felt that she would find it ultimately satisfactory to live in Japan, for all the reasons she left Japan in the first place.

I have gone to see my mother four times a year every year in between my numerous Board meetings, taking her to her biannual scans and check-ups. She was always waiting for me to come so that we could go out to restaurants. As soon as I arrive she would say "Are we going out?" We would go some distance away to an up-market Chinese restaurant in Hayama, forty minutes away or to a tempura restaurant at Akiya, and we invited our friends Furuno-san and the Okamis who then had a flat in Aburatsubo to join us. We found many agreeable restaurants much closer to Sonorous as well and went out virtually every day while I was visiting. The carers would get her ready, properly dressed with a string of beads from her jewel box, put powder and lipstick on her and comb her hair. Furuno-san took us out for drives to see the sea at Jogashima and the early spring cherry blossom in the nearby hills. She loved those outings and invited him to tea afterwards back at Sonorous. Dugald would also come with us whenever he came to Japan with me; he painted the scenery around the bay and went sailing with Yoshiaki on his boat – almost always on Boxing Day. Chahchah has been brave enough to take her to lunch in Tokyo in a taxi and invited our relations to join them; Mother was absolutely thrilled.

Those were the happier years but as time passed with little progress in recovering her mobility, frustration and boredom set in until Yoko became overwhelmed with loneliness. Her friends' visits to her room grew gradually less frequent, until finally no one came. The few visitors from Tokyo – her sister-in-law Mariko and niece Kinuko, who had her own mother to look after in a care home in any case – increasingly found the two-hour journey to Aburatsubo too demanding. But would they have gone more often if she was in Tokyo? With deteriorating eyesight she found it increasingly hard to concentrate for long enough to read her favourite novels or newspapers. The television programmes were boring (as indeed they are even to us, the younger generation). The novelty of care centre activities wore off and the games and quizzes were too easy and dull too. I tried to get her to paint in pastels in her room but she wouldn't, saying she could not concentrate so hard. I tried getting her to knit, which she was good at when we were young as she knitted many of our jumpers and cardigans, beautifully stitched with complex embroidered patterns. She tried for a while, saying she would knit a scarf for my birthday. But that too became tiring.

She said that dark thoughts kept her awake at night and she tried to think of names of flowers to send her to sleep. She would say to me "You should start to think about your old age; why not buy an apartment here – the one next to mine is empty – you could live there…" She would torment me, unintentionally, saying "When you were young you were always calling 'mama, mama,' and would not leave my side…" as if to say that now it is her turn to ask me to stay with her. As her loneliness increased she became introspective and depressed about the past; every time I went to see her she would say "I was a bad Mama, I am sorry I left you alone in England when we went to the Philippines; how lonely you must have been … you looked after the family when I was ill, you were a good daughter… I was not good at looking after my mother-in-law when she became incapacitated in old age; I couldn't look after her like I am being looked after here, they are very kind to me... I don't want to remember the past, I hate it..." It is more than one can bear to hear of the anguish that torments her late at night. Loneliness can take a toll in many different ways. For decades she has never had the company of her children close by and she was very self-sufficient emotionally and mentally. But she became badly insecure. She would be forever looking in her handbag to make sure her credit and ID cards were there. She was always well informed on world affairs and managed her investments and her numerous bank accounts by herself. When I told her a few years ago that negative interest rates were coming in, she immediately said "Shouldn't we put our money in cupboards rather than in bank accounts?" She feels helpless and anxious that she can no longer be in control of her own finances and frequently asks where her money is.

Even at mealtimes, the new regime sits people far apart so that there is no conversation to share memories. The change of management five years ago brought new carers, mostly from Fukuoka in Kyushu where the new management is headquartered, who had little cultural affinity with the residents. Sonorous Court had previously been owned by Shimizu Corporation, a major construction company, and it was an unprofitable sideline in the property investment business. It decided to sell to a nationwide specialist care home management company. To improve efficiency and profitability, the new regime streamlined its model, dramatically reducing the ratio of staff to residents and lowering the quality of food. It would be not just surly and discourteous but incorrect to imply that the competence of care has declined; mother frequently reminds me how much she appreciates their kindness. But she has little to do or talk about to anyone all day and increasingly she just wants to lie down in bed all afternoon. I warned the new carers that she must be helped to sit up in a chair as much as possible so that her muscles do not weaken, but to no avail. Food deteriorated so that she became alarmingly weak and her mental agility declined; at the local hospital where she was being treated for a minor infection, she was diagnosed as protein-deficient. Chahchah and I made a major protest to the management and the food issues were resolved. Within a month her mental and physical strength returned. We were reminded how important nutrition can be. I remember her surprising the chef at a sushi counter when he remarked she seems to like fish roe – sea urchins, caviar, salmon roes, etc. – and she responded "Do you know that each single egg, whether of hens or of fish, contains all the nutrients required for a human to live?"

Yoko continued to hope that she might one day leave the care centre and come to live with a daughter in London or New York. As recently as four years ago, aged ninety-eight, she made a tremendous effort to become more mobile; when I arrived she immediately pulled herself up on the bed and wanted to show me she could drive her wheelchair by herself, along the corridor and into the lift to go down to the tea lounge with me. She had clearly worked out in her mind that I would be more cooperative about her coming to live abroad if she was more mobile. She wanted to bring one of the carers from the centre with her and had been discussing it with one of them; she had asked about a prospective salary and confirmed in her mind that she could indeed afford it. "So is it OK? Can I confirm it with him?" She looked saddened when I replied "Let's discuss it with Chahchah…" The next day she said "I will stay here until I die."

Even so, she couldn't let go of the thought. She would say on the phone "You can get my passport renewed if you ring our friend at the Foreign Ministry who would arrange it; and you will come and collect me, won't you? I wouldn't be able to get on the plane by myself now…" Yet the practicality of bringing her over eluded us. Neither of Chahchah's or my homes were suitable to accommodate her and a carer, who would become lonely in a foreign country with a different language and food; she might not be able to tolerate the long flight; but most importantly she would not be able to have medical insurance in either the US or the UK. Old age national insurance for care and medical needs is not transportable across national boundaries. (Unless you are within the European Union!)

As time passed, and none of her suggestions were taken up by her daughters, she became morose, wanting to spend more and more time lying in bed. The more time she spent lying down, the less able she was to stay sitting up in a chair. I would say to her "If you lie down so soon after eating, as the saying is in Japan, you will turn into a cow." She always replied "I don't mind, I don't have anything else to do..." Even last year she was asking if she could get an electric wheelchair so that she could move around by herself.

Time passes quickly; the traumatic collapse which very nearly killed her was already eight years in the past. No one, including the doctors, then imagined that she would still be making efforts to try and travel at the age of over 100. Her mental fortitude and determination to live are more than impressive. We sisters had our commitments to jobs, husbands and children and did not think Mother would have wanted us to make sacrifices on her behalf; after all, that was the very reason she had bought into the retirement home/care centre at Sonorous Court. But these were her rational and brave thoughts, showing foresight in her early 70s. Once actually placed in the situation of being alone when ill, even her amazing mental endurance has been put to the test. Yet, she has never lost hope that she would one day get better and be able to leave the care centre. So often sentences started, "When I get out of here, I am going to..." My father in his last days in intensive care at the Red Cross Hospital in Tokyo said to me "You are the eldest, you must look after your mother." I promised him that of course I would. But I did not appreciate then how complex it would become with all of us living abroad.

Yoko's only remaining pleasure is food – virtually the last topic left that she is interested enough to concentrate on. She says herself that she is a "gluttonous foodie". She has often said she would teach the young chefs at Sonorous how to cook, as she found the new chef wanting. For Christmas three years ago Dugald and I took her to the best French restaurant in Hayama, and she ate all of a five-course lunch that was almost too much for us. Every time I go to Japan to see her, I take a small pot of caviar, which is her favourite. The joy on her face while eating it, exclaiming how delicious it is, gives me great pleasure. In recent years Dugald provides this present for her and she says repeatedly, "Please thank Dugald, it's my favourite … it's very extravagant…" Her eyes light up when I say "Do you know what I have brought for you?" She replies "Is it caviar?"

On the phone she tells me what she is craving: recently she said fresh sea urchins, smoked salmon, artichokes, avocados, ham, cheese and other things not served at the care home. I send her parcels of cheese and smoked salmon, hoping that the carers know how to present them to her. One afternoon she said "There is something called *foie gras* which Grandmother Sumiko took on picnics in Karuizawa." I asked her if she liked foie gras. She said she liked it very much but it is expensive and her grandmother would share it only in small pieces with her granddaughters. I take it for her and we have it together on crackers; she remembered that her grandmother ate it on brioche, which of course is the best way.

The Covid Pandemic and 100th Happy Birthday

One of Yoko's natural strengths has been the capacity to accept the unacceptable. That was the fate that came to pass, at the end of the war, for her and all of her friends. All of them were told at the end of the war to be mentally disciplined, 'to bear' and 'to endure the seemingly unbearable with patience and dignity'. I was brought up that way myself. She has been an example of that. But it has been a cruel coincidence that the Covid pandemic should engulf the world as she approached her hundredth birth-day. It suddenly became virtually impossible for her children to make those regular visits. Her aged and fragile emotions have, not surprisingly, been severely tested as Japanese government policy to close the border to all foreigners continued for two years. Sonorous Court has remained shut to visitors and even the residents in the retirement apartments are forbidden to go out. Under 'special circumstances' provisions I finally managed to get a visa when travel restrictions were slightly eased for a little while in the autumn of 2021. It was two years since I had last seen her.

When the first 'lockdown' came in the spring of 2020, our mother knew in the corner of her brain that there was this ter-rible disease spreading; she nevertheless kept asking for us to come straight away. She sometimes said "Isn't the virus disease over now…?" She said it was safer in Japan than in England or America and certainly at Sonorous. I would comfort her, saying "I will come just as soon as the pandemic subsides. You have lived through the war years; it's nothing compared to that…" No one expected then that the pandemic would still be spreading fast two years on.

Months went by with her crying out on the phone "When are you going to come? Please come soon; I am lonely…" Was it a defensive mechanism for enduring her loneliness that she clammed up as soon as I said "I will come just as soon as I can; but at the moment it is not possible with the travel restrictions, so wait for me?" On good days she replied "Yes, I am waiting; you don't have to worry about me, I am very well looked after here and I have nothing to worry about; they are wonderful to me…" but on other days there was only silence. It became excruciating to bring myself to ring her, as one could feel her psychological anguish so strongly.

When Sonorous opened briefly to visitors in a circumscribed way after more than six months of total closure, our kind friends

Okami Hiroko and Yoshiaki went to see her. (Yoshiaki's mother Yoshiko was my father's first cousin and niece of the old admiral Yamanashi.) Mother was overjoyed with their visit and happily chatted with them for over an hour, holding onto Hiroko's hand throughout. A few hours later, when I phoned by chance, she said immediately "Guess what? The Okamis came to see me today!" It revived an enthusiasm for life that lasted for several weeks. On one of the calls soon afterwards, she said to me "We have had to live separately for a long time in our family; we will be able to see each other again soon." I was so happy to hear her say that.

As the pandemic progressed with the new Delta variant, initially from India, border restrictions tightened ever further. Chahchah, who still holds a Japanese passport, managed to go and see her briefly when travel became easier from the US in the autumn of 2020. That was the only visit Yoko had from her children that year. On one of our calls she asked "How is Dugald?" He had been on chemotherapy for multiple myeloma and I thought how sweet it was of her to ask after him; later I wondered if she in fact had been thinking I had not come because Dugald was ill. When I answered "He is all right, continuing with his treatment" she said nothing more. We were in lockdown in the UK, forbidden to travel except in emergencies, Japan was closed to foreigners except in extreme circumstances, Sonorous was closed to visitors altogether into most of 2021. Of course, none of our other relations would contemplate risking infection to go to see Yoko.

At that age powers of concentration progressively decline in the absence of any verbal stimulus. With hardly any conversation with anyone at the care home, with no visitors allowed and staying all the time in the limited area of her room and the dining area, it is not surprising that Yoko became uncommunicative, withdrawing into herself. Our telephone conversations shortened: she would say only "Please come, I am lonely …

please think of coming to play with me sometimes…" followed by silence, whatever I said.

As the pandemic unfolded it suddenly dawned on me, far too belatedly, that we had to recognise the limits of an international family life, and short of going back to Japan we should make better arrangements to be with her for longer periods, so that at least one of her daughters would be there to keep her company. At the age of a hundred she deserves that, irrespective of the pandemic or any other unforeseeable circumstances. Wave after wave of the Coronavirus across the globe and the ever-changing travel restrictions in Britain and Japan made it impossible to put my idea into practice.

A Centenarian Now

On 14 March 2021 Yoko celebrated her hundredth birthday. She had been expecting that all of us would come for that day and kept saying "I don't want any presents; your coming will be the greatest present for me." I had been intending for months that we would have a special luncheon party at a Japanese restaurant nearby. The place I had in mind was Hogyo, where there is a large ground floor room looking over the lovely Japanese garden, serving excellent *kaiseki ryōri* (formal traditional Japanese cooking). We have gone there several times before and she enjoyed the ambiance as well as the cooking. We would have invited some of the staff that Mother has known for many years and those few friends who were still left there, as well as our relations from Tokyo. As the pandemic continued, such an idea receded further and further into the distance. By January, it was clear that I certainly could not be there as the UK went into a long lockdown with the rampant Delta variant spreading fast. Japan was not letting anyone from the UK enter the country. All care homes were closed to visitors throughout Japan and Sonorous Court was particularly meticulous in following government guidelines about not allowing visitors nor even allowing the residents to move around the complex. Chahchah got her vaccination in February 2021 and felt more confident about travelling. As she still has her Japanese passport and Japanese citizens could enter the country from America, we asked for special permission from Sonorous for her to visit on a very restricted arrangement for our mother's hundredth birthday.

Making a Herculean effort to meet the draconian restrictions of the Japanese government, Chahchah rented a self-catering apartment in Tokyo for the fourteen days' quarantine, as most hotels would not accept guests in quarantine. Sonorous allowed her to stay in Yoko's apartment but not to use the communal facilities such as the dining room, and to meet Mother only in a specially segregated visiting room for one hour twice a day. They would not permit her to go to Tokyo too often during her ten-day stay. She made a tremendous effort to please our mother by bringing in her favourite food each day and having lunches and dinners with her. On her birthday, Sonorous made a special lunch with a cake topped with '100' in sugar-coated biscuit in gold. Chahchah organised a Zoom meeting on her laptop so that Eiko and I could join in. Before lunch was served, presents were opened, and we were able to celebrate with her. Mother seemed somewhat bemused and said "Thank you," but was not very forthcoming. Not being used to video meetings, it was difficult for her to relate to us. She just said "Is this a *terebi denwa?*" (TV telephone). When a present of caviar from the Okamis was shown to her, she wanted to open it herself and ate it immediately. Two of her friends at Sonorous, who had not visited for years, were allowed to come briefly with their presents, and mother seemed moved to see them, reaching out with her arms. The staff at Sonorous made a tremendous effort to make it a special day, decorating the room with all the flowers and cards that had been sent to her, with the presents displayed on the side table. Chahchah opened each and every present with her, explaining who they were from.

When it became clear back in January that I could not be there, I wanted to make sure that I did everything possible to ensure that her birthday was remembered and celebrated. As is an old Japanese custom, I decided that we must mark the occasion by sending to our relations and very close friends some commemorative gift. For myself, it was a way of showing both my devotion to my mother and my appreciation for their friendship. I looked for a suitable gift, spending hours Googling. I found an old-established silversmith which made fine *sakazuki* (small vessels for drinking sake) in the shape of Mount Fuji with damascene work. I telephoned the maker, and they were more than assiduous in meeting my requirements as to boxing, wrapping, ribbons, cards etc. and sending them to arrive the day before mother's birthday. For the two staff members in the front office, who have been there from the very beginning thirty years ago, I chose pearl brooches; and for all the carers a large birthday cake and flowers for them to share on the day. For the three remaining friends in the Sonorous painting group, I arranged for Fortnum & Mason to send tins of biscuits that played music on opening – the postage cost more than the biscuits! Everything arrived on the appointed day and I was satisfied that I had done what I wanted to. It was also a way of showing that the Fukuda family was still intact, even though we live in different countries.

100th birthday, but the family could gather
only by Zoom.

EPILOGUE

~

It was terribly bad luck for our mother that in her twilight years the Coronavirus pandemic should strike. It was an unimaginable fate, depriving her of seeing her children for years, not just months. From her daughters' perspective the progress of time was no longer benign. Turning a hundred was a watershed; a slow decline set in and, though her cognitive powers are still intact, it is now an effort to speak and hold conversations. She was no longer making much effort: it was now urgent to be with her to give her pleasure in her last years.

Immediately after the birthday celebrations Eiko, having had her vaccinations, made a valiant effort to get a visa. It was a moment of triumph for Japanese bureaucracy: it took nearly three months but her persistence was rewarded. She was able to go and see Mother for the first time in over a year in the early summer, just before the Olympic games and Japan being put into an emergency with heightened infection rates in their aftermath. Eiko found Mother frailer and less communicative, but happy photographs of joyful smiles came flying in. My desire to go soon after her in the summer, when our lockdown in Britain was finally eased, was thwarted. The Japanese consulate warned me that it would take at least six weeks to get a visa and I would have to stay at a government-designated facility for six days; I should wait until the 'dangerous' situation had eased.

My anxiety and sadness were haunting as I heard Mother calling at the other end of the line each time I phoned her

"When are you going to come? Please come! I am lonely..." sometimes almost bellowing. I pitched the timing of my visit for late October or early November, by which time I reckoned that the Japanese emergency would be lifted. I was by then braced to have to spend some days at a government facility in quarantine: I had to go whatever the situation; after all it had been almost two years since I had last seen her. As anticipated, the Japanese government slightly eased the border control measures and I was able to get a visa before the end of October. But then not only did British Airways cancel all flights to Japan but I was suddenly struck down by an acute case of sciatica and could not travel. I had to delay my departure to the end of November and manage my mother's expectations, saying each time "I am *definitely* coming in a few weeks; wait for me." Eventually she appeared to understand that I did mean it and when I phoned on arrival in Tokyo she said "Where are you staying?" On hearing that I was at the Okura, she sounded relieved. When I finally arrived after the ten days of quarantine, with arduous reporting by app several times a day of my whereabouts and condition to the Ministry of Health, and she saw me waiting for her in the special meeting room at Sonorous, she was deeply moved, extending her arm to grip my hand and saying "Thank you for coming a long way ... I am so happy..." She would not let go of my hand for a long time. She kept saying "So glad you could come..." Some days she was more communicative than others; she would say "Haruko-chan, Haruko-chan, how have you grown up so much?" and "I am so happy you have come..." When I was not there one day, she said "Where have you been? Don't go away. Please stay here, here at Sonorous..." One afternoon I asked if she would like us to ring Chahchah together; she nodded enthusiastically. When I dialled the number on my iPhone, she read out "It says Sakiko Fukuda Parr..." then when Chahchah appeared on FaceTime she happily talked: "Hello! How are you? Where are you now? I guess Nicholas has now graduated from university..." Chahchah told her she was coming very soon and had already got her ticket. Mummy said "Ah so ... I will be waiting." It was the first time since I had arrived that she engaged in a conversation lasting as long as five minutes. It was the happiest moment of my visit. Some days later she asked me "Is Chahchah definitely coming? Is it true?"

Poor Chahchah had to contend with the gruelling restrictions the Japanese government introduced against the Omicron variety. The draconian measures, addressing every possible loophole over the last two years in Japan, have protected their citizens, as the rate of infection there has been far lower than in Europe or America. The customarily clean habits of the Japanese and the regular use of face masks have of course helped. Unlike in the West there has not been a total closure of shops and restaurants. Japan continued its border restrictions for far longer than Europe or the US, but, in the early summer of 2023, it is finally downgrading Covid status to the same level as influenza. At last we will be able to see our mother again more often – but no longer can she engage in much spontaneous conversation.

I admire her. A woman of enormous courage, she shows an amazing will to live. The fortitude with which she overcame her critical illness was more than remarkable; she surprised doctors with her clarity of mind and her physical strength. Our parents accepted the consequences of living abroad and so of their daughters pursuing international lives; they always put their children's happiness and fulfilment first. Yoko has written that she devoted her life to her husband, to their children, and to protecting the Fukuda family lineage. This was, in one sense, a source of regret: with no sons, our generation will be the last of the Fukudas. Since our father's death she has always said that she was living for us. So, she says: "I am waiting for you".

ACKNOWLEDGEMENTS

~

The writing of this book has been a journey of discovery as well as of nostalgia. The prolonged and repeated lockdowns during the Covid pandemic gave me the opportunity to spend uninterrupted hours going through crates of family papers and letters, reading numerous books from my library, many of which were memoirs and autobiographies of my relations and family friends, and opening old albums of photographs that belonged to my parents and grandparents. I wanted to share my discoveries and memories of happy childhood, most of all with my own sisters and friends. As it progressed, the task of writing it into a book became increasingly challenging.

It would not have been possible without the collaboration of Dugald Barr. His friends know him as *the master of words* and a perfectionist editor. Many an hour he spent going over endless drafts: rewriting, restructuring and choosing photographic images from numerous old albums, sacrificing precious time from his own writing and painting. His remarkable perseverance was matched by the advice and insights he offered from his great knowledge of Japan, its people and history, and his personal friendship with my parents over forty years or more. When I became a stockbroker, it was Dugald who made it possible for me to reconnect with my own country, from which I had become alienated. His patience and kindness, with a charming sense of humour, made it possible for me to overcome a vexing anxiety. Fifty years on I have now been able to write about my old country with objectivity and happy remembrances.

The production of this book could not have happened without

the tireless efforts of Sam Carter. He not only improved the text with further editing, making sure the meaning was clear to non-specialist readers, his professionalism and skilful attention to layout and the design of the cover as well as the reproduction of the photographic images resulted in this elegant volume. I am much indebted to him. My gratitude extends to his indexer and proof-reader, as well as to Elizabeth Vickers who photographed my mother's painted screen for the dustjacket.

I am grateful to my late Aunt Mariko who provided me with the flash drive of the Tanaka family photographic collection. Some of the photographs are taken from it. Sadly she died suddenly a month after her ninetieth birthday last year.

In the writing of this book I have been reminded how much I have benefited from many friends, without whose kindnesses my life in England would not have worked out as it has. I would like to extend my renewed gratitude and respect to them. It goes without saying that members of my family in reading this book may find their recollections differ. I ask for their forgiveness as I have given truthfully my own personal memories.

Finally, I thank my parents for the life we have led and I dedicate this book to them.

June 2023
London

Index